NATIONAL INSTITUTE SOCIAL SERVICES LIBRARY

No. 3

SOCIAL POLICY AND ADMINISTRATION
REVISITED

National Institute Social Services Library

1. SOCIAL WORK AND SOCIAL CHANGE by Eileen Younghusband
2. INTRODUCTION TO A SOCIAL WORKER
3. SOCIAL POLICY AND ADMINISTRATION by David Donnison and others
4. SOCIAL WORK WITH FAMILIES *Readings in Social Work, Volume 1* compiled by Eileen Younghusband
5. PROFESSIONAL EDUCATION FOR SOCIAL WORK IN BRITAIN by Marjorie J. Smith
6. NEW DEVELOPMENTS IN CASEWORK *Readings in Social Work, Volume 2* compiled by Eileen Younghusband
7. THE FIELD TRAINING OF SOCIAL WORKERS by S. Clement Brown and E. R. Gloyne
8. DECISION IN CHILD CARE: A STUDY OF PREDICTION IN FOSTERING CHILDREN by R. A. Parker
9. ADOPTION POLICY AND PRACTICE by Iris Goodacre
10. SUPERVISION IN SOCIAL WORK by Dorothy E. Pettes
11. CARING FOR PEOPLE The *'Williams'* Report on the Staffing of Residential Homes
12. SOCIAL WORK AND SOCIAL VALUES *Readings in Social Work, Volume 3* compiled by Eileen Younghusband
13. MOTHER AND BABY HOMES by Jill Nicholson
14. EDUCATION FOR SOCIAL WORK *Readings in Social Work, Volume 4* compiled by Eileen Younghusband
15. CHILD CARE: NEEDS AND NUMBERS by Jean Packman
16. THE VOLUNTARY WORKER IN THE SOCIAL SERVICES Chairman of Committee: Geraldine M. Aves
17. A PLACE LIKE HOME: A PIONEER HOSTEL by David Wills
18. ADOPTION OF NON-WHITE CHILDREN by Lois Rayner
19. HELPING THE AGED: A FIELD EXPERIMENT IN SOCIAL WORK by E. Mathilda Goldberg et al.
20. VOLUNTEERS IN PRISON AFTER-CARE by Hugh Barr
21. HOMELESS NEAR A THOUSAND HOMES by Bryan Glastonbury
22. HUMAN DEVELOPMENT: AN INTRODUCTION TO THE PSYCHODYNAMICS OF GROWTH, MATURITY AND AGEING by Eric Rayner
23. PLANS AND PROVISIONS FOR THE MENTALLY HANDICAPPED by M. Bone, B. Spain and F. M. Martin
24. SOCIAL WORK IN GENERAL PRACTICE by E. M. Goldberg and J. E. Neill
25. CLAIMANT OR CLIENT? A Social Worker's View of the Supplementary Benefits Commission by Olive Stevenson
26. COMMON HUMAN NEEDS by Charlotte Towle
27. THE POINT OF ENTRY A Study of Client Reception in the Social Services by Anthony S. Hall

SOCIAL POLICY AND ADMINISTRATION REVISITED

STUDIES IN THE DEVELOPMENT OF SOCIAL SERVICES
AT THE LOCAL LEVEL

BY

DAVID DONNISON

VALERIE CHAPMAN, MICHAEL MEACHER, ANGELA SEARS
AND KENNETH URWIN

London
GEORGE ALLEN & UNWIN LTD
RUSKIN HOUSE MUSEUM STREET

First published in 1965
Second impression 1967
Third impression 1970
This revised edition first published 1975

This book is copyright under the Berne Convention. All rights are reserved. Apart from any fair dealing for the purpose of private study, research, criticism or review, as permitted under the Copyright Act, 1956, no part of this publication may be reproduced, stored in a retrieval system, or transmitted, in any form or by any means, electronic, electrical, chemical, mechanical, optical, photocopying, recording or otherwise, without the prior permission of the copyright owner. Enquiries should be addressed to the publishers.

©George Allen & Unwin Ltd., 1965, 1975

ISBN 0 04 360037 9 hardback
0 04 360038 7 paperback

Printed in Great Britain
in 10 on 11 point Times Roman type by
The Devonshire Press, Barton Road, Torquay

PREFACE 1974

I was surprised to find that a lot of people still read *Social Policy and Administration*, although it was written a decade ago. Since the structure of the social services and the literature about social policy have both been transformed in that time, they deserve something less obsolete.

The original book presented a set of case studies of innovations in local units of the social services, dealing with events which took place in the 1950s and the early 1960s. In this book I have not altered those studies or tried to bring them up to date in comparable detail. Instead, I have added a postscript to each, briefly outlining the main subsequent developments which throw light on the original story and the conclusions drawn from it. In most cases the innovating trends we identified ten and even twenty years ago have persisted; in several they have become nationwide orthodoxy. But at least as interesting are the few cases in which there have been new and unexpected developments.

I have added an extra case study, dealing with the university department in which I was working ten years ago, which was written but not published at that time. This was the longest and one of the most interesting studies in the series and it contributed a good deal to the conclusions we drew from the original book. I am glad it can now be published.

The second chapter of our original book, called 'The Development of Social Administration', was an introduction to our field of study. It needed thorough revision, partly to make it more relevant to today's concerns, and partly because a set of case studies which have been transformed into history by the passage of time must be placed in a more lasting intellectual context if they are to retain their interest. The result is Chapter 1 of this book, 'What Social Administration Is About'. At the end of that chapter I have tried to pose some of the larger questions upon which studies of Social Administration should throw light, and I return to these questions at the end of the final chapter which has also been pretty thoroughly recast. Chapters 1 and 3 of our original book and its two appendices now seem redundant and have been omitted from this new version.

The changes produce a slightly longer but more simply organised book than its predecessor. Chapter 1 is an introduction to social policy and administration and to some of the literature about this field. Chapter 2 explains the purpose of our case studies and the way in which they were chosen and compiled. The following chapters present nine case studies, each followed by the conclusions drawn from them ten years ago, and a postscript about developments since then. Chapter 12 draws on these studies to present conclusions about the process of

PREFACE

innovation in local units of the social services and the people who play a part in it, ending with a discussion of the practical lessons and broader theoretical implications which may be derived from this research. Some readers will start at the beginning of the book and work their way to the end; but others will prefer to start with the conclusions, in which the thread of the argument can be clearly distinguished from the examples strung along it, and turn back later to the chapters which furnish the examples that interest them most.

For help with the revision of this book I owe thanks to an even larger number of people than before—far more than I have space to mention here. David Jones, Principal of the National Institute for Social Work, assembled a group of his colleagues for a lively discussion of the original book and the revisions it needed. My colleagues at the Centre for Environmental Studies made helpful criticisms of my first attempts at revision in a seminar and in working notes exchanged between us: I was especially grateful for the help of Peter Marris, Richard Minns and Harold Wolman. Kay McDougall, Dame Eileen Younghusband, Adrian Webb and many other colleagues of ours from the London School of Economics and Political Science gave me a lot of helpful advice. Jef Smith, Frances Cook, Alma Hartshorn, Derek Oulton, Antony Flew, Michael Zander, Maurice Kogan and Jean Donnison commented helpfully on particular chapters. I concluded my work on the book during six weeks spent as a guest of the Research School of the Social Sciences at the Australian National University where I was given further help in seminars and informal discussions.

My final thanks go again to my four co-authors who contributed to our original book, and wished me well in this attempt to rewrite it.

D.V.D.
Centre for Environmental Studies

PREFACE 1964

Many people have contributed to this book. The research on which it is based began for the purpose of teaching future social workers taking the course in Applied Social Studies at the London School of Economics and Political Science. Thanks to a grant from the School's research funds, Mrs Valerie Chapman was able to spend two years exploring the literature and making five of the case studies presented here. These were used for several years by students, at the School and elsewhere, whose comments helped to improve the presentation and discussion of the cases. At a later stage two more case studies were made by Michael Meacher,[1] Miss Angela Sears and Councillor Kenneth Urwin,[2] who were then graduate students at the School. The book was completed during a period of leave from the School which I spent at the National Institute for Social Work Training. I owe a great deal to Robin Huws Jones, the Institute's Principal, and his colleagues. Besides providing secretarial services and shelter from visitors and the telephone, they joined in regular and critical discussions of my drafts, inviting three others who also made exceedingly valuable contributions to these meetings—Miss Geraldine Aves, CBE, recently Chief Welfare Officer at the Ministry of Health, Dr Roy Parker[3] of the London School of Economics, and Derek Newman,[4] Principal of the Glacier Institute of Management. Meanwhile the whole project depended from start to finish on the directors and staff of local units of the social services who permitted us to study their work and record their endeavours to develop these services. They gave a great deal of their time and experience to the making of these studies and to the correction and improvement of successive drafts. Their generosity must not be allowed to implicate them in any errors that remain, all of which are the authors' responsibility.

D.V.D.
London School of Economics and Political Science

---

[1] Now Member of Parliament for Oldham West.
[2] Now Director of Social Services for the London Borough of Camden.
[3] Now Professor of Social Administration at the University of Bristol.
[4] Now Director of the Centre for Organisation Analysis.

CONTENTS

Preface 1974	*page*	7
Preface 1964		9
1	What Social Administration is About	13
2	The Case Studies	44
3	Slum Clearance Begins Again in Bethnal Green	47
4	The National Assistance Board Takes on New Duties	64
5	The First Ten Years of a Home Help Service	84
6	The Development of Casework in a Children's Department	103
7	High Flats in Finsbury	133
8	Crisis in a Canadian Service for Children	168
9	Consultation Among Social Workers in the Family Welfare Association	193
10	Formulating a Policy for Secondary Education in Croydon	221
11	Taking Decisions in a University	253
12	Conclusions	286
Index		317

CHAPTER 1

WHAT SOCIAL ADMINISTRATION IS ABOUT[1]

Why and how do innovations in social policy come about? The case studies in this book were designed to throw some light on this question at a particular time, place and scale—the time being the 1950s and 1960s, the place being mainly the eastern part of London, and the scale being local rather than regional or national. But the question is central to the study of Social Administration and should first be placed in that broader context to show the larger lessons which may be learnt from microscopic research of this kind.

The teaching of Social Administration began in Britain before the First World War in university courses like the one provided at the London School of Economics and Political Science in 1912 'for those who wish to prepare themselves to engage in the many forms of social and charitable effort'.[2] The subject now appears in all sorts of courses, and it is many years since future social workers constituted the majority of the university students studying it. But the social services are still the main things they study. That means they are also interested in people's living conditions, the processes which lead to the recognition of human needs and problems, the development of organised means for meeting needs and resolving problems, and the impact which social services and social policies have on living conditions and on society in general. This is not a discipline; it is a field in which many disciplines must be brought to bear.[3]

More fundamental questions underlie these studies. Urban, industrial, bureaucratic societies like Britain have been shaped by the growth of an economy and a culture which gave individuals greater freedom than hitherto to sell their labour in the market, to acquire and use property of their own and, if they were lucky, to experiment with new ideas, new

---

[1] An earlier version of parts of this chapter is to appear as a chapter in Brian Chapman (Ed.) *Political Questions. Essays in Honour of W. J. M. Mackenzie*, Manchester University Press, 1975.
[2] Calendar of the London School of Economics and Political Science.
[3] For a fuller account of the context and character of the subject see D. V. Donnison 'The Teaching of Social Administration', *British Journal of Sociology*, Vol. 12, No. 3, September 1961; and Joyce Warham 'Social Administration and Sociology', *Journal of Social Policy*, Vol. 2, No. 3, July 1973.

products and new life styles. Closely related to this individualism, both as cause and as effect, were two other developments: the growth of science—meaning the pursuit of rational inquiry and the publication, criticism and reformulation of its findings—and the drive for greater equality in civil rights, political power, property ownership and living conditions. Together, these developments and the ideals they generated are often described as Liberalism.

Liberalism poses recurring dilemmas. The triumphant march of individualism made it increasingly difficult to justify the fact that some individuals reaped so much more of its rewards than others.[1] Since each individual was supposed to have equal value, Liberalism had radical implications which could not be evaded. But progress towards equality threatened to provoke social conflict which might destroy freedom itself. These conflicts exposed the frailty of the claim to objectivity on which was founded the authority of science and of the professions which were expected to advance knowledge and apply it. These professions could not extricate themselves from the battle, nor clearly distinguish their knowledge from the ideologies of the contenders. All the social sciences are involved in these dilemmas, but students of Social Administration are more deeply involved than most because the things they study—such as the attempts of governments to redistribute incomes, reorganise educational systems and reform offenders—are often the very arena of battle.

This chapter attempts to show how these large and difficult questions arise in the field of Social Administration, and to introduce some of the disciplines which may throw light upon them, dwelling particularly on literature which has too often been neglected and hence paying too little attention, perhaps, to disciplines such as Sociology and Psychology which have a well established place in the courses taken by students of Social Administration.

We distinguish half a dozen approaches to problems of social policy. 'Approach' is for our purposes a usefully vague word because it covers three distinct but closely related dispositions. People who adopt a particular approach tend: (a) to pursue particular kinds of research, using characteristic methods to explore characteristic *questions*; (b) to adopt characteristic assumptions about society and its workings, refined and reinforced by research which produces characteristic *descriptions* of the world they study; and (c) to espouse particular attitudes and aspirations which lead to characteristic *prescriptions* for action. Often it is difficult to discern the point at which exponents of a particular approach move from questions to descriptions or from descriptions to prescriptions: they may themselves be uncertain how

---

[1] Continuing attempts are nevertheless made to justify a measure of inequality, (albeit much less than that which we have ever experienced). See, for example, John Rawls, *A Theory of Justice*. Oxford University Press, 1972.

far their findings are due to their research methods and their prescriptions to their findings. We shall try from time to time to distinguish these three phases of each approach to our subject, to show how one leads to the next, and to note the biases which may result.

The first two approaches we have named 'institutional' and 'policy-oriented'. Although they differ in important ways, both fall equally within a liberal, humane and rational tradition which is familiar to students of Social Administration because most of the books about their subject are of this kind.

The next two approaches we consider have developed more recently, particularly among operational researchers and political scientists in the United States. We describe them as a 'systems' and a 'pluralist' approach, although many other terms have been applied to them ('synoptic' and 'incremental', for example). Between them they include many of the most important contributions made to this field during the last decade. They differ in many ways—indeed, in the academic journals they have often been cast as antagonists—but they also have a good deal in common: both generally stop short of explicit prescriptions for social policy, yet they imply attitudes and priorities which may be the harder to challenge because they are unexplicit.

Then we turn to another pair of approaches which we have described as 'Marxist' and 'structuralist', although the latter might perhaps have been named 'neo-Marxist'. They are old and new standpoints on a continuum, and it would be a mistake to distinguish them too sharply. Together they provide the most telling criticism of the liberal tradition with which we began.

We cannot do justice to so large a literature in one chapter. Any reader familiar with it will at some point feel that we have over-simplified and caricatured sophisticated ideas, and crammed into one category works which deserve to be more carefully distinguished. We can only hope that our quotations and footnotes may introduce other readers to sources which they can read and appraise for themselves.

Towards the end of the chapter we try to summarise and contrast the main approaches we have discussed by comparing examples of each in one field of social policy. Urban planning is the field we have chosen, but others would have served as well.

We conclude by noting some of the central problems which emerge from this review of the literature. They are much too big to resolve with evidence derived only from nine local studies. But if our research has been worth doing it should throw some light on them. We return to these issues at the end of our final chapter to see if it has done so.

From an Institutional to a Policy-Oriented Approach
We have said that Social Administration is a field of study (rather than a discipline) dealing with the social services. But what is a social service?

A well-known pamphlet of the mid-fifties gave a confident answer. 'The essential marks of a social service are: (a) that it is rendered by, or on behalf of, the community *to an individual* or at most *to a family*, and appropriated to his or its exclusive use; and (b) that it contains an element of redistribution, i.e. that the majority of the individuals or families who avail themselves of it are receiving more than they give.' This view is individualistic and philanthropic. It is natural to continue: 'The question therefore which poses itself is not, "Should a means test be applied to a social service?" but "Why should any social service be provided *without* test of need?"'[1] The textbook most widely used by British students of Social Administration at that time—and for many years after—gave a more uplifting account: 'the generally accepted hallmark of social service is that of direct concern with the personal wellbeing of the individual' and its 'basis . . . is . . . to be found in the obligation a person feels to help another in distress'. This leads to another characteristic question. Has the 'multiplication of statutory social services' produced a 'decline in initiative and repudiation of personal and family responsibility?'.[2]

With variations of detail and emphasis, it is widely assumed by those who adopt this approach that the social services—'the moving frontier of social conscience'—were first established by religious and charitable pioneers and later consolidated by the state, under Acts of Parliament which were often due to pressure from the Labour movement. The services provide benefits for the relatively poor at the expense of the relatively rich—benefits which enable the poor to have some of the things that the rich can furnish for themselves unaided.

Within these assumptions there is still plenty of room for disagreement. At one extreme are those who regard the social services as a charitable burden borne on the back of the 'productive' institutions of the economy. To them these services are a 'residual' function of government, a temporary expedient to be dispensed with as soon as growing wealth and enlightenment enable the poor to meet their own needs through the 'normal' mechanisms of the market. At the other extreme are those who regard these services as a necessary and growing feature of a 'progressive' economy, producing an increasingly just and efficient society in which the major decisions will be based on rational and humane criteria. But, whether they look upon them as a dangerous intrusion upon normality or as a good deed in a naughty world, advocates at both extremes tend to regard the social services as distinctive institutions operating according to economic, political and moral rules which differ from those that apply elsewhere. These

---

[1] Iain McLeod and Enoch Powell, *The Social Services. Needs and Means.* Conservative Political Centre, 2nd edn 1954, pp. 5 and 9. (Italics in original.)

[2] Penelope Hall, *The Social Services of Modern England.* Routledge & Kegan Paul, 1959, pp. 3–4 and 7.

assumptions encourage the beliefs that the institutions currently described as social services are the subject matter of Social Administration, and the study of these institutions constitutes a distinctive academic discipline which will eventually furnish distinctive 'principles of social policy'.

History gives scant support to this point of view and it is to history that we must turn in order to grasp its limitations. Any study of the development of social policies soon reveals many tangled strands in the story. One strand is the continuing endeavour to provide the environment required for industrial development. Social services did not begin with industrialism: the guilds preceded the friendly societies, the Elizabethan Poor Law preceded the New Poor Law, and who knows when charity began? But the industrial revolution brought new demands which had to be met in new ways. It called for increasingly clear-cut distinctions between those who were in work and those who were not—between the self-supporting and the dependent. It called for a mobile, disciplined and increasingly educated labour force. As a labour market developed from which the young and the old were gradually excluded, and as rising living standards extended the expectation of life and hence the number of elderly dependants, so the poverty cycle afflicting children, their parents and the aged was greatly intensified.

Industrialisation brought the ruin of obsolete industries and the threat of recurring unemployment in every industry; it also created the big city, with its new problems of public health and public order. 'The age of great cities', said Walter Bagehot, 'requires strong government.'[1] But neither working men nor their employers could wait on government. In the friendly societies working men endeavoured to organise their own labour exchange, medical service, sick pay, unemployment benefits and funeral grants. Employers, too, attempted to create the conditions for more orderly and profitable industrial development when the opportunity arose. In the nineteenth century new towns built to serve the railways and other industries, showed the kind of environment which industry required, with police forces, medical services, savings banks, schools, pension schemes and housing—all provided or supported by the companies that established them. These communities were no Utopian experiment, but a hard-headed business investment. When at last the state assumed responsibility for elementary education, the Grand Junction Railway Company increased its contributions to the denominational schools of Crewe, the town it had created, for reasons that were frankly explained by its chairman: 'What is done at Crewe . . . in subscribing to schools, is only done after most careful consideration as to whether it is cheaper for the shareholders to pay a subscription or

[1] Mrs Russell Barrington, *Life of Walter Bagehot*, Longmans, 1914, pp. 393–5 Quoted by O. R. McGregor, 'Sociology and Welfare', *Sociological Review Monograph*, No. 4, 1961.

to pay the rate necessary to support a school board, the only consideration moving the directors being the economy which can be effected to the shareholders.'[1]

This strand in the development of social administration is still to be seen today as continuing industrial change throws up new needs and intensifies old ones. In Britain company chairmen may bewail the crippling weight of taxation and the debilitating effects of the state's welfare services in the opening paragraphs of their annual reports, but they go on to record the increasingly generous pension schemes and health services, the cheap canteens, the interest-free loans for house purchase and the other benefits they provide (at the consumer's expense) for their employees. Employers in other countries have gone even further in providing for the welfare of their workers. They point out that such benefits reduce absenteeism and labour turnover, help to recruit managerial staff and key workers, improve morale and promote efficiency. Meanwhile private insurance to meet the costs of education and medical care is booming, often with more help from employers, and the state has been called in to alleviate the poverty cycle amongst the rich and the middle income groups by redistributing their income over the life-span with the aid of increasingly elaborate tax allowances.

Clearly there is no argument about the necessity—the growing necessity, amongst rich and poor alike—for collective action of many kinds to redistribute income, to spread the risks and meet the needs that cannot be effectively met through personal expenditure. But who should distribute the benefits and levy the payments for them, and on what principles should they proceed? That is what people argue about.

The defence of the nation against economic and military rivals forms a second and closely related strand in the history of the social services. Sweat and courage were devalued by the industrialisation of production and warfare. A century ago it was clear that a nation must also be equipped with health and trained intelligence if it was to survive, militarily or economically. The Prussians, it was being said, had defeated the greatest military power in Europe because their soldiers could read and write and the French could not. To such requirements 'total war' has added a concern for 'civilian morale' derived from a sense of common purpose and confidence in the justice of the nation's social and political systems. The implications of these discoveries for social policies have been spelled out in the reforms which followed every major war.

The continually rising aspirations of ordinary people—aspirations often created by the social services themselves—form a third strand in

[1] W. H. Chaloner, *The Social and Economic Development of Crewe, 1780-1923*. Manchester University Press, 1950, p. 224.

the story. In Britain the first school attendance officers had a difficult task compelling hostile parents to send their children to school, with the uncertain backing of magistrates who might themselves be employing the children concerned. But in the first decade of this century this problem seems to have dwindled to a numerically trivial scale—intractable though it still remains.[1] That change probably came about because the first generation for whom a universal system of elementary schooling had been provided were by then sending their own children to school. The numbers of people seeking help from the health services—particularly the mental health services—appear to be increasing in many countries, though there is no evidence of a comparable increase in the disorders to be treated. The provision of new and better services has raised the aspirations, or lowered the 'pain thresholds', of the afflicted. Many forms of education and medical treatment must now be regarded as consumption goods for which demand will grow to match any increase in supply. Homelessness remains an obstinately insoluble problem.[2] Sixty years ago, thousands had no home, but they and their children hung on to life as best they could, starving in cellars and garrets. Today neither parents nor landlords are willing to tolerate housing conditions which used to be commonplace. Thus families become 'homeless', confident that in the last resort the government must shelter them. If it cannot do that, the family may disintegrate and more expensive forms of care will eventually have to be provided in children's homes or elsewhere.

Meanwhile, for technological and other reasons, the prices of the services upon which these rising aspirations are focused—particularly the prices of labour-intensive services like education and medical care —tend to increase more rapidly than other prices. Thus the development of social services does not hasten the day when people can provide for themselves through the 'normal' mechanisms of the market but makes it less likely that this will ever happen.

Britain embarked on her industrial revolution early, towards the end of a period in which the powers of central government had been severely and deliberately limited, at a time when the sea and the Royal Navy relieved the state of its most onerous responsibility—the maintenance of a standing army. With such a rudimentary government machine, collective action to soften the hardships of industrialism had often to be initiated by friendly societies, employers, and religious and charitable bodies, and for many years the state confined itself mainly to relieving the destitute. But in countries with stronger central governments and countries which have been industrialised more recently the development

---

[1] Julia Dixon, *School Attendance Officers*. University of Manchester, MA thesis, 1956.

[2] J. Greve, D. Page and S. Greve, *Homelessness in London*. Edinburgh, Scottish Academic Press, 1971.

of social services has often preceded industrial revolution; partly because collective action for the advancement of social welfare was seen to be a means of promoting and sustaining economic development. Britain too has occasionally experienced this reversal of its own traditional pattern. It has often been forgotten that the proposals made in the Beveridge Report for larger insurance benefits, financed by contributions which could be varied at short notice, gained support partly because they would help to maintain consumer demand through the post-war depressions then widely anticipated.

The creation of public services requires the recruitment and training of a growing number and variety of workers who in turn play a major part in extending and shaping the services themselves. The contribution of these groups—particularly those we call 'professions'—is a fifth strand in the story. Their history is a record of conflict—conflicts between the younger and older generations within the profession, conflicts with laymen and well established neighbouring professions, and conflicts between the sexes. All are to be seen in the letters of Florence Nightingale. 'The whole reform in nursing . . . has consisted in this:' she said to one of her protégées who had just been appointed a hospital matron, 'to take all power over the nursing out of the hands of the men, and put it into the hands of *one female trained* head and make her responsible for everything . . . Usually it is the medical staff who have injudiciously interfered . . . How much worse it is when it is the chaplain . . . *There is no worse matron than a chaplain.*'[1] Sometimes the professionals do battle with the administrators—the staff who are responsible for the management of the organisation rather than for the provision of services for individual clients. Thus a medical commission, investigating London's Poor Law infirmaries in 1865, reported that 'with regard to the powers entrusted to the surgeon we are of opinion that great need for reform exists. At present, owing to his nominal inferiority of rank to the master [of the Poor Law institution], an official who is nevertheless (save in exceptional instances) socially below him, an antagonism is often set up, and in many cases leads to the most vexatious and mischievous interference of the master with the purely medical orders of the surgeon . . .'[2] A sphere of expertise— 'purely medical'—is being carved out, and its practitioners seek the status needed to secure their hold upon it.

In their plan for the break-up of the Poor Law, the Webbs—those inveterate technocrats—proposed a wholesale eviction of laymen from positions of power in local administration, and their replacement by paid professional and administrative staff who would be co-ordinated

[1] Letter from Miss Nightingale, 1867. Quoted by Brian Abel-Smith, *A History of the Nursing Profession*. Heinemann, 1960, p. 25. (Italics hers.)

[2] Report of the Lancet Sanitary Commission for Investigating the State of the Infirmaries of Workhouses, 1866, pp. 31–2.

and supervised in every county borough by a new official, the Registrar of Public Assistance. One of their opponents attacked the scheme, saying that Englishmen would become 'sheep shepherded by an enormous and apparently irresponsible bureaucracy. . . . But stay—did I say irresponsible? To whom should an official be responsible but to an official? Behind the local superintendent there looms a greater figure—the unique glory of the Minority Report—that bureaucrat of bureaucrats, the Registrar—peripatetic, absolute and wielding, as the sword of his spirit, nothing less than a card index.'[1] The conflict between the minority and the majority in this Commission—two groups who agreed on so many radical reforms that their disputes now seem tragically trivial—can only be understood if we bear in mind the division between those who put their faith in the salaried public official and those who preferred unpaid volunteers and committeemen.

The commitment of professional groups to the development of their work and status has repeatedly led them to demand more and better social services—larger and more expensive services, too, which may not be best for the consumer. They have been disturbed by the knowledge that children cannot be taught unless they are first fed, that patients cannot be cured unless they are decently housed, that young delinquents cannot be tamed if they have no legitimate playground—for their primary responsibilities are not to the tax-payers or the organisation that employs them, but to their profession and the people whom they serve. The erosion of the Poor Law, as more and more of its functions were taken over by new services, was partly due to the lack of any generally enforced system of training for Poor Law officials, and their failure to acquire the expansive outlook and influential status of a profession.[2]

Each profession seeks to stress and develop those features of its work which are peculiar to itself, which distinguish it most effectively from other groups, and protect it from what are seen as extraneous or 'unprofessional' commitments. Partly as a result of this tendency to specialisation—sometimes fruitful, sometimes merely protective—each tends to promote the growth of satellite specialisms whose practitioners later seek professional status on their own account. The cluster of medical occupations offers the most highly developed example of this, although the same process can be seen elsewhere. Doctors needed trained nurses and medical social workers to assist in their work. The qualified midwife would not do the domestic chores often undertaken by her unqualified predecessors, and home help services developed partly to take over these functions. Now home help organisers have

[1] T. Hancock Nunn, *The Minority Report*. National Poor Law Reform Association (undated), p. 10.
[2] R. C. Mishra, *A History of the Relieving Officer in England and Wales from 1834 to 1948*. University of London, PhD thesis, 1969.

their own association (and an international association) and are pressing for training and registration. Meanwhile medical social workers are appointing specially trained assistants to relieve them of their clerical and routine welfare work.

Sometimes the process of multiplying sub-professions can be seen at work, together with some of the motives carrying it forward—as in the Plowden Report which advocated the appointment of 'teachers' aides' (trained ancillaries) in every primary school. 'The effectiveness and status of teachers will eventually be improved by their having assistants who can be used as they judge best.' If aides have to be left in sole charge of children they must be supervised by teachers, and 'responsibility allowances should be paid to teachers whose duties are increased in this way'.[1]

The struggle for the resources needed to provide an effective service and the struggle for 'professional freedom' (freedom, largely, from lay control) have frequently led the professions to call for bigger administrative units and increasing intervention on the part of central government—as witness, for example, the contribution of the medical profession to successive reorganisations of the health services, and the parts played by many professional groups in the debates about the reform of London's local government in 1965. Thus the growth of a new social service depends on the growth of new professions and new administrative organisations which then proceed to expand, subdivide and multiply. Thereafter the service can only be modified with their consent. It may be easier (as the Curtis Committee[2] concluded) to create a new service and a new profession than to make radical changes in the habits of existing organisations and professions.

To sum up: the social services are not an optional extra or an unproductive frill tacked on to the economy as a charitable afterthought; they are an integral and (in some form or other) a necessary part of an urban, industrial society—forms of collective regulation and provision which are required to meet the needs of a changing economy, to protect its citizens and to assure a market for its products. They are developed, differentiated and developed again in accordance with the changing aspirations of those who work in them and those whom they serve.

But since they are so deeply embedded in society, it follows that the social services cannot grow in a stable, liberal democracy without the consent of the major interests—political, industrial, religious or administrative—that hold power in such a society. These pressures produce

[1] *Children and Their Primary Schools*, a report of the Central Advisory Council for Education (England). HMSO, 1967; paras 921 and 926.
[2] *Report of the Care of Children Committee*, Cmd 6922, 1946. After reviewing the wide range of departments and professions with some responsibility for deprived children, the Committee concluded that all these responsibilities should be brought together in one new service.

WHAT SOCIAL ADMINISTRATION IS ABOUT

further strands in their history as people endeavour to meet changing or newly perceived needs without disrupting the social order. Some services—the penal system and much of the Poor Laws, for example—were established wholly or partly as means of social control; but similar motives appear in surprising places. 'An ill-educated and undisciplined population', the House of Commons was once told by one of its members, '... is one that may be found most dangerous to the neighbourhood in which it dwells, and ... a band of efficient schoolmasters is kept up at much less expense than a body of police or soldiery.'[1] Octavia Hill opposed the building of houses in courts or culs-de-sac for 'the poorer class of London labourers' because '... it is much more difficult to keep order in them. Where I own them, I feel very much more strongly the difficulty of keeping any public opinion or order in them, than the difficulty of getting air ...'[2]

Many social services have revolutionary potentialities. Thus the schools teach the illiterate to read Tom Paine as well as the Bible; they call for taxation on a new scale, and take over some of the social functions hitherto performed by the family, the church and employers—or so people have feared. Such services cannot develop until those with the power to prevent them are satisfied that they present no serious hazard to the existing order. In Britain the provision of elementary education was delayed for a generation as a result, and the secondary schools are only now beginning to free themselves from the assumption that there are three kinds of Englishmen—officers, NCOs and other ranks, as it were—for whom different types of schooling must be provided. Until recently the universities, too, still tailored their size and functions to the needs of the late nineteenth-century society in which their traditions took shape—bearing in mind, perhaps, that classic statement of their duty to preserve the existing order pronounced by one of Oxford's most distinguished sons. Cardinal Newman's ideal university would be a place in which 'people should be taught a wisdom, safe from the excesses and vagaries of individuals, embodied in institutions which have stood the trial and received the sanction of ages, and administered by men ... supported by their consistency with their predecessors and with each other'.[3]

Sociologists, fascinated by the capacity of socially stratified societies to preserve their hierarchies and privileges despite every attempt to democratise and equalise them, have sometimes concluded that without constant and aggressive pressure from the Labour movement social policies will only repress the poor and protect the rich. Although many

---

[1] Quoted in *Education in Wales, 1847–1947*. HMSO, 1948. p. 5.
[2] *Royal Commission on the Housing of the Working Classes 1884–5*; Minutes of Evidence. C 4402, para. 8886.
[3] John Henry Cardinal Newman, *The Idea of a University*. Longmans Green, 1893, p. xii.

examples lend support to this view, the reality is more complex. Shocked by scandals, armed with the Victorians' voluminous statistics of social conditions, and moved by humanitarian feeling, reformers within society's élite groups and bureaucracies have often taken steps to protect the most deprived, even when there were no political pressures or inducements to do so. Irish emigrants on their way to distant lands were utterly powerless and disfranchised, and no major campaign was ever mounted on their behalf in Parliament or the press. Yet they were eventually protected by the Passenger Acts which regulated conditions on passenger ships.[1] Similar stories could be told about many of the reforms which have led to the regulation of working conditions and housing standards, and the protection of groups such as canal boat families and gypsies. Popular pressure, when it occurred, was sometimes hostile to these developments.

This brief sketch of the evolution of the social services does not completely discredit popular assumptions about their origins and functions which are characteristic of an 'institutional' approach to this subject. Its purpose is to show that scholars with a sense of history have taught us that studies of social policy must go much further and deal with the evolution of a whole society—its private as well as its public sectors, its economy and politics as well as its individual human needs, its civil rights and social conventions as well as its social services. There is nothing new about this approach; it would have been familiar to Sidney and Beatrice Webb—or, much earlier, to Jeremy Bentham. But the establishment since their days of Social Administration as a recognised subject for study within the universities has too often confined its students to more restricted questions.

T. H. Marshall and Richard Titmuss played leading parts in enabling their students and colleagues to escape from this residual or philanthropic delineation of their field, confined too closely to the institutions which happened to be classified as social services. They formulated a more comprehensive approach dealing with the impact made upon society by government departments and policies of every kind. Marshall pointed out that the most significant effect of the development of the social services was to extend the meaning and rights of citizenship, and modify the social mechanisms which determine the distribution of lifechances, power and status.[2] Richard Titmuss showed that these distributions were determined not only by the government's explicit social policies and the institutions which happened to be labelled 'social services', but also by taxation and the conventions of the fiscal system, and by the rights and benefits attached to contracts of employment

[1] Oliver MacDonagh, *A Pattern of Government Growth*, MacGibbon & Kee, 1961.
[2] T. H. Marshall, *Citizenship and Social Class, and other Essays*. Cambridge University Press, 1950.

which he described as the occupational welfare system.[1] Later he went on to argue that the arrangements a society makes when it seeks or provides help for people in need—and particularly the extent to which it relies on the mechanisms and morality of the market place—have pervasive effects on the community's values and human relationships, and on the distributions of opportunities, power and status.[2] Marshall, Titmuss and their colleagues were concerned with the long aftermath of the industrial revolution and the continuing response of urban, industrial, bureaucratic societies to the massive transformations it has brought about. They placed the subject of Social Administration in a historical context and turned it into the study of equity—an exploration of the ways in which society formulates problems of distribution or social justice, and attempts to resolve these problems. They were unashamedly concerned about the character of their society, and expected students of the subject to propose policies for the future when they could responsibly do so.

Yet, at a more fundamental level, those who adopt this comprehensive, policy-oriented approach are at one with those whom we have described as having a more restricted institutional or residual approach to the subject, for all of them believe that their fellow citizens recognise human needs with a fair degree of consensus, that social priorities can be rationally debated, that social policies can help to make the world a better place, and that their own work can help to clarify these problems and make the policies more effective. All of them work within the liberal, social-democratic tradition of scholarship. It is a tradition with important political implications. Inheriting a utilitarian conviction that the ultimate test of a policy is its effects upon people and that the people themselves will generally be the best judge of their own interests, liberals assume their prescriptions will not deserve to be applied unless they win the approval of the electorate through the ballot box.

A 'Systems' Approach and a 'Pluralist' Approach

These have often been regarded—particularly by some of their own exponents—as conflicting approaches to the problems of government; but although they pose different questions about society, to which different kinds of answers are given, they have a common point of departure. Both are modes of analysis, not designed to formulate any general social philosophy, concerned with the processes of decision-making rather than their outcome.

'Systems' approaches of various kinds were originally devised to help practical men, but they have their roots in earlier academic work.

[1] Richard M. Titmuss, *The Social Division of Welfare*, Eleanor Rathbone Memorial Lecture. Liverpool University Press, 1956; reprinted in *Essays on the Welfare State*, Allen & Unwin, 1958.
[2] Richard M. Titmuss, *The Gift Relationship*, Allen & Unwin, 1970.

Decision-makers responsible for larger organisations and bigger decisions needed help in weighing up the growing numbers of factors about which they could secure information. They found that students of social policy (concerned with wider questions of equity) and economists (whose rather abstract theories about the behaviour of firms were designed to throw light on the workings of markets rather than individual organisations) both tended to ask the wrong kinds of questions, and work at too large a scale to provide the help they needed. Sociologists studying bureaucracy and industrial psychologists concerned with human relations often worked at too small a scale, and also asked the wrong questions, often concentrating on irrational behaviour and bureaucratic pathologies. So help was sought from mathematicians accustomed to rigorous analysis of complex problems. The questions posed for them were those that worry organisations whose bosses know roughly what they want but have difficulty in deciding how to attain it. Their advisers often proceeded by defining self-contained 'systems' of linked processes or activities which provided an accounting framework for the analysis of inputs and outputs of people, money, information or other things, and the changing stocks and flows at different points within these systems. Over time, changes occurring anywhere in the system had to be balanced by other changes occurring elsewhere in it.

Many different procedures have been devised.[1] The term 'systems analysis' is generally used to describe methods for formulating strategies in situations where aims may be initially unclear, many factors have to be considered, and the problem is complicated by uncertainty and risk. Cost-benefit analysis can help decision-makers to choose between different programmes of action once general aims have been agreed. At a smaller scale of complexity, operations research can identify the best techniques for attaining clearly specified objectives. These and other procedures (social accounting, zero budgeting, planning-programming-budgeting systems (PPBS), management by objectives, the analysis of interconnected decision areas (AIDA),[2] and so on) have been entitled 'programmatic analysis' in a recent review by Hugh Heclo.[3] 'Synoptic' and 'rational-comprehensive' are other labels which have been given to the more ambitious of these approaches. In each case the organisation's aims, and other requirements defining a solution of the problem, are prescribed from sources outside the analysis (possibly by the analyst himself, working in another capacity). The analyst's tasks are

[1] For an account of those applied to the fields of urban and regional planning see George Chadwick, *A Systems View of Planning.* Pergamon, 1971.
[2] J. K. Friend and W. N. Jessop, *Local Government and Strategic Choice.* Tavistock, 1969, Part III.
[3] 'Review Article: Policy Analysis', *British Journal of Political Science,* Vol. 2, 1973, p. 83.

to find ways of solving the problem more quickly, cheaply, safely—or in any other manner prescribed. In the course of his work he may show that the organisation's aims are contradictory, excessively expensive or unattainable within the rules laid down for solution of the problem, but it will be for others to approve modifications of these aims.

The flavour of a systems approach is well conveyed by Professor John Stewart who commends this large-scale version of it to those who manage local government. It is characteristically addressed to 'the organisation', rather than to smaller-scale entities (such as committees or chief executives) or bigger ones (such as society at large). It is thus best suited to problems which 'the organisation' can in fact solve unaided.

'1 The organisation identifies certain needs, present and foreseen, in its environment.

2 It sets objectives in relation to those needs, i.e. the extent to which it will plan to meet those needs.

3 It considers alternative ways of achieving those objectives.

4 It evaluates those alternatives in terms of their use of resources and of their effects.

5 Decisions are made in the light of that evaluation.

6 Those decisions are translated into management action.

7 The results of the action taken are monitored and fed back to modify the continuing process; by altering the perception of needs, the objectives set, the alternatives considered, the evaluation, the decision made or the action taken.'[1]

If exponents of this approach have a characteristic moral stance, it combines, among the best of them, a commitment to rigorous and honest decision-making procedures with a determination to give elected representatives (or other duly constituted authorities) greater scope for making their own choices.[2] These are the virtues of the good consultant. It would be an insult to their intelligence to say they assume that the world is rarely riven by irreconcilable conflicts and usually produces solid majorities for attainable objectives, but their methods certainly work best under these conditions. They work best, too, in organisations with clear aims, and well trained and highly disciplined members who can be relied on to act promptly and predictably when decisions are taken. It was no accident that PPBS was first applied successfully on a large scale in the US Defense Department.[3] A systems approach is less

[1] J. D. Stewart, *Management in Local Government: A Viewpoint*. Charles Knight, 1971, pp. viii–ix.
[2] This point is cogently made by Charles L. Schultze, *The Politics and Economics of Public Spending*. Brookings Institution, 1968.
[3] Aaron Wildavsky, 'Rescuing Policy Analysis from PPBS', *Public Administration Review*, Vol. 29, No. 2, March/April 1969.

effective when major consequences of decisions are difficult to forecast or likely to fall outside the operations of the system to be studied, and when the aims and interests of the people involved are in conflict.

The characteristic strengths and weaknesses of this approach can be briefly illustrated. If a city council knows all about the volume of the city's domestic refuse and has sufficient tips, trucks and men to dispose of it, and opportunities for securing more when they are needed, and if it has the necessary legal powers and there is general agreement about the standards of service which should at current costs be maintained, then a systems approach will be well suited to the questions to be resolved—questions such as what size of truck to choose? Which tips to use and in what order? And how should the drivers' schedules and routes be organised? The scope of the analytical methods matches the scale of the problem to be analysed. These are the sort of problems which operational researchers enjoy working on: the Local Government Operational Research Unit solves similar ones every week. (It tackles more interesting problems too.)

But suppose local pressure groups complain that the city council's refuse trucks endanger their children and pollute the district; suppose local tips are filled up, the city starts dumping its refuse elsewhere, and neighbouring authorities bitterly resist this invasion of their territory; suppose labour shortages compel the council to find new ways of disposing of its refuse, but the dustmen threaten to strike if labour-saving equipment is installed, and the central government will only permit the council to buy this equipment if equivalent cuts are made in expenditures already approved for other council services. The scale of the council's problems has then expanded beyond the scope of a systems approach.

It was for the study of this kind of situation that various approaches which may be called 'pluralist' were devised. The two approaches have more in common than their most ardent advocates recognise. David Easton, whom we shall class amongst the 'pluralists', says his own approach 'can best be described as a systems analysis',[1] and both approaches owe a great deal to Herbert A. Simon, a pioneer in the analysis of decision-making under conditions of uncertainty.[2]

Unlike systems approaches devised by operational researchers to help practical men solve their own problems, pluralist approaches were devised by political scientists to explain how political processes work, and how practical men decide what to regard as a solution to their problems. Those we describe as pluralists generally argue that we live in a society in which there can be no lasting consensus. Policies evolve piecemeal as the unforeseen outcome of decisions made in different places by different élites under pressure from different quarters. Policy-making does not call for the specification of clearly defined objectives or

[1] *A Framework for Political Analysis*. Prentice-Hall, 1965; p. ix.
[2] *Administrative Behaviour*. 2nd edn, Free Press, 1957.

broader social aspirations; indeed it rarely permits either. Such supposedly rational strategies are precluded by the dizzying variety of options open to policy-makers, the profusion of unpredictable primary, secondary and subsequent consequences of their decisions, and the conflicting political pressures which must be accommodated every time something has to be done. The costs of gathering and interpreting all the information required to operate in the way prescribed by Professor Stewart are usually too great, the pluralists argue, for anyone to attempt the task. Moreover the clarification of aims—an essential feature of a systems approach—tends in practice to be counterproductive, because people who might agree about the immediate action to be taken fall out as their longer-term differences are revealed, while others who can at length be induced to agree about aims may not agree about immediate action.

In the field of social administration, pluralists would conclude, decision-makers attend to the most troublesome complaints and problems arising from current practice; they compare the immediate, predictable implications of a few marginal adjustments, and choose the course of action which seems most likely to resolve these difficulties, to gain political support and secure the assent of other people whose collaboration they need in order to implement the next few decisions to be made. Marginal changes can be tried out, their results examined, and modifications made before the next step is taken. This 'strategy of disjointed incrementalism' (or 'the science of muddling through') is not just a cynic's view of government; it may be a rational attempt to reduce risks and the costs of information gathering and analysis, to attain a tolerable rather than a perfect outcome, to minimise the probability of disaster rather than maximise the probability of bliss—an attempt to 'satisfice' rather than to 'optimise'.[1]

Before commenting on the pluralist approach we must distinguish three different things it may mean. First, it may amount to a penchant for particular research questions and methods which political scientists have sometimes called 'the group approach', central to which is a concern for interest groups and the interplay of pressures in the political market place. That approach has produced some revealing studies, and invigorated a political science which was dying for lack of any real understanding of human behaviour.

Secondly, it may be argued that accounts of the political process such as those I have briefly introduced provide the best descriptions of decision-making and government: this is how things actually work. That is an empirical question to be settled, case by case, in the light of

[1] This line of argument is well summarised by one of its critics, Charles L. Schultze, in *The Politics and Economics of Public Spending* (op. cit.). It is most briefly expressed by Charles E. Lindblom in 'The Science of Muddling Through' (*Public Administration Review*, Vol. 19, 1959, pp. 79–88) and most fully by David Braybrooke and Charles E. Lindblom in *A Strategy of Decision* (Free Press, 1963).

the evidence, and we shall consider it in the chapters which follow. But the pluralists will often have the best of the argument because the alternative of 'comprehensive' or 'synoptic' planning which they contrast with their own account of the political process is an 'Aunt Sally', described in terms much too ambitious to be taken seriously.[1]

Thirdly it may be argued that a pluralist society and pluralist styles of decision-making will generally be the best we can have. Some of the father figures of current social science have been quoted in support of this view. Sir Karl Popper, for example, rejected 'Utopian engineering' which 'claims to plan rationally for the whole of society, although we do not possess anything like the factual knowledge which would be necessary to make good such an ambitious claim', and called instead for 'the piecemeal engineer' who 'will . . . adopt the method of searching for, and fighting against, the greatest and most urgent evils of society, rather than searching for, and fighting for, its greatest ultimate good'. Again, '. . . blueprints for piecemeal engineering are comparatively simple. They are blueprints for single institutions. . . . If they go wrong, the damage is not very great, and a readjustment not very difficult.'[2] Popper rejected comprehensive social planning because it is dangerous.

Professor Oakeshott went further, arguing that aspirations for a planned society are not feasible at all. 'In political activity men sail a boundless and bottomless sea; there is neither harbour for shelter nor floor for anchorage, neither starting place nor appointed destination. The enterprise is to keep afloat on an even keel; the sea is both friend and enemy; and the seamanship consists in using the resources of a traditional manner of behaviour in order to make a friend of every hostile occasion.'[3] His poetic statement is both a description and a prescription.

David Braybrooke went further still. Whereas Oakeshott had described himself as a sceptic 'who would do better if only he knew how',[4] Braybrooke argued that 'the strategy of disjointed incrementalism' will 'rehabilitate utilitarianism' by providing 'a practical substitute' for Jeremy Bentham's felicific calculus.[5] In a telling phrase, David Easton later described 'the *responding* political system'[6] in which government attempts to maintain an equilibrium between competing demands for its 'outputs' and the reluctance people feel to make the 'inputs' required to sustain these outputs. Neither of these authors can

[1] See, for example, Braybrooke and Lindblom, *op. cit.*, chapters 3 and 4.
[2] *The Open Society and its Enemies*, Vol. 1. Routledge & Kegan Paul, 5th edn, 1966, pp. 158, 159 and 161.
[3] Michael Oakeshott, 'Political Education. An Inaugural Lecture', in *Rationalism in Politics*. Methuen, 1962, p. 127.
[4] *Political Education*. Bowes & Bowes, Cambridge, 1951, p. 7.
[5] Braybrooke and Lindblom, op. cit., Part 4. The quotations are taken from the titles of their chapters.
[6] Title of the concluding chapter in *A Framework for Political Analysis*. (Italics added.)

readily incorporate in their analyses the political leadership which may *change* demands and rally support for *new* policies.

At this stage it is clear that a school of thought which began with a penchant for asking certain kinds of questions (about the impact of competing interest groups on government, for example) and led on to descriptions of society (generalising about the way in which government works) has begun prescribing pretty boldly for our future. David Braybrooke and Charles Lindblom argue that the pluralist substitute they propose for Jeremy Bentham's principles is neutral—as useful to the Left as to the Right [1]—and it is of course true that pluralist descriptions of the world, if accurate, will furnish tactical guidance which can be as helpful to radicals as to conservatives. But to go a step further and argue that pluralism is 'good', in the sense that the pressures transmitted through pluralist social and political systems provide the most authentic or wisest guidance to action, is a different matter. Since this assumption now exerts a pervasive and powerful influence, it deserves further discussion before we turn to consider other approaches.

Many have argued that in democracies the needs of majorities are communicated to their rulers pretty effectively through the political market place. Robert Dahl, a leading pluralist, goes further. He concludes his classic essay on the American political system by saying that 'with all its defects' this system 'does . . . provide a high probability that *any* active and *legitimate* group will make itself heard effectively at some stage in the process of decision.'[2] Lindblom said much the same: 'Almost every interest has its watchdog. Without claiming that every interest has a sufficiently powerful watchdog, it can be argued that our system often can assure a more comprehensive regard for the values of the whole society than any attempt at intellectual comprehensiveness.'[3] Most Englishmen would probably be less confident about the virtues of their own constitution. But all we should note at this point is that these are empirical statements which call for verification in specific cases before they can be relied on.

If democratic politicians listen to majorities (a more modest, though still questionable claim) we may find they are only majorities of those 'present and voting', and we need not look as far as Marxist critics of a class-dominated society to discern some of the conservative biases lurking in this arrangement. Anthony Downs, one of the most perceptive analysts of pluralist politics, points out that it takes more than votes to exert any continuing influence on governments: it calls for information, contextual knowledge and the power to communicate opinions,

---

[1] Braybrooke and Lindblom, op. cit., pp. 106–10.
[2] Robert A. Dahl, *A Preface to Democratic Theory*. University of Chicago Press, 1956, p. 150. (Italics added.)
[3] 'The Science of Muddling Through', *Public Administration Review*, Vol. 19, 1959, p. 85.

all of which are very costly to attain and keep in working order. Since we specialise as producers but 'generalise' as consumers, producers will always have greater incentives and opportunities than consumers have to arm themselves with knowledge and the means of communication.[1] This may be equally true for the producers and consumers of welfare services, medical care, education and other social services. It would be naïve to adopt pluralist descriptions of the political market place as prescriptions for political organisation without troubling to find out whether those who succeed in such markets differ from those who succeed in the economic market place.

Even when majorities do get their way, the outcome may be discouraging, for governments can attend most successfully to the needs of majorities only if they neglect minorities. Some minorities gain a good deal of power—particularly if they muster enough votes in marginal constituencies—but the fate of minorities in general depends in the long run on the willingness of majorities to adopt social and political conventions—or ideologies—which protect them. Children, prisoners, mental patients, gypsies, emigrants, and immigrants who have yet to acquire a new citizenship are among the more obvious groups who lack a vote. For them, ideologies are vital. Easton notes that governments operate within a 'general culture' which 'helps to mould the constraints within which political discussion and competition take place . . . lends colour to the style of political life, and signalises the kinds of issues that will be considered important by the members of the system'[2]—but these ideologies are not a central concern of his kind of political scientist. That is indeed one of the blind spots of this political science. But what is no more than a distressing blind spot when presented as a description of reality becomes a dangerous bias when the description is transmuted into prescriptions for civilised government in societies where 'the end of ideology' is to be welcomed.

The techniques of economic analysis are now fashionable amongst political scientists, some of whom adopt a common economists' assumption that the marginal voters and consumers who withdraw their support from a political party or their demands from a public service will be those who have least to lose from the switch: they have, in economic terms, the smallest 'consumer surplus'. But reality may be more complex, and less reassuring. In the political market place the dissatisfied may complain, or transfer their custom to another shop— what Albert Hirschman has described as the options of 'voice' and 'exit'.[3] Those most likely to use each option will often be those who feel

[1] Anthony Downs, *An Economic Theory of Democracy*. Harper, 1957, p. 254.
[2] Easton, op. cit., p. 113. In an earlier book, *The Political System* (Knopf, 1953) Easton explains his mistrust of political scientists who give ideology—rather than equilibrium—a central place in their work.
[3] Albert O. Hirschman, *Exit, Voice, and Loyalty*. Harvard University Press, 1970.

they have most, not least, at stake, and those whose economic strength gives them both options. If the rich choose the 'exit' option—moving out of poor and ill-served neighbourhoods, and transferring to private doctors, private transport and private schools, rather than using the public services—their departure may further impoverish the poor by transferring the support of aggressive 'voices' from the services on which poor people depend to more affluent neighbourhoods and private services from which the poor are excluded. Once again, pluralist descriptions can be revealing, but when they are adopted as prescriptions (for example, by those who would replace expenditure on the social services with 'vouchers' intended to enable individual consumers to choose their own medical care and education in what is called 'the open market') their effects will usually be conservative if not reactionary. Economists themselves no longer make this mistake: they try to take account of the fact that public goods are supplied in 'packages' to groups of consumers who gain access to them only if they can join the appropriate 'club'.[1]

Another concept taken over from the economists which has given a conservative bias to pluralist political prescriptions is 'Pareto optimality'. It began as a rule for decision-making which served as a useful warning to economists that, no matter what its benefits, a change could not be classed as unequivocably desirable if any individual suffered from it. In the minds of some, this rule has gained the authority of a moral imperative: do not act if anyone will suffer. Yet it is only one of many potential rules for decision-making and not inherently more rational or convincing than its opposite: act if anyone will gain.[2]

Other procedures encouraged by pluralist prescriptions tend to have similar biases. The multiplication of representative bodies and layers of government—at regional, county and district levels—and the dispersal of power among them can both be advocated on pluralist grounds. But such policies raise the price of change by increasing the costs of getting things done—the costs of securing and imparting information, mobilising support and 'buying' political agreements. It is not surprising that corruption often flourishes most outrageously in supposedly 'weak' city governments of an avowedly pluralist kind where the costs of legitimate political decision-making can be so high that corruption may be the only alternative to paralysis. But it is less appealing to find pluralist analysts commending this pattern.[3]

The pluralist approach to social policy, and its supposed rival the

[1] Loudon Wingo, 'The Quality of Life: Toward a Microeconomic Definition', *Urban Studies*, February 1973.
[2] For a revealing analysis of these problems, see Brian Barry, *Political Argument*. Routledge & Kegan Paul, 1965.
[3] Martin Meyerson and Edward C. Banfield (*Politics, Planning and the Public Interest. The Case of Public Housing in Chicago*, Free Press of Glencoe, 1955), provide examples. L. J. Sharpe in 'American Democracy Reconsidered' (*British Journal of Political Science*, January 1973, pp. 1–28; and April 1973, pp. 129–67) gives others.

systems approach, are both blinkered in a more fundamental fashion. They are unhistorical. They concentrate on the present and do not place the problems they study in the context of the longer-term development of the societies concerned. These scholars have together produced the most important contributions to political science during the last twenty years. But they perceive the aims, values and loyalties of individuals as 'inputs' to the systems and processes they study, and seldom ask where these ideologies originated, whether they are appropriate to the needs of the time, or what contribution they will make to the future development of the wider society.[1] Neither do they feel much obligation, in their capacity as social scientists, to contribute to public debate about the future of their country and the ideologies which should inform its development and protect its most vulnerable citizens. What is will be—till something else turns up. And both in their time will be right. These limitations distinguish both approaches from those we have already discussed, and from those to which we now turn.

From a Marxist to a 'Structuralist' Approach

For Marx and his followers social problems could not be understood until they were placed in their historical context, and it was the scholar's duty not only to understand his society but to change it. With that, radical liberals would agree; but they and the Marxists thereafter part company. Marxists see man as a producer, not only of goods and services but of society itself, for 'the act of reproduction changes not only the objective conditions—e.g. transforming village into town . . .—but the producers change with it, by the emergence of new qualities, by transforming and developing themselves in production, forming new powers and new conceptions, new modes of intercourse, new needs, and new speech'.[2] In a capitalist society men's opportunities and status depend on their access to means of production belonging to property owners who form with their associates a ruling class whose power is maintained from generation to generation by the transmission of inherited wealth through the family, and by selective recruitment of able people from lower classes who conform to the dominant culture. 'The ideas of the ruling class are in every epoch the ruling ideas . . . The ruling ideas are nothing more than the ideal expression of the dominant

---

[1] This does not mean that pluralists are personally callous about values, ideologies or the future—only that their political science does not readily lend itself to an analysis of these things. For 'a venture in social forecasting' by a member of this school, see David Bell, *The Coming of Post-Industrial Society*. Heinemann, 1974.

[2] Karl Marx, *Pre-Capitalist Economic Formations*, E. J. Hobsbawm (ed.) (Lawrence & Wishart, 1964, p. 93). We have been guided to a number of references used at this stage of the discussion by Graeme Duncan's thoughtful book, *Marx and Mill: Two Views of Social Conflict and Social Harmony*. Cambridge University Press, 1973.

material relationships . . .'¹ Thus Marxists see the freedom, creative individuality and scientific knowledge so prized by liberals as merely the ideology and privileges of the bourgeoisie. In a society stripped of communal, patriarchal or feudal restraints—a mere labour market— the capitalists degrade workers into appendages of machines and capture much of the value they produce to invest in new capital and the continuing enrichment of the ruling class. Government itself belongs to this class, for 'the executive of the modern state is but a committee for managing the common affairs of the whole bourgeoisie.'²

Thus, it is argued, while capitalism survives, the social policies of governments can only be designed to maintain the existing social order; they are the product not the creator of that order, and 'the public interest' can be no more than the interests of the ruling class. Debates about social priorities, in which liberals delight, are pointless. Engels explained as much in the principal Marxist text on housing policy: '. . . it does not occur to me to try to solve the so-called housing *question* any more than I can occupy myself with the details of the still more important *food question*, I am satisfied if I can prove . . . that there are houses enough in evidence to provide the working masses for the time being with roomy and healthy living accommodation. To speculate as to how a future society would organise the distribution . . . of dwellings leads directly to Utopia.'³ (He did not take the trouble to discover whether there *were* 'houses enough'.)

Latter-day exponents of this view are convinced that the social services tend only to institutionalise and legitimise social injustice, keeping the working class in subjection and conferring their most generous benefits on the bourgeoisie.⁴ The 'welfare state', they argue, is a sham. The problems it purports to solve are a product of capitalism; they can only—and then readily—be solved when capitalism is destroyed. Scholars working in the field of Social Administration may open their students' eyes to the world's iniquities, but within a bourgeois democracy they can make few practical contributions to the development of the social services unless they are content to be docile servants of the existing order. Not surprisingly, the purer forms of this view are more often found in neighbouring disciplines—among sociologists and political scientists, for instance—than in University Departments of Social Administration. It furnishes its advocates with a very comfortable intellectual posture, for they are burdened neither by the

---

[1] Karl Marx and Frederick Engels, *The German Ideology*. Lawrence & Wishart, 1965, p. 60.
[2] *The Communist Manifesto*.
[3] Frederick Engels, *The Housing Question*. Lawrence & Wishart, 1936, p. 98.
[4] Although he himself does not belong to this school of thought, Brian Abel-Smith's much quoted exposé of the inequitable effects of social policies ('Whose Welfare State?', in Norman Mackenzie (ed.), *Conviction*. McGibbon & Kee, 1958) is still one of the best things of its kind.

philanthropic duties of a conservative *noblesse oblige*, nor by the social democratic obligation to soil their hands with the compromises of reformist politics, nor—in Britain—by the danger that there might actually be a bloody revolution. They are not even required to formulate concrete priorities and policies for a communist society—what Engels contemptuously called 'the details'—for that, as he explained, would lead 'directly to Utopia'. Comfort, however, is no proof of error.

We should beware of saying that Marxism is simply wrong, for this is a more fully articulated ideology than any of the others we have considered, and its propositions—rather like those of religion or Freudian psychology—can be interpreted to explain almost any outcome. Manual workers and their children, it is said, rarely achieve 'the big leap into higher business and independent professional occupations'. If they do gain positions of power, 'it is all but inevitable that recruits from the subordinate classes into the upper reaches of the state system should, by the very fact of their entry into it, become part of the class which continues to dominate it'. If, against all the odds, 'a dramatic extension of the system of welfare' is brought about, we can be sure that 'it did not, for all its importance, constitute any threat to the existing system of power or privilege' because reform, once it has occurred, must by definition accord with the ideas of the ruling class for they are the ruling ideas.[1]

Although they sound like a series of verifiable assertions these propositions amount in fact to a rambling tautology which is true by definition. They are also a kind of metaphor—an 'as if' statement. Few would assert that the ruling classes engage in a continuously successful plot to protect their privileges and the existing social order; it is only claimed that history unfolds *as if* something like this was going on.

Few social theories offer much more than tautologies and metaphors of this kind. Economists who formulated the traditional theory of the firm also offer us a set of propositions which are true by definition. They do not assert that entrepreneurs actually equate their marginal costs and revenues—or even know what they are. They tell us only that the market as a whole tends to behave as if they did, because those who persistently fail to do so are eventually replaced by others who (wittingly or unwittingly) come nearer to achieving that. The first question to ask about theories of this kind is not 'are they true?' but 'are they revealing, and will they help us make better predictions?'

Marxist metaphors of class conflict are often revealing when predictions must be made about the social outcome of reforms—such as the reorganisation of secondary education on comprehensive lines, for example. Without anyone plotting the subjection of the working class or the protection of privilege, society tends to evolve as if something of

[1] The quotations in this paragraph all come from Ralph Miliband, *The State in Capitalist Society*. Quartet Books, 1973, pp. 37, 60 and 99.

that sort was happening, and those who try too aggressively to reverse these trends tend before long to lose power. Inequality is complex, pervasive and deeply rooted in the social order.

But we should also ask how well such theories match the realities examined by their authors. If the match is a poor one, the analyses and predictions they furnish will grow increasingly misleading as time goes by. The traditional Marxist story is now apt, a century after his times, to mislead us at many points—a fact which would not have surprised Marx himself. A few of the anachronisms and inconsistencies which bear most directly on problems of social policy should be noted.

Marxists have criticised industrial society for converting medieval concepts of property, regarded as *claims*—often communal claims—to a *benefit* of some kind, into capitalist concepts of property, regarded as the exclusive and unlimited possession of *things* which give power over the labour of others.[1] But some have failed to notice that under social democratic government property is again changing its character. Access to housing, an income in retirement, education, and medical care—needs which used to constitute four of the main reasons why people sought property—now depends increasingly on rights assured and distributed by government, or at least through communal action, in ways which differ from those characteristic of the 'open market'. Even when these things are still purchased for cash, access to them depends increasingly on the buyer's tax status (and tax reliefs), his employment status (with which go occupational pensions and welfare services) and other collectively regulated factors of various kinds. More and more people are employed by the state, and rights to practise in many trades and professions—as teacher, doctor, engineer, taxi driver, farmer, bookmaker, docker and so on—are collectively regulated. Growing proportions of income—from family allowances, unemployment pay, student grants, supplementary benefits, farming subsidies and other payments—have nothing to do with individual contracts of employment. Ownership of land, which was simplified during the nineteenth century into something that often came close to unlimited, personal possession, is again becoming an increasingly complex, communally regulated bundle of rights—rights to occupy, to develop for various purposes, to lease, sell or inherit, to pay taxes at varying rates and to secure capital gains or to vote in elections, and so on. Like the leaves of an artichoke, the meaning of land ownership is being endlessly unfolded, subdivided and elaborated.

These are the kinds of development which led T. H. Marshall to examine the changing meaning of citizenship, and Richard Titmuss to discuss the social division of welfare. Neither assumed that things would necessarily grow better—in some respects they seemed to be

[1] The transformation is traced by C. B. Macpherson in *The Political Theory of Possessive Individualism: Hobbes to Locke*. Oxford University Press, 1962.

growing worse—but they pointed out that it was no longer possible to understand what was happening in urban, industrial, bureaucratic societies without careful study of these new forms of property or rights. With distinguished exceptions,[1] Marxist observers tend to be so obsessed with older forms of property characteristic of their traditional enemy, old-fashioned capitalism, that they fail to pay sufficient attention to these developments.

New forms of power are emerging—powers such as those of the planners who regulate land uses and development rights, and those of the various 'gate-keepers' who allocate access to public housing, secondary schools and universities, hospital beds, and other things which may determine the course, and even the length, of people's lives. These powers work in ways which cannot be adequately explained in traditional Marxist terms.

New forms of oppression arise from the use of these powers. Marxist propagandists who draw on the evidence of reformist bodies such as Shelter, the National Council for Civil Liberties, and the Child Poverty Action Group often fail to notice that many of the injustices they deplore are due to the exclusion of minorities from rights accorded by the state to majorities through social services originally introduced by spokesmen of the Labour movement. The exclusion of mobile households and fatherless families from municipal housing, immigrant workers from jobs in the docks, and gypsies from the camping sites they used to occupy are recent examples of problems which will not be automatically resolved by capturing power for the workers. Far from it.

Fortunately, younger neo-Marxists, trying to appraise such developments in various countries, are beginning to examine Eastern Europe as critically as the West,[2] and to recognise the price which the centrally planned economies have paid in lost liberties for the progress they have made in equalising the distribution of wealth and housing. (In equalising the distribution of income and medical care, the scores of East and West are much more equal.) The early Marxists offered revealing observations about urban, industrial, bureaucratic societies which were in their day capitalist—what else could they be? But now that we have more models to study it is clear that the overthrow of capitalism will not necessarily put things right. Ralf Dahrendorf has argued that 'the abolition of property merely replaces the old classes with new ones ... ' 'The origin of inequality is ... to be found in ... norms of behaviour to which sanctions are attached.' For '... all men are equal *before* the law but they are no longer equal *after* it. ... ' In any society 'the system

---

[1] C. B. Macpherson has revealingly analysed some of these developments in 'A Political Theory of Property', Chapter 6 of *Democratic Theory* (Oxford University Press, 1973).

[2] E.g. Frank Parkin, *Class Inequality and Political Order*. MacGibbon & Kee, 1971, pp. 171–83.

of inequality that we call social stratification is only a secondary consequence of the social structure of power'.[1] Ralf Dahrendorf's approach may be better described as 'structuralist', rather than neo-Marxist. He and others echo earlier pessimistic analyses by scholars who accepted that we are unlikely to escape from highly stratified societies and their ruling classes.[2]

Conclusion
We must now draw this essay to a conclusion and note some of the questions it poses for discussion in the course of the case studies which follow. But first, since so condensed a survey of such a varied literature is bound to be confusing, it may be helpful to show how the approaches we have been discussing have been applied to one field of Social Administration. For this purpose we have chosen the field of urban studies and planning, but similar examples could have been found in many other fields of social policy. All the examples we have chosen are impressive books, worth careful study. They are not competing approaches, analytically speaking, for they deal with different questions in different ways. We only have to choose between them when their authors move on from analysis and description to evaluation and prescription.

Although narrowly institutional approaches to urban planning can be found, they offer the scholar and the practising planner so little help that we can turn straight to Hugh Stretton's study, *Ideas for Australian Cities*,[3] which provides a historically informed and boldly comprehensive survey of planning policies in four of the biggest Australian towns. Stretton traces the political development of these cities, showing how their economic and social structure have evolved within the constraints of their geography. He proposes policies for the future whenever he can responsibly do so. To attempt so comprehensive a task within the covers of a small book he has to speculate at many points where evidence is lacking. To anyone with a less perceptive grasp of the social sciences and the history of his own country (which means nearly everyone) the task would be impossible. But Stretton is explicit about the kind of criteria against which he would expect to see his own proposals tested. Will they help to extend and equalise people's access to jobs, shops, social services and recreation? Will they prevent massive segregation of the rich and poor? Will they enable children, old people

[1] Ralf Dahrendorf, *Essays in the Theory of Society*. Routledge & Kegan Paul, 1968, pp. 160n. and 169.
[2] In their different ways James Burnham, *The Managerial Revolution* (Putman, 1942) and R. Michels, *Political Parties: A Sociological Study of the Oligarchical Tendencies of Modern Democracy* (Free Press, 1958) illustrate these views.
[3] Melbourne, Georgian House, 1970. William Ashworth, *The Genesis of Modern British Town Planning* (Routledge & Kegan Paul, 1954) might have served as another example.

and others who do not drive cars to get about conveniently and safely? In short, will people—and particularly the poorest people—like the results?

When it comes to the tactics of action, Stretton is quite prepared to use a disjointedly incremental approach, and admires others who have done likewise in a good cause. But he attempts throughout his study to formulate a broader, humane consensus about planning policies based on rational understanding of the ways in which cities work. Although he examines the detail of housing layouts and pedestrian movements he always has an eye for more complex problems and the simplifications which may help to clarify them: 'very big cities are both physical and psychological devices for quietly shifting resources from poorer to richer, and for excusing or concealing—with a baffled but complacent air—the increasing deprivation of the poor'.[1]

Brian McLoughlin's book, *Urban and Regional Planning. A Systems Approach*,[2] is a rigorous but pragmatic example of the approach it claims to represent. He explains how activities and communications between their locations are related to each other in an urban system, and how these changing relationships may be analysed in order to clarify the options open to planners. He is confident that 'the fundamental principles of control in complex systems are universal, irrespective of the actual nature of the system . . .'[3] At this level of generality he naturally does not attempt to propose policies, other than policies of an organisational and methodological kind for the improvement of analytical and decision-making procedures. Neither does he explain where the creative spark of design originates or how the aims of a plan are generated. This is neither Genesis nor Revelations but The Acts of the Apostles: 'Plan formulation, in essence, is the choice of those projected or simulated future states of the system which yield optimum conditions. These optimum conditions are described by reference to the performance criteria derived from the goals.'[4] Others will choose these goals.

In *Urban Dynamics*[5] Jay Forrester, a more ambitious and less fastidious systems man, starts from a simple set of policy objectives and some assumptions about the relationships between three main groups of variables representing population, jobs and housing. He then

[1] Stretton, op. cit. p. 310.
[2] New York, Praeger, 1969.
[3] Ibid., p. 17.
[4] Ibid., p. 231. 'I am indebted' says McLoughlin 'to Dr G. F. Chadwick for this form of words.' In his own book (*A Systems View of Planning*, Pergamon, 1971) George Chadwick says' "Widening the range of choice" is perhaps the best and only way of describing what town and regional planning *ought* to be about . . .' (p. 332). But in a world of scarcities, widening the choices of some necessarily implies restricting the choices of others.
[5] MIT Press, 1969.

simulates the growth of a city over a period of 250 years. Since the supply of land is fixed and many other elements in his system have exponential rates of growth, Forrester's city heads inevitably for crises which for some reason are described as unexpected or 'counter-intuitive'. To social democrats many of his assumptions will appear unrealistic or distasteful, but he would reply that it is up to them to propose better alternatives: his purpose is only to trace interactions in an urban system through time, and point out their implications for policy-makers. To Forrester, correlations are explanations, and all are potentially reversible. Thus, since poor people are attracted to cheap housing, removing it will make them go away again. Where they go, once outside the city, is no concern of the planner because his analytical system, and hence his social responsibilities, do not extend beyond the city's boundaries.

Politics, Planning and the Public Interest. The Case of Public Housing in Chicago, by Martin Meyerson and Edward C. Banfield[1] still provides a classic account of the disjointedly incremental process of planning in a plural society, followed by a shrewd analysis of its three main terms—'politics', 'planning' and 'the public interest'. 'We are not interested', they say, 'in making specific recommendations having application to the Chicago scene ... but in developing a perspective for the analysis of decision-making processes in general.'[2] They defend 'machine' politics and pluralist political styles fairly vigorously, for 'the survival and prosperity of the machine depended on its ability to find settlements which both sides would agree represented the public interest or something approaching it'.[3] But the basic craftsmanship of their report enables the reader to form judgements of his own about the character of these processes and the interests they are most likely to serve.

The purer forms of Marxist urban research will generally be confined to the analysis of urban problems, since in a market economy their authors would not expect to be able to propose policies for the future which could be accepted by the ruling class. David Harvey's *Social Justice and the City*[4] presents a series of essays by this widely read geographer which record his abandonment of a liberal for a Marxist standpoint and his subsequent attempts to analyse urbanism, social change and the meanings of more specific concepts such as income and rent. He shows how whole disciplines have been created for the analysis of problems posed by a particular kind of society and the interests that dominate it. This is the recurring problem of the social scientist who

---

[1] Free Press, Glencoe, 1955. Another good and more recent example of this approach is Alan A. Altshuler's, *The City Planning Process: A Political Analysis*. Cornell University Press, 1965.
[2] Op. cit., p. 14.
[3] Ibid., p. 300.
[4] Edward Arnold, 1973.

wants to get to the bottom of his subject—how to ask questions about it which do not by their unexamined assumptions preclude him from understanding essential features of his material. Harvey discusses these philosophical questions usefully.

Unfortunately the faith he has adopted seems to impose new blinkers on his vision even more confining than the old ones. Every aspect of urbanism must be treated as a fresh opportunity for contrasting socialist and capitalist cities (always to the disadvantage of the latter). The structuralist view that the socialist and the capitalist versions of urban, industrial, bureaucratic societies both face similar problems which neither copes with very well has no place here.

Harvey rejects 'positivist method' and 'traditional bi-valued Aristotelian logic to test hypotheses' which 'are either true or false . . .' For him the conventional rules of scholarship are 'mere liberalism'.[1] He proceeds by assertion, unsupported by empirical evidence, to propositions which become increasingly difficult to verify. Thus, the 'surplus value' required for investment in urban development—a destructive process under capitalism—is transformed under socialism because 'a socialist surplus arises, in principle at least, out of unalienated labour. The surplus so redefined loses its class character; all members of the society who are able to yield up a certain quantity of their surplus labour for socially defined purposes. It is from this theoretical perspective that we have to gauge the emergence of new urban forms'.[2] Capitalist investment is bad, socialist good.

But who invests, in what, and for whose benefit? Clearly there is little point in seeking the views of the electorate on such questions because they will reflect 'the ruling ideas' which—as we have been told—are merely the ideas of the ruling class. As in the previous approaches we have considered, analytical style and descriptive content shape the prescriptions which follow. The human implications of Harvey's faith are frightening. We are reminded of Engels' assertion that housing problems will be readily solved once capitalism has been destroyed. Yet between 1923 and 1950 the urban population of the Soviet Union grew from 21·6 to 74·5 millions, and urban dwelling space grew from 139 to 297 million square metres. Space per head fell from 6·4 to 4·0 square metres. Although the war played a part in this story, the decline continued throughout the period with no intervals of improvement. A radical change in policy followed after 1952: none too soon—for by then there had been a reduction of nearly 40 per cent in the housing space available for urban workers.[3] A social disaster of these dimensions could not have occurred in a parliamentary democracy which, despite

---

[1] Ibid., pp. 130 and 146.
[2] Ibid., p. 235.
[3] Timothy Sosnovy, *The Housing Problem in the Soviet Union*. Research Program on the USSR, New York, 1954.

its faults, tests policies and the theories on which they are based by enabling those who experience their effects to get rid of their rulers from time to time. Researchers whose work deals with human needs and social policies have a comparable obligation to phrase their hypotheses in human terms and test them with empirical evidence when they can. Their assertions must at least be wrong—not merely unverifiable.

Finally, what questions should this chapter leave in our minds to be considered in the case studies which follow? These questions are too big to answer in any conclusive fashion, but we may be able to throw some light on them.

Was any comprehensive ideology brought to bear in making the decisions we have studied? Who contributed most to these ideas, and where did they get them? What parts were played by politicians, administrators, professional staff and the users of the services concerned? Were rigorous systems analyses attempted or feasible? Did the process of decision-making proceed in a disjointedly incremental fashion and could it have been otherwise? What political pressures were brought to bear—by whom and on whom? Whose needs are likely to be neglected? Were latent or overt class conflicts present, and how were they settled? Does the presence of working-class movements affect the outcome? How far were the interests of the poor and powerless taken into account? Difficult though they are, these are some of the more practical questions to bear in mind.

Behind such questions lie larger issues. Can urban, industrial, bureaucratic societies realise the promises of equality and social justice implicit in their liberal origins? Can there be a sense of the public interest in such complex societies? Can they formulate a humane consensus—or any lasting consensus—about the needs of their citizens? Can any fundamental change be wrought within such societies, or is radical reform precluded by the political power and the intellectual monopoly of their ruling classes—until revolution comes to break the mould? What contribution, if any, can the research worker make to resolving these dilemmas? Can the study of Social Administration enable him to help in making the world a better place?

CHAPTER 2

THE CASE STUDIES

Our social services are not a self-contained, static or completed edifice. They are part of a more general and continually evolving collective response to the changing needs of an industrial society. Their objectives, derived from diverse pressures and motives, are continually developing and continually disputed. Their organisation has no validity in its own right; it can only be evaluated in the light of the tasks it has to perform. Thus neither the ends nor the means of social administration can be taken as 'given'; they must be considered, and questioned, together. Moreover these ends and means are not determined, once and for all, by Parliament: they are repeatedly reshaped and reinterpreted by people at all levels in the social services and by the changing needs and expectations of their customers.

The central purpose of our studies is to throw light on the evolution of the aims, functions and methods of the social services, and the contribution made to that evolution by different groups and individuals. They deal with change, and the manner in which it comes about. We have made no attempt to pass judgement on these changes: although the reader may form his own judgements from time to time, our purpose has been to explain, not to evaluate, the development of social policies. These studies are a small part of the broader academic enterprise of exploring the ways in which societies evolve. They call for the aid of other disciplines that deal with human behaviour and social structure, and their debt to these disciplines will be obvious.

The administrative units which formed the starting point for our studies were local offices of social services provided by central and local government and by voluntary organisations. All but one of these units operated in the London area. We approached the officials responsible for them and asked: 'What are the most important developments or changes which have taken place in your department (or local office) in the last few years?' In some cases we were assured that no 'developments' or 'changes' had occurred for many years. If this view was maintained in subsequent discussion we proceeded no further—even though we were sometimes aware that changes of some importance had taken place. In other cases, one or more developments were mentioned, and we then selected whatever seemed the most important (and accessible to research) in consultation with the head of the local unit concerned. Clearly these developments cannot be regarded as a random sample of the administrative process, or of the work of London's social services. They may have been chosen because they were expected to interest a University Department of Social Administration, or because they were easily identified and analysed, or because they were unlikely to discredit the service being studied. Nevertheless they were chosen not by outsiders who might have misapprehensions about the most important features of the work to be studied, but by those directly responsible for the administrative units concerned. The outcome may prove less dramatic than a series of studies chosen because they were 'interesting' or likely to provide 'good teaching material', but it may afford a more realistic and representative picture of important local developments in social administration—developments more important than the reorganisation of record-keeping procedures or a typing-pool, but more local than a change in central government policy or the nationwide implementation of new legislation. Having selected our material in this fashion, we felt bound to publish all the studies we made: to exclude any because they seemed uninteresting or untypical would destroy whatever merits our selection procedure may have.

Our methods of research were simple though laborious; we read all the relevant documents we could find and interviewed those who had been most closely concerned with the events to be traced. Some of the developments chosen were still in progress, but most of them had been completed months earlier. Human forgetfulness or reticence and the failure to make or preserve records inevitably prevented us from securing the complete story in some cases. Publication had then to be approved by senior officials, and at times it seemed that our studies were either dull, because we had not discovered the full story, or unpublishable—because we had. But with the passage of time we have arrived at publishable versions of the studies which include all we were able to discover that appeared to us to be of real importance.

These studies were written without theoretical presuppositions or technical terminology. While there is nothing more revealing than a good theory, few things can be so stultifying and misleading as a bad one. Since it was the lack of enlightening and tested theories of administration which prompted this research in the first place, it seemed best to present our studies in a descriptive fashion, without attempting to illustrate or prove any general conclusions, so that the reader could be enabled, as far as possible, to draw his own conclusions and reject ours. During the decade since these studies were written research on administration has made great advances, but it still tends to be weakest when called upon to explain how and why the functions and policies of a service change. Each of our studies is followed by a brief discussion of the light it throws on the evolution of social policies—a marginal commentary that is drawn together and reappraised in the last chapter of the book. To these discussions have been added postscripts, completed early in 1974, which briefly outline subsequent developments that throw light on the original studies. The differing interests of our readers will prompt them to look for different things in these studies, and some may be bewildered by the points we have chosen to explore in our discussions and postscripts. Our purposes may become clearer if the last chapter of the book is read before the case studies.

We owe a great debt to all those who helped us compile and revise these studies. Any errors and distortions still to be found in them are the authors' responsibility. The officials who helped in this research knew it was unlikely to be of any immediate practical value to them and might even prove harmful—if only in the demands it made on the time of busy people. We hope their patience and generosity may encourage others to help in future work of this kind. Meanwhile it must constantly be borne in mind that our studies do *not* provide a complete or typical picture of the organisations and services concerned, nor were they intended to do so; they deal only with particular developments within them and particular phases of their history. Their purpose is not to provide an account of current social policies, but an analysis of the manner in which such policies are formulated, implemented and modified at the local level.

Our accounts of administrative processes often make them appear deceptively systematic and continuous. In practice the performance of a particular task, or the carrying through of a particular development, seldom fills the working day of those responsible for it. It more typically consists of one item towards the end of a crowded committee agenda, a telephone call made the following month, a paragraph in a memorandum prepared over the weekend dealing mainly with other matters, then a hurried departmental meeting followed by a chance conversation between two people on their way to lunch. Such are the scattered incidents—if the researcher is fortunate enough to trace them—which should be threaded together to produce what the participants may later regard as an unrecognisably coherent story.

Finally we must draw attention to an omission so obvious that it may too easily be overlooked. Our resources only permitted us to read records and interview many of the staff who participated in the developments examined. We did not seek the other side of the story—the views of the social services' clients and consumers. The contribution they made to the development of these services is glimpsed from time to time, but to explore it systematically would have taken far more time and labour than were available to us. This book presents an analysis of social administration which is derived from one side of the counter only.

CHAPTER 3

SLUM CLEARANCE BEGINS AGAIN IN BETHNAL GREEN

The first study in this series provides a useful introduction to the framework of local government which forms the setting for several subsequent studies. A change in the resources available for a service brought about a redirection of policy, the character of which was dictated by the aims of the elected Council. The administrative processes involved took place in various departments of the local authority, and at other levels of government too. Co-ordination of the whole development depended heavily on one official. The change in policy was perceived in different ways by those concerned.

This study, carried out in 1958, began in the Housing Manager's Department of the Metropolitan Borough of Bethnal Green. The Housing Manager had no hesitation in naming the most important recent development in the work of her department: it was the return to slum clearance or—as she first described it—the change from rehousing people selected from the Borough's waiting lists to rehousing people whose houses were to be demolished. This development was traced through the records of the Borough—those in particular of the Housing Committee and its Housing Management Sub-Committee—and in discussions with the Chairman of the Housing Committee, the Housing Manager and her staff, the Deputy Town Clerk, the Medical Officer of Health and his staff of Public Health Inspectors.

Our report begins with a brief outline of housing policy in England between 1945 and 1958, followed by an account of the bodies responsible for implementing various aspects of this policy in the Borough. The changeover to slum clearance is then described.

But first a warning should be given. 'Slum clearance', the Chairman of the Housing Committee reminded us, is a technical term, referring to the demolition of houses unfit for human habitation: it implies no evaluation of the people who live in this property. These people have lived longer in Bethnal Green than anyone else and are the Borough's most respected citizens; if there *were* any 'slum people' in Bethnal Green, he remarked, they would be found elsewhere in the Borough.

Housing Policy since the War

For about eight years after the war, housing *policy* presented few problems; the problems were mainly of *method*—how to build houses as fast as possible in all parts of the country with the resources available, and how to restrict the programme to a level these resources would permit.[1] The Housing (Temporary Provisions) Act of 1944 extended to 'general needs housing' the subsidies provided for slum clearance under the Housing (Financial Provisions) Act of 1938. The Ministries of Works and Health were empowered by further legislation to construct, distribute and erect prefabricated houses that were to go on sites provided by local authorities. In 1946 the Housing (Finance and Miscellaneous Provisions) Act established the basis for new and more generous subsidies which were continued, with minor modifications in 1949 and further increased in 1952, until the Housing Subsidies Act of 1956 drastically reduced 'general needs' subsidies (as a first step to abolishing them altogether) and concentrated Exchequer contributions for new building on slum clearance projects, on 'overspill' housing built in new and expanded towns and in other places outside the authority for which the houses were provided, and to a lesser extent on housing for old people. Until 1954, housing policy for most authorities was, in principle at least, a fairly straightforward matter: Mr Tomlinson, introducing the first post-war housing Bill, said housing 'should be tackled as one would tackle a military operation'. Mr Bevan, introducing the 1949 Housing Bill, had no doubts about the aims of this operation: 'We shall, of course, go on providing additional houses until we have reached the position of providing a separate home for every family in the country . . .' The local authorities were the chosen instruments for this operation—their programmes could be planned and controlled, and they could allocate the new houses to those most in need of them. When private building began again, the local authorities were told (by Labour and Conservative Governments alike) that new houses built for private owners 'must go and be seen to go to persons in need of homes'.[2] Provisions were made in the 1949 Housing Act for the encouragement of repairs and improvements to existing houses (through loans, grants and technical advice). This policy was developed further in the 1954 Housing Repairs and Rents Act and in a number of subsequent Circulars and policy statements, but it had achieved little by 1958. During the period covered by this study, proposals for slum clearance thus constituted the only seriously considered alternative to the overriding policy of increasing the country's stock of homes. These proposals were first taken up with conviction in a Circular issued in March 1954,

[1] D. V. Donnison, *Housing Policy Since the War*. Occasional Papers on Social Administration, No. 1. Welwyn, Codicote Press, 1959.

[2] Ministry of Health Circular, 108/48 of 25 June 1948. Similar instructions were given in the Ministry of Housing and Local Government's Circular 73/51 of 27 November 1951.

which withdrew earlier instructions to hold up clearance projects and asked local authorities to 'take up again, as a matter of urgency, the campaign of slum clearance which the war interrupted.'[1] The Housing Repairs and Rents Act of that year required all authorities to submit slum clearance proposals to the Ministry of Housing and Local Government, and there followed a period of discussion and planning brought to a head two years later—amidst bitter political controversy—by the Housing Subsidies Act which compelled many authorities to switch their efforts from 'waiting list' rehousing to slum clearance rehousing.

Under slum clearance procedures local authorities may deal with individual buildings by serving demolition orders. Larger areas containing a sufficient proportion of unfit houses can be declared to be 'clearance areas' with the approval of the Minister. The authority may then compel the owners of property in the area to demolish it and later make compulsory purchase of the land if they fail to redevelop it; or it may (and normally does) acquire the land by agreement or compulsion and itself demolish and rebuild. Alternatively, large groups of buildings in urban areas may be declared to be 'redevelopment areas', provided they contain at least fifty 'working class' houses of which at least one-third are unfit for habitation or congested or overcrowded; or the declaration may be based on grounds of overall planning needs, regardless of the character of the property involved. The procedure for redevelopment is the same as that for slum clearance.[2] Objections may be made to compulsory purchase or clearance orders and these are considered at public local inquiries conducted by a representative of the Minister.

In this study an attempt will be made to show how one Metropolitan Borough came to make the change from building for 'general needs' to slum clearance and rebuilding. It is not suggested that developments in this Borough were typical of those taking place on a national scale. This development was not chosen as an example of housing policy, but as an illustration of administrative processes. Since the time of this study there have been further developments in national housing policies and a radical reform of London's local government, but they need not be recorded here.

Housing Administration in Bethnal Green

Bethnal Green covers a compact 760 acres between Shoreditch, Stepney, Hackney and Poplar in the east end of London. Its population in 1955 was 54,000—just half what it was in 1931. Ninety-three per cent of those in work were in skilled (55%), partly skilled (13%) or unskilled (25%) manual jobs.[1] Rows of two-storey terrace houses are crowded

[1] Ministry of Housing and Local Government Circular 30/54 of 2 March 1954.
[2] The Town and Country Planning Act of 1947, and Part III of the consolidating Housing Act of 1957 contain the relevant powers for redevelopment and clearance.

amongst small factories and workshops, a few squares and parks, new council flats, Victorian tenement houses, and the main railway lines running eastwards and northwards from Liverpool Street Station. In Bethnal Green a penny rate raised less revenue than in any other London Borough. Many of the Borough's houses were condemned as long ago as 1920 when its first thorough survey of housing conditions was made.

Unlike some of the other public services considered in this series of studies, the provision of housing is not the responsibility of a single authority or department but of several. The smaller Metropolitan Boroughs presented an extreme example of this system.

In 1958 the London County Council and the Metropolitan Boroughs had joint housing powers. Major questions of planning, the allocation of responsibility for redevelopment areas, major building projects, and building that took place outside the County Council's boundaries were among the more important issues to be decided by the County Council, working to a considerable extent through the District Offices of its Housing Management Department. The Eastern District Office covered the Boroughs of Stepney, Poplar, Hackney, Bethnal Green, and parts of Shoreditch, Finsbury and Woolwich. Bethnal Green's surveys and the five-yearly development plans called for by the Town and Country Planning Act of 1947 were discussed with the London County Council, and areas for clearance and redevelopment were divided between the two authorities—the County generally taking the largest. The Borough was not compelled to secure the County's approval for its housing programme, but in practice the two collaborated closely, partly owing to the fact that the Borough had to rely on the County Council for help in rehousing any families that could not be accommodated in Bethnal Green. Unlike other housing authorities, the Metropolitan Boroughs were not permitted to build outside their own boundaries. A Borough as densely populated as Bethnal Green could seldom find homes for all those whose houses were to be demolished in clearance schemes, but the County Council normally provided for half the resulting 'overspill'. Owing to its small population, limited resources and serious housing problems, Bethnal Green had always relied on close collaboration with the London County Council for help in its housing programmes. Boroughs with less daunting problems to face, larger resources and a different political complexion, tended to collaborate less happily with the County.[2]

The Ministry of Housing and Local Government and its predecessors, the Ministry of Local Government and Planning and the Ministry of

---

[1] Census 1951.

[2] Evidence submitted to the Royal Commission on Local Government in Greater London by the Boroughs of Hampstead, St Marylebone and Bethnal Green illustrates this contrast.

Health, used to exercise detailed control over the numbers, types and location of houses to be built, the volume of building licences to be issued, the purposes for which they were to be used, and so on. But building licences, 'zonal conferences' of local housing authorities, housing allocations and restrictions on the use of materials had come to an end before the period with which this study is mainly concerned. At that time the size of the housing programme was mainly limited by the rising cost of building, the high level of interest rates and the restriction of subsidies. The Ministry still supervised building standards, approved all plans for demolition, clearance and redevelopment, and sanctioned loans raised by the local authorities.

The Borough's Housing Committee, through its Housing Manager and her assistants, was responsible to the Council for preparing a building programme, selecting the tenants to go into Council flats, and arranging transfers and exchanges between tenants in Council and private property. The Borough had no architect of its own, and its buildings were designed by four private firms of architects who worked closely with the Borough's officers, attending Housing Committee meetings when necessary and conducting negotiations on the Borough's behalf with contractors, the County Council and the Ministry. For the actual construction of houses and flats the Borough normally employed private contracting firms, but some of its new building and much of its maintenance work was carried out by its Surveyor's Department. The Borough Treasurer was responsible for raising loans—at one time from the Public Works Loan Board but in 1958 from the open market—in order to finance building schemes. He was also responsible for collecting rents on Council property and for advising the Committee when they fixed these rents. The Medical Officer of Health was responsible for the selection and 'representation' of unfit buildings and areas. This work was largely handled by the Public Health Inspectors in his Department; they attempted to make regular surveys and inspections, but this was difficult owing to the acute shortage of these officers, only two of whom were available for housing work. Decisions about the 'fitness' of housing had to be made in consultation with the County Council but in practice the Medical Officers of the two authorities applied rather different standards. The County's criteria had to be applied throughout its territory, but a Borough which had made good progress with its clearance programme could afford to apply more rigorous standards.

It should now be clear that the provision and management of housing do not constitute a separate, self-contained 'service', directed by one official and his committee; they are the responsibility of half a dozen independent bodies, including private architects and various Departments of the London County Council, working under the general supervision of the Ministry. In this Borough the co-ordination of the activities of these different bodies was largely due to the Clerk's

Department and in particular to the Deputy Town Clerk.[1] A few examples may illustrate how the system worked.

Slum clearance projects begin with the selection of sites suitable for clearance. Every five years a 'preliminary survey' was made of the whole Borough and a general plan of action discussed and agreed with the County Council. Detailed surveys were then made by the Public Health Inspectors who brought bad spots to the attention of the Medical Officer of Health. He might also receive information from other sources, official and unofficial. The position was discussed with the Deputy Town Clerk, and the Medical Officer himself made a survey of the areas selected. He would then prepare an 'official representation' of certain areas which was submitted to the Public Health and Housing Committees and then to the Council. The Medical Officer might be asked to make changes in the general programme derived from the preliminary survey, and he was usually prepared to accept some modifications of the original scheme, perhaps altering the priorities for demolition or increasing the size of the whole clearance programme. Since this Council was entirely dominated by one Party, the effective debate on such questions occurred in Committees and in Labour Party Group meetings where the representatives of different wards might call for prompter action in their own areas. Clearance plans for individual areas were communicated to the London County Council and then went to the Minister for approval, with a census of the population involved and an undertaking to rehouse the people within a specified period. The Borough had at the same time to publish its plan for the area to be cleared and within six months serve clearance or compulsory purchase orders on the owners of the property concerned. The latter might make objections to the Minister who notified the Borough (which then made a further survey of the area) and conducted a public local inquiry. At this inquiry it was the Town Clerk's responsibility to present the Borough's case; his Deputy generally handled this, though counsel might act for the Borough in some cases. The Borough Surveyor and the Medical Officer of Health were the main expert witnesses called on the Borough's behalf. The order would then be confirmed, amended or rejected. The administrative procedures required before demolition could begin normally took more than a year to complete.

Decisions about the type of housing to be built on the site were made by the Council, on the recommendation of the Housing Committee where the matter was discussed with the Deputy Town Clerk, the Housing Manager and the architects. Usually there was considerable discussion of these problems before they reached the Committee—the architects perhaps favouring larger flats which are more economical to

[1] All reports made to the Council on housing questions appeared over the name of the Town Clerk, but in practice the Deputy Town Clerk assumed responsibility for preparing these reports.

build, and the Housing Manager hoping for an increase in the scarce supply of small dwellings. The Housing Committee was unlikely to be faced with a difficult decision unless its officers and the architects had been unable to reach agreement. The sizes and types of dwellings built were related as nearly as possible to the character of the households to be catered for, but since plans for flats might have to be drawn up four or five years before the tenants moved in this was an extremely difficult task. It is not surprising that in the days of the waiting list an applicant's chance of being rehoused depended to a considerable extent upon the size of house he needed. The selection of tenants was made by the Housing Manager from a waiting list compiled according to the 'points' system devised by the Committee (up till 1955), or (later) from the property due to be demolished. In 1953 there were about 2,800 households on the Borough's waiting list. Since then the numbers are likely to have become increasingly misleading because many who knew of the slum clearance policy and the abandonment of the waiting lists would not have bothered to put their names on the list. Tenants were not necessarily transferred direct from condemned to new property; much of the Housing Manager's time was spent in arranging exchanges —sometimes three- or four-cornered exchanges—which made for greater flexibility in rehousing policy than might at first appear possible. It frequently happened that people whose homes were to be demolished ('decanted' tenants, in official language) preferred to move to repaired property or to pre-war flats rather than to more expensive new buildings which might be in a less favoured part of the Borough or might call for an embarrassing jump in living costs. Exchanges were sometimes arranged with the London County Council, or with other Boroughs within or beyond the London area. These arrangements were designed to meet individual needs, and did not necessarily involve new property. Where they did, the principle was observed that in each set of transfers one new dwelling must be provided for someone whenever a household was moved from condemned property. Rents were fixed at levels comparable with those currently charged for London County Council property, though neither authority kept in step with subsequent changes made by the other.

Slum Clearance Begins Again
By the end of 1953 repairs to war damaged houses capable of further use had been completed (though general deterioration could not be so easily set right) and 643 new houses had been built by the Borough. Few Boroughs had suffered so much destruction—altogether 3,120 homes had been destroyed and practically every house had suffered in some way—and for some time there was no shortage of sites. Those rehoused were selected from several waiting lists (drawn up for households of different sizes) ranked according to points systems which changed from

time to time but in general gave priority to those overcrowded or with no home of their own, those with children, those who had been waiting longest, and those suffering from illnesses likely to be exacerbated by their housing conditions.

In 1951 Bethnal Green, like other Metropolitan Boroughs, embarked on a five-year housing plan, worked out in consultation with the London County Council. The Borough's officers were already aware that the policy of building new houses and flats as quickly as possible could not go on much longer, for there would soon be no more sites left to build on. They demolished 236 unfit houses during this period, but clearance would soon be needed on a larger scale. Rehousing from the waiting lists must therefore be brought to a halt while there were still sufficient unallocated houses in the course of construction to take the growing numbers of people whose homes were to be demolished.

The second five-year plan came up for discussion in April 1954, just after the appearance of the Ministry's Circular urging authorities to resume slum clearance. The Deputy Town Clerk, Medical Officer of Health and Housing Manager discussed the situation and there followed a joint meeting of the Housing and Health Committees at which plans for slum clearance were considered. The Deputy Town Clerk presented a report on the situation, pointing out that '... the housing programme of the Council was, in effect, only the consequent redevelopment upon this slum clearance programme ...' The Council was eager to set about clearing the slums, particularly in view of the failure of the London County Council to fulfil its own (considerably larger) plans for clearance in this area. The Borough's officers persuaded the Council to reduce its first ambitious estimates since the resources available for this work were unlikely to be sufficient, and somewhat reluctantly agreement was reached on a more modest demolition programme during the second five-year programme. The Medical Officer of Health and the Deputy Town Clerk were responsible for working out these figures. Between 1956 and 1960, 510 unfit houses were demolished in Bethnal Green by the County and 550 by the Borough. Large numbers of 'grey' houses (not technically unfit) were pulled down in the same clearance areas.

In October 1955 the Deputy Town Clerk presented a report to the Joint Public Health and Housing Committee outlining the five-year plan finally agreed with the London County Council and submitted to the Minister. In it '... members' attention is specifically drawn to the following assumptions upon which the programme has been devised: (1) That no dwellings becoming available during the next five years will be allocated to the housing waiting list unless such persons on the waiting list, by coincidence, happen to be in clearance areas ...' Since this decision was the inevitable concomitant of the clearance programme which all were determined to start on, it was accepted

SLUM CLEARANCE BEGINS AGAIN IN BETHNAL GREEN 55

without much comment and discussion was confined to the timing and details of the programme. No new flats were completed between June 1955 and April 1957, a long gap that seems to have been due mainly to the ambitious nature of the project completed in 1957, which included a number of high flats requiring extensive piling. The meeting in October 1955 thus constituted a watershed between the old policy and the new. The last block of flats completed in 1955 was let to people moved from a clearance site, and after that only one new letting and two 'relets' were offered to families on account of their position on the waiting list. Two of these families were flagrantly overcrowded and the third moved from a house which could then be used for rehousing a large family whose home was due to be demolished.

Each year thereafter, the Deputy Town Clerk presented a report on the housing programme to the newly appointed Housing Committee. Each year his report repeated the assumptions on which the policy was based. But while no serious objection has ever been offered to what constitutes, in effect, a closing of the waiting lists, no public announcement of the decision to abandon the lists was ever made.[1] Indeed, strictly speaking, no such decision was ever taken—it was merely the outcome of the decision to switch resources to slum clearance which was forced on an authority that had no more vacant building sites and was not permitted to build outside its own boundaries. After the Housing Subsidies Act of 1956 many other authorities were encouraged or compelled by the central government to adopt similar policies and the abandonment of the waiting list was then more explicitly recognised by the Bethnal Green Council.

The outcome of this change in policy appears in the distribution of new housing and of vacancies in existing housing. Between 1953 and 1958 the Borough had an average of 135 new lettings and seventy-five vacancies in older housing to dispose of each year. During the first three of these years, 24 per cent of all lettings were allocated to the waiting lists, and 43 per cent went to tenants 'decanted' from slum property or to others exchanging flats in a manner designed to meet the needs of decanted tenants. During the next three years decanted tenants and exchanges organised on their behalf accounted for 75 per cent of all lettings, and only two lettings went to the waiting lists—though many of those who were rehoused on account of slum clearance were also on the waiting lists. The remaining lettings during this period were exchanges and transfers unrelated to slum clearance, and a small number provided for caretakers, for people moved out of requisitioned property, and for special cases of various kinds. The shift from waiting list to slum clearance rehousing took place in the new lettings about a year

[1] This may be contrasted with the policy of the London County Council and other authorities which have publicly announced their decisions to curtail or abandon the rehousing of those on waiting lists.

earlier than in the re-letting of older property, but the change was effectively complete in both types of letting by 1956, and began several years before that.

The Housing Manager described this development as a change in the selection of tenants involving the virtual elimination of the waiting lists as an instrument of selection. The Deputy Town Clerk described the development in rather different terms. The growing shortage of building sites and the fact that the Borough was restricted to building within its own boundaries compelled the Council to choose between abandoning its housing programme or embarking on slum clearance. The Council's determination to press on with building left the choice in no doubt. This implied an end to rehousing from the waiting lists, but no formal decision was taken, or required, on that question. The smooth progress of this change in policy was largely due to the Deputy Town Clerk's work as co-ordinator of the various departments and authorities who were required to play a part in it. The central government's policy took a similar turn at about the same time, but Bethnal Green's change in policy was dictated by other necessities and was not greatly affected by developments in Whitehall.

DISCUSSION

The change in policy traced in this brief study may not appear momentous. Yet it deprived many families whose cramped housing conditions placed them near the top of the waiting lists of the opportunity of securing a new flat, transferring these opportunities to people living in condemned housing. The County Council's waiting lists remained open and continued for a time to provide an avenue of escape from bad housing conditions. But as other Boroughs were compelled to make the same choice that had faced Bethnal Green, and as the County's own slum clearance programme got under way, that avenue dwindled to a narrow path through which few could be admitted. This change in policy, coupled with the effects of the 1957 Rent Act, the disposal of requisitioned property (virtually completed in 1960) and the continued growth of employment in the London region, made it increasingly difficult to provide adequate housing in central London for families previously catered for through the waiting lists. It was no accident that the rising numbers of homeless families seeking the County Council's help and the growth of illegal and undesirable practices in London's rented housing market attracted increasing public attention from 1960 onwards. But although the development we have traced was part of a longer and more drastic trend affecting the whole of London, it presented no serious problems in Bethnal Green at the time. Once the blitzed building sites were exhausted, the legal powers of the housing authority (restricted to building within its boundaries), the densely populated area it was responsible for, and the determination of the Council to press on with the rebuilding of the Borough permitted only one course of action. The change in policy was provoked by a change in the resources (of land) available to the service, and its outcome was dictated by the structure and powers of the administrative system and the general objectives of all concerned. The Borough's housing powers might conceivably have been changed—by conferring on Bethnal Green the powers available to the nearby County Borough of West Ham, for instance—but since this would have called for a radical change in the principles of London's local government at a time when the central government was intent on persuading local authorities throughout the country to adopt the changes in policy already taking shape in this Borough, it was not surprising that no attempt was made to do this.

No more need be said here about this change in policy, but several features of the administrative organisation bringing it about should be noted. This case vividly illustrates a point made in our preliminary discussion of administrative concepts—the fact that administrative 'organisation' does not exist in its own right, but is simply a useful way of summarising the relationships between people performing a specific task. Most of the actors in this story—the Chairmen of Housing and Health Committees, the Deputy Town Clerk, the Medical Officer of Health, the Borough Treasurer, and so on—were responsible for many other things besides the particular development studied here. The relationships between them—the patterns of communication, authority and influence that constitute the 'organisations' in which they played a part—could not be traced or described without specifying the work or task to which the organisation is relevant. Even the most carefully drawn 'organisation chart' can only be valid for specified tasks. Other work—the administration of the Food and Drug Acts, or the calculation of next year's rates, for example—would call a different pattern of organisation into being, even if the same people appeared in it.

It is clear, too, that the development described could only have been brought about through the collaboration of many different administrative units. Different departments of the Borough, the County Council and the Ministry each played a part in the story, while the implementation of this change in housing policy called for an even wider collaboration, including firms of private architects, contractors, property owners, and the institutions of the money market. Bethnal Green had an exceptionally decentralised pattern of housing administration, arising from its past history and the relatively modest size of its housing programme. But even in authorities which have brought rent collection and much of the design, building and repair of housing within one department, there remain many aspects of this development which would have to be handled by separate administrative units, owing to the technical skills needed (in the field of local government finance, for example), the requirements of the law (only the Medical Officer can classify housing as 'unfit', for example), or the division of powers between separate levels of government (responsibility for town planning rests with the County Council, for example). Such a development cannot, therefore, be carried through within the framework of a single administrative hierarchy in which each person has only one superior and all are ultimately responsible to one person or group; it can only be carried through by a constellation of individuals working in parallel or completely independent administrative units, and subject to no single system of authority, sanctions or loyalties. Some authors have regarded such patterns of administration as abnormal or undesirable. Our own studies were not designed to evaluate administrative structures and do not provide the systematic assessments of administrative performance that such an evaluation demands. But it is clear that many important developments in policy *are* carried through in this way, and under a system of independent local government they must be. Only those concerned with organisation for its own sake would make a general condemnation to such a system.

Since many of the people concerned in this story worked in independent units and were subject to no common authority, it follows that 'formal authority' played a fairly small part in bringing the development about. Other forms of administrative relationship had to be employed. The task of maintaining these relationships and bringing them into play in the proper time and sequence fell largely on the Deputy Town Clerk. Although exercising scant formal authority, he had great influence owing to his technical and diplomatic abilities, his seniority, and his general responsibilities for co-ordinating housing policy and preparing the necessary correspondence and memoranda. The initiation of discussions, the arrangement of informal meetings, the preparation of reports and draft decisions conferred on him the roles of adviser, influential colleague and 'filterer' of communications—used to crucial effect, for example, in securing (and repeating annually) the Housing Committee's formal decision to press on with slum clearance, and hence to abandon the waiting list as a means for the selection of tenants. The experience of comparable housing authorities suggests that this field of social administration, calling for the collaboration and co-ordination of so many different units and levels of government, generally depends heavily on influential and far-sighted 'middlemen' of this kind. Where they are found is often a matter of chance: in other boroughs it may be the Surveyor, the Housing Manager or even a member of the Council who do most of this work.

The role of the Council and its Committees is difficult to trace. Over the period in question the Labour Party held all the seats on the Council and was thus able to confine discussion of contentious issues to closed meetings of the Party Group, consisting of Council members and local representatives of the Labour movement. Thus there was no public recognition of the fact that the waiting lists were effectively closed. The battle between different wards for priority in the slum clearance programme and the resulting pressures occasionally exerted on the Medical Officer of Health were one outcome of the Group's discussions. The Council also compelled their officers to revise and increase the provisional clearance programme prepared for the years 1956–60, though they did not secure as large a programme as they had first hoped for. A considerable amount of the Housing Committee's time was devoted to consideration of individual problems of housing management and the Chairman of the Committee—always an influential figure in the Council—took a close interest in the Department's work. (One of the Chairmen during the period covered by this study was a bus conductor on a route passing close to the Town Hall, which enabled him to make frequent and unexpected calls on the Housing Manager.) But the influence of an elected Council and its Committees cannot be determined solely from its recorded decisions. It is clear that the officers of this Borough were never in doubt about the general determination of their Council to press on with rebuilding as fast as the available resources would permit. The Council is also responsible for the Borough's public relations—communicating official views and intentions to the electorate, the County Council and other bodies, as well as communicating the electorate's views to their officials. This work may be inadequately performed (other Councils have played a much more active part in explaining their abandonment of waiting lists, for example) but it can never be entirely forgotten—as can be seen from the remarks of the Housing Committee chairman quoted at the beginning of this report. Meanwhile the very existence of a Council and its Committees, and the regular monthly meetings they hold, provide a means for establishing and registering policy decisions, and for reconciling and codifying the views of the chief officers who must prepare the evidence and recommend the decisions to be considered by elected members.

POSTSCRIPT

The development of housing policies and programmes in this part of London during the next sixteen years would fill a large book. This postscript is not a condensed version of that book; it only notes a few points in the story which throw some light on the themes of our original study. The size and powers of the Borough, and the organisation of its services have been transformed, but its social and political character have not changed; indeed they seem all the clearer now that they operate on a larger scale.

Under the London Government Act of 1963 the old Metropolitan

Borough of Bethnal Green was combined with two of its neighbours, Stepney and Poplar, to form the much larger London Borough of Tower Hamlets in 1965.[1] For a few years the new Council included a small opposition of two Communists, but since 1971 the Labour Party has held every Council seat. Above them in the hierarchy of local authorities, the new Greater London Council covered a larger area than the old London County Council, but shed much of its work to the Boroughs. Tower Hamlets took over the Home Help and Children's Services, described in Chapters 5 and 6 of this book. This postscript should therefore be compared with those added to these Chapters, and with Chapter 7 which deals with housing in Finsbury—a Metropolitan Borough which was incorporated in the new Borough of Islington in 1965.

The populations of all these inner London Boroughs continued to fall faster than anyone foresaw at the time the first edition of this book was written. The population of Tower Hamlets fell from 206,000 to 165,000 between 1961 and 1971. The Borough, which is the heart of the traditional 'East End', remained the most solidly working-class area in London.[2] The decline in the numbers to be housed eased pressures on the stock of housing, and progress was made towards eliminating the worst conditions, but councillors and officials were still keenly aware of huge unmet needs. At the time of the 1966 Census, 8·2 per cent of Tower Hamlets' households lived at more than 1·5 persons per room. (In Greater London the average was 3·8 per cent; in Islington, the worst Borough, 9·6 per cent.) In Tower Hamlets 48·9 per cent of households lacked exclusive use of hot water, bath and inside water closet. (In Greater London as a whole the figure was 34·4 per cent; in Islington, worst again, 67·1 per cent[3].)

The loss of population from Tower Hamlets was partly brought about by the movement of younger people to better housing in less crowded suburbs. It was hastened by the loss of manufacturing, warehousing and dockside employment, and the demolition of small factories and workshops in slum clearance and redevelopment schemes: even when new working space for this sort of industry was provided, small employers were often unable to pay the higher rents which had to be charged for it.

The new Boroughs had greater powers than their predecessors. Soon after the reorganisation of London government they took over the administration of waiting-lists for public housing from the Greater London Council. Five years later they began taking over much of the

---

[1] For an account of the reorganisation and its outcome, see Della Adam Nevitt and Gerald Rhodes, 'Housing', in Gerald Rhodes (ed.), *The New Government of London: The First Five Years*. Weidenfeld & Nicolson, 1972, pp. 213-62

[2] See David Donnison and David Eversley (eds), *London: Urban Patterns, Problems and Politics* (Heinemann, 1973), particularly chapters by Margaret Harris, Peter Willmott and Michael Young.

[3] John Greve, Dilys Page and Stella Greve, *Homelessness in London*. Scottish Academic Press, 1971.

GLC's stock of houses too. They can build houses outside their own boundaries. Along with other authorities throughout the country, they have gained increasing powers to acquire and improve large areas, to make grants for improvement and loans for house purchase to private owners, to provide housing subsidies for private tenants in the form of rent allowances, and to make rate rebates which help to adjust local tax burdens to the tax-payer's ability to pay. In one respect, however, their discretion was later reduced: the Housing Finance Act of 1972 prescribed a nationwide system for the fixing and mutual alignment of rents in public and private housing, and for the rent rebates and housing allowances which were intended to relate to the incomes and requirements of tenants in each sector.

The main policies of the old Metropolitan Borough were taken over and carried forward by the new combination. Bethnal Green's slum clearance was being completed at the time of the amalgamation, but a lot remained to be done in Stepney where the problem was complicated by a large number of densely packed nineteenth-century tenements. The priority given to the programme of clearance and closing orders means that people to be rehoused in other parts of the Borough generally have a prior claim on new housing and relets in Bethnal Green. At first people were reluctant to cross the old Borough boundaries, but they have gradually become more willing to do so. Unlike Islington and some other inner Boroughs, Tower Hamlets has never tried to build outside its own boundaries. Since handing over its waiting-list to the Boroughs, the Greater London Council has allocated space in its own estates to them. In 1974, Tower Hamlets had a 'decant quota' of about 300 units a year to help with its clearance programme, and a 'general needs quota' which had recently been reduced to about 250 units a year owing to the progress made in solving the Borough's most pressing housing needs. Since the Borough has been building less than 500 houses a year, and normal mortality and movement only create vacancies in $2-2\frac{1}{2}$ per cent of its stock of houses each year, this help is essential to keep its programme moving.

Slum clearance is Tower Hamlets' top priority. Next it seeks to improve its own older property, and to transfer or rehouse tenants with special claims on grounds of ill-health or crowding. Unlike some other inner London authorities with large Labour majorities, it has been reluctant to help people buy their own houses. The waiting-list has been reopened again—indeed, the London Government Act of 1963 obliges London Boroughs to keep these lists open—but the claims of those on the list generally have to come last in the queue.

Some accommodation has to be set aside for a few of the families who are homeless or in danger of becoming homeless, but the Housing Department believes these crises generally arise from domestic disputes rather than from eviction or harassment by private owners. Our postscript to Chapter 7[1] shows a different pattern in Islington. Tower Hamlets has provided less accommodation than other Boroughs for homeless families and has tended to allocate most of it to cases of the 'fire and flood' type in which the households concerned are most obviously blameless. During the year ending on 30 September 1970, Tower Hamlets admitted fifty-six families to temporary accommodation—fewer than in any other inner London Borough (Islington admitted 273). Most of these families hope eventually to secure a council tenancy. In Tower Hamlets fourteen homeless families achieved that during the year—again fewer than in any other inner Borough (in Islington 110 secured council tenancies.) Some believe Tower Hamlets' policies have laid additional burdens on the Borough's Social Services Department which must often meet the needs of homeless families not rehoused by the Housing Department.[2]

A growing majority of the houses in this part of London belong to public authorities—in 1971 about two-fifths to the Greater London Council (a larger proportion than in any other Borough) and one-fifth to Tower Hamlets.[3] Most of the rest belong to small private landlords who expect their houses and their tenants to be taken over by the Borough before long. Like many other Boroughs, Tower Hamlets has opened a centrally placed and comfortably appointed Housing Advice Centre to provide information and answer questions about such matters as rent regulation, housing allowances, improvement grants, opportunities for rehousing, loans for house purchase, and the rights of private tenants. This Centre is not heavily used. Those who are badly housed in Tower Hamlets usually face daunting but essentially simple problems: can they buy their way out to the suburbs, or survive in Tower Hamlets till the Council rehouses them? There are few other solutions to their housing difficulties, and the Borough's policy towards the private sector of the market shows that it is not anxious to provide other solutions.

Tower Hamlets is little troubled by the operations of speculators, controversy about the demolition of older housing, or invasion of its territory by middle-class outsiders prepared to spend large sums on buying and improving houses—all of which provoke debate in places like Islington. Attempts to consult the public about proposals for redevelopment and other matters have generally gone smoothly, probably because most people have been in general agreement with their Council's policies. Local people are not incapable of mobilising against public authorities to demand their rights, as occasional rent strikes in GLC housing, and a major uproar over bus services and other amenities on the Isle of Dogs have shown. Borough councillors are capable of imposing

---

[1] Page 161.   [2] For a discussion of these problems see J. Greve, *et al.*, op. cit.
[3] *Annual Abstract of Greater London Statistics*, 6, Section 8. Greater London Council.

their policies on officials, as can be glimpsed in the postscript to Chapter 6, but they have in general been hostile to community action intended to bring pressure on public authorities. The Borough's grant to its own Council of Social Service was cut off after that Council got involved in incidents of this kind.

Although its housing services are now far more extensive than its predecessors', Tower Hamlets disperses these responsibilities as widely as ever.[1] The Deputy Town Clerk, who played a major part in our original case study, left the Borough years ago, but the Housing Manager was appointed to the same post in the new Borough and continued till her retirement shortly before this postscript was written. A review of the whole system was then being made and changes are expected shortly, but we can only describe things as they stood early in 1974. Perhaps as befits an authority putting slum clearance first, housing management and lettings are dealt with by a combined Health and Housing Management Committee which is to be reorganised when health services are transferred in April 1974 to the new Area Health Authority. The Housing Department comes within the Directorate of Community Services along with local health services, baths, libraries, entertainments and other functions. The head of this Directorate, for a few weeks longer, is the Medical Officer of Health. The Housing Department has three Divisions, responsible respectively for general administration, lettings and estate management. The condemnation of unfit housing, and thus the selection of areas for redevelopment, is still the responsibility of public health inspectors working under the Medical Officer of Health. Plans for new building are prepared and implemented in the Development Directorate which has its own Committee. The Director of Finance and his Committee are responsible for rent collection and arrears, and for the new housing allowances for private tenants, but the administration of rent rebates for Council tenants (allocated according to the same rules as those applied to housing allowances) remains in the Housing Department. Improvement grants are administered by the Director of Technical Services, loans for house purchase by the Chief Executive, and action on the (very rare) cases of harassment of private tenants by the Solicitor to the Council. The Housing Aid Centre is separately administered within the Directorate of Community Services. Collaboration between the many different officials and committees responsible for these different aspects of housing policies seems to be reasonably good. In this as in other fields, any major question of policy is referred to the Council's Policy Committee. But that is not often needed: Tower Hamlets' main priorities for housing have been clear for a long time.

[1] Some other authorities, such as Lambeth, have brought many of these powers together under one Chief Officer and Committee. See Michael Harloe, Ruth Issacharoff and Richard Minns, *The Organisation of Housing*. Heinemann, 1974.

CHAPTER 4

THE NATIONAL ASSISTANCE BOARD TAKES ON NEW DUTIES

The next study deals with an entirely different situation. A national organisation, with local offices operating throughout the country under close central control, was called upon to assess the incomes of people seeking a service provided by another agency. On the local level at which this study was conducted the task to be performed was clearly specified, presenting problems of a purely 'technical' nature. But the subdivision of responsibilities for different aspects of the service posed a number of difficulties; and the rules drawn up for the assessment of incomes may have restricted the scope of the service in ways not originally intended. Major new developments, unforeseen at the time of the original study, are recorded in the postcript.

Unlike the others dealt with in this series, the National Assistance Board's services are provided by the central government and subject to uniform, centrally determined policies applied in a similar fashion throughout the country. In order to meet local needs some flexibility is permitted in the interpretation of the Board's rules, but major innovations in policy do not originate at the local levels where this study was made. In 1959, after discussing various proposals for research with the NAB's East Ham Area Officer, the Regional Controller and a member of the Headquarters staff, it was decided that the organisation and reorganisation of 'assessments' for Legal Aid in the East Ham Area Office constituted the most suitable recent 'development' for our purposes. The authors interviewed officials concerned with the Legal Aid Scheme at these three levels of the hierarchy, and read various documents on this subject prepared by the Board and others.

The National Assistance Board
The NAB was set up in 1948 to carry out provisions of the National Assistance Act of that year which deal mainly with financial assistance for those lacking adequate means to support themselves. The Board itself consists of six members appointed by the Crown. Like its predecessors, the Assistance Board and the Unemployment Assistance Board, it is supposed to be independent of direct Parliamentary control in carrying out its work. But its spokesman in Parliament is the Minister

of Pensions and National Insurance and its status and powers do not in practice differ appreciably from those of other central government departments. Day to day administration is carried out through a network of Area offices, numbering 427 in 1959, to which were attached 83 Local Advisory Committees whose members are selected for their local knowledge and status. Area Offices are grouped into Regions, nine of which covered England and Wales.

The Part Played by the NAB in the Legal Aid Scheme in 1959
Two years after it was set up the NAB took on additional duties under the Legal Aid and Advice Act of 1949. This Act empowered the government to assist people involved in litigation not covered by existing free legal aid schemes,[1] and the sections dealing with actions originating in the Supreme Court came into effect in October 1950. Since the scheme was intended only for those with 'small or moderate means', there were two aspects to its administration: legal and financial. Other services, such as the child care and home help schemes dealt with in this series of studies, also call for payments that are determined by means tests. But in those the provision of the service and the administration of means tests are carried out by the same organisation: in this case, however, the two tasks were sharply distinguished and given to different organisations. The administration of the scheme's legal provisions rests in the hands of the Law Society, and is carried out through the Society's Area and Local Offices, subject to the requirements of the Act and the Legal Aid (General) Regulations. The financial sections of the Act, however, require the assessment of applicants' resources and their liability for contributions, and this function was allotted to the Board. The procedure is complicated; its general outline, including specific financial limits, is laid down in the Act itself and amplified by the Legal Aid (Assessment of Resources) Regulations. These Regulations are issued by the Lord Chancellor, with the Treasury's approval. The Board has no statutory part to play in drawing up or revising Legal Aid Regulations, although it does prepare the rules for its own services—the Regulations for Assistance issued by the Minister under the 1948 Act.

All applications for legal aid were made in the first instance to the Area or Local committees of the Law Society by whom they were sent to the appropriate NAB office if the applicant appeared to have a prima facie case. The Law Society's Areas generally corresponded to the Regions of the NAB, which was administratively convenient, but in 1948 there were less than half as many Local committees as NAB Area Offices. It was realised that administration would be simplified were each local Law Society committee to refer to one NAB office only, and for this reason it was hoped either to concentrate legal aid work in one Area

[1] Under the Criminal Appeal Act 1907. S. 10, Poor Prisoners Defence Act 1930, S. 1 & 2, or Summary Jurisdiction (Appeals) Act 1933, S. 2.

office in each committee's district, or to arrange for one office to provide for liaison with the committee. More important, however, was the Board's recognition that the new functions would require special knowledge and skills among the officers concerned and that the volume of legal aid work would not be great enough to occupy a full-time officer in each Area office. From the beginning, therefore, it was envisaged that in appropriate districts assessments for legal aid might be concentrated in a few specialised offices.

The procedure for assessment can now be described in greater detail. If the legal merits of the case appeared to be adequate, the part of the application referring to financial circumstances was sent from the local branch of the Law Society to the appropriate NAB office. All assessments (although, as will be shown, not all interviewing) had to be done by the office 'designated' for this work in the district where the applicant lived.

Interviews normally took place in the office but might be carried out at home if applicants were ill or disabled. In exceptional cases travelling expenses could be paid for applicants who lived a considerable distance from the office. At the interview the person applying for legal aid had to declare and prove all sources of income and capital, and all liabilities. Except in matrimonial disputes, this information was given for both the husband and wife. From this information the 'disposable income' was calculated—that is, the income likely to be received during the twelve months following the application, from which were deducted allowances made on account of major expenses necessary for the support of dependents, for rent, and so on. Capital assets had also to be taken into account, and after deductions for dependent relatives and other responsibilities a calculation was made of 'disposable capital'. In 1959, anyone with a disposable annual income of less than £156 and anyone receiving national assistance was entitled to free legal aid. A disposable annual income of more than £420 or (with a few exceptions) a disposable capital of more than £500 disqualified the applicant from receiving any legal aid. With a disposable income between £156 and £420 and a disposable capital under £500 he was liable to make a maximum contribution of one half of the amount by which the disposal income exceeded £156, plus the amount by which the disposable capital exceeded £75.[1] The more generous provisions subsequently made in the Act of 1960 are shown in a footnote on page 69.

A 'determination' giving three figures (the disposable income, the disposable capital and the maximum contribution) together with other information relevant to the collection of contributions, was sent to the branch of the Law Society referring the case, which decided on the

[1] For example, if the disposable income was £356, and the disposable capital £100, the maximum contribution would have been £125—that is, £100 from income and £25 from capital.

NATIONAL ASSISTANCE BOARD TAKES ON NEW DUTIES

precise amount of the contribution and the way in which it was to be paid. Unless the applicant's circumstances changed sufficiently to warrant a re-assessment, that was the end of the NAB's part in the procedure. The Law Society had no power to amend or overrule the NAB's assessment, although it had some discretion in allowing assistance to people with disposable incomes below £420 who had been refused help because they had more than the maximum amount of capital.

The method of computation, the maximum allowances permitted for major items such as dependants and rent, and the amounts of supplementary income from pensions and insurance benefits which might be disregarded were laid down in the Act and in the Lord Chancellor's Regulations—unchanged between 1950 and the date of this study. Little discretion was allowed to the Area's officers, and particularly close control was exercised in the early years of the scheme.

Assessments were verified by the designated Area Officer before being returned to the Law Society, and some queries could be dealt with at that point. More serious problems, and cases falling into categories reserved for Headquarters' decisions were passed on, in the first instance to the Regional office. Originally such referrals were fairly heavy and in the office of the London (Outer) Region, which included East Ham, the Legal Aid staff consisted of at least two full-time executive officers. The Region's discretion was also fairly limited. About 10 per cent of the cases referred to it were decided there and returned to the Area, sometimes after informal consultation with Headquarters. Collaboration between Regional and Headquarters staff was comparatively easy since both occupied the same building. The few fraudulent applications were returned to the Law Society for action. The remaining cases bearing the Region's preliminary opinion were sent to the Legal Aid Section at Headquarters. This consisted of an assistant secretary, a principal, a higher executive officer, executive officer and clerical officer. At first the section received problem cases at the rate of approximately sixty each week. By 1958, with better training, growing expertise and greater discretion allowed to officers in the Areas, the number had been halved.

Most of these referred applications fell into two groups: first, those in which there might be a case for allowances more generous than those permitted under local discretion (for example, where there were large payments to be made to separated dependants, or heavy and necessary hire purchase commitments); and second, those in which complications arose from comparatively unusual factors (involving income tax, trust monies, or the resources of a step-father in a case involving a wife with a child from a previous marriage, for example). Difficulty commonly arose where the applicant's income was drawn from his own business— a man may run a Jaguar yet have a declared personal income of only £10 per week. These cases went to specialists in the Finance Division.

Where legal problems arose, the Headquarters staff consulted the Board's Solicitor or the Law Society. Once a decision had been taken, cases were returned to the Area via the Regional Office. A straightforward assessment was dealt with by the Area within a fortnight (although much depended upon the co-operation of the applicant). Difficult assessments might take as long as three months.

The Development of Assessment Work in East Ham
The East Ham Area office was originally given responsibility for carrying out assessments for nine Areas in the metropolitan fringe of Essex, and for this purpose an executive and a clerical officer were added to its staff of twenty executive and clerical officers. Along with their colleagues in other parts of the country, the special officers were given short training courses organised by Headquarters to equip them for their new duties. After the first rush of applications, reaching a total of 1,549 in 1951, the numbers of cases dealt with by these two officers fell steadily to an annual rate of 850–900 between 1955 and 1957. Most of the Area offices designated for this work elsewhere in the country had far fewer cases: in a sample fortnight in 1954 half of them received fewer than five applications. At that time the Board's Organisation and Methods Division found the standards of assessment in the quieter Areas were disturbingly uneven and urged that the number of designated offices be reduced by about a half in order to achieve greater specialisation and uniformity in this work. This step was delayed because the Government was considering extending the Legal Aid scheme to suits originating in County Courts, and the Board and the Law Society could not predict how caseloads would be affected. The extension came into effect on 1 January, 1956, and applications rose by only 6 per cent in the following year—in East Ham by even less.

Regional Controllers were then encouraged to bring about a further concentration of assessment work in Area offices close to the Law Society's offices. Meanwhile the picture was complicated by the Government's drive to reduce the number of Regional offices in all government departments. Two of the NAB's Regional offices in south-eastern England were abolished, and in 1958 the East Ham Legal Aid section was given responsibility for assessments in nine more Areas. The applications dealt with doubled in that year and an extra clerical officer was appointed to help with the work. This growth in the territory to be covered hastened another development that had already gone a considerable way: the collection of the information required for assessment was separated from the assessment itself, and the special officers had to rely increasingly on their colleagues in other Areas to secure this information, bringing them together from time to time to explain what was required. Shortly after this study was concluded a further step was taken in this direction by transferring assessments for Essex to the South

Kensington Area office and leaving East Ham to collect and pass on information about applications in the surrounding Areas. Legislation was introduced later to raise the income and capital limits governing the assessment procedure so that Legal Aid could be provided on a more generous basis, but that most important development, which brought an appreciable increase in the scope of the scheme and the number of cases dealt with, falls outside our study.[1]

Conclusion

This study traces the manner in which new duties were assumed by a service responsible for a much larger volume of different work. At the beginning the assessment procedure was unfamiliar and complicated. The volume of work to be done was unpredictable. The applications to be dealt with constituted a tiny and widely scattered fraction of the Board's total caseload. In 1954, besides the two assessment officers in East Ham, there were only twenty-seven others in the whole of England and Wales employed full-time on this work; the rest of it had to be done by a much larger number of officers, equivalent to seventy-one full-timers, most of whom spent only an hour or two a week on these assessments. It was therefore extremely difficult to maintain the standards of precision, promptness and uniformity required.

The Board adopted three approaches to the solution of these problems. (a) Short initiation and refresher courses were arranged for the staff doing the work. (b) The work itself was increasingly divided into two parts: the collection of the information required from applicants, and the calculation of the figures that formed the basis for assessing applicants' contributions. (c) The work of assessment was gradually concentrated in a reduced number of designated Area offices, to achieve greater skill among the officers thus enabled to specialise in it, and closer collaboration with local offices of the Law Society.

The Headquarters staff were responsible for these developments, and they were convinced that they improved the standards of work: certainly the proportion of unresolved cases that had to be sent to the Region and on to Headquarters for final decisions fell off considerably, and with growing experience staff in the Area offices designated for assessment work could be given greater discretion. But the maintenance of uniform and efficient standards of work among the interviewing officers who collected information from applicants remained a continuing problem which could never be finally resolved.

---

[1] The Legal Aid Act of 1960 increased the disposal income limit of £420 to £700 and reduced the contributions from income to one third of the excess over £250 and from capital to the amount by which disposable capital exceeds £125. The revised Legal Aid (Assessment of Resources) Regulations also provided for a more generous definition of capital resources.

The principal objectives and methods of the assessment procedure could be clearly defined and were not changed during the period studied. Having no responsibility for the broader social and professional aims of the Legal Aid scheme, NAB staff could devote their energies to perfecting the procedure. In the Region studied the officials carrying out the work remained in the same posts for considerable periods of time, and such specialist training as they had was planned and provided by the NAB, not by independent professional institutions. Thus the development called for an intelligent organisation and deployment of resources for the attainment of defined and agreed ends. Though technically complex, it was logically simple—and more completely a matter of administrative 'technique' than any of the others studied in this series.

But it should not be forgotten that the logical simplicity of these problems arose from the distinctive structure of the Legal Aid scheme. The scheme itself and the service it was designed to provide, were administered by the Law Society and its members. It was they who actually decided whether Legal Aid should be granted. The Board only provided the information required by the Society for determining the contributions to be made by applicants whose cases were regarded by solicitors as meriting legal representation. Yet the NAB's task, though merely 'technical' in appearance, went far to shape the character of the whole scheme; for the assessments effectively determined who was entitled to Aid. But these assessments were performed according to prescribed rules, drafted by the Lord Chancellor's Department and the Treasury, which could not be altered without fresh legislation. The Law Society's first Report on the operation of the scheme pointed out that the contributions demanded of assisted persons were too high. A scheme originally designed for people of 'small or moderate means' was in danger of being restricted to the very poor. But these contributions remained unaltered through a decade of inflation that continually eroded the scope of the scheme. It was our impression that the Board's officers were well aware of this problem, and often did their utmost to exercise discretion in favour of applicants.

But the division of responsibilities for the operation of the Legal Aid scheme between the Law Society, the Lord Chancellor, and the NAB might have been designed to obscure these problems by ensuring that each of these authorities would concentrate its attention upon its own contribution to the scheme and none would be in a position to assess the service as a whole. The NAB's administration of assessments was simplified—and possibly rendered more 'efficient' in a technical sense—by the exclusion of these broader questions of policy from its sphere of responsibility. But some may conclude that the applicants and potential applicants paid a considerable price for this achievement.

The Legal Aid service itself lay outside the scope of our study, but those responsible for it were keenly aware of the restrictions imposed

NATIONAL ASSISTANCE BOARD TAKES ON NEW DUTIES 71

on it by the means test regulations. Rarely can an official advisory committee have made its views so monotonously clear:

'We have said in previous Reports that the rate of contribution in some cases imposes too great a hardship on assisted persons. The cost of living is still rising and, though in some cases wages and salaries have risen proportionately or more, there are many prospective litigants whose incomes are fixed and to them the rate of contribution is an increasing burden as the cost of living rises.' (*Fifth Report of the Law Society on the Operation and Finance of Part I of the Legal Aid and Advice Act, 1949, and the Comments and Recommendations made by the Advisory Committee.* London, HMSO 1956. *Comments*, para. 19.)

'Nothing has occurred to alter the view expressed in our last four Reports that the rate of contribution does impose too great a hardship on some categories of assisted persons.' 'The basic figures in the Act and the Assessment of Resources Regulations have not been amended to take account of the changed economic circumstances. [Yet] Since the Regulations were made, the subsistence levels or "scale rates" contained in the National Assistance (Determination of Need) Regulations have been increased on four occasions.' (Ditto, 1957; paras. 11 and 12.)

'We cannot but take the view that after the thirteen years of rising prices, the scheme no longer adequately covers the section of the community, regarded in terms of income groups, which the Rushcliffe Committee intended' [in its Report of 1945[1]]. (Ditto, 1958; para. 13.)

'The value of the £420 disposable income limit compared with 1949 money values is therefore only about £280. To bring it back to its real value in 1949 would require raising it to about £650, £50 more than we recommended in our last Report . . .' (Ditto, 1959; para. 5.)

But some relaxation was permitted at last, and the Advisory Committee was able to report in 1961:

'During the year, by the Legal Aid (Assessment of Resources) Amendment Regulations, 1959[2], your Lordship amended the . . . Regulations so as to make more favourable to applicants the rules for computing the allowances which are taken into account in determining their incomes and eligibility for legal aid. Largely as a result of those measures, there was, during the year under review, a considerable increase in the volume of legal aid work . . .' (Ditto, 1961; para. 2.)

DISCUSSION

The developments outlined in this case have more general implications that should be noted. The Legal Aid scheme is the only major independent service for which the NAB has been called on to carry out the

[1] *Report of the Committee on Legal Aid and Legal Advice in England and Wales.* Cmd 6641; para. 147.
[2] S. 1. 1959/1350.

investigation of means and the determination of contributions. But from its own resources the Board can also refund payments for National Health Service prescriptions, some have argued that it should carry out means tests to determine the rents paid by Council tenants, and those wishing to impose or increase payments for medical care and education sometimes have similar procedures in mind. This analysis of Legal Aid assessments may indicate some of the problems such procedures would pose. Our discussion of the case, however, is not designed to pursue its long-term social and political implications, but to throw light on the administrative processes involved.

The structure of the NAB differs from that of the other agencies dealt with in this series of studies. Its services are provided by Area offices within each of which individual officers and specialist sections are subject to the authority of one Area Officer; Areas are grouped under Regional offices, within each of which there are specialist sections responsible to a Regional Controller, and they in turn are subject to Headquarters and the Board itself. Throughout the country there is a clear 'line of command' from the officers interviewing applicants, through Area Officers and Regional Controllers, to Headquarters. Auxiliary and specialist services are required at these three levels, but although those providing them communicate with similar specialists at other levels of the hierarchy, they are directly responsible to the 'line' officer in charge of their unit and official communications pass through him. The complexity and variety of Legal Aid cases compelled some modification of this system (in that the Area office at East Ham, designated for assessment work, relied on officers in the surrounding Areas to gather much of the information it required), but difficult cases were passed for decision to the Region and on to Headquarters through the Area Officer and Regional Controller, and returned by the same route. Specialist staff at each level were given considerable, and increasing, discretion to make their own decisions on these cases but this discretion was interpreted in the light of the NAB's general policies, on the understanding that cases in which these policies afforded insufficient guidance would be passed to the 'line' officers who could forward them when necessary to more senior levels of the hierarchy.

In some of the earlier literature on administration this type of structure, typical of military organisation, was regarded as a normal pattern and one to be widely advocated.[1] It clearly has many advantages. Necessary specialist services can be incorporated at appropriate points in the system and effectively co-ordinated without infringing the principle that everyone should be responsible to one known superior. A variety of knowledge and skills can be brought to bear on particular

[1] E.g. L. Urwick, 'Organization as a Technical Problem', *Papers on the Science of Administration*: L. Gulick and L. Urwick, (eds), New York, Institute of Public Administration, 1937.

problems while ensuring that the duty of making decisions in each unit rests with one person who is responsible for the attainment of the more general objectives to which each specialist makes his contribution. The service to be provided can be deployed over a wide area, and staff who are transferred to different parts of the country and to different levels of the hierarchy can quickly get their bearings within units whose structure is already familiar to them. Without infringing the authority of 'line' officers, senior specialists can maintain effective contact with similar specialists in subordinate units, thus keeping abreast of developments in the field, ensuring adequate standards of performance, and watching over the careers of junior staff.

The NAB has certain characteristics which make it peculiarly well suited for such a system. It must provide prompt and effective help to meet needs which can potentially be a matter of life and death to the people concerned, and its work is subject to close and critical public scrutiny. The same could be said of hospitals and other services but the NAB's call primarily for humanity, devotion to duty and a good working knowledge of rules and procedures—not for advanced technical skills derived from a high degree of training. More specialised skills, such as those provided by the Board's legal and financial officers, for example, can be treated as auxiliary or advisory services supporting the provision of assistance that is the Board's main task. The Assistance Regulations and the practical principles accumulated for their interpretation are the main criteria for the guidance of individual officers. These officers do not have the discretionary powers, the protection from public criticism or the opportunities for alternative employment which expert status and membership of a profession confer. Their education and experience is often fairly limited and the turnover of staff is considerable: those seeking promotion are often compelled to move to other departments of government. One of the Board's senior officers reports that there has been 'an exceptionally heavy and sustained turnover of staff'. '. . . one Area office in two years had thirty-nine departures and forty-one arrivals: the complement of the office is forty. At a smaller office, with a complement of twenty-five, there were twenty-three departures and twenty-five arrivals. These are offices in Central London, and they are not untypical.'[1] It is essential that the services these officers provide should be immediately available in all parts of the country, and subdivision of the work to be done must therefore be based mainly on geographical considerations, rather than on distinctions in expertise, techniques, the types of client to be served or other factors. At the same time close control, prompt communication and uniform practice must be ensured throughout this network of local offices. If the system appears to restrict discretion and the exercise of judgement, it should

[1] K. R. Stowe, 'Staff Training in the National Assistance Board: Problems and Policies'. *Public Administration*, Vol. 39, Winter 1961, p. 331.

be remembered that discretion can be employed 'against' a client as well as 'for' him—particularly in cases involving litigation (in which divorce proceedings are the most common type of action). None of the other services considered in this book have this combination of administrative requirements or the structure that arises from them.

The provision of legal advice and the decision to embark on litigation in cases where the client's costs are partly or wholly met from public funds (while his opponent is likely to be meeting his own expenses) clearly pose technical, professional and ethical problems of the highest order. Only trained lawyers could provide such a service. Had they been recruited on a full-time salaried basis for this purpose, like the professional staff of other social services, eligibility and payment for the service could more easily have been determined by the organisation responsible for providing it. But although some of them draw a large part of their income from this service, the lawyers remained in independent professional practice. Thus it was that another organisation, equipped with the necessary expertise, was called upon to carry out the assessment of applicants' incomes.

This subdivision of responsibilities for the scheme, dictated by the legislation establishing it, focused the attention of the NAB's staff on the perfection of assessment procedures, and the need to ensure prompt and uniform decisions gradually brought about a centralisation of the work in offices remote from the applicant himself. Meanwhile the lawyers devoted themselves to the professional services they were to provide. The manner in which responsibilities for the scheme were distributed among different authorities appears to have prevented effective reappraisal of the total scheme and probably restricted the operation of Legal Aid in ways which Parliament had not originally foreseen or intended. As in other cases considered here, the administrative structure established for a service played a large part in determining the work, the outlook and the general frames of reference of those engaged in providing it—and hence the contribution they were enabled to make to its development.

POSTSCRIPT

There has been little change in Legal Aid assessment procedures during the thirteen years since our original study was made; they have evolved slowly in the directions we traced. But the scale of the Legal Aid scheme has been transformed. We will briefly note the development of the procedures we studied, and then consider the growth of the scheme itself.

Under the Social Security Act of 1966 the Ministry of Social Security began bringing together the administration of its means-tested benefits and the less stigmatising contributory benefits provided under national insurance. All will eventually be administered through the same local offices. Two years later the Ministry itself was brought into the new and much larger Department of Health and Social Security. The 1966 Act abolished the NAB, setting up in its place the Supplementary Benefits Commission (or SBC)—a body with more modest legal powers, although its personal influence with Secretaries of State appears to be at least as great as its predecessor's. In the Department's publications and regulations 'applicants' for 'assistance' became 'claimants' for 'benefits', and a determined and fairly successful attempt was made to convince people of their right to social security payments. Growing demands for an increasingly elaborate array of benefits added to the burdens on the SBC and its staff.

Important though they were for the social security services, these changes had no effect on the Legal Aid scheme. The Annual Reports of the Law Society and the Lord Chancellor's Advisory Committee for the year 1967-8 make no comment on them and reveal the transition only in the terminology they use. During the following years the strain on the social security services, and particularly on their London offices (already noted in our original study[1]) grew more severe. As we foresaw they might,[2] governments relied increasingly on supplementary benefits staff for the administration of means tests for prescription charges, family income supplement and more generous exceptional needs payments and allowances of various kinds. These developments meant more, and more difficult, work. Staff increased in numbers—there were about 26,000 working on supplementary benefits by 1973—but turnover was high and undermanning common. To maintain tolerable standards of service the Department had to 'industrialise' its operations by breaking the work down into increasingly specialised sections, each handled by different people. A claimant seeking supplementary benefit would normally be given an appointment for an interview by one officer and be interviewed by a second, his needs might be assessed by a third, payment approved by a fourth and despatched by a fifth, and he would be visited if necessary, by a sixth. If his case involved missing 'liable relatives', prolonged unemployment, suspected fraud or difficult welfare problems, each would be dealt with by other specialists from local or regional offices.

Thus tendencies, which we noted years ago, to separate the tasks of information gathering and assessment and to concentrate the latter in more specialised units now appear not as a temporary response to new and sparsely scattered Legal Aid work but as forerunners of a pattern that was to become more common throughout the social security system.

In the Legal Aid scheme these tendencies have gone still further.

[1] Page 73.
[2] Page 72.

Assessments are carried out in twelve offices—approximately one for each Region—which work only on Legal Aid. Interviewing and information-gathering are left mainly to local offices whose managers are asked to give the job to people who specialise in it, usually along with other work. A programmed learning 'kit' is sent to local offices for the instruction of these interviewing officers. For London and the surrounding region there are two assessment offices, one in Fulham and the other in Croydon, each with about fifty staff—mainly clerical officers. A smaller group of about eighteen officials looks after the administration of the scheme at Headquarters.

The Research Unit set up by the Law Society in 1971 examined the workings of the scheme and found that the average time taken to issue a certificate for Legal Aid 'is 48 days of which 25 are taken up by sending the papers to the Supplementary Benefits Commission, their investigation and the return of the papers to the local office' of the Law Society. (Much of this time is spent in getting applicants to produce documents or come to interviews, and in waiting for letters to come through the post.) This, said the Lord Chancellor's Advisory Committee, 'seems reasonable'.[1]

The assessment procedures have occasionally been challenged in the High Court[2]—most recently when the Court overturned the SBC's ruling that gifts 'in the order of £17,000' to 'a member of the Singer sewing machine family' living in Vieux Cagnes, France, should be regarded as giving the litigant too large an income to qualify for Legal Aid. To be treated as income, said the Lord Chief Justice and his colleagues, such gifts must display 'an element of periodic recurrence'.[3] But assessment has generally worked smoothly and provoked no complaints.

In the last decade the Legal Aid scheme has grown into a substantial social service. Applications for Legal Aid from England and Wales rose from 105,000 in 1961–2 to 261,000 in 1972–3. In addition, free Legal *Advice*, first introduced at the beginning of this decade, was provided for 111,000 people.[4] All this work dealt only with civil proceedings. Alongside it, Legal Aid in criminal proceedings, provided under the Criminal Justice Act of 1967, was widely used in the magistrates' courts, quarter sessions, assizes and other courts up to the House of Lords.[5] Unlike aid for civil cases, this was provided without any test of the merits of the action, and with very informal means tests in which the SBC played a much more limited part.

[1] Twenty-Second Report of the Lord Chancellor's Advisory Committee on Legal Aid and Advice, 1971–2. HMSO, 1973, p. 33.
[2] For examples, see E. J. T. Matthews and A. D. M. Oulton, *Legal Aid and Advice Under the Legal Aid Acts 1949 to 1964*. Butterworths, 1971, pp. 430 and 433.
[3] *The Times*, 30 March 1973, p. 20.
[4] Twelfth and Twenty-Third Reports of the Law Society on Legal Aid and Advice, 1961–2 and 1972–3.
[5] Matthews and Oulton, op. cit., pp. 52–3.

Our original study dealt with the NAB's assessment procedures, not with the service itself. But we pointed out that the early development of the service was restricted in unforeseen ways by the separation of assessment from the provision of Legal Aid, and the inflexible financial scales adopted. Despite those constraints, the service subsequently grew faster than any other major public service in Britain. This is the only case in this book in which major trends or patterns identified in our original studies were reversed. We should briefly consider how and why that happened.

Growth came about in four different ways. (a) The Divorce Reform Act of 1969 which came into force on 1 January 1971 enlarged the opportunities of many people (whether assisted or not) for litigation, and hence the demand for advice as well as aid. This had a considerable impact on the scheme: matrimonial causes always constituted much the largest group of aided cases.

(b) The scales adopted for assessments have been raised three times since the changes of 1960 reported at the conclusion of our original study. In 1970 the statutory income disregard was raised to £300 and the upper income limit to £950. In 1972 the capital disregard was increased to £250 and the upper capital limit to £1,200.[1] Finally, from 1 January 1974, the income disregard was raised again to £375 and the upper limit to £1,175, and the scales for Legal Advice and Assistance went up too.[1] These changes had an immediate impact, but they were usually overtaken by inflation before long and are unlikely to have greatly enlarged the proportion of the population financially eligible for aid. In their Report on the year 1970–1 the Lord Chancellor's Advisory Committee proposed (surprisingly for the first time) that the income limits for the scheme should henceforth be made inflation-proof by tying them to the more regularly revised SBC scales, and that capital should be treated more generously. Two years later they called for an annual review of these scales and in October 1973 the Solicitor-General told the Commons that 'In future, it is proposed that they should be reviewed annually, so as to ensure that they do not compare unfavourably with, for example, the periodic increase in supplementary benefits.'[2]

(c) Far more important than these developments was the extension of the scheme to cover a larger range of proceedings—particularly the provision of legal advice and assistance (tentatively beginning in 1959 and greatly enlarged in 1973), the provision of legal aid for a growing range of matrimonial, domestic and other proceedings in magistrates' courts

---

[1] Legal Aid (Financial Conditions) Regulations, 1970, 1972 and 1973; Legal Advice and Assistance (Financial Conditions) Regulations, 1973. These rules apply to civil Legal Aid. For criminal Legal Aid the rules are different: see Criminal Justice Act 1967, S. 73, and *Legal Action Group Bulletin*, January 1974, p. 17.

[2] House of Commons Official Report, Parliamentary Debates (Hansard), 23 October 1973, col. 1207.

(beginning in 1961), and the first venture into tribunal proceedings (beginning with the Lands Tribunal in 1970).

(d) Less dramatic, but perhaps equally important in the long run, was the increasing willingness of the public to use the service. In its Reports the Law Society often noted growth in long-established branches of the work occurring alongside extensions of the scheme to new types of proceedings—usually in years when inflation was reducing the proportion of the population eligible, under fixed income and capital limits, to benefit from the scheme. Poor people were gradually learning to use the rights offered by Legal Aid.

These developments were reviewed by the Law Society in their Report for 1963–4. In the previous year they had said that 'virtually all practising barristers are members of the legal aid panels'.[1] Now they estimated that more than 50 per cent 'of the more serious cases in all the Courts in this country are legal aid cases'.[2] But the Rushcliffe Committee's original aim had been 'to enable persons of small or moderate means to obtain, as of right, all those services of a solicitor and barrister which a prudent man who had sufficient means to do so would obtain at his own expense' and no prudent man would embark on litigation without first consulting a solicitor. The opportunity of doing this did not become fully available to the poor 'as of right' (i.e. without relying on the charity of lawyers) until legal advice and assistance were brought within the scheme in April 1973. Part I of the Legal Advice and Assistance Act 1972 then enabled solicitors to provide without charge any service they were qualified to offer (including things like writing a letter to a landlord or viewing the scene of an accident) up to the value of £25—subject to a greatly simplified version of the usual kind of means test which they administered themselves without the help of the SBC. Whether the poor can readily get to a solicitor will in many areas depend on the use that will eventually be made of Part II of the Act which provides for the establishment of neighbourhood law centres in places where none are available.[3]

The Legal Aid service was also exerting a more general influence on the courts. It drew the attention of the legal profession to branches of the law previously neglected—some of them very important branches. (Rookes v. Barnard, for example, was a legal aid case taken eventually to the House of Lords which in 1964 reached a decision with profound implications for the rights of workers and the powers of trade unions.[4])

As the work of the courts came increasingly to be financed by taxpayers, the Government and all concerned with the law were obliged

---

[1] Report of the Law Society for 1962–3, p. 2.
[2] loc. cit.
[3] A. F. Seton Pollock, *Legal Advice and Assistance—The New Deal*. Law Society, 1973.
[4] See Matthews and Oulton, op. cit., p. 20, for further examples.

to seek ways of simplifying proceedings in order to economise in the use of this expensive service.[1] Critics would have added, however, that the failings of the courts had long ago compelled the British to invent other procedures for settling disputes in which lawyers played little part: '... over 2,000 administrative tribunals ... hear more cases than the High and County Courts combined ... The total value to the individual of awards of social security benefits or of reductions in rents can greatly exceed the common law jurisdiction of County Courts; while decisions on compulsory purchase, a road haulage licence or permanent disability, may alter a man's whole future.'[2] But despite these limitations the scheme had become a major service, with a major influence on the legal system. We should note some of the factors which played a part in achieving that: several of them reappear in other studies in this book.

The Rushcliffe Committee's aims, mentioned above, have been repeatedly quoted in official reports on Legal Aid. For those who wanted to extend the scheme these aims had the advantage of being simple in principle, difficult to oppose, and almost indefinitely extensible in practice. No one can define exactly who are 'persons of small *or moderate* means, or prescribe exactly what are '*all* those services' which 'a *prudent* man who had *sufficient* means ... would obtain'. The meaning of such terms grows as time goes by. Indeed, the growth can sometimes be seen going on: 'The Act of 1949', said the Lord Chancellor's Advisory Committee in 1972, 'was designed to provide legal assistance not only for the poor but also for those of moderate means. This expression covers the middle income group who have as yet hardly benefited from the scheme.'[3]

But in its first decade growth was slow, first under a Labour administration which gave priority to houses, incomes, food subsidies and other necessities, rather than to professional services, and then under Conservatives initially suspicious of anything which could be interpreted as 'state interference'. The judges themselves were often hostile to the scheme.[4] Then the general climate of opinion grew more favourable in several ways. Publicly-debated issues, ranging from police corruption to race relations, poverty, public participation in planning, the rights of women and the troubles in Northern Ireland, repeatedly reminded people of the importance of their civil rights and extended the meaning of such concepts—beyond court proceedings into pre-trial investigations and the work of public inquiries and tribunals, for example. The spread of more permissive conventions about sexual behaviour made

---

[1] See, for example, Comments and Recommendations of the Lord Chancellor's Advisory Committee for 1966–7, p. 66.

[2] Brian Abel-Smith and Robert Stevens, *Lawyers and the Courts*. Heinemann, 1967, p. 462.

[3] Comments and Recommendations, 1971–2, p. 34.

[4] See Abel-Smith and Stevens, op. cit., Chapter 12.

people less hostile to divorce—always the bread and butter of Legal Aid work. The scheme was supported with growing conviction by an articulate and powerful profession with a great deal to gain from its extension. In response partly to pressure from younger men with a sharpened social conscience and more urgent need of work, the lawyers provided the trained manpower which made successive extensions of the scheme possible.

As important, perhaps, as these favourable winds has been the lack of any strong contrary wind. Opposition has been kept at a low level, partly because abuse is rare—'litigation is not inherently attractive to the vast majority of the public'[1]—but also because the Law Society achieved success rates of 82 per cent (in 1972–3)[2] by careful control of the use of Legal Aid, and because the Society did its best to keep costs down. By contributing from Legal Aid funds to the costs of successful opponents of assisted clients,[3] the Government eventually took steps to meet one of the recurring criticisms of the scheme.

Leaders of the movement to extend the scheme kept it out of party politics. Even when lawyers in different parties made different proposals—for the development of legal advice and assistance, for example —it was clear that all wanted to extend the scheme and attain the same general objectives.[4] It is often assumed that a reform can be hastened if it gets the backing of a political party, but a later chapter, describing attempts to reorganise secondary education in Croydon, shows some of the difficulties that afflict a public service which becomes a focus of party conflict.

The Legal Aid scheme was set up by lawyers and has always been administered by the Law Society and its local branches. That has given it a professional and strictly non-political style which might be described as élitist. The Lord Chancellor's Advisory Committee illustrates this style. It has nine members, including a professor of sociology and leading figures of the voluntary social services and charitable foundations, besides lawyers. The authorities they quoted when considering an extension of the scheme to cover proceedings in the juvenile courts were 'the Bar Council, the Law Society, the Children's Officers' Association, the National Association of Probation Officers, the County Councils' Association, the Association of Municipal Corporations and the Home Office'.[5] Of these, only the CCA and the AMC could be described as

---

[1] Report of the Law Society for 1963–4, p. 3.
[2] Report of the Law Society for 1972–3, Appendix 5. Success rates for matrimonial cases were 93 per cent, and for the remainder 69 per cent; 7 per cent of all cases were settled out of court.
[3] Under the Legal Aid Act 1964.
[4] Compare, for example, *Rough Justice* (Conservative Political Centre, 1968) and *Justice for All* (Fabian Society, 1968).
[5] Comments and Recommendations of the Lord Chancellor's Advisory Committee for 1962–3, p. 47.

representing the public—but in this case they had a more immediate interest in speaking for the local authorities' social services. None of them could speak single-mindedly for the children or parents involved.

The Secretary to the Lord Chancellor's Advisory Committee plays a crucial part in the administration of the scheme—a part, characteristic of its operations, which probably explains much of its success and some of its limitations. He is always a lawyer, and the present holder of the office is co-author of the principal reference book on Legal Aid and Advice. He acts as the Lord Chancellor's representative on the Law Society's Legal Aid Committee where he must listen sympathetically to those who provide the service; he consults the staff of the SBC about their part in the scheme and the financial implications of any change in the means tests; he drafts annual Reports for his Advisory Committee; and he advises the Lord Chancellor who must decide how to respond to this advice and later convince the Government and the Treasury if the service is to be expanded. Anyone who does this job successfully must show a remarkable combination of integrity, discretion and diplomacy. It is not a job which could be done in a public, contentious or overtly political fashion.

Nevertheless the scheme is beginning to provoke more explicit political concern. Most of this is focused on the development of legal advice and law centres. The first recognition of the need to consult clients more directly which appears in the Reports of the Law Society or the Lord Chancellor's Advisory Committee was a modest proposal made by the latter in its *Comments and Recommendations for 1971–2*. When considering the experimental law centres then being set up, they said 'It is important that every legal centre should gain the support of the community in which it works. To this end we think each centre should invite appropriate representatives of the community to join an advisory committee where the problems facing the centre could be discussed.'[1]

Michael Zander, a lecturer in Law at the London School of Economics and Political Science, intruded on discussions of Legal Aid in a more abrasive style when he asserted (first in *Socialist Commentary*[2]) that 'for most of the population, going to a lawyer seems to be about the equivalent of going to the moon' and called for 'Neighbourhood Law Firms' with resident staff to work in districts where there are no solicitors. The Lord Chancellor's Advisory Committee invited him to meet them but they remained opposed to anything resembling a full-time, salaried public legal service. The Law Society also opposed the idea at

[1] Page 39.
[2] Quoted in Comments and Recommendations of the Lord Chancellor's Advisory Committee for 1965–6, p. 50.
[3] *Second Memorandum on Legal Advice and Assistance*. Law Society, 1969.

first, but later agreed³ to administer the law centres provided for by Part II of the Legal Advice and Assistance Act 1972, which has yet to be brought into force. A number of experimental and voluntary centres of this kind are now working with support from charitable foundations, central and local government.¹ At first the Lord Chancellor's Advisory Committee publicly opposed the grants made by the Home Office from Urban Programme funds to voluntary law centres which, in effect, compete with more conventional forms of Legal Aid and Advice; but before long they too called for more law centres.

Zander, it should be remembered, is an academic lawyer, like several of his closer collaborators. Although his proposals were more radical, he had no demonstrably better claim to speak for litigants, the poor or the public at large than any other member of his profession.

In a service of this kind the professionals may have to take the lead: 'the disgruntled layman simply does not know enough about the system to be able to press effectively for changes'.² Lawyers in the recently formed Legal Action Group are doing that through their journal, *The LAG Bulletin*. Nevertheless, the élitist character of the Legal Aid movement may have blinded its leaders to needs which would have been more quickly perceived by people who were directly accountable to clients and potential clients of the scheme. Instead of beginning with the Supreme Court and taking nine years to start on Legal Advice, eleven to reach the magistrates' courts, and twenty to reach tribunals, such people might have begun from the other end, first making legal advice available in poorer neighbourhoods, and then helping people appearing before tribunals—particularly those dealing with supplementary benefits, industrial injuries and housing. (From the point of view of the poor, the Lands Tribunal was an odd place to start on tribunal work.) They might not have waited twenty-five years to ensure that the value of the income and capital scales used in assessments is not continually eroded by inflation. They might also have been more alert to the social implications of one of the crucial principles used to decide whether an action should be legally aided. That depends on the merits of the case, which are usually decided by asking 'whether a prudent unassisted party who had adequate but not over-abundant means of his own would choose to risk them by bringing or defending the action'. This 'has the effect of *individualising* all conflicts and preventing the use of litigation and the legal system as means to advance group interests'—a restriction not mposed on others who are at liberty to take joint action through trade unions, resident's associations, companies and similar groups.³

[1] Richard White, 'Lawyers and the Enforcement of Rights' in Pauline Morris, Richard White and Philip Lewis, *Social Needs and Legal Action*. Martin Robertson, 1973.

[2] Letter from Michael Zander to the author, 18 January 1974.

[3] Richard White, op. cit., pp. 18 and 19. See also Matthews and Oulton, op. cit., pp. 124 et seq.

But it cannot be assumed that a service more directly accountable to its clients would have grown faster than the present scheme or that it would necessarily benefit more people. Whatever its deficiencies, the Legal Aid and Advice scheme has been this country's fastest growing social service and has become, by comparison with other countries, one of its best.

CHAPTER 5

THE FIRST TEN YEARS OF A HOME HELP SERVICE

This study traces the development of a new social service. The service began to take effective shape when full-time organisers were appointed to run it. They were given considerable freedom to work out their aims and methods. The outcome, a decade later, appears to have been dictated largely by the demands made on the service by its clients and by 'neighbouring' organisations which needed its help in their own work.

When the possibility of making a study in one of the nine geographical Divisions of the London County Council's Public Health Department was first discussed with the County Medical Officer of Health and senior members of his staff, half a dozen topics were suggested for research. After further discussion with the Divisional Medical Officer and members of his staff, it was decided that the evolution of the home help service provided the most suitable development to study in his area—Division 5 of the County Health Department. The research was carried out in 1959, and was based on interviews with the Medical Officer of Health and administrative officers at County Hall, the Divisional Medical Officer and his senior colleagues, the three Home Help Organisers in the Division and the President of the Institute of Home Help Organisers, and also on a number of departmental reports and memoranda, and on reports and circulars issued by the Ministry of Health.

Home Help Services before 1948
The home help service became nation-wide after 1948, but its origins lie sixty years further back. These origins are probably to be found in the growth of a specialised body of qualified midwives and the displacement of the old fashioned 'handy-woman' who not only delivered the baby but also cared for the home and family during the mother's confinement. This was work that a trained midwife would not do, and the gap had to be filled by someone—usually by the mother's relatives.[1]

[1] See *Report of the Working Party on Social Workers in the Local Authority Health & Welfare Services*. HMSO, 1959, p. 57.

In London at the turn of the century a voluntary society concerned with infant welfare started to provide household helps to look after families during the mother's confinement. Results were good enough for the Local Government Board, predecessor of the Ministry of Health, to take up the idea in November 1914 when a circular was issued on the welfare of expectant and nursing mothers in wartime, recommending local authorities to consider among other things the possibility of employing and training 'household or, as they are sometimes termed, sick-room helps'. Four years later the Maternity and Child Welfare Act of 1918 gave general powers to local authorities to arrange for the care of expectant mothers and young children. It was followed by a circular explaining that one of the services which could be given under the Act, with the aid of a 50 per cent subsidy from the exchequer, was the provision of suitable women to take over a mother's ordinary domestic duties during the puerperium. Voluntary associations might be used as agents for this purpose.

During the next year, eight local authorities and thirteen voluntary societies started such schemes, but recruitment was difficult and by 1924 only forty-two local authorities were providing this service, on a widely varying scale and with varying types of staff. At no time did the service absorb more than £7,000 per annum, or 0·5 per cent of the total subsidy for maternity and child welfare services. The Ministry realised that success depended upon constant supervision, and that local authorities could not afford to allot administrative staff solely to this work. The service dwindled to very small proportions: even after the renewal of powers under the Public Health Acts of 1936 only seven authorities in England and Wales had schemes, dealing in 1937 with a mere 262 cases.

The second world war placed a great strain on services for civilians and a Ministry of Health circular of November 1942 urged local authorities to maintain and improve home help schemes as a vital part of their maternity and child welfare services. Since recruitment was then more difficult than ever, the Ministry of Labour and National Service gave such work equal priority with hospital domestic duties. War-time conditions intensified the difficulties of all kinds of sick and disabled people, including the aged whose problems attracted the keenest attention. In 1944, Defence Regulation 68E gave Welfare Authorities the power to provide 'domestic helps' for non-maternity cases. A subsequent circular[1] explained the Ministry's intensions more fully. The service was intended for the kind of case where a wife was ill or had to leave her home to visit a husband in hospital, for cases in which illness struck several members of a family simultaneously (at this time the Ministry feared outbreaks of epidemic illness), and for the elderly infirm. Like the home help service it would be subsidised, could be operated through voluntary agencies, and the Ministry of Labour and National Service

[1] 179/44, 14 December 1944.

would assist with recruitment. Again the Ministry realised the need for special administrative staff, but did nothing to encourage such appointments. The service was regarded as experimental and thought to be unnecessary in rural areas.

The response was patchy and generally inadequate. A Ministry survey made in 1946 found that in the whole of England and Wales only two authorities—one metropolitan borough and one provincial city using the WVS—were operating fully successful schemes, and that their success largely depended on the existence of a full-time organiser. Recruitment still presented problems, but it was hoped that the establishment of the National Institute of Houseworkers would help to solve them by raising the status and quality of domestic work.

In November of the same year the National Health Service Act reached the statute book. Under Part III (Local Authority Services), Section 29 gave local health authorities power to supply domestic help to households where someone was ill, lying-in, expecting a baby, mentally deficient or aged, or where there were children under school leaving age. These powers replaced those granted under the 1936 Acts and Defence Regulation 68E, and amalgamated the home help and domestic help services. A Ministry circular (118/47) pointed out that although these powers were permissive the absence of such a service would greatly reduce the effect of other local authority services that were compulsory. In the event, all local health authorities provided the service. Like its predecessors, the service is grant-aided, but those able to pay for it may be called upon to do so. The circular stressed the need for full-time organisers.

The Structure of the Service in 1959
The National Health Service Act of 1946 came into operation on 5 July 1948. It transferred to the London County Council some of the health services which had previously been administered by the Metropolitan Borough Councils, the City of Westminster and the City of London Corporation. The services transferred included those for maternity and child welfare, the prevention of tuberculosis, after-care for the tuberculous, chiropody and a restricted form of domestic home help, but some Boroughs did not operate all these services. Henceforth the day to day supervision of these services was carried out in nine newly created Health Divisions (co-terminous with similar Divisions for Education and, later, for Children's Services). Each Division covered the areas of a number of Metropolitan Boroughs. Health Division 5, in which the developments to be described took place, covered the City of London and the Metropolitan Boroughs of Bethnal Green, Poplar and Stepney.

The Public Health Department was directed from County Hall by the Medical Officer of Health, who was also the Principal School Medical

THE FIRST TEN YEARS OF A HOME HELP SERVICE 87

Officer. He had a staff of medical, nursing, technical and administrative officers in County Hall and the Divisions. Matters of policy were dealt with by the Health Committee (subject to the approval of the Council) and the Committee's decisions transmitted to Divisional Health Committees. Each Divisional Health Committee consisted of about eighteen members; three or four (including the Chairman) were members of the Health Committee, ten (one of whom was the Vice-Chairman) were nominated by Metropolitan Borough Councils in its area, and the rest were nominees of the Local Medical Committee, Dental Committee, Pharmaceutical Committee, District Nursing Associations and the Royal College of Nursing. The Divisional Committee was responsible to the Health Committee for the service in its area. It framed its own budget, subject to ratification by the Health and Finance Committees (at the time of this study the budget for Division 5 amounted to over £250,000 a year); it was responsible for certain staff appointments and could sanction expenditure (within the approved estimates) up to £1,000 in any one case, and reported quarterly to the Health Committee on the action taken under delegated powers. The Divisional Committee was also empowered to consider any of the services within its jurisdiction, and report to the Health Committee on them.

The Divisional Medical Officer directed the services in his Division and was assisted by three senior officers: the Divisional Administrative Officer, the Divisional Nursing Officer and the Divisional Treatment Organiser. Their work entailed frequent communication with professional and administrative staff in County Hall. The central office provided guidance on matters of policy, and advice and information flowed both ways between those in the Divisional Office and their opposite numbers in County Hall. General responsibility for the Home Help service lay with the Divisional Medical Officer, but the Divisional Administrative and Nursing Officers and their staff carried out most of the work done at the Divisional Office in connection with this service—the latter being concerned with particular problems arising in connection with illness and the visiting of recipients of the service, and with the 'special home help service' to be described later.

The Division was split into three districts for the purpose of this service: North (Bethnal Green, the City and part of Stepney) East (Poplar and part of Stepney) and South (most of Stepney). Each district had its own office run by a Home Help Organiser. At the time of this study the Organisers each had one full-time Assistant Organiser, one full-time clerk, and (in Poplar and Stepney only) a part-time Assistant Organiser. The organiser was responsible for the recruitment and briefing of her home helps. She visited new clients to assess the amount of help needed, and made the initial assessment of the charges (if any) which they were to pay. She allotted and supervised the work of the helps. Monthly returns on the work of the office were made to the Divisional Medical Officer, and the Organiser gave estimates of the service's cost which were used in drawing up the Divisional budget.

The three Organisers attended bi-monthly meetings on the home help service with the DMO, the Administrative Officer and the Nursing Officer. They also attended the Divisional Co-ordinating Committee on the fairly infrequent occasions when one of their cases was being discussed. This Committee consisted of social workers and others from statutory and voluntary agencies who met regularly to consider particularly difficult cases. The DMO was its chairman but frequently left the Area Children's Officer—its vice-chairman—to conduct the proceedings. The Treatment Organiser was secretary to this committee—the main capacity in which she had contact with the Home Help Organisers.

Twice yearly a meeting was held at County Hall, which was attended by all Organisers in the County, and the Principal Clerk and other officers of the central office Division responsible for the home help service (and much else besides). The meetings were chaired by the Chief Administrative Officer of the Public Health Department, and covered a wide range of general topics concerning the service given and the recruitment and training of its staff. Home Help Organisers also attended the periodic, informal meetings arranged between social workers in voluntary and statutory agencies in the various Boroughs. In Division 5, as was usual, they were members of the Old People's Welfare Committees for each Borough.

The structure we have described had changed very little since it was first established by the County in 1948. The development of the Home Help service over the previous decade can now be traced.

The Development of the Service

Before the National Health Service Act came into force, each of the three Boroughs making up Division 5 had employed a few home helps who had worked with maternity cases, under the direction of the Borough's Superintendent Health Visitors. Bethnal Green had five part-time helps, Poplar one full-time and six part-time helps. Stepney had been helping 'general' cases as well, and employed altogether seven full-time and fifty-three part-time workers. The City, which is also included in Division 5, had had a small home help service run by its Welfare Officer, who was invited by the LCC to carry on with the service. But she did not wish to organise a service for which the clients might have to pay, and it was therefore agreed that she would continue to deal with old people's cases in the City (since these were not likely to involve any charge), and all others would go to the Bethnal Green office. There were very few of the latter—perhaps four in a year. The division of work between the County and the City appeared to operate very well; co-operation between the two services was good, and they had been able to help each other out during difficult periods. Owing to this arrangement the City does not feature significantly in the following account.

The three Borough services were taken over by the new Division in 1948 and plans were made to combine and extend them. During the next twelve months an Organiser was appointed to each of the three district offices and given the assistance of one clerk. They faced a difficult task, having to build up a new service whose dimensions and precise functions were unclear, evolving their own methods of working, recruiting and training staff, and at the same time trying to meet heavy demands with inadequate resources and experience. The Public Health Department as a whole was then in the throes of major reorganisation and expansion as a result of the National Health Service Act, and the home help service, having a comparatively minor part to play, was left to develop along its own lines without interference or precise guidance. A Departmental committee, set up in October 1948 to inquire into this rapidly developing service, made a number of recommendations concerning its organisation, but it was decided to allow the service to gain experience and establish itself before making any changes.

The Bethnal Green office in Division 5 was set up at the beginning of 1949 by a young woman who was still in charge there at the time of this study. She had received in-service training in a neighbouring Division where the borough service had been fairly well developed. She had a clerk, but no assistant. Recruitment was exceedingly difficult, and although the Ministry had urged organisers to conduct intensive campaigns, most were too overburdened to use more elaborate tools than the Employment Exchange and notices in local shops. Many of the early recruits seem to have been unreliable; some disappeared without ever doing any work at all (having merely gone through the motions of job-hunting in order to satisfy the Employment Exchange), some falsified their time-sheets or skimped their work if not closely supervised, others gave notice after experiencing the squalid circumstances or uncertain tempers of some of those they were asked to help. The work was heavy and the strain of travelling round the district could be serious. As the service became better known and more effective, unreliable workers became comparatively rare but the other factors continued to produce a wastage rate of 50 per cent over a full year.[1]

The other two district offices experienced similar difficulties, but those of Stepney were even greater. This was partly because the larger heritage to be assimilated from the pre-1948 services presented considerable problems, and partly because the proximity of the City provided a

[1] We made enquiries among three large office cleaning contractors and two University institutions employing cleaning staff. Office cleaners work different hours from home helps and are required to do less travelling (usually confining their work to one building). Turnover rates vary widely, but an annual figure of 50 per cent does not appear to be abnormal among large agencies employing staff of this kind.

ready source of easier, better paid cleaning work for potential home helps. But the main difficulties seem to have arisen from the nature of the area—poor, congested, housing many nationalities and religions with widely varying standards, customs and attitudes. Stepney had a larger population, producing more cases, more difficult cases, and relatively fewer workers to help them. In July 1950 the Division re-drew the boundaries of the districts, transferring part of Stepney to the other two in order to distribute the work more evenly.

When the LCC took over the service the demand for it was expected to increase, though to what extent and in what ways could not be foreseen. From the initial response of hospitals and general practitioners when the service was proposed it could be inferred that there would be many more chronic sick and elderly patients. In 1949 the Health Committee approved the following order of priorities for the types of cases then appearing: (1) confinement, (2) acute or chronic illness, (3) the aged, infirm or blind, (4) households including a mentally deficient person or large numbers of children under school leaving age. It was made clear, however, that this order should not be too rigidly applied. During the early stages, the demand for help greatly exceeded the supply available. Maternity cases, with first priority, were always helped, but the Medical Officer's annual reports on the whole County give high figures for 'other' cases refused—3,500 in 1949, 1,560 in 1950. But in Division 5 it is claimed that no one who was entirely without other sources of help has ever been refused, although occasionally there has been some delay in giving service, and the amount given may frequently be less than is required. We made no attempt to verify this claim by enquiring elsewhere.

Two changes arising from the operation of the National Health Service were soon reflected in the caseload of the home help service. The first and lesser of these was the preference shown by mothers for hospital confinement. Although help can be given to the families of women confined in hospital as well as to those confined at home, and also to expectant mothers during difficult pregnancies, the proportion of help devoted to maternity cases declined during the first four years, and remained low thereafter. Of the 500 households helped during the second half of 1948, 14 per cent were maternity cases. This proportion fell to 3 per cent of the 2,254 cases dealt with in 1952. Since then the proportion of maternity cases had not changed, but the total number of cases helped each year had risen to over 3,000 by the time of this study.

The second influence concerned the aged and chronic sick. Until July 1948, they had been cared for in two ways. The chronic sick—that is, those who are bed-ridden or virtually so, needing daily and continuous medical treatment, 'and also extremely aged persons who although suffering from no specific disease, are confined to bed on account of extreme weakness'[1]—had been admitted to local authority hospitals. These hospitals were now administered by the Regional Hospital Boards and were struggling to care for much larger numbers of acute cases with many near-acute cases waiting for admission. There was a shortage of nursing staff, and among physicians geriatrics was a much neglected speciality, with the result that a 'chronic case' once admitted was likely to occupy a hospital bed for years. Even when the patient was fit enough, discharge was difficult unless relatives were willing to provide a home, for housing was scarce and accommodation in old people's homes was at least as scarce as that in hospitals. Until 1948 old and infirm people had been cared for in Poor Law institutions; these 'homes' were now run by the Welfare Department and debarred by law from accommodating those in need of constant medical care. They were full, with waiting lists—a situation aggravated by the acute housing shortage—and since the hospital chronic wards were so congested, many were driven to maintain 'illegal' wards for chronically sick residents who could not be transferred to hospital.

In this situation a good deal of the strain was taken by the home nurses and home helps. During the first quarter of 1949 the Public Health Department examined a sample of nearly 11,000 patients treated by district nurses and found that 30 per cent of them should have been in hospital—most of them elderly people suffering from respiratory, heart or artery diseases. At the end of the same quarter over 6,700 non-maternity cases were receiving home help in the LCC area; some 3,900 of them were chronic sick cases and 780 were having home nursing care as well. As the care of the aged and chronic sick became the subject of increasing public and professional interest, it was accepted that domiciliary services were essential, not merely to eke out inadequate institutional care or to deal with crises, but because many old and sick people preferred to remain in their own homes as long as possible, and should be helped to do so. This view was endorsed in a Ministry circular of January 1950 which called on local authorities to co-operate with voluntary bodies in extending such services. At this time the LCC made a survey of the care of the aged chronic sick, asked Divisions to provide additional domiciliary services where possible (washing, shopping and chiropody services, for example) and urged them to make the maximum use of existing home nursing and home help services. In the autumn of 1952 the Committee approved a scheme to provide night attendants for households where elderly sick people were cared for by relatives, to enable the family to have two nights uninterrupted sleep per week. Division 5 was able to introduce the scheme with volunteers from the existing staff of home helps. This service has never been drawn on

---

[1] Definition taken from a report to the Council made on 21 October 1952, by the Special Committee on the Welfare of Old People (Minutes, p. 506).

heavily—normally, none of the Districts carries more than one or two such cases—but it is of great value to those who do use it.

This was the only deliberate extension of the scope of the service during its first five years. The number of home helps in Division 5 (expressed as an approximate measure of their 'full-time equivalent') rose from 90 in 1949 to 145 in 1953. Numbers continued to increase until 1955 (with a full-time equivalent of 162), fell off slightly in 1956, and then rose again considerably in 1958 (to a figure of 191). Over this period the population in the Division fell steadily from 240,000 in 1948 to 216,000 in 1958, but the numbers of old people were probably increasing. (Figures are not available for the Division, but in the County as a whole the population fell during this decade while the numbers in the pensionable age groups increased.)

In Division 5, unlike the rest of the country and some parts of London, the factor limiting expansion of the service was not its cost but the scarcity of home helps. This was particularly true of Stepney. Although the numbers employed in Division 5 were below the establishment permitted, the Division nevertheless helped more cases per thousand of the population than the London average. As time went on, help was refused or postponed in fewer cases, and each year more long-term cases remained on the books.

The cost of the service rose steeply, though income from the charges made for it remained at a low level. The Department, making a random check on information supplied by applicants, was shocked to discover how many people understated their incomes. A check made in 1950 on 36 per cent of the applications arising during one year throughout the County showed that 48 per cent of applicants understated their incomes. After that all statements of income were verified, usually direct from employers.

The information needed for assessment was gathered on the initial visit which was usually made by the Home Help Organiser herself. The assessments were done either by her or by her clerk, and were checked by a member of the Divisional Administrative Officer's staff. The assessment scales were complicated. They depended on the joint income of husband and wife, plus whatever was paid for household expenses by children, lodgers, or other non-dependants. Allowances were made and living expenses deducted at rates used by the NAB, and a proportion of the remaining income was regarded as available for payments—one-third of the first pound, one-half of the second and two-thirds of the remainder. In cases of prolonged illness the weekly payment could be reduced to one-third of the first pound and half of the remainder. In addition the hourly charge varied according to the amount of service given; for example, the charge for the first ten hours was 1s 6d per hour, but the cost of twenty hours' service was one guinea. In 1959 the maximum charge was 3s per hour (though the home helps' wage alone

THE FIRST TEN YEARS OF A HOME HELP SERVICE

was 3s 5d per hour at this time) and there were always some people who preferred to pay the full amount rather than have their incomes investigated. Those receiving national assistance were automatically given free service.

By the beginning of 1954 the home help service was well-established and its value recognised by other branches of the health services. It then entered a period of expansion to meet new, specialist demands made upon it by other services, and its administrative structure was overhauled. The special schemes will be described first.

The County Children's Department was set up in 1948, and its activities soon reflected the growing belief that every effort should be made to enable families to care for their own children before removing them from home. During 1952 these problems were discussed among officers and committees of the Children's and Health services and it was suggested that home helps might have a part to play in this connection. Divisional Medical Officers were consulted and their opinions (based on discussions with their Home Help Organisers) reported to the Health Committee, together with those of the Children's Officer. The Committee approved the scheme suggested and it came into operation on 1 December 1953, for an experimental year.

This scheme provided for 'child helps' to be sent to families referred by the Area Children's Officers, although direct application to Divisional Medical Officers has since been encouraged. The families catered for were those in which two or more children under school-leaving age were temporarily deprived of care at home and likely to be received into the Council's care if this help was not available (for example, children with mothers in hospital, and fathers working away from home or on night-shift). The child help would live in, sleeping in the home at night and generally taking the place of the parents. It was found at the same time that in some cases the father or a relative could sleep in at night, but that help was still required to get the children off to school and care for them on their return until the father finished work in the evening; this need could be met by ordinary home helps provided outside the usual hours—from 7 a.m. to 9 a.m. and from 5 p.m. to 7 p.m. for example—and this 'early morning and evening help' scheme thus grew as an off-shoot of 'child help'.

Morning and evening help was found to be extremely effective in the cases where it could be used, but Division 5 scarcely ever supplied residential helps, and after the experimental year annual figures for residential helps in the whole County did not exceed five. It was also realised that in a number of cases home helps working on 'general' cases were intrumental in preventing families breaking up. As early as November 1954 the Ministry of Health issued a circular (27/54) commending the child help service—which then operated only in London and one or two other areas—and encouraging all health authorities to follow suit.

After receiving reports on the first full year, the Health Committee accepted the scheme as a permanent and integral part of the home help service in June 1955. A few amendments were made—families with only one child became eligible for help and the helps no longer had to be drawn from the normal staff; thus, if a friend or relative of the client were prepared to give up a paid job in order to do the work they could be employed by the Division for that purpose.

In the following year a further step was taken. Ministry of Health circular 27/54 had mentioned the need to prevent 'problem families' breaking up, and suggested the use of home helps to teach housecraft to mothers of these families. 'Problem families' were a source of concern to the Health and Children's Departments at this time, and in March 1956, after consulting the Divisions, the Health Committee approved a scheme whereby a small number of 'special home helps' from each Division would receive training for work with these families. The first group, including ten from Division 5, took a five-day course of instruction in simple home management, cookery, child care, and teaching methods. The families to whom they were sent were referred by health visitors and social workers who continued to work with them, while the Home Help Organiser retained full responsibility for service matters. The special home help attended monthly meetings with the Home Help Organiser, the health visitor and other social workers concerned with the family. This scheme demanded the closest co-operation between all those involved. The Health Committee did not alter the order of priorities established in 1949, but left the allocation of these cases to the discretion of the Organisers. Ten cases were dealt with in the first six months of the scheme. The Division claimed that five showed clear improvement, and some improvement took place in three others. The special service continued and further groups of helps joined it. They were chosen by the Divisional Medical Officer on the recommendation of the Home Help Organisers and the Divisional Nursing Officer. The Nursing Officer reported that the service would be much more extensively used but for the difficulty of winning the co-operation of the families. Comment from other agencies suggested that the location of this and other home help services in the Health Department may have encouraged families and the social workers serving them to assume that they were designed only for 'health cases', thus discouraging applications from people who might have benefited. But we have no other evidence that this was the case, and the Department did its best (in the LCC's 'Directory of Social Services', for example) to publicise the full range of needs dealt with by the home helps. On several occasions a special home help from this Division worked in close collaboration with the local Family Service Unit—a voluntary organisation working intensively with a small number of 'problem families'.

These developments brought no reduction in the numbers of old people assisted by home helps. The number of 'special' cases always remained very small, and the aged and chronic sick continued to take much the largest proportion of the service. The aged and chronic sick were not distinguished from other non-maternity cases in the Division's statistics until 1953, when they accounted for 86 per cent of all cases—a proportion maintained until the time of this study. A Ministry survey made in 1954–5 (The Boucher Report)[1] stressed the importance of local authority domiciliary services, including home helps, and even suggested they might mask deficiencies in the hospital services—though the Organisers in Division 5 did not believe this was happening there at the time of our study. The Ministry's circular issued after the publication of the Report urged local authorities to extend their services for old people and to encourage voluntary activity in this field.

While the special schemes were evolving, the arrangements for the service came under scrutiny. During 1954 and 1955 the Organisation and Methods Branch of the LCC Clerk's Department carried out a thorough survey of the work of the Public Health Department and the report made by its Reviewing Committee to the Health Committee suggested that the home help service in the County had developed in a way that led to considerable variations in working methods and standards of service. It also remarked on the rapidly increasing cost of the service. Whereas in the first nine months the total cost of the service was £200,340 and in 1955–6 it had risen to £756,635, income from clients over the same period had only risen from £26,670 to £44,740. These comments were referred to a Departmental working party under the chairmanship of the Administrative Officer and including the Principal Clerk of the relevant Central Office Division, 1 Divisional Medical Officer, 1 Divisional Administrative Officer, 1 Divisional Nursing Officer and 2 Home Help Organisers. The working party was appointed in May 1956, and presented a detailed report to the Health Committee in February 1957.

The Reviewing Committee had suggested that variations in standards within the County arose through confused lines of supervision both within the Divisions, and between the Divisions and County Hall. As far as the Divisions were concerned, the working party found it was not clear whether the Divisional Medical Officer's responsibility for the home help service should be channelled through the Divisional Administrative Officer or the Divisional Nursing Officer—the arrangement within any Division depending rather on the amount of interest shown by the officers concerned. The working party decided for a 'tripartite administration', with the Divisional Medical Officer at the head of the service, and the two other officers responsible for supervision of those parts of the service connected with their work. This decision made no

[1] Ministry of Health Reports on Public Health and Medical Subjects No. 98. *Survey of Services Available to the Chronic Sick and Elderly*, 1954–5.

significant change in the organisation of Division 5. The working party urged that regular meetings be held between the Home Help Organisers and the senior officers of the Division, with the result that the periodic meetings hitherto held in Division 5 were now arranged on a formal, bi-monthly basis. The problem of the Home Help Organisers' isolation from the central office was tackled, not by the appointment of a County Organiser as suggested by the Reviewing Committee and the Organisers themselves, but by arranging twice-yearly meetings between the Organisers and administrative officers at County Hall which enabled the Organisers to give their views to Headquarters more directly. These meetings also afforded a useful opportunity for contact between the Organisers themselves, who tended only to be acquainted with colleagues working in neighbouring areas.

When considering the uneven distribution of service between one area and another, the working party showed that during the previous three years there had been increasing uniformity in the amount of service given, but pointed out that local variations in need—as between a relatively scattered residential area like Eltham and a congested area like Stepney, for example—would inevitably lead to variations in service. The working party agreed that major economies could not be made without a fundamental change in policy which would be a matter for the Council to decide, and that an increase in cost was to be expected if the service was to form an effective complement to other health and welfare services.

Much of the working party's time was devoted to the detail of organisation and changes were recommended which would simplify and standardise administrative routines, so reducing confusion and making it easier to transfer staff from one Division to another. They also provided for a much more detailed system of statistical recording in order to make closer supervision of the service's development possible. The earlier, simpler forms of record keeping had not shown changes in the Division's work in any detail.

Schemes of training were recommended for Assistant Home Help Organisers—post-entry training under the supervision of selected Organisers, and a more theoretical course, possibly leading to a formal qualification, to be arranged after consultation with the Institute of Home Help Organisers. The Institute was not officially represented on the working party, but one of its chief officers was a member in her capacity as a Home Help Organiser.

The Institute of Home Help Organisers had its origins in a small group of London and Home Counties Organisers who in 1948 created an informal association which met to discuss ways of raising the standards of training and performance among Organisers then being appointed. By 1954 the association was incorporated as the Institute of Home Help Organisers (affiliated to the National Association of Local

Government Officers) and had established good contacts with similar bodies in other countries. In 1959 the Institute claimed a membership of over 300, organised in eleven regional branches, and its International Secretary (an LCC Organiser) had been elected first President of the International Council of Home Help Services—a body formed that year with the approval of the governments concerned.

During the previous two years the Institute had been instrumental in persuading some authorities to set up in-service training for Organisers and in 1958 the LCC began a course of in-service training for newly appointed Assistant Organisers. The Institute also had plans for a brief training for home helps along the lines of the courses for 'special' home helps, and a more ambitious plan for a six-month postal course leading to an examination that would confer a certificate on Home Help Organisers. This plan had been approved by the Chairman of the Society of Medical Officers of Health and it was hoped that local authorities would give it their support. Thus the Organisers, originally a group of women chosen (often rather haphazardly and with little or no training) for a harassing and scarcely understood job, were beginning to emerge as a recognised body, concerned with their professional standards and reputation.

Conclusion

This is the story of a new service, created from a patchwork of schemes taken over in 1948 and developed into something more comprehensive and much bigger than had ever been envisaged before. It was several years before the scope and purpose of the service emerged clearly. Then there was a phase of reorganisation: administrative procedures were standardised, specialist branches were identified and developed, regular statistics were prepared, links with other services were forged, a new professional group took shape, and training was begun. By the time of this study the service had settled down into recognised routines; the numbers of cases helped continued to rise slowly, but the distribution of help between different types of case had remained remarkably stable for the previous seven years. The service was still experimenting, but fresh developments now appeared as modifications of a well established pattern.

Before 1948 the service had in most places been a rudimentary affair, designed for the purpose of helping families in which the housewife was temporarily incapacitated. Then three major changes took place. The County authority was given powers to provide domestic help to meet a much wider variety of needs. It was accepted that the service could not succeed without a competent staff of organisers. And it was recognised —more slowly—that the home helps were neither an independent, self-sufficient service nor a frill upon the fabric of the welfare state, but an essential ancillary to the hospitals, the domiciliary health services, the old people's welfare services and the child care service. Thereafter the growth of the service depended mainly on the number of home helps who could be recruited and kept on the job.

What the principal functions of the service would be was still an open question—but not for long. Priority was always given to the family in which there was confinement or serious illness, and the aged and chronic sick were not separately identified in the statistics for five years. But it is clear that the old took the lion's share of resources from the beginning. Maternity cases fell steadily from 14 per cent to 3 per cent of all cases. After 1953 the aged and chronic sick constituted 86 or 87 per cent of the caseload each year, and all other types of case continued to provide the remaining 10 per cent of the caseload. These figures understate the importance of the maternity cases, each of which demanded more hours of service per week than were required by other cases, but the trend is clear. This pattern of work is typical of that found in other LCC Divisions and many other local authorities.

The principal factors shaping the course of this development lay outside the service: the growing demand for home help among the aged and chronic sick arose from the growing proportion of elderly people in the local population, the growing numbers in this group who were able to continue living in their own homes, and the scarcity of accommodation for them in hospitals and residential institutions. This demand was directed and supported by hospitals, general practitioners and the welfare services whose patients and clients needed the service. Being based in a Public Health Department, the service is likely to have been particularly attuned to the demands of the chronic sick and particularly responsive to the pleas of medical authorities. Priority was accorded to young families, but the growing proportion of mothers having their babies in hospital provided an alternative means of meeting their needs. Meanwhile the system of charges (although it was exceedingly complex, and raised only a small fraction of the total cost of the service) demanded relatively high payments from households with a full-time wage earner needing several hours help each day, and negligible payments from households with no wage earner needing only a few hours help each week. Thus the aged and infirm may have been more willing to seek help than were mothers with young children. Moreover the provision of occasional help for elderly people, many of whom lived alone, must have entailed a more easily sustained pattern of personal relationships (for helper and helped alike) than the provision of more intensive help in a family of young children.

The Council, its Health Committee and senior staff gave the Home Help Organisers great freedom to develop the service in response to the demands made upon it, and subsequently devoted their attention to the development of special branches of the service and the general improvement of its administrative structure and procedures. The pattern that

THE FIRST TEN YEARS OF A HOME HELP SERVICE

eventually took shape in response to the demands of clients and the social services assisting them was accepted and confirmed, rather than initiated, by those ultimately responsible for the direction of the service.

DISCUSSION

The previous studies in this series dealt with tasks that formed a part of a longer or larger administrative process. But this one deals with the origins and subsequent development of a particular local branch of the social services. It therefore provides an exceptional opportunity for studying the manner in which the functions of such a service take shape. Our discussion of the case will be restricted to a few general features of this process which reappear in later studies of similar developments.

Many attempts had been made to establish a service of this kind since the government first gave its blessing to such schemes during the first world war. But it was not until the National Health Service was introduced in 1948 that the appointment of full-time Organisers provided a corps of junior administrators who were wholly devoted to the development of the service and backed by a local authority prepared to provide the financial resources it would require. Despite initial difficulties and a continuing scarcity of labour, the staff of the service was rapidly built up in the area studied, and ideas which had been discussed for close on fifty years became viable at last.

Nevertheless the functions of this service, derived from disparate needs and traditions, were not specified at all precisely in the National Health Service Act or in the initial directives issued by the County Health Department. Its eventual extent and scope and the priority to be accorded to different needs were uncertain. This uncertainty, and the freedom given to the Organisers to develop the services in their own way, were increased by the overwhelming urgency of other tasks which engrossed the attention of the Committee and its senior officials at the time.

The influence of other bodies which made demands on the Health Department, referred clients to the home help service, and provided general support for its growth at central and local levels of government constituted one group of factors which played a part in shaping the development. A service of this kind cannot develop without spending money and recruiting staff, but these must be secured in competition with other potential users of the same resources. To compete successfully for resources the service must convince those who control them that it does—or will do—valuable work. The people to be convinced are not themselves directly responsible for the service but their support for it is crucial. In this case the service required the initial backing of the Ministry of Health and the Ministry of Labour, and the sustained support of general practitioners, the hospitals, the medical services represented on the Divisional Committee, the County Welfare Department and the Children's Department. Its functions were partly shaped by the needs and expectations of these bodies.

A second major influence shaping the service was provided by the increasingly confident and coherent group of Organisers managing it. Within the broad limits assigned to them, it was they who interviewed applicants and determined how much help they should have and how soon they should have it; it was they who selected home helps and assigned them to households, drew up budgets and distributed resources. In a perfect world it would no doubt have been recognised from the start that those responsible for these complicated and onerous tasks required some training, adequate assistant staff and opportunities for regular consultation with each other and with senior officials. But in real life a group of workers must struggle to gain recognition for such needs, first among themselves and then at more senior levels of the services in which they operate. Hence it took time—and the creation of national and international associations—for the Organisers to secure these things and to ask for further developments, such as the appointment of a County Home Help Organiser with direct and permanent access to senior staff in the central office, which had not been achieved at the time of this study. From the start, individual Organisers played an important part in shaping the service; in future their professional association and the climate of opinion it creates may play an increasing part in this process, though its operations will doubtless be guided by the more influential administrative and professional interests (represented by the chairman of the Society of Medical Officers of Health, for example) whose support it requires.

It has been suggested that the number and character of the applicants coming to ask for the service played the most important part of all in shaping its development. But these demands are a complex phenomenon depending on the motives and behaviour of people on both sides of the counter, and the relationships between them. We have only examined one side of that process. But it seems likely that demographic changes, the general climate of opinion affecting the growth and function of services for people living in their own homes, the growing interest in the needs of old people, scarcity of alternative social services and the home helps' close links with the whole system of health services, all played a part in determining the volume and types of applications received and the priorities accorded to each of them. Unlike the charges made for Legal Aid, dealt with in the previous study, the charges made for the home help service were entirely under the control of those providing the service itself, and the assessments were to a considerable extent designed to accord with the priorities laid down for the service. We have no reliable evidence about the effects of this system of charges (and neither had the LCC) but it seems likely that these effects were appreciable and partly unforeseen, producing a larger proportion of elderly and infirm applicants than would have been expected had the service been provided free.

This brief outline of the principal features of the development may be summarised in the form of hypotheses to be tested in subsequent studies. The creation of a service calls for considerable resources which can only be secured with the agreement of influential bodies outside the group responsible for providing it. The variety of these bodies and the diversity of their interests may partly account for the broad and ill-defined terms of reference with which the service begins. To secure the growing volume of resources it needs, those providing the service are compelled to enter into general, if ill-defined, commitments that command the approval of those whose support they require in competing with other potential users of these resources. The staff directly responsible for managing the service find they have common problems and common interests in their daily work of dealing with their clients, their subordinates and seniors. They formulate general principles for their own guidance and for the training of their successors, and they seek direct access to more senior officials and greater influence over the development of the service. Meanwhile staff providing the service can exert considerable influence on the character and volume of the demands made on it by the public, through selection procedures, deliberate or accidental, and through the reputation they create for it. But to develop extensively, the service must go a long way towards meeting the needs expressed by its clients and by those who play a part in directing clients to it.

In conclusion it may be noted that the principal relationships in this simplified model—particularly those between the people providing the service, their clientele, and the external 'backers' controlling the resources they require—are not unlike those to be seen in the development of industrial and commercial institutions. The price mechanism plays a smaller (though by no means a negligible) part in the transactions of the social services; but, although money may not be the principal medium of exchange employed, the relationships between the parties to these transactions are similar in many ways to those which are to be seen in the market. In order to grow, the service must both meet a demand and maintain its creditworthiness among those controlling the resources it needs.

POSTSCRIPT

Since our original study the work done by home helps has changed very little, but the place of the service within local government has been transformed by two major reorganisations. The reform of London government which took place in April 1965 abolished the London County Council and returned the home help service to the Greater

London Boroughs—a lower tier of larger and more powerful authorities than the old Metropolitan Boroughs which had been responsible for the service before 1948. Six years later, in April 1971, the service was transferred from the Borough Health Departments to the new Social Service Departments. Amongst the other services incorporated in the new Departments was all the work previously done by the Children's Departments which were abolished at that point.

Since our next chapter deals with the Area Office of the LCC Children's Department which later joined forces with this Division of the Home Help Service in the Social Service Department of the Borough of Tower Hamlets, we deal with both in a postscript to Chapter 6.

CHAPTER 6

THE DEVELOPMENT OF CASEWORK IN A CHILDREN'S DEPARTMENT

This study, like the previous one, deals with the first decade of a new social service, but it is restricted to selected developments within the organisation. As before, the scope and objectives of the service were initially unclear. They were gradually worked out by the staff providing the service, through successive adaptations which had to be reconciled with the expectations of external interests controlling the growing volume of resources required. The 'vagueness' of the service's objectives appears to have been a necessary condition for successful evolution. As the work developed, changes occurred in the structure of the organisation, affecting the relationships between those working in it. But considerable differences in outlook could be tolerated, provided new developments went some way towards satisfying the aspirations of all concerned.

This report deals with Area 5 of the London County Council's Children's Department—the same geographical area as that served by Division 5 of the Health Department which formed the subject of the previous study. When asked to select the most important developments that had taken place in the work of her office during recent years, the Area Children's Officer chose two: first, and most important, a reorganisation which delegated responsibility for casework with children in the Council's care to whichever Area Office received the children into care and dealt with their families; secondly, an experiment in 'intensive' casework which had been made in this and one other Area Office. The Home Area Scheme was introduced in October 1953, and the first intensive caseworker was appointed in January 1955. Since each formed a part of the same general evolution of the service, this study deals with both of them. It was carried out in 1957 and 1958.

Neither of these innovations can be understood without some account of the structure and history of the whole Department. Our report therefore begins with an outline of the Department's origins and early growth. The development of the Home Area Scheme and the intensive casework service are then traced in turn. In both these sections of the report the description of developments at County Hall generally precedes the description of developments in the Area Office, but it is the work of the Area Office which forms the focal point of the study. After a summary of the situation as it was in 1957, the report closes with some general conclusions.

The main sources for this account were the people who took leading parts in the developments described—the Chairman of the Children's Committee and about ten of the Council's staff, including the (then acting) Children's Officer, the Area Children's Officer of Area 5 and her predecessor. The Department also provided a report on its work made by the Organisation and Methods branch of the Clerk's Department and a number of other reports and directives. Three cautions should be borne in mind while reading this study. The Area Office chosen for the study was not typical of the other eight in London County, for although all followed the same general principles each was free to develop its work in response to local needs and problems. Considerable further growth and change took place in this Area shortly after the completion of the study, but although a note on these later developments appears at the conclusion of this report we have not attempted to bring the story up to date. The term 'casework', frequently used in this report, can have several meanings: here it refers simply to 'work on cases' carried out by child care officers and others in the Area Children's Office—which is the sense in which the phrase was normally employed in the Department.

The Establishment of the Department

The administrative structure to be described originated in the Children Act of 1948 which amended and extended the responsibilities of Local Authorities for deprived children. The Act provided for the creation of new departments to carry out these functions and those imposed on Local Authorities under Parts III and IV of the Children and Young Persons Act 1933, the Adoption of Children (Regulation) Act 1939, and (in the case of the LCC) Part XIII of the Public Health (London) Act 1936. Among their responsibilities were the reception into care of children orphaned, deserted or for other reasons deprived of proper care in their own families (including those committed to the Authority's care by the courts under 'fit person' orders) and the provision of foster homes or other residential establishments for them. For children in their care they were also given wide powers in the field of adoption, and enabled in certain circumstances to assume the rights and duties of parents. The Children's Authorities also have other duties—those under Child Life Protection Regulations, for example—which are not elaborated here as they played no part in the developments to be described.

In November 1948 the London County Council appointed its Children's Committee to which all this work was referred, and the

Department itself came into being in the following year. Many of its functions were inherited from other Departments; hitherto the Social Welfare Department had been responsible for decisions about the reception of children into care, the form of care to be provided for them, and the assumption of parental rights; it also assessed and collected parental contributions. Of the children received into care and placed in institutions, those under two years had been put into residential nurseries run by the Public Health Department, and those over two years had gone to residential nursery schools, residential schools and homes run by the Education Department. The latter Department was also responsible for selecting foster homes, placing and supervising the children who went into them, providing after-care, and generally implementing the decisions made by the Welfare Department. Along with these functions, thirty-two residential establishments were transferred to the new Department, and 1,440 staff, of whom 70 worked 'in the field', 140 were in office grades, and the remaining 1,230 were in residential homes and schools. Field workers and residential staff were transferred *en bloc*, but when a new service is carved out of existing departments in this way, it is natural for the parent departments to endeavour to retain their most efficient office staff.

The administrative centre of the new Department was at County Hall, but work on individual cases was decentralised to nine offices set up in Areas corresponding to the Divisions already existing in the Education and Public Health Departments, each Area covering about three Metropolitan Boroughs. Most of the records, field workers and office staff were transferred to these offices.

The Department was thus faced with multiple problems, having not only to build up a new service, but also to assimilate and modify a patchwork of inherited functions, attitudes, staff and records. The Area Offices were undermanned, and contained many people trained under the Poor Law or in the Education Department who had been uprooted from their accustomed settings. The Department had to begin by creating a new set of loyalties and a clear understanding of its enlarged responsibilities throughout this heterogeneous team. Moreover the legislation establishing it had been directly prompted by popular concern about the fate of children in public care, and no provision had been made for helping children still living in their own homes. Placed like an ambulance at the foot of a cliff, the service had no power to prevent the casualties it awaited. This restriction could not be maintained indefinitely.

Up to this time residential institutions had been accepted as the normal and desirable means of caring for children, but the Children Act required the new Department to use foster care whenever possible. This was in accordance with recently developed ideas about child care, but was also made necessary by the acute shortage of space in residential establishments. This was the most important change made during the first few years. The Department had its work cut out to get the new service going, and there was no time to spare for other tasks.[1]

The Department in 1953

The beginning of 1953 forms a convenient starting point for this study. The numbers of children in care had by then risen from 5,681 (in 1949) to 8,027; the numbers in foster homes had almost doubled, raising the proportion boarded out from 18 per cent to 25 per cent.

The Children's Committee was responsible to the Council for all questions of policy and for interpreting the work of the Department to the Council. It met monthly and had twenty-one members, some of whom were co-opted. Members sat on the managing committees of residential homes and schools, and visited these establishments from time to time. The duties, membership and procedures of these managing committees still remained largely unchanged, but the establishments to which they were attached were henceforth to play a less predominant part in the service than they had done previously.

At County Hall the Children's Department consisted of four Divisions. Two of them, responsible respectively for child care and work on individual cases, and for the management of residential establishments, came under the Chief Assistant Children's Officer. The other two Divisions—one dealing with staff and the other with finance and the general organisation of the Department—came under the Department's Administrative and Establishments Officer. All four Divisions were staffed by administrative and clerical officers. In the course of time three Inspectors of Child Care were appointed to supervise the residential establishments and to advise on child care generally.

The Area Offices handled direct relations with the public, receiving children into care, and finding and filling foster homes. Each was responsible for liaison with a particular group of residential homes and schools, principally for the purpose of boarding out children from them, and they were gradually expected to extend their 'casework' as far as their limited resources allowed. In January 1953 Area 5 had a staff of seventeen, ten of whom were social workers. The Area Children's Officer was responsible for both the administrative and casework aspects of the Area's work and, like all Area Children's Officers appointed before 1955, she was graded as a Senior Assistant in the administrative class of officers (though we have included her among the social workers numbered above). She had started her career in residential work at the time local authorities first took over children's homes from the Boards of Guardians. During the war she ran special schools for evacuees, and in 1944 joined the LCC Education Department as a

[1] For an account of the early development of this Department, see Donald Ford, *The Deprived Child and the Community*. London, Constable, 1955.

boarding out officer. She was responsive to new ideas and enjoyed experimenting. Moreover her experience had given her great respect for the advantages a child can gain from his own home, and considerable reluctance to place children in institutions whenever this could be avoided. She was supported by a staff that was anxious to use opportunities for innovation. Like all but two of the Area Children's Officers she had had little administrative experience. Like some of the others, she had come from the Education Department which had established standards of boarding-out work widely considered to be in advance of anything comparable at that time.

There were nine child welfare officers in the Area. Three of them were 'special duties' officers dealing only with court cases, including adoption, for which they undertook the work of 'guardians *ad litem*'. Each of the others was responsible for liaison with one or more establishments, and two of them also undertook 'aftercare'—that is, the supervision of children in care who had left school. The three 'special duties' officers and one other had worked for the Council for many years but had no paper qualifications. The remaining five held University Social Science Certificates, and two of them held a professional qualification— the Home Office Certificate in Child Care—as well.

The administrative staff of the Area consisted of one Administrative Assistant, two male clerical officers who dealt with new applications for children in need of care, another who assessed parental contributions, and two general clerical officers, one of whom did some local visiting as well as clerical work. Much of this would have been regarded as social work, even at that time; thus there was no clear distinction between the activities of administrative staff and social workers.

The methods employed by the Department at that time were still based on those used before 1948. All establishments and the allocation of vacancies in them were controlled from County Hall. Applicants coming to the Area Office in Bethnal Green Road were interviewed by a clerical officer—a former relieving officer, experienced in record-keeping and in dealing with 'difficult' clients. If a child was to be received into care he collected the information needed to fill up the application form, and telephoned to County Hall for a place appropriate to the age, sex and special needs (religion, length of stay, etc.) of the child. The child was only accepted into care if an appropriate vacancy could be found or created. In practice about one in four seem to have been accepted—the desperate shortage of places meant there was room for the most urgent cases only, and the rest had to be placed on a waiting list. It was generally felt that places went to whoever put in most applications and pushed hardest, and the staff tended to react accordingly. The procedure placed a great strain on everyone. Thus the clerk responsible for this work in the Vacancies Section at County Hall was at one time christened 'Molotov' by staff in the Area Office. But when child welfare officers were brought into County Hall for a short period to take over these duties the position was just as bad. All concerned were the victims of a system devised years before which could no longer cope with the increased demands being made on the new service.

Social workers in the Area Office took no part in this procedure, for child welfare officers assumed no responsibility for children until they had been placed in care. Children were sent to establishments in all parts of the County and far beyond, and they then became the responsibility of the Area Offices to which the establishments were attached, while any dealings with their families and with children returning to their homes were the concern of the Areas in which their parents lived. Often several children from one family were placed in different establishments, and two or more Area offices dealt with a single family. Satisfactory liaison between Areas was difficult, and mountainous paperwork resulted.

In 1952 the extension of boarding out came to a halt, and for the next five years there were fewer children in foster homes. Most foster parents wanted a child of a specified age and sex, free from close ties with his own family. Few would take children for short periods, few would take more than one child (and the Department's policy was to keep brothers and sisters together) boys were harder to place than girls, Roman Catholic foster parents were always scarce, and children with behaviour problems had to be cared for in the Department's establishments. Foster parents resembled hesitant adopters and were treated as such.

Meanwhile the rising numbers of children in care and the larger staff required was making the service increasingly expensive. Although officers in the Areas recognised these financial problems, they were primarily the worry of those in County Hall who stood nearer to the Committee. The Area Children's Officers' main complaint was that the system for placing children was cumbersome, some felt that if they themselves controlled the vacancies they would be able to develop a better policy for reception into care. As early as 1951 a few of the leading members of the central office had come to believe not only that it was cumbersome and expensive, but that more stress should be placed on the welfare of children in their own homes, and relatively less on the 'child minding' aspects of the service. At County Hall the principal advocates of this approach were found in the Child Care Division and the inspectorate. But several other senior administrators felt that if Area Children's Officers controlled reception they would bring much greater numbers of children into care, and cause a calamitous drain on the Department's inadequate resources. The Children's Officer himself was reluctant to subject a newly established Department to the radical change implied by such a step. It was a heavy responsibility to justify such trouble and expense to his Committee and the Council.

The Home Area Scheme

Plans for the new system originated in the Child Care Division at County Hall, and the details were thrashed out in informal discussions. After two months or so the Area Children's Officers were brought into the talks. At first it was not clear whether the proposed scheme was to be regarded as a change in administration (and therefore to be left to the officers of the Department) or as a change in policy (and therefore subject to the Committee's approval). The officials took the view that it was an administrative change; the plans were discussed with the Chairman of the Committee, and after long debates within the Department in September 1953 the Children's Officer issued a directive outlining two plans: the 'Home Area Scheme' for regrouping Area offices and establishments and the 'decentralisation of vacancies', both to come into force on 1 October 1953.

The nine Areas and their outcounty regions were grouped into four 'Sectors'. Area 5, with Area 6 and their contiguous outcounty regions constituted Sector C, and they were given control of vacancies in the group of homes and schools in that Sector. But since these two Areas were divided by the Thames they agreed to operate autonomously, each using the establishments in its own outcounty region; Area 5 was therefore able to work as a more or less independent unit. Responsibility for cases and the allocation of children to establishments was to be settled by the Areas amongst themselves—County Hall declined to act as arbitrator over the details of individual cases, and only consented to receive appeals on questions of exceptional difficulty. The central office remained responsible for providing and running establishments, for negotiations with other local authorities, and for authorising the use of private and voluntary establishments. The immediate aim was for children to be placed within their own 'home' Sector, though a few big specialist establishments were to be temporarily available to all Areas. It was intended that the officer making the initial contact with a family should be in charge right through a child's time in care, and that the child *and his family* should be regarded as the 'child care unit' for which the service was provided. 'Anticipated results' of the scheme, outlined in the Children's Officer's directive, included a speedier and more elastic procedure requiring less paper work, and a greater sense of personal responsibility among officers; child welfare officers would be brought into close touch with reception work, and there would be closer contacts both between children, parents and the Service, and between Area Offices and establishments. Finally, it was hoped by some that there would be opportunities to begin 'preventive work', leading to the growth of a casework service dealing as much with families as with children. The directive added that 'All officers will be aware of the long term child care principles and aims underlying the scheme'.

Differing views of the new situation were found in different parts of the Department. In practical terms what had happened was that the Vacancies Section at County Hall had disappeared. Instead there was an informal grouping of the nine Areas and their outcounty regions into four Sectors, and each Area had been allotted space in a group of homes, schools and so on; within Sectors, each child had become the responsibility of its receiving Area (which, potentially at least, was also the establishment Area) and families were no longer split between several Areas. Ultimately the effect of these changes would be that the children in any group of establishments, together with those boarded out in the same Sector, would (with a few inevitable exceptions) be those received into care by the Area offices of the Sector. Each of the four Sectors would then form a self-contained unit.

But in October 1953 this scheme had hardly begun to take shape. The children from one Area's territory were still scattered throughout the four Sectors since it had been decided that none would be transferred simply for the sake of administrative convenience. Two years later, when the pattern had begun to grow clearer, further complication was caused by the creation of three subcommittees of the Children's Committee, known as District Committees, which substituted a three-part division for the original four-part system. Another continuing source of untidiness remained in the reception and assessment centre at Poplar, a short-stay home in Wandsworth, after-care hostels, and a large home named Wood Vale; these were still used as 'all-London' establishments and small homes for disturbed children were added later to this group since it was not possible to make every new experiment in triplicate.

The Committee seems to have been most concerned with the redistribution of children brought about by the Home Area Scheme, laying less stress on the reallocation of responsibilities between County Hall and the Areas, and between individual Areas. Caseworkers recognised the importance of these administrative changes, but more important to many of them was the fact that this development held out hopes of making the 'long-term principles of child care' a reality. The Areas had been given considerable freedom in interpreting their new powers, and Area 5 was particularly responsive to the opportunity offered. Before the Home Area Scheme was introduced it had already given its child welfare officers the task of dealing with applications for admission to care. Developments in this Area were worked out in staff meetings which were frequent, though at that time irregular and unrecorded. These meetings included all members of the staff—clerical and administrative officers and social workers. The Area Children's Officer commented that the plans discussed were to alter the policy and procedure of the whole office, and it was therefore important that everyone should accept the new methods and contribute to them.

At these meetings it was decided that reception into care should be the responsibility of social workers rather than administrators, and that something more than a formal interview was required if the needs of a family were to be understood. That is, all stages of the work—not merely boarding-out and aftercare, but also reception and eventually 'preventive' work—should be conducted by those experienced in applying 'the principles of child care'. The first step had been taken when a woman clerical officer, originally a Welfare Department worker who had done local visiting, took over reception interviewing, while each application was followed up by a home visit from a child welfare officer. In order to share this extra work and to economise on travelling time, the Area was divided into 'patches', and one child welfare officer made responsible for all investigations in each. Child welfare officers began to gain effective control over reception policy in June 1953 when the clerical officer was withdrawn from reception work altogether and a new division of duties was made: all preliminary visits of investigation were undertaken by one half-time child welfare officer; all short-stay and rehabilitation cases were allocated to another, and the remainder of the child welfare officers undertook reception interviewing for one-week periods on a rota system, in addition to their work with the establishments.

This system for dealing with applications for care created new problems, but visits to applicants and the discharge of short-term cases were handled more quickly, and social work criteria could be brought to bear on the crucial decision to receive children into care. The introduction of the Home Area Scheme completed the picture. Within the limits determined by the policy, powers and resources of the department, the Area now had full control of residential placements, and reception into care depended on social workers' assessments of the needs of children and their families. It also became administratively feasible to make one social worker responsible for a family and for any of its children that might be in care.

The Area then had to assimilate its new functions and deal with the snags in its reception system. These snags were in part a reflection of the large case loads and inadequate staffing the Department had always had to contend with. Developments were therefore determined as much by the peculiarities of the staffing position as by deliberate policy. (The Council's Organisation and Methods Branch made a study of the Department in 1955 and found the situation bad enough to call for an interim report recommending the appointment to the Department of twenty additional child welfare officers, bringing their total numbers to 108.) The solution reached in Area 5 was partly due to administrative reorganisation and partly a reflection of changed thinking about the functions of social work within the service.

The 'patch' system had the disadvantage that decisions were delayed whenever the officer responsible for one of the patches was absent; moreover it was not easy to demarcate boundary lines. In September 1954 the Area was divided into three 'sections' within which were grouped more clearly defined patches. (These Area 'sections' must not be confused with the four Sectors into which London's nine Areas were grouped. They will be escorted by inverted commas to mark the difference.) Officers still worked their own patch as before, but in addition had an overall responsibility for a whole 'section' and thus could more easily deputise for each other. A clerical officer was assigned to work for each 'section'.

Meanwhile, interviewing by rota had given rise to serious difficulties, for there was no uniformity or continuity of treatment. This created difficulties for the visiting officer and caused confusion and frustration for social workers elsewhere—almoners, for example, who might have to deal with different reception officers on different days of the week. The public was also affected, and some people were quick to spot the idiosyncrasies of different officers and vary their tactics accordingly. It was not unknown for parents to put their heads round the door, say 'Oh, it's you!' and come back another day.

It was decided that all reception interviewing must be done by one child welfare officer, and the job was given to a new member of staff who was slightly lame and therefore unable to do much visiting. (She had more positive qualifications too, being a trained and experienced social worker.) This arrangement smoothed the internal and external relations of the office, but continuity and uniformity had still to be achieved, for office interviews and home visits were handled by different workers. The staff continued to discuss the whole problem. Then in July 1955 the interviewing officer left unexpectedly, and in the emergency the Area reverted to the rota system of interviewing, while a half-time officer took over all visits of investigation.

Finally it was agreed that a permanent team of officers should be responsible for initial interviews and the home visits that followed. But it was felt that short-stay cases should not be transferred to other officers for the few days or weeks while such children remained in care, and the team ought not to be limited to reception work. But who was to draw the line between 'short-term' and 'long-term' cases?

An opportunity for reorganisation came in February 1956 when two more child welfare officers were appointed to Area 5—one half-time and one full-time. The Area's three geographical 'sections' were retained to deal with long-term cases, and a fourth 'section' created: 'section 4', consisted of two (later three) child welfare officers who took over all reception interviewing, investigation visits, and short-stay cases. 'Section 4' officers collaborated with those in the other 'sections' and could consult the appropriate workers at a very early stage in any case that seemed likely to present long-term problems. The precise moment of transfer from one officer to another was decided between them. That is, the demarcation of officers' responsibilities—which might well have been regarded as a purely administrative question—had become a 'casework' decision, left to the two officers directly concerned. This system was felt to work well, and had not been changed up to the time of this study (though it has since been abandoned).

'Intensive' Casework

The second development to be described is the experiment in 'intensive' casework. We have seen how the social workers extended their sphere of work 'backwards' from the supervision of children already in care to the investigation of new applications and the selection of those to be accepted. But concern for the welfare of children could not be halted there. Throughout this period child welfare officers became increasingly interested in the cases in which it seemed that intensive work might forestall the breakdown of normal family life or in other ways prevent children coming into public care. The seeds of this development had already been set when the first changes in reception procedure were made, and after the introduction of the Home Area Scheme one officer began to give special attention to this kind of work. But though all child welfare officers had done fairly intensive work with some families, heavy case loads prevented them from devoting much time to it.

The Child Care Division at County Hall had already recognised the whole family as the proper focus for preventive and rehabilitative work, and those responsible for the preparation of budgets acceptable to the Council had pressing reasons for supporting any measure that would reduce the number of children in care. The interest of the Chairman of the Children's Committee was sharpened by conferences and discussions, including a paper read at a conference of children's workers on the unit experimenting with intensive casework in Oxfordshire. The example of the Family Service Units, which had for long been developing intensive work with specially difficult cases, must also have been in the minds of many people. In the spring of 1954 the Chairman and the Senior Inspector of Child Care visited the Oxfordshire unit, and in July a report was presented to the Committee suggesting that two people should be appointed to attempt similar work in London. The scheme was submitted to the Director of Establishments—a chief officer of the Council to whom proposals for new staff positions in all LCC Departments were referred at that time.[1] He advised the Committee that the project lay outside the scope of their work: the Children Act provided no basis for it. But he suggested that comment be invited from the recently formed Joint Special Sub-committee on Children Neglected or Ill-treated in their own Homes. This Sub-committee consisted of the Chairmen of the Public Health, Education, Housing, Welfare and

[1] This office was concerned with the Council's general staffing policies, not with the Children's Departments residential 'establishment' previously referred to. It was later abolished and at the time of this study its duties were carried out by the Clerk's Department.

Children's Committees, together with other representative members, and was attended by the chief officers serving these Committees. It was appointed to investigate the co-ordination of services for neglected children. If it reported favourably on the plan (which it did) the Director of Establishments said he would have 'no further observations to offer'. The Chairman of the Children's Committee (who was also Chairman of the Joint Special Sub-committee) had a special interest in the project and was able to do a good deal to put the idea over. It was arguable not only that the scheme was good child care, but also that it would save more money than the amount required for additional salaries.

At a meeting in July 1954, the Children's Committee approved the experimental appointment of two intensive caseworkers for one year. The scheme was then sanctioned in turn by the Establishment Committee, the Finance Committee and the Council. Areas 5 and 8 were asked to take part in the experiment, but since the worker in Area 8 withdrew after a very short time the experiment was in effect confined to Area 5.

There the intensive caseworker took up her appointment on 1 January 1955. She was fiftyish, extremely alert and brisk. She had no paper qualifications, but plenty of relevant experience, having worked in a County Children's Department, helped in the founding of Spofforth Hall,[1] and run what she called a 'spare-time, private FSU'.[2] At the outset she was given a case load consisting mainly of well-known 'hard-core' cases, and was left free to develop her work as she chose. Monthly case reports were submitted to the Child Care Division in County Hall and a full report was presented to the Committee at the end of the year. It was soon discovered that it was a mistake to take on so many 'hard-core' cases, when other families in difficulties were able to respond more quickly to a comparatively short period of intensive help. It is remarkable that the worker achieved as many 'successes' as she did: the report on her first year's work claimed that out of 24 cases, 5 had been satisfactorily closed, 5 still needed 'close supervision and support', 4 'less frequent supervision', and the remaining 10 were making 'slow progress'. Financially, too, the experiment proved successful; the Area Children's Officer estimated that a net saving of nearly £1,000 had been made in the first year. These results gave general satisfaction, although it was realised that twelve months was too short a period in which to assess the real effectiveness of such work.

During the year an interim report of the Joint Special Sub-Committee had given warm support to this work, and the Public Health Department

---

[1] A residential institution which provided rest and re-education for mothers and children from families with very low standards of house-keeping and mothercraft.

[2] The Family Service Units work with small numbers of families needing the most intensive help. There were three operating in London at that time (later four), one of which worked in Area 5.

was ready to start a similar venture. As a result there were extensive inter-departmental discussions, and the formal decision by Council to maintain and extend the Children's Department experiment had to be delayed until the end of 1956, although the worker in Area 5 was in fact able to continue with her duties during this interval. Two intensive caseworkers were then appointed to Area 8, and a second one to Area 5. The latter joined the Area in July 1957. She had a Social Science Certificate and had worked in the Education Department until 1948, when she transferred to a County Children's Department and there worked closely with its 'Part III accommodation unit' for homeless families. These two workers appeared to form a largely independent unit within the Area office. Potential cases were passed by 'section 4' (the reception officers) to the Area Children's Officer who decided whether or not they might be suitable for intensive help. It was then left to the intensive caseworkers to decide which families to work with. Much of their work was devoted to families who might be enabled to take back children already in the Council's care. They kept their case loads down to twelve families each, and considered anything beyond fifteen would be unwise. The Area Children's Officer called case conferences to discuss these families with outside agencies when necessary. Monthly case reports were still prepared for the Child Care Division, and a more general report was made to the Committee each year, for the work was still regarded as experimental.

General Development of the Department

Area 5's experience was only a small part of the developments that were taking place over the same period in the Department as a whole. Many of these arose from the report made in 1955 by the newly created Organisation and Methods Branch of the Clerk's Department. The Children's Department was chosen for the first O & M investigation conducted outside the Clerk's Department because it was the youngest Department and expanding rapidly. The report distinguished two aspects of the Department's work: administration and casework. The latter was described as a specialised function with a policy derived from professional and administrative considerations. It was the casework aspect of the work that was found to be in need of strengthening. The report also drew attention to the lack of effective links between Areas and County Hall. All the main recommendations were based on these two points.

The Chief Assistant Children's Officer and his two Divisions were replaced by a Senior Child Care Officer (replacing the Senior Inspector) who was to advise on child care and run a Policy and Casework Division with the assistance of an administrative officer. This new Division was the former Child Care Division, shorn of its routine administrative responsibilities which were transferred to the Department's Administrative and Establishment Officer who now supervised three Divisions: Finance, Staff, and General Administration. The Senior Child Care Officer, and the Administrative and Establishment Officer were to be of equal rank, but it was the former who would deputise for the Children's Officer in his absence. The inspectorate was increased, with one Inspector to work in each of the new Districts.

The LCC region, including the out county zones, was divided into three Districts, with new District Offices (situated in County Hall) responsible for each. The O & M report had accepted the existing informal four-fold division into Sectors as the basis for the new system, but the Children's Committee had for some time been considering a decentralised committee structure that would enable Councillors to maintain closer contact with local units of the Department. The three-part division proposed in the Committee's plans was eventually adopted.

With the help of District Administrative Officers the new District Committees took over some of the functions hitherto exercised by the central committee, notably the provision and maintenance of establishments and certain general responsibilities for children in them. The District Committees consisted of members of the Children's Committee and co-opted members. Most members also chaired House Committees attached to the establishments. They carried as much responsibility as could be delegated without threatening the main Committee's overall responsibility for the service.

It was decided that Area Children's Officers should henceforth be classified as social workers and not as assistants in the administrative class. Each Area was to have one Administrative Assistant, who would deputise for the Area Children's Officer in administrative matters only —a point which had not been clarified before. It had been found that in practice one child welfare officer tended to act as deputy in child care matters, and this situation was given official recognition by creating the post of Senior Child Welfare Officer with this responsibility. No ruling was made about the officer who should act for the Area Children's Officer in the latter's absence, though it would not have been surprising if practice tended to follow the precedent set in County Hall where the Senior Child Care Officer was the Children's Officer's deputy.

By the end of 1957 a child welfare officer who first joined Area 5 in 1950 had become the Area Children's Officer. She had taken a Social Science Certificate at the University of London and had some experience in the probation service. Most of the other eighteen social workers on her staff had University qualifications in the social sciences, but only six had any formal professional training for social work. On the Administrative side the Area Children's Officer's deputy was graded as an 'Assistant I (a)'. After resort to arbitration, the salary scale for Senior Child Welfare Officers had recently been raised to £815–£1,140, placing them slightly above the I (a)s' £815–£1,090, and this was assumed by some to establish the Senior CWO's authority to act for the Area Children's Officer in her absence. (In fact the increase was granted in order to relate Senior Child Welfare Officers' salaries to those of other social workers. When the I (a)s sought, unsuccessfully, to regain parity, the Council specifically stated that there was no relation between the scales for administrators and social workers—hence differences in salary were not to be taken as an indication of differences in status.) A clerical officer was attached to each of the four 'sections', and five others dealt with parental contributions, statistics, a case review system and other matters. Thus there were nineteen social workers and ten administrative and clerical officers in the Area, responsible for 992 children. In 1953 there had been ten social workers and six administrative and clerical officers responsible for over 1,100 children.

Conclusions

The two innovations traced in this study were but a part of a more general development of the whole service: a Department originally formed to care for children without adequate homes of their own was beginning to provide more general forms of help (of which child care still formed by far the major part) for families having difficulty in caring for their children. The family, rather than the child, had become the focus of the service, and from a child care service there had emerged the beginnings of a general social work service.

The extent of these changes should not be exaggerated, nor should they be visualised as a continuous and precisely planned development. It was a gradual shift of emphasis that took place. Three changes of emphasis were in fact discernible, bringing about redistributions of influence and status—from County Hall to the Area offices, from the residential establishments to the Area offices, and from administrators to social workers. In 1949 it was inevitable that the new Department should rely mainly on its central office, its residential establishments and its inherited administrative patterns: the Area office's job was simply to deal with the public. But as the Areas gained experience, skill and staff, more and more powers were delegated to them. This decentralisation began at once. By the following year the Areas had already been given responsibility for administering holiday grants, and grants for children with special abilities and disabilities. Soon they were responsible for parental contributions (their collection and assessment, including discretion to waive claims) and for boarding-out allowances paid to foster parents. They made recommendations to the courts on the necessity for 'fit person' orders, and they were empowered to prosecute or take other action necessary in the rare cases of cruelty or neglect. The decentralisation of vacancies formed an important part of this trend. Interwoven with this was the development of casework and the growth of a professional child care 'interest' within the Department.

Before 1948, child care was provided and administered by three different Departments; it was a relatively minor feature of the education, public health and poor law services. The attitudes and expectations that arose from this system were not changed overnight by the creation of the Children's Department. But gradually it was accepted—within the Department at least—that casework in child care was a service in its own right, for which special skills and training were required. An important contribution to this development was made by the group of administrative officers within the Policy and Casework Division—the former Child Care Division. These 'administrators of casework' became a source of information and guidance on the legal and administrative aspects of the Department's work. They interpreted Committee decisions about casework to the Area Offices, they explained to the Committee the implications of central government policies, circulars and reports dealing with child care; they kept in touch with the Children's Department of the Home Office, and briefed the Council's spokesmen in Parliament when child care legislation was to be debated. Meanwhile the District Officers did similar work for their District Committees. These activities were carried on as a side-line by the old Child Care Division, but the reorganisation that followed the O & M report enabled the new Policy and Casework Division to devote itself entirely to such work. This new Division only consisted of four administrative and two clerical officers, but it performed a vital co-ordinating function, interpreting the principles of child care and casework in workable administrative terms. An important part was also played by the so-called Inspectors, who were given rather loosely defined duties and acted as casework consultants: they urged the delegation of powers to Area offices, and stressed the need to make the family the focus of the service—a policy which implied a corresponding stress on Area offices within the structure of the Department.

Within Area 5, too, the balance of power between social workers and administrators was altered. Child welfare officers became more numerous and tended to have rather more formal training: in 1958 thirteen out of nineteen held a University Social Science Certificate or comparable qualification, compared with five out of ten in 1953, but the proportion having further professional training for child care remained more or less the same. A growing discrepancy appeared between the responsibilities they carried and their official status. They took on reception, preventive casework and other duties, yet the status of their chief was still an administrative one, and her sole official deputy was an administrative officer. The O & M report found, however, that in Area offices generally the administrative officers received comparatively little attention and consequently tended to lack enthusiasm. The reorganisation following that report was designed to relieve difficulties arising from these shifts of emphasis and responsibility within County

Hall and the Area offices. By regrading officers and by reorganising the central department the growing importance of the social workers was recognised, the casework side of the work was strengthened, and responsibilities were clarified. The District Committees were formed to enable Children's Committee members to keep in closer touch with the new work going on in the Area offices from which they had felt increasingly remote.

For Area 5 the crucial steps in the story were the withdrawal of clerical officers from reception work, the creation first of the three geographical 'sections' and then of 'section 4', and the agreement to take part in the intensive casework experiment. These developments were long debated, but their character and timing were in large part determined by the exigencies of the staffing position. The final separation of short-term from long-term casework came about almost as a last resort—indeed, the Area Children's Officer felt at the time that her decision was taken in defiance of 'sound casework principles'. The intensive casework experiment formalised and accelerated a trend that had developed during the previous twelve months from a growing awareness of the problems posed by certain families and the difficulty of providing adequate help for these families owing to staff shortages and heavy caseloads. The attempt to develop preventive work had been germinating for several years and naturally suggested further development in the directions leading towards a family casework service.

The main decisions taken at County Hall (about the Home Area scheme, the intensive casework experiment, and the steps arising from the o & m recommendations) emanated from a policy-making unit and were formulated in directives to the whole Department, though the long-term implications of these developments were not made very explicit—often for diplomatic reasons.

These changes were often interpreted differently by the various groups involved. The Home Area Scheme was seen by many of the administrators as a redistribution of responsibility between offices; Committee members tended to regard it as a redistribution of children over the region; and among social workers, the inspectors and the administrators in the Policy and Casework Division it was seen as an avenue to a new and more comprehensive approach to child care. Similarly the intensive casework experiment was for some Committee members an exciting new departure, for the Policy and Casework Division and some of the social workers it represented a step in a long term and much-discussed development of the Department's work, while for some of the administrative officers and for various groups outside the Department it was a doubtfully relevant innovation. Nevertheless, all those favouring these schemes felt not merely that they accorded with their own ideas but that they originated directly from their own efforts.

No attempt has been made here to evaluate the services of the

Department or the success of the developments studied. Indeed, until recently there would scarcely have been sufficient agreement about the functions of the service to form a basis for evaluation. What *is* evidence of success in such a service? Higher numbers of children in care, or lower numbers, or an increase in the proportion boarded out? The speed at which the children are returned to their own homes, or the number of children enabled to remain in their own homes? If children are kept out of care is this being achieved by a 'goal-keeping' technique or by skilled casework? How should the costs of the service be measured; and how important is it that the service be understood and accepted by public opinion—even if important developments may be delayed as a result? The Committee and its staff attempted to reconcile these considerations and create a policy from them. The Department was aware that more information was needed before much progress could be achieved, and attempts were made to collect and analyse relevant statistics, particularly at Area level. Research had begun, for example, on new applications to Area offices in an effort to determine what criteria should be used in evaluating the Department's policy and allocating its resources.

Some of the pressures making for change emerge fairly clearly from this account. The limited resources of the Department were at once restrictive and stimulating. The very size and complexity of a London-scale service meant that extensive delegation of powers was necessary, and indeed such a tradition had already been established by the Public Health, Education and other Departments. The Committee and the central office were willing, once the teething stages were over, to allow Area Children's Officers to develop what amounted almost to their own departments. Individual attitudes and experience and the outlook fostered among the staff of each office thus became very important and produced marked differences between Areas. When the first Children's Officer of Area 5 moved to another Area office she commented that it was hard to believe she was in the same service, administering the same Acts of Parliament.

The early growth of boarding out came to a halt because of the scarcity of appropriate foster homes. With larger numbers in residential homes and schools the cost of the service increased, and the building programme of the LCC could not provide sufficient new, small homes for children requiring institutional care. The Department was thus forced to pay more attention to the prevention of family breakdown, and the rehabilitation of families whose children might return home from the Council's care. Meanwhile, Area offices had to search for any redistribution of duties that would ameliorate the effects of staff shortage by making better use of the available social workers and improving liaison with outside agencies such as the courts and hospitals.

Underlying these changes was the development of new ideas about children and social work, expressed by an increasingly numerous and confident group of social workers within the Department, and supported by a more widely disseminated climate of opinion. 'We were aware of Bowlby, "A Two-Year-Old Goes to Hospital", the Oxfordshire experiment, and the general swing to family casework,' said the Area Children's Officer. Meanwhile, many of the staff attended conferences and refresher courses which helped to crystallise and circulate ideas first formulated a little hazily on the job, and students from new professional training courses in the University came to the Area for field training, and some of their supervisors attended seminars at the University.

Subsequent developments in the Department, many of them beginning in this Area office, show that the events traced in this study were the forerunners of much further change involving a reappraisal of rules and procedures, large increases in staff, and the introduction of further intensive caseworkers and a new grade of supervisors within the Area offices. New factors played a part in these developments, including a study of the Department made by the Home Office inspectorate, changes in senior staff, and a renewed increase in the numbers of children coming into the Department's care, due partly to growing stresses in the London housing situation. But most of these later trends flow directly from the developments to be seen in this study.

DISCUSSION

The services taken over and incorporated in the new Children's Department were more extensive and had a longer history than those that formed the basis of the Home Help scheme considered in the previous study. But the terms of reference the Council approved for the Department and the terms of the Children Act that established it were again of the most general kind, leaving plenty of scope for interpretation—particularly in the work of the Area offices which formed the subject of this study. The 1948 Act and the Government Reports from which it sprang offered scant guidance for the development of this work; they only provided a basis for experiment—and until the new legislation of 1963 many regarded this as a very slender basis for the edifice erected upon it.

The Children's Departments were new and small. The services they provided were of the most vital kind, but in the Area studied the number of families served was less than a third of the number served by the home helps who themselves provided only a small fraction of the Health Department's services. In the years immediately following the war the London County Council gave first priority to housing and education and the new Department—viewed with some suspicion by neighbouring empires out of which it had been carved—could not expect a generous share of the County's resources. The resources it secured depended on the backing of Council members on the Children's Committee and on the support of other sections of County Hall, the Clerk's Department, the Health Department and the O & M Branch, for example. The latter gave decisive support for increases in Area office staff in its 1955 report, and the consent of the Director of Establishments and of members and officers representing the Health, Housing, Education and Welfare Departments was eventually secured for the appointment of intensive caseworkers.

The Home Office appears to have exerted little influence on these developments—partly because it was more wary of intervening in the affairs of the LCC than in those of smaller authorities, but largely because the Act provided a flimsy legal basis for preventive social work. Such work could be justified by arguing that reception into care under Section I of the Act called for considerable investigation of the family situation before decisions could be taken; and later the Children and Young Persons (Amendment) Act of 1953 provided further scope for it. But until the new legislation of 1963 the Home Office was frequently aware that a benevolent silence was its most helpful contribution to the efforts of Children's Departments to make good the omissions in the original Act.

Increases in staff—particularly social work staff—were crucial at every stage in the development of the Area office; many of the most important changes in procedure and in the work these procedures permitted sprang directly from the gain or loss of one or two workers. Some of the additional resources secured by the office were provided for the fulfilment of existing legal commitments for the supervision of foster children. Others were secured by entering into new commitments; the appointment of intensive caseworkers, for example, was justified on the grounds that they would cover their costs by reducing the numbers of children in care, and procedures were devised to ascertain whether this claim had been justified. But on the whole, the Area office's objectives retained their general character, providing ample scope for subsequent interpretation in the light of experience. Within the Department, the realisation of 'long term child care principles and aims' was one of several phrases used to indicate general objectives without clarifying these too precisely. Though the lack of precision about objectives was partly an unavoidable aspect of the kind of work the Department was doing and the uncertain legal basis for doing it, this was also a necessary tactical device for sustaining continued expansion of the service without provoking dissension inside and outside the Department. Some vagueness about objectives is often an essential means of maintaining consent and collaboration among a large and varied team of people.

Objectives were gradually, though never completely, clarified in the practical day-by-day work of the Area office. The participants approached common problems from different points of view and defined them in different ways, according to their past experience and training, and their current status and duties within the organisation. Thus different people ascribed differing meanings and significance to the developments brought about. This, too, is a recurring feature of administrative studies, but there may be special reasons for it in units employing new and developing professions.

The gradual growth of a distinctive professional group in the Area office, supported by some members of the central office, made an important contribution to the developments studied—as it did in the previous case. Initially these staff had little training, and although later arrivals had rather more preparation many were young women and there was a considerable turnover among them—as in nearly all Children's Departments. In this situation people may have a special need to isolate and identify the tasks, skills, attitudes and principles which distinguish them and their work from other people and other work to be seen all round them. It would not be surprising if a professional group tended during this stage of its development to overemphasise its distinctive characteristics and to neglect general administrative work that does not have a distinctly professional content. If so, this stage should be succeeded by a phase of reintegration during which the profession achieves closer collaboration—a rapprochement—with others engaged in providing the service.

The principal developments studied were accepted or welcomed by people who differed considerably in outlook and aims. Many of these people—Council members, senior administrators and social workers—not only participated in these developments but subsequently claimed in discussion with the authors that they themselves had played a major part in conceiving and initiating the schemes studied. This, too, was a feature of other studies in this series. It suggests that different objectives derived from different frames of reference—even extreme diversity, amounting to mutual incomprehension—need cause no serious conflict or administrative breakdown, provided the objectives of all concerned can be reconciled, and provided many are left with the conviction that the achievements of the service are in some sense their own.

Nevertheless, the development of an organisation usually imposes stresses of some kind since its benefits are seldom evenly distributed. The Area office doubled its staff and reduced its caseload in five years. At the end of that time it was not simply doing the same job more efficiently or with less effort; it had assumed duties previously performed in County Hall, embarked on entirely new tasks, and modified and extended its work—or at least its objectives. In the course of these developments the social workers who did the bulk of the new work had gained greater influence in the affairs of the office, just as those concerned with casework had gained greater influence in County Hall. Meanwhile administrative and clerical staff, despite increases in salary, were feeling neglected and 'lacked enthusiasm', the Children's Committee became increasingly isolated from the work of the Area offices, and communications between Area offices and County Hall were weakened. The O & M report proposed means for easing these stresses, but there could be no return to the roles or the balance of power of previous years. It will be shown again in later studies that additional resources cannot for long be treated simply as an improvement in the means available for performing unchanged tasks. They often lead to changes in the tasks themselves—changes in the character and scope of the work done—and these in turn bring about changes in relationships, communications and status amongst the people concerned—changes, that is to say, in the structure of administrative organisation.

The smooth progress of such developments depends heavily on those responsible for communication with, and supervision of, the groups with divergent and potentially conflicting interests and attitudes. It is they who have to reconcile these differences or suffer the consequences. In the first case examined, a Deputy Town Clerk bore these responsibilities. In this case the small Casework and Policy Division and their predecessors in the Child Care Division clearly did the same. They, and others at similar levels, exercised great influence in advising senior officers and members, consulting officials in neighbouring Departments, preparing memoranda for submission to those with the formal authority to make decisions and subsequently preparing explanations interpreting the meaning of these decisions, besides generally directing and filtering the flow of communications.

One further point deserves comment at this stage. Distinctions between the work of 'policy-making', assumed to take place amongst senior officials, and the 'implementation' of policies that is assumed to take place at humbler levels, tend to be misleading—and particularly so in an organisation conferring considerable discretionary powers on the staff actually providing the service for which it is designed. What could appear more trivial than the selection of the people to sit at the the reception desk in the Area office, the arrangement of their rotas of work, and the invention of procedures to determine when a short term case should be reclassified as a long term case? Yet it was decisions on such issues that brought about some of the main developments in the work of the Area offices and called for a reappraisal of the objectives of this work. An approximate distinction can be made between 'more important' and 'less important' decisions: it rests on the implications of the decision—particularly on its long-term and irrevocable implications. But it may be difficult to predict precisely where the important decisions will be made, and the policy and character of a service is not determined by such decisions alone.

The features of this case we have chosen to comment on may be briefly summarised. Many will already be familiar from previous cases. The purpose of the Area office was initially ill-defined. The struggle for the resources such offices required in order to develop their work could only succeed with the support or consent of senior officials in other services and, ultimately, of Council members. To convince 'outsiders' of the justice of their cause, staff in the Children's Department had to commit themselves to certain objectives approved by members and officers responsible for neighbouring services. Nevertheless the objectives of the Area office remained unexplicit and capable of being interpreted in different ways.

This 'unexplicitness', or vagueness, was a necessary feature, enabling the Department to maintain unity within its own ranks, to avoid conflict with other bodies and to preserve opportunities for (and a choice of) future developments. Differing objectives and interpretations persisted within the Department, but could generally be reconciled without the necessity for disruptive choices. The formulation of the Area office's aims and methods was worked out gradually and empirically in day-by-day discussion and modification of working procedures. The growth of professional loyalties and working principles among the increasingly numerous and influential group of social workers played an important part in this process. This group derived some of its ideas and aspirations from association with wider professional and academic circles. The development of the Area office's work and the acquisition of the resources required for it also depended heavily on administrators—mainly without specialist training—at the 'upper middle' levels of the hierarchy. These officials needed a thorough understanding of the interests and aspirations of elected members, of staff in neighbouring Departments and of their own professional staff, and the ability to reconcile these aspirations and render them administratively and politically viable. Thus the growth of resources led to gradual but important changes in the objectives and character of the service, bringing about simultaneous changes in the structure of the organisation. In the Area office and in County Hall the policies of the service took shape in the course of changes in the deployment and management of these resources. Thus the structure and functions of the service—its management and policy—could not be understood in isolation from each other, but were closely related aspects of the same general process of development.

POSTSCRIPT

As we explained at the end of the previous chapter, the home help and children's services were combined in one department in 1971. We therefore deal with both in the same postscript. For these services the past decade has been a period of constant change.[1] The Children and Young Persons Act of 1963 gave the Children's Departments a general duty to do preventive work among children who might otherwise come into their care or appear before the juvenile courts. That gave them powers to extend preventive work and family advice services on which the LCC and other authorities had already made a tentative start. The LCC itself was abolished in 1965 when the new Greater London Boroughs took over the home help and children's services. The jurisdiction and powers of the courts over children were changed by another Children and Young Persons Act of 1969 which laid heavier responsibilities on the Children's Departments for children previously dealt with by the courts and the Probation Service. The Children's Departments were abolished in 1971 when their work was brought into the new Social Services Departments together with the Welfare Departments' Services and home help, mental health and other services from the Health Departments. New responsibilities are still being laid on these Departments.

Meanwhile the environment in which these services work has been changing too. The population of inner London has continued to fall, but many of the poorest and most vulnerable people have been left behind. New and more aggressive forms of community-based political action have made an impact on the social services, and social work training and practice have been modified by growing concern about problems of poverty, homeless families, civil rights and other questions which were considered less often—or less explicitly—during the period we studied. This postscript makes no attempt to trace all these developments: it provides no more than a brief outline of some of those that bear most directly on our original studies and the conclusions we drew from them.

Some features of the old system were carried forward into the new. The London Borough of Tower Hamlets covered almost the same area that had been served by Area 5 of the LCC Children's and Health Departments—the old Boroughs of Stepney, Bethnal Green and Poplar, together constituting London's traditional East End, but not the City of London. The Children's Department's Area Officer was appointed Children's Officer for the new Borough and most of her staff were transferred at the same time. The senior staff responsible for the home help service also continued to serve the new Health Department under a Medical Officer of Health who had been MOH for the old Borough of Stepney.

We briefly described the new Borough and its Council in our postscript to Chapter 3. The Labour Party dominated it to an even greater extent

[1] For accounts of their development within the reorganised government of London, see chapters by Betty Tate ('Personal Health and Welfare Services') and Roy Parker ('Children's Services') in Gerald Rhodes (ed.) *The New Government of London: The First Five Years*. Weidenfeld & Nicolson, 1972.

DEVELOPMENT OF CASEWORK IN CHILDREN'S DEPARTMENT 127

than the old LCC, capturing all but two Council seats. Those were held for a while by the Communists, but they too fell to Labour in 1971. Battles were fought privately within the Council between spokesmen of the old Boroughs, reluctant to abandon their loyalties, and between different denominational groups—Catholic and Jewish, with deeply felt but differing attitudes to the family. Initially several academic and professional experts were co-opted from outside the Borough to help the Children's Committee; one had been the LCC's last Children's Officer, and another became a member of the Seebohm Committee whose influential Report on Local Authority and Allied Personal Social Services[1] led later to the creation of the Social Services Departments under the Local Authority Social Services Act of 1970.

The Area 5 team had been widely regarded as one of the most innovative and enterprising in the LCC Children's Department. Successive national developments, starting with the 1963 Children and Young Persons' Act, enabled them to press on in the directions traced in our original study. The service was encouraged to undertake preventive work which led to the creation in Tower Hamlets of new forms of family advice service and later to the devolution of increasing responsibilities to area teams in the new Social Services Department.

The new Social Service Department, set up in 1971, had a much bigger job to do. In a report to his Committee, prepared in October 1970 in advance of the Department's formal inauguration, the Director-Designate of Social Services estimated his seven Area Groups would be dealing with about 17,000 cases. That was the combined total of clients of the services he was taking over, which included an unknown but probably small number of overlapping cases on the books of two or more services. It was a larger caseload than the total handled by the whole LCC Children's Department. Elderly people, previously helped by the Welfare Department, accounted for 44 per cent of these cases—much the largest group. Other welfare and social work for the deaf, the physically handicapped, the blind and partially sighted—many of them elderly people too—accounted for 12 per cent. The home help service—also mainly for old people, as we have seen—accounted for 15 per cent and the mental health services for 4 per cent. The minority remaining were often the most demanding and time-consuming cases: this was the work inherited from the Children's Department which we studied—social work with deprived children (23 per cent of the caseload) and families that were homeless or in arrears with their rent (2 per cent). The Department is still accumulating more responsibilities: it is taking on work previously done by approved schools, it is expected to do more for the disabled, and in April 1974 it took on the medical social workers previously employed by the Health Department.

During its first years, staff of the new Department felt overwhelmed

[1] Cmnd 3703, 1968.

by the needs of the elderly and physically handicapped. But although the numbers of children living in the Borough fell steadily, and the numbers in the Borough's care fell from 1,379 in 1965 to 1,130 in 1972, there was no decline in the work to be done for deprived children. In London generally, among staff of the old Welfare Department 'the majority were, though experienced, untrained'.[1] 'In child care however the position in London [was] comparatively favourable . . .'[2] In Area 5, the numbers, training and morale of child care officers were higher than elsewhere. Thus staff from the old Children's Department tended to exert most influence in the new service and to secure many of its senior posts.

Demands on the Department have always exceeded the resources available to meet them. The acceptance of new cases is the responsibility of the seven Area Offices, each of which differs somewhat, in organisation and character. Within these Offices, intake teams—not unlike the group described in our original study—usually decide which cases to take on. The decision to give longer-term care, provided by other staff, is taken after consultation between intake workers and senior social workers. Social workers have in general gained more responsibility for discussing and deciding these questions than they used to have.

But much of the Department's work is still done from its headquarters—more than in many other Social Services Departments which have gone further in delegating work to Area Teams—and the Committee plays an unusually active part in decisions about individual cases. The Children's Department had feared that the pressures of current work might lead to the neglect of long-stay children in their care, so responsibility for them was transferred to a new section in the headquarters office.[3] The new Social Services Department retained this arrangement. Headquarters staff also look after homeless families, and do much of the work of finding and selecting foster parents and adopters as a service for the Area Teams. Home teachers of the blind, originally placed in the Areas, are also coming into headquarters. But pressure on the Area Teams remains severe. The Department recognises that in addition to the people on its 'caseload' there are others whom they should serve but for whom they can do little or nothing owing to more urgent demands. These numbers, colloquially known as the 'guilt load', are divided as fairly as possible on a geographical basis between the Area Teams. Pressures on the Department must be increased by the relatively small amount of temporary accommodation for families in Tower Hamlets (less than one-quarter of the amounts provided in

---

[1] Betty Tate, op. cit., p. 91.
[2] Roy Parker, op. cit., p. 138.
[3] Elizabeth Ney and David F. Tomlinson, 'Children in Long-Term Care: A New Approach', *Social Work Today*, Vol. 3, No. 2, April 1972.

Lambeth or Islington, for example)[1] and the relatively hard line taken with such families by the Borough's Housing Department.[2]

The home help service has continued with remarkably little change through these years. Its staff of home helps, measured in full-time equivalents, was almost exactly the same in June 1973, at 193, as it was in 1958 (when it was 191). The distribution of the service appears to have changed very little too. At the time of our original study the aged and chronic sick accounted steadily for between 86 and 87 per cent of those helped each year. In 1973 people aged sixty-five or more—a slightly different category—constituted 86 per cent of those helped. The Council and the staff of the Service are familiar with the needs of frail, elderly people, and happy to help them. Other people, as we saw in our original study, are harder to serve. The distribution of this service, continuing the trends observed in our original study, is typical of the country as a whole as the following table, prepared by the Department of Health and Social Security, makes clear.

Home Help Service (England)

PERCENTAGE OF CASES IN WHICH SERVICE WAS GIVEN

Type of case	1969	1970	1972
Maternity	3·7	3·1	2·3
Elderly (65 or over)	83·0	84·2	85·3
Chronic sick and tuberculosis	7·0	6·9	6·8
Mentally disordered	0·4	0·4	0·5
Other	5·9	5·4	5·1
TOTAL	100	100	100
Number	427,849	443,208	473,883

Source: Department of Health and Social Security, *Review of the Home Help Service in England*, September 1973 (duplicated).

In England as a whole, during these years, the elderly gained an even more dominant position among the users of the service, at the expense of mothers with young children. 'Predominantly help is still provided for the elderly and for the acute and chronically sick, especially on discharge from hospital', commented the Department. 'All areas', said the Report, 'confirm the continuing decline in maternity work. This is attributed to the cost of the service to users (usually a full assessment), increased reliance on hospital confinements, better equipped homes and more accessible launderettes. Also husbands are more prepared to take time off to give help in the home . . .'[3]

In Tower Hamlets the home help service is directed from the Depart-

---

[1] Betty Tate, op. cit., p. 97.
[2] See pp. 61–2 above.
[3] Department of Health and Social Security, *Review of the Home Help Service in England*, p. 12.

ment's headquarters by the Senior Home Help Organiser who is responsible to a Principal Officer within the Field Work Services Group. Three Area Teams have their own Organisers who are responsible both to the Area Officers and to headquarters, and the Department hopes to adopt this arrangement in other Areas when they have enough staff to do so. This arrangement falls between two common patterns of organisation identified in the review already quoted: 'the centrally organised service', and 'the service which is more or less fully integrated with the Area Teams'.[1]

Thus far, the central government has not played a major part in these developments. That is partly because the amalgamation of the personal social services was paralleled by a concentration of responsibility for the relevant services in a new central Department of Health and Social Security which has had its hands full in coping with these central and local reorganisations. Moreover the Department's traditions, inherited from the Ministry of Health, were not particularly intrusive at the local level and the Conservative Secretary of State who took over in 1970 was known to be opposed, like most of his colleagues, to interference in local affairs. Staff in Tower Hamlets commented that when the Department has had time to consider the ten-year development plans now being submitted by the local authorities, it may adopt a more innovative role. They believe that the scale of the new service, symbolised by the high salaries paid to local Directors, means that central government treats Social Services Departments with greater deference than it extended to the old Children's Department. Officials of the Social Work Service in the Department of Health and Social Security said, 'We are now trying to monitor and carry out some control of quality across a much broader field. Inevitably this means different techniques and sampling rather than overall coverage.'[2]

The Borough's Children's Committee and its successor, the Social Services Committee, differed considerably from their predecessors in the LCC, and have probably wielded a stronger influence on their service. Since the beginning of the century when George Lansbury and the Poplar Guardians of the Poor set a pattern of revolt against the Local Government Board—a pattern which became known by the 1920s as 'poplarism'—the elected spokesmen of the East End have been suspicious of central government, the professions and outsiders who intervene in their affairs. (Our original study of slum clearance in Bethnal Green conveyed a glimpse of this spirit.[3])

Before long, the new Council shed the co-opted members of its Children's Committee and its graduate Chairman departed. He became

[1] Ibid., p. 6.
[2] Letter to the author from the Deputy Director, Social Work Services, 6 February 1974.
[3] See pp. 47 and 62–3.

a Member of Parliament for an Essex constituency. Social workers found the Council was often generous to old people, the sick and the physically handicapped when providing services for them or making grants to local voluntary bodies working for them. Its 'meals on wheels' service provided more meals, in relation to the Borough's population of elderly people, than any other Borough in London.[1] But it was less generous to 'multi-problem' families and those whom councillors regarded as 'feckless'. They had always been suspicious of philanthropic agencies led by outsiders, and were often hostile to the new politics of community action and to militant spokesmen of the poor and the outcast. Some of the Department's staff were aware that the growth of their service gave it an increasingly dominant position and they, therefore, sought to work constructively with groups acting as advocates for clients or providing alternative forms of care for them; but the Council's policies sometimes made that difficult.

In our original study we noted that social workers in Area Offices were gaining more power—partly from the central administration and its political leaders. In Tower Hamlets that was bound to cause trouble sooner or later, and it was not long before there was a confrontation between the Council and its staff which was reported on television and in the national press. The Children's Officer was directed by her chairman to remove a child from her mother because of the Committee's disapproval of the mother's moral standards. The child had been placed in the Council's care by the court under a 'fit person' order, so the Chairman was acting *'in loco parentis'*. Later the Council summoned its professional staff to make clear to them its determination to control the work of their Children's Department. Soon after, the first Children's Officer left to take an advanced course at the London School of Economics and Political Science,[2] and many professional staff resigned during the next two years. Her deputy took over as Children's Officer. Later the man who had previously been Assistant Borough Treasurer was appointed to the new post of Co-ordinator of Social Services, created to prepare the way for the new Social Services Department. The first Director of that Department was a man recruited from another authority's Welfare Department.

Conclusion

We shall attempt only to draw a few conclusions which bear on points considered in the original study. In this Borough and across the country as a whole, the main trends we noted in the LCC Children's Department[3] continued—although Tower Hamlets retains more centralised Social Services and home help services than many other authorities. History

[1] Betty Tate, op. cit., p. 107.
[2] This was the course mentioned on pp. 281–2 below.
[3] See p. 117.

has generally been on the side of those who pioneered these developments.

The LCC Children's Department, like many others, had been placed in an unavoidably competitive relationship to the Public Health Department and other services represented on the Council's Joint Special Sub-Committee[1] which did intensive casework or provided competing forms of care for children and their families—all potential substitutes for the Children's Department's services. The amalgamation of many of these services within the new Social Services Department, where they were subject to one Director and his Committee, did not necessarily resolve these conflicts, but provided more effective means for making and enforcing choices between competing needs and competing services.

As the Seebohm Committee foresaw, amalgamation has created a service which works on a scale that enables it more effectively to withstand outside pressures and to secure resources for growth. But public demands on the service have grown even faster, leaving professional staff in the Area Teams with the main responsibility for determining priorities between different needs and deciding which clients cannot be served. The growing scale and complexity of this work has thrown greater burdens on supervisory staff—the middle (and 'upper middle') management of the Department.

The central government has remained an important but generally latent influence on the Department's development. That influence has been strongest where capital expenditure is involved because the Department of Health and Social Security determines how many, and which, residential homes are to be built. But it exerts less influence on professional services and current expenditure.

Although it has not initiated new developments, the Council plays an active part in shaping the evolution of the service. The 1963 Act gave the Children's Departments and their successors considerable powers for providing material help for families in need, and the Committee has made more generous use of these powers than most have done. But staff, some of whom are paid £5,000 a year or more, are not permitted to spend more than £25 on any person or family without their Committee's approval. Although this approval, given through the Casework Sub-Committee, is rarely withheld, staff are well aware of Council policies and attitudes governing the allocation of this money. These attitudes are not, in any simple sense, due to Party politics. (The leading figures in the LCC and its Children's Committee were also Labour Party members.) The Council is expressing deeply felt, and sometimes conflicting, views about behaviour and social obligations within the family and the community—views which would probably be widely endorsed among their electorate.

[1] See p. 113 et seq.

CHAPTER 7

HIGH FLATS IN FINSBURY[1]

The next study is the only one in this series which deals with a construction project—the building of some Council flats in central London. Many organisations, public and private, have to collaborate in the process, and some of them have little or no interest in the project for its own sake. Their participation has to be organised through prolonged discussion and bargaining, and occasional resort to arbitration and coercion. Formal decisions required at various stages in the development have to wait on the outcome of these informal negotiations. The architect acting as the Council's principal professional adviser bears most of the responsibility for the management of the whole process and he needs a sensitive grasp of the timing and phasing of the decisions required. But decisions that call primarily for an assessment of risks remain the responsibility of the Council.

A feature of the first study in this series which particularly interested us was the major part played by firms of private architects in the management of a public housing programme. We therefore resolved to take a firm of architects engaged on public housing programmes as the starting point for one of these studies. The firm of Emberton, Franck and Tardrew provided this opportunity and they suggested we examine one of the most important of their recently completed projects—the building of 240 flats for the Metropolitan Borough of Finsbury. The Borough agreed to participate in the study which was eventually carried out in 1963, two years after the completion of the flats. In the early stages of the project the firm consisted of three senior architects and four assistants, specialising in large-scale developments with high flats, mainly built for local authorities. They normally had about four projects in hand—typically one under negotiation, one going to tender, one under construction and one on the point of completion—amounting to a little over a million pounds' worth of building each year. Over the preceding decade much of this work had been done for the Borough of Finsbury.

[1] The study presented in this chapter was carried out by Michael Meacher and Angela Sears, and the account presented here is a shortened version of a report they prepared.

The data for the study were provided by the Architect in charge of the project, officials and members of the Borough Council, officials of the London County Council and the Ministry of Housing and Local Government, the Secretary of the Guinness Trust and the caretaker of a Trust estate adjoining the site. Further evidence was gathered from the reports, correspondence and working papers prepared in the course of the project, and from a number of published articles dealing with it.[1] We also had the benefit of a thoughtful analysis of our report prepared by staff at the Building Research Station who are making studies of the administration of urban planning.

The study traces the principal stages of the development in chronological order. The first of these led to the acquisition of the site under compulsory powers; this could well have formed an independent study in its own right, but the brief account presented here is only designed to explain some of the problems arising later when rebuilding began. Next we deal with the preparation of detailed site plans, negotiations for securing the approval of the London County Council for the height and layout of buildings, and negotiations with the Ministry leading to the provision of subsidies and permission for the Borough to raise the necessary loans. The progress of building operations and the resolution of problems arising in the course of building are then described, and the study concludes with a brief account of the completed scheme. Its purpose is to trace the principal decisions that had to be made in the course of building these flats, and to analyse the criteria and the evidence brought to bear on these decisions.

Finsbury lies near the centre of London, immediately north of the City. It was the smallest of the Metropolitan Boroughs, except for the adjoining Holborn, and the population of its 587 acres had fallen from an estimated 57,000 in 1939 to 33,000 in 1961. But its daytime population was estimated at 150,000, for this is one of the most highly industrialised areas of London. Its eighteenth-century dependence on the manufacture of clocks and watches had almost been abandoned, but Finsbury can still claim pre-eminence in clock repairing and in the supply of parts and tools for the trade. Manufacturing and repairing opticians and jewellers are also common, and the Borough's numerous other trades include light engineering, machine and other tool dealers, silver, electro and chromium dealers, and the production and distribution of surgical and scientific instruments, ladies' and children's garments, radio accessories, tobacco pipes, printing, process engraving, bookbinding and stationery. During the war Finsbury lost many offices, warehouses and factories, most of which have now been replaced by new buildings. The area's commercial and industrial future

[1] Articles by Dr C. Franck in the *Architect and Building News* (31 December 1958, and 17 August 1960), *Official Architecture and Planning* (April 1959), and *Interbuild* (January 1963).

is assured since it lies near London's northern railway termini, adjacent to the City, and not far from the docks. Wartime losses of housing were also extensive, but the Council had carried out an extensive rebuilding programme, helped by the LCC. In the first fifteen years after the war, nearly 3,000 flats had been built in the Borough, in twenty-four different projects of varying sizes. The Borough itself owned about 2,600 dwellings, consisting of 600 built before the war, 180 acquired from the City Corporation at a very high density of 500 persons to the acre, 440 in miscellaneous property due for demolition and 1,400 post-war flats. At the beginning of 1963 plans had been prepared for the building of another thousand dwellings.

Administrative Procedures

When a development scheme is taken in hand there is no single national set of rules to be followed by the authorities involved. The procedure varies according to the type of development and the location and powers of the housing authority. As in many fields, the regulations applying to London differed slightly from those for the rest of the country. At the time in question the administrative procedures for a scheme of slum clearance and redevelopment fell into five distinct but over-lapping stages.

(a) First of all, the local authority applied to the London County Council for *planning permission*. The density and type of development proposed in this request would accord with the general intentions of the current London Development Plan. This plan, revised by the County Council every five years after consultation with the Boroughs, included the areas to be designated for clearance and redevelopment. Although it delegated certain powers to the Boroughs, the County, as planning authority, was responsible for final decisions on the development plan which had then to be approved by the Minister of Housing and Local Government who might consider any objections made by the Boroughs.

(b) Once outline planning permission had been granted by the LCC, proceedings for *compulsory purchase orders* were set in motion, and at the same time the architect's first detailed site layout schemes were drawn up. A compulsory purchase order must be submitted to the Ministry with details of the properties involved and their status—'fit' or 'unfit'—as decided by the Borough's Medical Officer of Health. Once the order had been submitted to the Ministry, the Borough was required to give public notice in the local press and to every owner, mortgagee or tenant involved. Objections against the order might then be lodged with the Ministry. The Ministry is bound to hold an inquiry if there appears to be substance in any of these complaints. The most frequent objection is that properties have been wrongly classified as 'unfit' and in such cases a final assessment is made by government inspectors. Site plans were usually provided by the Borough at such enquiries to refute suggestions that no development would take place if compulsory purchase were permitted. These negotiations normally took at least six months.

(c) Meanwhile, the *detailed site plan* would be in preparation. Certain features of the plan are pre-determined by the shape of the site, its surrounding landscape, and the proximity, character and height of adjacent buildings. The final scheme was the outcome of influences exerted by the Borough Housing Committee, the LCC Planning Department and the Ministry. Conflict might arise if these authorities employed divergent criteria in judging the architect's plans. The original brief from the Borough Council normally included the types of dwellings required and the costs likely to be allowed by the Ministry. The latter would be based on the Council's experience and the advice of the Borough Surveyor, the Engineer or the Architect. The Architect then outlined successive schemes for the site as a whole. The Housing Committee might ask for changes in the size of flats, the numbers of rooms or other features of the plan, relying mainly on its Housing Manager for such suggestions. Before the Borough could apply to the Ministry for loan sanction, approval of the detailed plans had to be granted by the LCC which would be mainly concerned with density, appearance and layout. Even then, the Ministry would only permit the Borough to raise the necessary loans if the final detailed plans conformed with certain standards and expenditure limits evolved by their own planning staff. Constant informal consultation was therefore necessary between the Architect and the three public authorities at each stage in the development of his plans, so that a compromise might be reached which would satisfy all concerned.

(d) When the final scheme had been drawn up, further permission was required for *buildings over 100 feet in height*. Consent was given provisionally in accordance with the London Building Act of 1930, and then public notification was posted at specified points on the site boundary and in other places. Notice was usually sent to all neighbouring owners and tenants within a radius specified by the LCC. Objections had to be made within twenty-one days of the issuing of provisional consent and they were considered by a Tribunal of Appeal where, if they were upheld, provisional permission for buildings over 100 feet would be withdrawn and the plans would have to be reconsidered. Normally, however, the LCC would reject most complaints as untenable, and the more substantial objections would be referred to the Borough Council in the hope that some compromise might be achieved to appease objectors.

(e) When these steps had been completed *invitations to tender* were issued. Once a tender had been accepted, application could be made to the Ministry for *subsidy and loan sanction*. This request was accompanied by the Borough's formal resolution specifying the tender to be accepted, enclosing a copy of the planning permission, the District Valuer's report, and certificates relating to land ownership. If reductions in tender price were required by the Ministry, satisfactory modifications were usually arranged without much delay and loan sanction was given for the whole capital expenditure, including fees for the Architect, quantity surveyor and consulting engineer, and the cost of site clearance which might already have begun. The loan was normally repaid over a period of sixty years. An Exchequer subsidy was provided according to graduated scales designed to meet the additional costs of high buildings and expensive sites. But the Ministry's anxiety to restrict expenditure to a minimum led to administrative pressures intended to counteract the encouragement for high buildings exerted by the subsidy system.

Certain features of these procedures should be noted before we examine their application in this case. Each stage of the development hinges on the attainment of some specific agreement between the Borough and other bodies. Many of these agreements take a very simple form, and their original intentions were often equally uncomplicated. But they have become the fulcrum on which the authorities concerned can exercise a much more extensive leverage, influencing the Borough's policies in their own interests and in the light of wider considerations of regional and national policy. Thus the central government, which is responsible in the last resort for the solvency of local authorities, must ensure that these authorities do not borrow more than they can repay. But the procedure for granting loan sanctions, originally introduced 130 years ago for this purpose, is now employed as a means of restricting the inflation of building prices, standardising the character of local housing policies, controlling the overall rate of public investment, and for other general purposes. Meanwhile each of its building projects is an integral part of the local authority's whole housing programme. Each may be held up by factors outside the local authority's control— by technical snags, labour shortages or bad weather for example. Any delay will upset the timetable for other projects which cannot proceed until housing is available for those whose homes are to be demolished in subsequent schemes. An authority the size of Finsbury has no buffer stock of vacant accommodation to absorb the effect of such delays, and it must often accept compromises over particular projects in order to keep its whole programme moving in an orderly fashion. Thus the right to object to some aspect of one project confers on the individuals and authorities prepared to use it a formidable bargaining power. The objector's principal concern may not be the detail objected to but the advantages to be secured from compromises on other points which the authority can be induced to accept as a price for the withdrawal of the objection and the avoidance of the delays it might cause.

The Galway Street Project
The housing project to be studied was built on the Pleydell Estate covering three and two-thirds acres on both sides of Galway Street. The area is densely packed with commercial, industrial and tenement buildings—mainly old and without aesthetic or architectural distinction. The scheme arose from the bombing of the French Hospital which occupied part of this site. Other areas to the south and west of the site were considered for slum clearance in 1949, but agreement was not reached with the County Medical Officer of Health, although they were included in plans for development made at that time. Galway Street was included later, however, and by 1955 planning permission for redevelopment on this site had been secured from the County Council.

In June 1955 the compulsory purchase order was submitted to the Ministry. It included 157 'pink' (unfit) houses with 685 occupants, two 'grey' (fit) houses with ten occupants and five other buildings, including a public house. After thirteen objections had been received, a public local inquiry was held in October, at which the Borough Council pleaded that the houses were unfit and that demolition was the best means of dealing with conditions in the area. Objections were lodged mainly against the Council's assessment of 'fitness', and on the grounds that certain properties were not houses but business premises. 'Unfit' property is purchased at the value of the cleared site, whilst 'fit' property is bought at its full market value for such purposes. Disagreement was rendered more acute because the terms for compulsory purchase at that time (since amended) were regarded by many as providing inadequate compensation for property owners. Hardship was argued by persons who had bought their properties within the preceding three or four years and still had mortgages outstanding. Thus a Trust complained that they had bought property consisting of 106 premises in 1951 with an unexpired lease of 765 years, after enquiries which revealed that the Council had no intention to acquire at that time. The Trust expected to lose about £10,000 in capital value, and had still to repay an outstanding mortgage of £28,000. The Ministry's inspector, however, recommended that the compulsory purchase order be confirmed with modifications to exclude a Methodist Mission Hall which was being acquired more economically by private agreement, and he asked for only one 'well-maintained payment' for a house classed as unfit. Most of the properties belonged to the Corporation of the City of London who made no objection. The order was accordingly confirmed in January 1956, after which the Council applied successfully for loan sanction of £110,240 to enable them to acquire the site. A further loan sanction for purchase of the Mission Hall by agreement was granted later in the year.

Soon after the compulsory purchase order was submitted, and before the public inquiry of October 1955, the Architect had begun his designs for a layout scheme for the site. The working relationship between the architect and the Council varies in different boroughs. In Finsbury the same firm of architects had been working for the Borough since the early post-war period and the arrangement had become traditional. Negotiations between the Architect, the Council and its Housing Committee were more direct here than in many London Boroughs. The Architect did not negotiate through the Surveyor, a Borough Architect or other intermediaries, but himself carried many of the responsibilities such officers would bear, preparing papers for the Council and discussing them with the Housing Committee. This encouraged the growth of mutual confidence between him and the elected representatives, since he knew that the arguments for any proposal had been adequately presented and understood, even if the Committee chose to reject them. Criticism of the Architect's schemes could be offered by an architect in the Borough Engineer's Department, but the latter played no part in project design and was concerned mainly with estate maintenance. The Housing Manager also had an opportunity to comment on the plans, but this was a recent development: one of her main responsibilities was to tell the Architect how many flats of various sizes, ranging from one to four rooms, were needed within a total determined by a specified density ratio. These proportions alter with changes in the types of households to be catered for. In this case the Architect provided flexibility in design that permitted a redistribution of rooms between neighbouring flats, both during building and (with minor modifications) after completion. An incidental contribution of the Housing Manager was the idea of using the basements of demolished houses as a sunken playground.

Two problems confronted the Architect on the Galway Street site. (See plan.) The first was the need to take full advantage of a permanent open space to the south of the west side of the site. The existence of this space clearly meant that as many units as possible should face in that direction, provided that there were not so many 'slab' blocks as to cut down the light and air between them. The need to avoid this latter danger was reinforced by the LCC's insistence on safeguarding the entry of light and air to Guinness Trust buildings adjoining the site to the north. The second problem was the need for compactness to leave room for adequate neighbourhood facilities such as play areas, parking space, service roads, pathways, access for fire engines, tree and flower landscaping, and a certain amount of open space for the residents' general use. This difficulty was accentuated by the high density for the area laid down in the London Development Plan, already approved by the Minister. In the case of Finsbury, 200 persons per acre had been decided on—London's highest planned density—and this, with a site area of 3·63 acres, permitted 726 persons to be rehoused. On the basis of the standard LCC figure of 1·1 persons per room, the total number of rooms was thus fixed at 660. The combination of the need to allow enough free ground

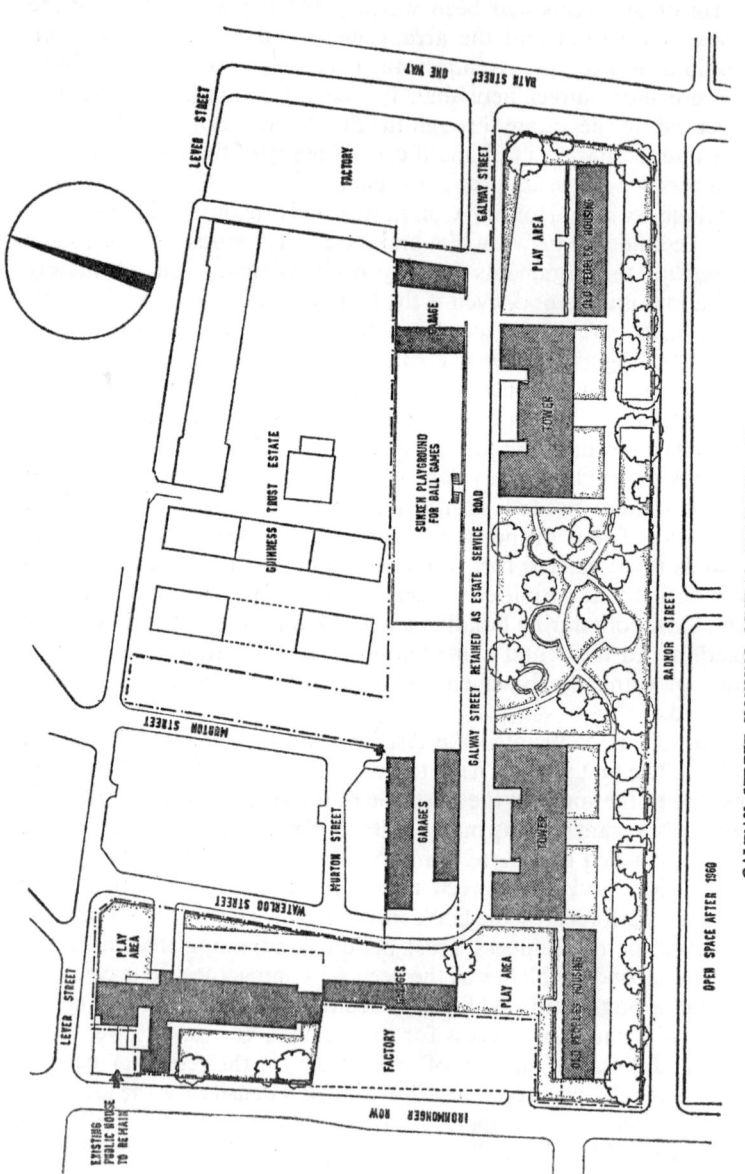

GALWAY STREET HOUSING SCHEME, FINSBURY—SITE LAYOUT
From a plan prepared by Emberton, Franck & Tardrew, Architects

space and the need to reach the total required density inevitably called for tall blocks of flats.

In October 1955 the Architect set about preparing layout schemes for the site. During the next twelve months three successive plans were prepared and modified in the light of discussions with officials in the County Planning Department. These discussions dealt mainly with the arrangement of blocks, the amenities to be provided in the area surrounding them, the heights of buildings (with an eye to the need for subsequent LCC permission for buildings over 100 feet), the appearance of the buildings, the provision of access and circulation space for vehicles and pedestrians, the obstruction of light and air, and the relation of the project to adjoining buildings. Officials in the County Planning Department could only offer their advice, and the Architect constantly met different planners who might disagree with each other or change their minds. Nevertheless it was essential to prepare a plan likely to be acceptable to the Council's Planning Committee whose decisions would depend mainly on the recommendations of these officers. In the event of disagreement it would be open to the Borough to appeal to the Minister—assuming the uncertainty of the outcome and the delay of six to nine months that this would involve could be tolerated—but Finsbury had never done this. If necessary, discussions could also be initiated between the elected members of both Councils. The majorities in each were drawn from the Labour Party. Some of their leading figures had known each other for many years, and Finsbury had the advantage of particularly forceful and experienced leadership. But that avenue was not tried in this case. The fact that an intervention of this kind was to be used to the full shortly afterwards in another Finsbury project may have restricted the scope for personal interventions at member level in this project. Informal agreement was finally reached over a layout based on three 'point' blocks (which the LCC's officers preferred to longer 'slab' blocks) having four flats on each floor and restricted to seventeen storeys in height. These towers would be linked by single-storey housing for old people, with garages, playgrounds and planted open space in the surrounding area. The Housing Committee then resolved to apply formally for planning permission and the Town Clerk made arrangements for the Borough to take possession of the housing that had been compulsorily purchased.

At this point, in November 1956, the architect in charge of the firm died. His two senior colleagues took over as partners by agreement with his executors and one of them assumed responsibility for the Galway Street project. He immediately made contact with the Ministry to ensure informal approval for the cost of the scheme before the LCC gave its planning permission. This move, which had hitherto been neglected, was in accordance with the policies of the Ministry which has since issued a circular (61/58) stressing the desirability of early consultation between a local authority's professional representatives and Ministry officials at the sketch layout stage, before either the layout or the detailed designs have been settled. The suggestions of the Ministry's architects do not necessarily prejudice the future acceptance of a scheme, though their criticisms obviously carry weight when the plan is formally submitted. Ministry approval is called for at all stages which require Government expenditure. The Galway Street project was eligible for a subsidy as a slum clearance scheme. Subsidies consisted of a fixed sum, paid per dwelling according to the number of storeys comprising the block. Under section 3 of the Housing Subsidies Act 1956, which was in force during the negotiations with the Ministry, dwellings other than a block of flats of four or more storeys qualified for an annual exchequer subsidy of £22 1s for sixty years, blocks of flats of four storeys for £32 per annum per dwelling, five storeys for £38, six or more for £50, increased by £1 15s for each storey by which the block exceeded six storeys. Since the additional costs of steelwork, lifts and other high-building devices heavily increase expenditures at high levels there was a strong incentive for local authorities either to keep their buildings low or to raise them so high as to recoup their losses from the very large subsidies available as the twentieth floor was approached: at seventeen storeys the subsidy was very nearly £70 per annum per dwelling. This incentive to build tower blocks clearly worked in opposition to the Ministry's desire to limit its expenditure by keeping heights down. The Ministry did not oppose high building on principle: the circular quoted above states that 'sometimes a limited amount of really high building will produce a saving of expenditure on the scheme as a whole, while in other cases the extra cost of high building may be well worth-while to preserve gardens and trees or to make the most of an open prospect. The aim in all cases must be to get value for money'. Thus the criteria employed by the Ministry in considering a scheme for loan sanction were that it be judged 'technically sound' and 'reasonable as to cost'. Architects coming at an informal stage for consultation were generally diverted to the Ministry's architects who provided them with a ceiling target figure of costs at which to aim. The Ministry has ceiling costs which are constantly readjusted in the light of different schemes being presented for approval, though the exact amounts vary from one region to another and are not made known to the architects. If at a later stage the Ministry feels that costs may be reduced in any part of the scheme they do not criticise particular items too specifically but merely suggest general areas where expenses may be cut.

When the Architect approached the Ministry for discussions in January 1957, he was received by their Principal Regional Architect and a Senior Architect responsible for an area including Finsbury. The latter was the main representative of the Ministry in the negotiations. He stated that they were greatly disturbed by the rising costs of flats in tall blocks and that a tendency was growing to reduce expenditure by building more flats per staircase—six flats instead of the four favoured by the LCC's planners. This arrangement would cut down costs considerably by greatly reducing the area of perimeter walling. He therefore strongly advised the floor plans recommended by the Ministry, with a long interior corridor to a staircase and lifts at either end. The Finsbury Architect, however, claimed that these corridors developed in practice into badly ventilated, dark and noisy tunnels which were liable to be treated as football pitches by the children. As to lay-out, the Ministry architects objected to three seventeen-storey blocks with single-storey old people's flats between them on the grounds that this would prejudice future development to the north. They proposed two seventeen-storey blocks at new angles and made several other suggestions about the old people's housing, the contrast between high and low buildings, the service road and pedestrian access. The Architect then returned to discuss the Ministry's recommendations with the Housing Committee at two meetings on successive days. Some, but not all, of these modifications were accepted, and he set about drawing revised plans in January 1957.

During January and February the quantity surveyor was engaged in working out estimates for comparison between the costs of the Ministry scheme or its revision, and that which had been submitted by Finsbury's appointed Architect. The Ministry's version was found to be more expensive and the quantity surveyor's comparative estimates were sent to Whitehall. This result was taken to provide grounds for intervention by leading members of the Finsbury Council to discuss the scheme with members of the administrative staff at the Ministry. At this stage the procedure was for administrators to put their Ministry's case and point out the reasons why, on the advice of their own professional staff, they did not consider the expense of the scheme to be justified. The Town Clerk was the equivalent in the local authority organisation of the administrative officers at the Ministry, and he would advise his Council. If the Council did not agree with the Ministry's decision, then they might have access to the Minister himself who would be advised by his administrators on the main points involved and the principles at stake, and by his professional staff on technical matters. On this basis he would make the final decision.

In this case the Ministry's divisional Senior Architect brought in the administrative section at an early point in the negotiations. This was quite usual when the professionals felt that complications were likely to obstruct progress when tenders were called for later, for costs would then have to be estimated accurately and loan sanction passed as quickly as possible. The Senior Architect, together with the Assistant Secretary in charge of London housing, a Principal and another administrator met the Chairman of the Finsbury Council, the Vice-Chairman of the

Housing Committee, the Town Clerk, the Borough Engineer, the Housing Manager and the Architect in March 1957. This meeting, amounting to a head-on clash, was called at the request of the Architect. Finsbury asked for the acceptance of the three point blocks in their plan on the grounds that the criterion of cost employed by the Ministry to reject their scheme ran counter to the Ministry's wish to reduce expenditure by introducing six flats per storey instead of four. But the Ministry's representatives again stressed the importance of opening up the site, they again objected to the number of single-storey old people's flats and they practically rejected three tower blocks (The discussion also dealt with the visual effect of three tower blocks standing not far from St. Paul's Cathedral, but this hardly constituted a decisive point of difference between the Borough and the Ministry since the latter were asking for two broader towers of the same height.) Finsbury still defended their scheme, but it was made clear that loan sanction would not be granted if three tower blocks were retained in the plans. The Ministry did agree at this meeting, however, that they would regard the site as a single unit. This was crucial because it meant that the single-storey old people's dwellings would not be treated separately, and a more generous 'expensive site' subsidy could be offered.

Two days later, Finsbury's Housing Committee rejected the Ministry's first revised scheme and a compromise scheme was submitted by the architect and approved by the Committee. The Ministry's demand for six flats per floor was accepted but the defects of an internal corridor structure were avoided by a novel disposition of the flats. The Ministry's objection to three tower blocks was also accepted and other changes were made, but resistance to various features of the new plan was still expected from the Ministry.

Later in the month informal discussions were held with the LCC's planners to discover their reaction to the revised scheme. These talks exposed a basic disagreement between the LCC and the Ministry over the point blocks. The Ministry disliked tall thin blocks because it wanted to restrict costs, while the LCC disliked highly directional slab blocks because they fitted less easily into the landscape, were less likely to produce satisfactory aspects from all directions, and were liable to obstruct light and air in the surrounding neighbourhood. Various other problems were discussed, but the LCC refused to permit an increase in height to nineteen storeys which—with six flats per floor—would have accommodated all the housing required except for twelve single-storey old people's dwellings. This restriction on height was relaxed shortly afterwards when the Architect gained the County's approval for nineteen storeys on another project, and still higher flats have been built since then. But at the time of the Galway Street project the planners would not go higher than seventeen storeys.

Meanwhile, at the end of March 1957, permission was received by

Finsbury from the LCC Planning Committee for the plans submitted in October 1956 before an approach was made to the Ministry. In its accompanying comments the LCC suggested the reduction or redistribution of play areas to avoid noise nuisance, and also the reduction of the large expanse of hard-paved areas between and along the old people's dwellings. The block in the north-west corner of the site was excluded from planning permission so that new designs might be made for the better inclusion of the public house standing there. Adjustments had also to be made to the fire escapes and it was stipulated that the site had to be cleared and the buildings erected in a single operation.

This consent was acknowledged by the Architect but at the same time he submitted the revised scheme, explaining the Ministry's refusal to accept three tower blocks, and arguing that changes introduced under pressure from the Ministry did not materially affect the LCC's planning requirements. He also included a shadow diagram which showed that in summer almost no shadow fell on adjoining properties and what fell on the site itself touched only the least important parts of it such as the car park and the playground for ball games.

The Architect then made a first trial of the Ministry's views about costs. In May 1957 he wrote to the Senior Architect there and presented information about the costs of foundations and dwellings. These were examined by the Ministry's quantity surveyor, who found one of the lower blocks to be extremely expensive. He estimated that the accommodation could be provided in a four-storey block at a saving of about £1,000 per dwelling, since such a height would obviate the need for lifts and certain structural strengthening devices. This conclusion was passed on to the Finsbury Architect who was told that the disputed block was too costly in its present form and he therefore agreed to redesign it. But this block remained expensive, owing to its brick dressing and other items, and the whole scheme came within the Ministry's cost ceiling only because of the economy derived from the unusual structural design of the tower blocks.

Having informally discovered both the LCC's and the Ministry's opinions of the latest plan, based on their different criteria, the Architect finally submitted a revised application for formal planning permission to the LCC Planning Committee in May 1957. With this request he included the suggestion of closing Galway Street, which ran through the middle of the site, and using it as an access road. He also asked for a waiver of the ruling that permanent ventilation must be provided since at seventeen storeys this would make the modest degree of central heating ineffective.

The LCC were clearly disposed to accept the plan except for their crucial disagreement with the Ministry over the desirability of point blocks as opposed to slab blocks. They accordingly consulted representatives of the Ministry about this. (Such informal contacts between the Ministry and the County became more frequent later, to avoid situations in which Boroughs played off one against the other. Meetings of this kind had nevertheless to be regarded as confidential to avoid suggestions of collusion, since if local authorities resort ultimately to appeals against LCC decisions the Ministry has to arbitrate and must preserve an impartial status.) Various points were made at the meeting, held in July 1957, but the crucial one was again the prohibitive cost of the three 'point' blocks and the saving to be achieved by substitution of 'wing' blocks with six flats per storey. The LCC's aesthetic preference for non-directional tall blocks was finally overruled.

After this encounter with the Ministry the LCC granted planning permission for the final scheme in July 1957. Discussion of the siting of the children's playground was requested, and attention was drawn to the new ruling, published two months previously by the Metropolitan Standing Joint Committee for Parking, which required provision of one garage for every two flats. The Architect responded to this by asking that parking space be increased only to the sixty-three-car maximum which the Borough Council regarded as the highest permissible number (about half the proportion recommended) and this permission was granted in February 1958.

Permission had also to be gained for extinguishment of rights of way and for the construction of buildings over 100 feet high, though the procedure was different in the two cases. For the former, all objections had to be heard *before* permission was considered; in the latter, provisional consent was given first, and only then were objections invited. Objections against proposed building heights must be made within twenty-one days, though this period was often extended until the actual day of the hearing. Petitions were lodged with the Tribunal of Appeal. Under section 52 of the London Building Act all owners and lessees within a radius of 100 yards of the proposed building (or whatever distance is specified by the LCC) had the right of appeal. They were notified of the proposal, a similar notice was published in *The Times*, two notices were posted in public view, and the LCC notified all tenants affected. If objections were raised—usually concerning light, access or outlook—it was essential that some compromise be reached to the satisfaction of the complainant, for if the case were pursued to a public inquiry, a delay of over six weeks might arise which could be very damaging now that preparations were being made for the start of building operations. The notices mentioned stated that copies of the detailed site plans were available for inspection at County Hall. Thus objectors were able, and entitled, to object to any feature of these plans, not only to building heights and rights of way.

Seven complaints were received. The first batch came from the factory at the north-east corner of the site, the insurance company who were the head lessees for the factory, and the Church Commissioners who were its ground landlords. The Commissioners sought further information. The insurance company complained about obstruction of light, and they and the factory complained about the closure of Galway Street and the difficulty that this would entail for the loading and unloading of the factory's lorries. This objection was pushed to an extreme at a later stage in the negotiations. Another firm, situated on the western boundary of the site was more favourable and after requesting information did not raise any complaint except about access to its loading bay. A third firm protested about the obstruction of light and raised questions about the possibility of the Borough buying its property. A further objection came from the Church Commissioners, this time in connection with their property interests in yet another factory; it was claimed that a restriction on height had been agreed in 1891 with the French Hospital (destroyed during the war) which limited the height of any building on the south-eastern fringe of the site to 44 feet. This light and air agreement was attested to be binding on the French Hospital, their successors, lessees and tenants. The final complaint was made by a tenant living on the top floor of one of the Guinness Trust blocks adjoining the site to the north, again on the grounds of the barring of light. It was true that one of the proposed buildings, 148 feet high, would overshadow part of the Guinness block at 9 a.m. (summer time). The objector's daughter was secretary of the Guinness Trust Tenants' Association, a body which first became active about this time, mainly for the purpose of securing a badly needed supply of electricity in the Trust flats: they felt that as ratepayers they could not reasonably be asked to contribute to expensive redevelopment when the basic amenities of their existing dwellings were neglected.

The Tribunal of Appeal disallowed all objections about light obstruction except the one from the Guinness Trust tenants, though this too, on investigation, proved to be too weak to uphold. As for the French Hospital's agreement, this was felt to be a matter for personal settlement between the Borough Council and the factory involved. Thus by the time that official permission was received for buildings over 100 feet in October 1957, all objections had been dismissed except those of the two firms appealing, for different reasons, against the closure of Galway Street. The actual application for extinguishment of rights of way was sent off by the Council in November for approval by the Ministry.

The objection by the factory on the western boundary of the site was that the inclusion within the redevelopment site of a strip of road 14 × 60 feet in area meant that their lorries had insufficient space to manoeuvre at their loading bay. The factory on the north-east, on the other hand, complained that the closure involved the inconvenience to them that their lorries, instead of being able to use the shorter route through the middle of the site from their unloading to their loading bay, would have to drive round the outside of the whole site. Finsbury was notified of these two objections by the LCC in January 1958, in the hope of some satisfactory settlement. This was made all the more urgent, if the Council was to avoid disastrous delays, by the vehemence and perseverance with which the management of the factory to the north-east pursued their case. They made representations to the Ministry, who referred the inquiry to the LCC, who in turn referred the objectors to the highway authority for the area (the Borough). Finally, by March 1958, the company approached the Guinness Trust and the Council with a proposal that if the former allow them right of way through the existing access road to the Trust estate, then the Council should make up at their own expense an exit road to the south to connect with Galway Street (see plan). Thus the Borough would provide the Company with a new road, partly on Guinness Trust property, linking existing streets and extending right round the factory building.

This agreement was extorted from a reluctant Council, and accepted by the Secretary of the Guinness Trust to help out the Council. Cooperation between the Trust and the Council over the exchange of tenants and other matters had been excellent for some years. It was this tradition which induced the Guinness Trust to concede right of way to the objector in the interests of the Council. But at the same time the Trust insisted that the right of way be fenced off, with a gate offering access for fire engines to their site. Further, the Secretary of the Trust arranged privately with the objecting firm that their lorries only use the road at certain stated hours of the day, so as to minimise the consequent noise and disturbance. As an additional check against unnecessary use, the firm and the caretaker of the Trust estate were each given possession of three keys to the gates at both ends of the access road over Trust property. On the Council's side, discussions in May 1958 showed that, apart from the construction of the end of the access road, the objector's requirements could be met by closing a small additional part of Galway Street that was not covered by the Council's previous resolution about extinguishment of rights of way. Permission for the change of plan, with right of way over Guinness Trust property, was granted by the LCC in July 1958. The factory on the western side of the site was sold the 14 × 60-foot strip of land they required so that it might be incorporated in their loading yard.

By October 1958, Finsbury's Town Clerk was able to report to his Council that both objections to the extinguishment of public rights of way and to the height of the proposed buildings had been withdrawn. Next month both companies withdrew their requests for payment of costs and fees incurred in the arrangements made with them to secure withdrawal of their objections. However, the company securing the new road over the Guinness Trust property never made use of it. The significance of the road to them had been its value as parking space for their employees, though this was partly frustrated because the Trust caretaker retained keys of the gates at both ends of the section of road on Trust property. Nevertheless the company gained permission in March 1959 to park in the unenclosed cul-de-sac at the south end of the road until site operations were completed in September 1960.

Meanwhile, on the assumption that negotiations with objectors would be successfully concluded, preparations for the start of building operations had gone ahead. The District Surveyor and the Metropolitan Water Board had to be consulted before building could begin. District Surveyors, appointed by the LCC in each Borough, were responsible for ensuring the structural safety of all new building. In this case the Surveyor's requirements caused some delay at a later stage in the project. The Metropolitan Water Board interprets and enforces by-laws in its field—by-laws which required, for example, two huge water storage tanks at the top of each tower block and a small tank in every flat. Again, demands made by the Board at a later stage in construction resulted in prolonged argument.

The consultant engineer collaborating with the Architect had to be satisfied that the ground would support blocks of the necessary height without subsidence. At Galway Street, trial borings were originally estimated for at a cost of £175, but in October 1957, they had to be made in the roadways at a cost of £630 because demolition had not yet started and further delay had to be avoided. In July 1958, however, the Architect was obliged to inform the Housing Committee that the trial borings showed very variable ground, and the consultant engineer now wished to sink eleven additional holes. These were accordingly approved provided the cost did not exceed £1,200.

Arrangements had also to be made with the London Electricity Board and the South-Eastern Gas Board for the supply of fuel and power to the flats. In another of the Borough's recent housing projects the flats had been equipped with gas water-heating except for one floor which was supplied with electricity. Later the tenants were asked for their comments and all favoured electricity. This was discovered at a time when gas ducts were already being installed in Galway Street. These ducts were required for gas water-heating in the kitchen, and had been chosen partly as a favour to the Gas Board who were anxious to experiment with them on tower blocks since they had previously been used only to a height of six storeys. Meanwhile the Council resolved in March 1958 to approve the terms of the Electricity Board for electricity supply; these involved an additional service charge of £2,400 for electricity mains and meters if the proposed installation did not conform with certain 'standard requirements' (agreed between the Board and the Metropolitan Boroughs' Standing Joint Committee) which excluded the use of gas planned for these flats. Thus the charge had to be paid before the Board would start installation, though the possibility of further negotiations about the charge was kept open.

Meanwhile, a sixty-year lease for an electricity transformer station was granted by the Council to the Electricity Board at a nominal rent of £1 per annum.

Once informal approval had been given for the detailed layout scheme by the LCC and the Ministry, the Borough Council set about obtaining loan sanction. In November 1957, the Architect reported to the Housing Committee that typical ground-floor plan working drawings for the main blocks and for the one-storey old people's flatlets had been completed and handed over to the quantity surveyor. Within six months the bills of quantity had been despatched and tenders were delivered by July 1958. The lowest tender, at a price of £669,331, was accepted, with the time of completion given as ninety weeks. This selection was based on a competition between some eight or ten large companies. Invitations to tender were not made public. These firms were recommended by the Architect and chosen to ensure they could cope with the size and building methods of the scheme. But before tenders were actually invited, the Architect had taken the precaution of informally contacting the Senior Architect at the Ministry in May 1958, to check that the cost of the seventeen-storey blocks would be acceptable. Their economic structural design would offset their height and might also offset the expensive smaller block. This economy was a considerable achievement. Having thus gained informal approval from the Ministry for the cost, the official application for loan sanction was made by the Council in August 1958, for two seventeen-storey blocks of 201 dwellings, one six-storey block and one three-storey block, together providing 29 dwellings, and two single-storey rows of flatlets providing 10 dwellings—240 in all. With this application were sent the usual documents required by the Ministry—notice of the tender to be accepted, a copy of the planning permission, the district valuer's report, and certificates showing that the local authority owned the land. The tender figures were examined by the Ministry's architects, who recommended that they should be accepted. Decisions to pass loan sanctions are made by the executive grade without reference to administrative officers, when no questions of policy are involved. The Minister is only called upon to play a part when the case is unprecedented. The Finsbury Council received a formal reply in September 1958, from a Principal on behalf of the Minister to say that he had no objection to the Council's acceptance of the tender; he also gave consent for the provision and maintenance at the site of forty-six lock-up garages.

The Exchequer subsidy for high building was requested in May 1960.[1] Finsbury was asked to show how many families had been displaced from unfit properties and how many houses had been built to rehouse them. At the end of the month a formal letter on behalf of the Minister was written to the Council approving 240 dwellings to be

[1] The rates of subsidy at that time are explained in Ministry Circular No. 33/1956

provided for the purposes of the Housing (General Purposes) Act 1958, and stating how much subsidy was payable for each dwelling. The application for 'expensive site subsidy' under section 7 of the Act was dealt with separately. The Regional Architect at the Ministry considered the application for the payment of £45,579 and approved this figure as reasonable. The application was then considered by the specialist division dealing with subsidies, and in a letter of July 1960 the Council was told that the cost of the site as developed had been provisionally determined at between £40,000 and £41,000 per acre. On behalf of the Minister it was agreed to pay an Exchequer subsidy of £4,661 per annum for sixty years.

Meanwhile building had begun on 1 January 1959, but not before an additional appointment had been made to the construction team. The engineer and the quantity surveyor had been appointed in January 1957, the sub-contractors were nominated by the Borough Engineer in November 1957, the main contractors were appointed in July 1958, and then, in October 1958, the engineer recommended that his company be permitted to appoint a resident engineer to assist him. The reason for this suggestion was that the reinforced concrete structure designed according to the specifications of experts allowed considerable savings in steel and concrete, but required a high degree of precision in construction. It was claimed that the additional cost of about £1,800 would be more than offset by the saving effected. The Council accordingly made an application to the Ministry for loan sanction for this amount, and after the Regional Architect had been consulted this was granted in December. The appointment was a fortunate one as the consultant engineer died that month and was not replaced till June 1959.

Tenders from a large number of sub-contractors for specific items were received during the last few months of 1958. These items included lifts, plumbing, electrical work, lightning conductors, heating, ventilation, pram lockers, external railings and gates, roof railings, kitchen fittings, timber doors, metal door frames, metal windows, door fittings and piled foundations.

Work on the site proceeded slowly at first. The contractor dealing with the 'stage one' demolitions did not satisfy the Council with the progress made, and so, in the negotiations with the Regional Architect in March 1959, it was explained that the Council were not accepting the lowest tender for future demolition work. Consequently, loan sanction was given by the Ministry for acceptance of the second lowest tender. The danger of such failures is always inherent in the tendering system. The advantage of working for considerable periods with the same architect who knew the needs and procedures of his clients was sacrificed in the case of the contractors. Building also began rather slowly, largely because of lack of experience in handling and fixing prefabricated parts. But after initial trouble with the construction procedure had been overcome and erection teams had been trained, a considerable saving in building time was achieved. The thirty-six prefabricated units, excluding edge beams, of the first floor built on the Galway Street site took three weeks to complete. Later this time was reduced to five-and-a-half days, including the construction of floors; the teams were able to cut down the fixing of one unit from forty-five to eight minutes.

Changes in the sizes of flats were requested by the Housing Manager in March 1960. By comparison with the schedule of accommodation fixed when the LCC approved the final lay-out scheme in July 1957, forty fewer three-roomed flats were now needed and more four- and two-roomed flats were wanted instead. Changes in the distribution of rooms were easily achieved on this site since the construction techniques employed permitted considerable flexibility. The system was based on staircases and lift shafts forming central load-bearing cores which, with concrete gable walls at the end of each block provided structural stability and wind-bracing. The perimeter of the building consisted of load-bearing columns set in the external walls, and a floor slab six-and-a-half inches thick spanned the area from the perimeter to the structural core. This large span of 23 feet, without structural crossbeams, provided an uninterrupted space enclosed by a concrete shell which made possible a wide variety of layouts. After completion of the flats further modifications remained possible through the provision of bedrooms with doorways opening into the corridors of two flats, and movable insulating and sound-proofing panels that could easily be fixed to the door not in use.

This system provided some badly needed elbow room for the Housing Manager whose selection of tenants for the flats available was complicated not only by normal changes in requirements arising during the period of five years that usually elapsed between the preparation of building plans and the occupation of the flats, but also by the tendency for people to move into an area as soon as it was known to be due for demolition. Under the terms of compulsory purchase orders the authority was bound to rehouse all who were living in the area when the order was made. Since the order may take nine months or more before it is confirmed by the Ministry, this gives ample opportunity for a considerable influx of relatives and friends and there is no legal means of preventing this. Even after the order is made, the local authority can only control the entry of tenants to privately rented property by taking out a 'notice of entry' which entitles them to take over the leaseholds from landlords of residential property. But this procedure has its drawbacks too, since the local authority then collects the rents and must compensate landlords fairly generously until the property is finally acquired from them. Some landlords realise that it would profit them to hold up negotiations for the compensation settlement so that they may continue to draw these payments, and compensation may not be settled for months or even years.

The final selection of tenants was made by the General Purposes Sub-committee of the Housing Committee after detailed study of the circumstances of individual households. Within the limits imposed by the Council's slum clearance requirements, the most important criterion governing the allocation of flats was the financial capacity of prospective tenants who must be capable of maintaining their rent payments. If they could not afford the higher rents that some of the newer blocks required, or if in general they were not felt to be suitable for new accommodation, then they were rehoused in older buildings at lower rents. Previous housing conditions were not a relevant factor; in any case, all the houses had been in bad structural condition. The process of selection began when the General Purposes Sub-committee were given lists of all those to be rehoused, stating their present rents, the amounts they said they were able to afford, the sizes of their families and their occupations. Prospective tenants were seen by the Housing Manager and her staff, who gave them details of the rents and flats, and finally they were interviewed by the Sub-committee who then made the selection. This was decided for most of the flats at Galway Street in May 1960, though further tenants continued to be chosen as late as October 1960, and January 1961, as more flats became available.

Rents came up for discussion at the time that changes in the sizes of flats were being considered. Council members who are also Council tenants are normally excluded from this discussion, but since about half Finsbury's Housing Committee lived in Council property this bar—but not the prohibition on voting—was waived, with the approval of the Ministry, as is normal in such cases. Finally the Committee recommended to the Council that the rents be calculated at two-thirds of the gross value assessed for rating purposes. This meant rents of £2 3s 1d, £1 17s 0d, £1 11s 6d and £1 3s 6d for four-, three-, two- and one-room flats respectively. The blocks were then named and in May a caretaker was appointed.

The progress of work on the site was interrupted early in 1960 owing to technical difficulties. When the flats were half-finished, the Metropolitan Water Board insisted that the over-flow pipe from each storage tank, which projected through the bathroom walls over the bath waste pipe, must be diverted the whole way round the wall to discharge over the 'head' end of the bath. This, they said, would ensure that tenants reported faults in the tank stopcocks promptly, for if the stopcocks failed cold water would fall on their heads and not on their feet. After weeks of argument the Board was persuaded to drop this unsightly and expensive requirement.

Further delays led to a meeting on the site between members of the Housing Committee's 'Progress of Site Sub-committee', Borough officials, the Architect and contractors in June 1960. The reasons given for the delay were: compliance with the District Surveyor's requirements, difficulty in obtaining bricks, modifications to the top floor of one block, the break enforced by winter frost in January, and the scarcity of plasterers. The contractors agreed to seek more men and to prepare a revised progress chart for the architect.

But the most serious challenge to the administration came from the association of tenants in the neighbouring Guinness Trust property who united to form a Social and Welfare Committee composed of about twelve people. Their principal motivation still appeared to be resentment at not having an electricity supply. They had already raised an objection against the height of the new buildings in May 1957. At the end of 1958 they protested over the facilities provided by the Council for the factory alongside the Guinness property which was given a new service road. The contractors had entered the site, six weeks before building operations began, to construct this access road to the rear of the factory. In December 1958, a deputation from the tenants made the first of many protests to the Council about the road. The tenants' association took their complaint to the Ministry in April 1959, after the completion of the road, claiming that it was dangerous because it was used as an access walk to the Guinness Trust estate, and also that it was not subject to permission granted under the town planning layout scheme which had been officially approved. The LCC knew of the proposed revision of the plans and gave formal approval for the road that month. The Ministry, however, offered to take the matter up with the Borough Council. Meanwhile, after the road had been built and despite the fact that it appears virtually never to have been used by the factory, the tenants' association complained that the lorry drivers could see into their bathrooms and that the lorries would disturb them. The Guinness Trust had arranged for use of the road only at stated times, and the Trust caretaker had keys to the gates at either end of the right of way which would prevent disturbance by car parking. Of the thirty-six windows overlooking the site, six were in bathrooms. The Council followed a policy of appeasement, and part of the fence dividing the road from the Guinness estate was replaced by a brick wall which was constructed in the latter part of 1959. The wall was intended to be six feet high and up to this height no planning permission would be needed for this change. But a request that the wall be raised to a height of eight feet was made by the caretaker of the Guinness Trust to prevent children climbing over it. (Not that it ever did.) This request was granted but the necessity for planning permission was overlooked by the Architect at this point. Meanwhile the tenants' association, having gained their wall, began to protest about its cost. They were helped, when their protests proved ineffective, by a Communist opponent of the Labour council. A QC was briefed and an appeal was fixed against the Council's action for July 1960. The Architect therefore hastened to arrange a meeting with planning officers of the LCC in May to discuss whether planning permission had covered the building of the wall on part of Guinness Trust property. It was they who drew his attention to the height of the wall and pointed out that no consent had been sought. The Architect apologised, saying that the increase in height had been made to keep on good terms with the Guinness Trust, and he at once applied for retrospective permission under the London Building Act which was soon granted and formally confirmed. At the public enquiry in July, held before the District Auditor, the Guinness Trust tenants objected on three scores. Their main one was that money had been spent on providing facilities for the neighbouring factory and that this expenditure was not in the ratepayers' interests, and that, therefore, the councillors should be surcharged £3,000—the full cost of the wall and the access road. This was a serious matter: a surcharge of this amount would have disqualified councillors from standing for re-election. But the District Auditor, the presiding Ministry representative, dismissed the charge that the expenditure was illegal and no negligence was found. Nor was the attempt to isolate the wall and the gate as impermissible expenditure successful, for they had always been intended as part of the access road provision. A further objection, raised by Guinness Trust tenants, was that fumes from trucks would cause sickness, that the noise would create a disturbance and the trucks would endanger the children. But the Medical Officer of Health did not agree that any detrimental effects on health would result. The one ground of appeal which succeeded, however was the discovery by the QC on the tenants' side that permission had not been obtained at the proper time for the eight-foot wall and the Architect was criticised by the Auditor on this score. But thanks to the retrospective permission given by the LCC, the councillors and officers concerned were released from the obligation of paying a surcharge of £831—the cost of the wall. This protracted and detailed hearing, which involved the Town Clerk, the Borough Engineer, the Architect, the Housing Manager and Medical Officer of Health for three days, therefore had no effect. Building operations continued and the Council was exonerated. The tenants' association lost its momentum after this and the movement ceased a little while later when they obtained an electricity supply.

The final request for planning permission on the site was made in September 1960, and concerned play areas. The LCC replied in October that no planning permission was required, as this item had already been covered in previous grants of approval but they assumed that contact had been made with the District Surveyor to seek his advice under the Building Act. They had no comment to make on the equipment provided, but noted that both the smaller play areas were partly overshadowed by old people's flats and that they might therefore be better placed to obtain an unobstructed southern outlook.

At the scheduled date for completion, in October 1960, the contractors were six weeks behind on site progress. Attempts were made to speed up the work but the lack of plasterers delayed the recently increased force of painters. By February 1961, however, instead of an official opening ceremony, a show flat furnished free by a local company was used to celebrate the public opening of the estate. Two blocks and the old people's flatlets were occupied in March and the others were taken over soon afterwards.

The completed project cost £35,000 less than was originally estimated. Both the principal problems of the site had been satisfactorily resolved. The longest boundary to the south overlooks an area scheduled to become an open park, and the blocks have been planned so that twelve out of the eighteen living rooms at each floor level have a southern aspect. The need for compact spacing to permit adequate neighbourhood amenities on the ground has been met by building six flats per floor and by enabling the perimeter of the blocks to be used as living space, for the core of lifts, stairs, WCs, bathrooms and ducts are grouped at the centre on each floor.

The areas around and between each block were planted and laid out with paths. A play area for small children was sited next to each block to make supervision easier. On the other side of the estate service road from the point blocks there is a large playground sunk four feet below street level to make use of existing basements, which is suitable for ball games. In the same area, with access from the service road, are forty-six lock-up garages with further open parking space for at least another sixteen cars. The finish and fittings of the blocks themselves are of high quality. Each flat has a gas water-heater and drying-cabinet which are ventilated into internal ducts. There is oil-fired central heating, with radiators in the two main rooms of each flat, giving a temperature of 65 degrees in the living rooms and 55 degrees in the halls. The roof, which is finished in asphalt, holds the lift motors and plant rooms, which have been housed in brick with a curving concrete canopy. Part of the roof can be used by residents as a sun terrace at the discretion of the Housing Manager, and a five-foot close-meshed railing was built round it. Each flat has its own balcony. There are no inter-connecting passages or corridors and the only covered space for circulation is provided by two open, well-lit lobbies on each floor between the lift and the staircase. Fittings included floor finishes of thermoplastic tiles, tiled window sills, special safety catches on all windows, generous tiling round baths, 'eating kitchens' seating up to five persons, plentiful power points, built-in electric wall fires, a built-in TV aerial, and special baths for old people. Much of the equipment was in fact specially made, for many of the advantages of large-scale production can be derived from a development of this size.

But ground floor storage appears inadequate and many tenants have to bring prams up in the lift; the lifts take one minute from bottom to top, and prams can barely be parked inside the flats. The two rows of old people's flatlets are rather exposed to the street. Though each flatlet has its own front garden and sun terrace, they have no private or even semi-screened open space. The balcony walls in the flats are too high and solid for children to see over and this may tempt children to climb on them. No lighting was installed in the sunken playground, and at the time of this study the cost of providing this, at £700, seemed likely to prove prohibitive.

The Architect in this case made unusual efforts to follow up his past work and assess its faults. When a scheme was completed, he made a point of visiting the caretaker each year for about three years to see what difficulties had appeared in running the buildings. He said, 'You must remember that 75 per cent of your reputation is made in the kitchen. That's where the housewife spends her time, and it's her opinion that counts—and she may be on the Council.' Several of the points we have criticised were corrected in the next project built for the Borough of Finsbury by this firm of architects.

DISCUSSION

This study differs from the rest in this series in dealing with a specific and concrete piece of capital investment. Though it formed a part of a continuing, long-term housing programme, this project had restricted and fairly well defined objectives. Thus the story has a beginning and an end.

The case clearly illustrates the distinction between studies which deal with the work of a particular administrative unit, and studies (like our own) which deal with the management of a particular task or the progress of a particular development. The participants in this development did not form a single administrative unit or group, and did not have any overriding common aims or any continuing relationship to each other. Indeed, many of them were unaware of the existence of others participating in the story. This kind of situation is typical of many that confront the more senior administrator. Moreover it has serious implications for the future housing policies of this country. It took twenty-six months to build 240 flats, from the start of demolition to the rehousing of the new tenants. But four years elapsed after the first planning permission given by the LCC before demolition could begin. The only delays in this process which might have been avoided arose from the postponement of informal consultations with the Ministry about the design and cost of the scheme, and the negotiations that led to the building of the access road for a neighbouring factory. The building industry appears to be capable of the greatly enlarged schemes of urban redevelopment now envisaged for the future, but whether our administrative system is capable of sustaining such a programme remains an open question.

The Borough and its Architect were subject to controls of various types imposed by the County Council and the Ministry. Placed in the thick of central London, this housing project brought about the movement—outwards, then inwards—of well over a thousand people, and it called for widespread changes in land use and ownership, the closing of streets, the diversion of traffic and the disturbance of many long established patterns of life. The individuals and groups involved—in the Ministry, the County Council, the Gas Board, the Water Board, and among local land owners, commercial organisations and residents—had all to participate in the scheme before the Borough's flats could be completed. Their interests were diverse and for most purposes they were subject to no common authority. Securing their participation was therefore a 'political' task—a matter of using, reconciling or defeating potentially conflicting powers—not simply a matter of organising available resources for generally agreed ends.

Such tasks call for the discussion and exploration of the interests of those concerned in an attempt to establish common objectives, and (where unity of aim is lacking) a process of bargaining designed to arrive at mutually satisfactory solutions, or (where even that proves impossible) a process for determining the balance of power. To the Ministry and the County Council the Borough could offer a contribution to the national housing programme and the relief of housing needs in London; from them it received subsidies, technical advice and authorisation for certain actions. To others the Borough could offer money, or special advantages of various kinds—space for parking or loading, an exchange of tenants, an opportunity for experimenting with gas services, a site for a transformer station, or a more attractive view. In return it received land, technical services and agreements to participate without causing undue delay. Where land uses are concerned, democratic rights have a cash value, and the objector's power to delay and disorganise a complex and costly programme sometimes constituted a crucial bargaining counter in the negotiations. The formal authorisations required at each stage of the project from the Ministry and the County Council frequently constituted the seal placed on a much more complex bargaining process covering issues, important or trivial, many of which had no statutory place in the proceedings. Similar processes of bargaining and arbitration operated elsewhere in this series of studies, but frequently in an informal manner, more difficult to discern. In this case the Ministry and the County planning authority were specifically required by the legislation to arbitrate between contending interests at many points: authorisations for action on building plans, building heights, closure of rights of way and the borrowing of money formally established the outcome of these arbitrations. Such discussions had therefore to be preceded by lengthy negotiations to determine the views, interests and bargaining strengths of all concerned. Even when different departments of government were responsible for assisting progress on the same project, their frames of reference—the Ministry's coloured by a concern for economy, the LCC's by a concern for the visual amenities of London, for example—overlapped but did not coincide. Thus there were important differences in the criteria they employed and the evidence they regarded as relevant for the decisions to be made.

In negotiations subject to arbitration or decision by official bodies it was often found that criteria which could be specified in numerical terms proved easiest to establish and apply—the density of rooms per acre, the heights of buildings, the obstruction of light (as measured in shadow diagrams), volumes of water storage and waste disposal, fire escapes and access for fire engines, the cost of buildings, the floor area of rooms and flats, for example. Some of these criteria were based on technical requirements that were liable to be rendered obsolete by further technical development; rules for water storage and the height and capacity of fire escapes, for example, appeared to reflect technical assumptions that might no longer be justifiable. Questions for which there were no quantifiable criteria often proved harder to settle— questions such as the choice between 'slab' and 'point' blocks, the 'preservation of the London skyline' and the disturbance of privacy among Guinness Trust tenants had eventually to be resolved by overriding legal authority. Issues over which the Borough had to satisfy two or more potentially conflicting interests also presented special problems. The prolonged conflict between the County Council's and the Ministry's views has already been mentioned, but such disagreements cannot always be foreseen so easily: the Borough's attempt to appease one objector by providing him with a road led to time-consuming and potentially damaging objections from the neighbouring tenants' association which probably originated from other discontents of which the Borough had no direct knowledge.

While most of the requirements which the Borough had to meet in the course of the project were established for good technical or political reasons, it should not be concluded that all relevant needs were therefore taken into account. Indeed, the impression was gained at times that the interests of the authorities responsible for technical services, subsidies, land uses and other matters were so precisely quantified and so effectively represented that little scope was left to attend to the general needs of the people who would live in the flats. If the share of a fixed total of resources which must be devoted to fire escapes, water storage, and other technical requirements is expanded beyond a certain point, the share left for the general purposes of living may be unduly restricted. More recent developments in housing policy, following the publication of the Parker Morris Report,[1] have gone some way to improve this situation.

The person principally engaged in reconciling all these interests, co-ordinating the resources they controlled and creating a habitable environment out of them was the Architect. He was manager as well as professional adviser to the Council. To perform his task he required a thorough and sensitive understanding of the administrative system, and the play of human nature and political and commercial interests within it—an understanding that was as essential a part of his professional equipment as his more specialised technical skills. The Housing Committee could advise him about the needs of tenants—half of them were Council tenants themselves—and the Housing Manager could also give useful guidance, though (extraordinarily enough) she had only recently been accorded the right to comment on building plans. Nevertheless a heavy social responsibility remained with the Architect for envisaging and meeting the needs of those who would live in his buildings—and regulations about the size and equipment of flats, layout, access and many other matters left him scant elbow room for responding to it. The traditions of professional training in this and many other fields were originally based on the assumption that the architect—like the lawyer, the doctor and others—was clearly and primarily responsible to an individual 'client'. In this case the client was the Borough Council, but the value of the project will depend on its success in meeting the needs of present and future tenants. Somewhat similar problems arise in other cases we have considered. (Are child welfare officers working primarily for children, for parents, or for the Council employing them?) These questions have major implications for research on the development of social policies and for professional education to which we return later in this book.

The 'timing' of each step in the project was a crucial feature of its management. Not only had each phase of the project to be completed in appropriate sequence, but many decisions could only be made when the necessary preliminaries of the bargaining process had been completed and the 'balance of power' clarified. Thus negotiations had to be started soon enough but could not be completed too hastily. The LCC's devotion to point blocks could be surmounted as soon as it became clear that it would preclude subsidies from the Ministry, but delay in ascertaining the Ministry's point of view postponed the resolution of this conflict. Meanwhile, once this decision was accepted, the Ministry agreed to make useful concessions on other points in return. The

[1] Ministry of Housing and Local Government, *Houses for Today and Tomorrow*. London, HMSO, 1961.

HIGH FLATS IN FINSBURY   161

administrator's need for a good sense of timing is a question that emerges again in later studies.

But important though the Architect was, owing to his central role in the network of communications and the phasing of decisions, it should not be forgotten that the project was the Borough Council's, not his. At critical points in the story it was the Council or its Housing Committee which had to decide—in the light of many other commitments—whether to compromise and when to do this, whether to resist and when to muster delegations capable of presenting their views. They relied on the Architect and their chief officers to advise them on such occasions, but once armed with this advice, the weighing of risks, potential delays and alternative costs was their responsibility, not their advisers'. Likewise, the Architect had always to know how far the Council was prepared to go in supporting him before undertaking negotiations on their behalf. Thus he consulted the Committee and its senior officials and assured himself of their support at every stage of the project.

POSTSCRIPT

We have already noted some of the changes which took place in the government of London in our postscripts to Chapters 3 and 6, and in the first of these we noted changes in the administration of housing. Finsbury, like Bethnal Green, was a small, central Metropolitan Borough which disappeared in the reform of London government. It will be useful to compare this postscript with the other two; it shows many similarities and a few interesting differences.[1]

The old Metropolitan Borough of Finsbury was merged in April 1965 with its larger and poorer northern neighbour to become the new London Borough of Islington with a solidly Labour Council and a population of nearly a quarter of a million, mostly housed in densely built, multiply occupied nineteenth-century property. Islington has less public open space than any other Borough in London.[2]

The new Borough has greater resources and powers than its predecessors. As the main planning authority for its area it is entitled to build houses without seeking the approval of the Greater London Council, unless main roads are to be closed. It is also entitled to buy land and build houses outside its own boundaries. If that land is acquired by agreement, not compulsion, the Borough only has to secure the approval of the local planning authority (like any private developer) and needs no permission from the Greater London Council. Finsbury's Town

[1] Della Adam Nevitt and Gerald Rhodes, in Gerald Rhodes (ed.), *The New Government of London: The First Five Years* (Weidenfeld & Nicholson, 1972) trace the general development of housing policy and organisation since the reform of London government.
[2] *1972 Annual Abstract of Greater London Statistics*, 1973, p. 301.

Clerk and Housing Manager became Deputy Town Clerk and Housing Manager respectively in the new authority, but the private architect responsible for the project we studied dropped out of the picture when work already commissioned by Finsbury had been completed. Shortly afterwards he retired.

Although Islington's housing conditions were repeatedly singled out as being among London's worst by the Milner Holland Committee, which reported on housing in Greater London in 1965,[1] the old Borough had had an unimpressive building record and its work was confined mainly to small sites, often purchased by agreement. A more ambitious policy, dealing with larger projects, was already beginning to take effect when the Labour Party was returned to power at Westminster in 1964 with a commitment to bigger housing programmes. Islington ranked fifteenth among the thirty-two Greater London Boroughs in the number of Council dwellings built each year between 1961 and 1964; it rose to tenth place during the years 1965-8, doubling its output.[2]

In 1968 the Conservatives captured the new Borough of Islington from Labour in an upset which probably surprised their own candidates as much as anyone. Not one of the new majority had served on the Council before, but they wanted to show that they could build still more houses and, thanks to the more generous subsidies now available from the central government and the larger programme put in hand by their predecessors, completions rose. The Conservatives also placed more emphasis on rehabilitation, which tended to slow down the building programme. Some councillors, elected by wards subject to major redevelopment, had a mandate to oppose wholesale demolitions.

Leaders of the new Council were dissatisfied with the conventional pattern of departments and committees which they found, and the difficulties it made for inexperienced councillors trying to reappraise needs and formulate policies in a far-reaching fashion. They called in a firm of management consultants to examine the system and make recommendations. The outcome for housing probably owed as much to political conflicts within the Council as to any theory of organisation and management: in the old Borough, housing had formed the power base of the leading figure amongst the Labour group of councillors and his personal supporters. That base had been strengthened even further in the new Borough by concentrating enlarged responsibilities for planning and housing in the same committee. The reorganisation brought about by the Conservatives abolished the Housing Committee altogether and distributed its responsibilities among several committees.

---

[1] Report of the Committee on Housing in Greater London, Cmnd 2605. HMSO, 1965. Figures quoted in the postscript to Chapter 6 show the position has not greatly changed.

[2] Rhodes, op. cit., p. 226.

This pattern survived the defeat of the Conservatives in 1971, when all Council seats were recaptured by the Labour Party in which new leaders and new alignments had by then begun to emerge.

The Housing Manager who appeared in our original study was still the senior housing official at the time we returned to the Borough, but the Director of Development had overall responsibility for the housing programme. The Housing Manager was responsible to the Public Services Committee for housing management and relations with tenants, and to the Social Services Committee for the selection of tenants from the waiting-list. Rent policies were dealt with by the Council's Policy Committee—a central co-ordinating group set up on the advice of the management consultants—but that Committee's powers to fix rents had recently been reduced by the Housing Finance Act of 1972 which introduced common criteria and procedures for rents and rent rebates for all authorities in England and Wales. Responsibilities for land acquisitions, new building and rehabilitation fell to a Deputy Director of Development, with special responsibility for housing, working in the Directorate of Development under the Town Planning and Development Committee. That Committee was responsible for the selection of those to be rehoused in clearance schemes. Other housing powers—to make loans to house buyers and grants for house improvement, for example—rested with other Departments and Committees. This was a highly fragmented system to retain at a time when Ministers and conference speakers were repeatedly calling for a more comprehensive approach to housing problems, making better co-ordinated use of all the influences a Council can exert on the housing market,[1] but it was no more fragmented than the Tower Hamlets system briefly described in our postscript to Chapter 3 on Bethnal Green.

The London housing market was changing in unforeseen ways. The population of the inner Boroughs, already falling at the time of our original study, was declining still faster. Islington's fell from 261,000 to 199,000 between 1961 and 1971 as more and more young families moved out to the suburbs and beyond. This helped to ease the pressure on space. But the unprecedented rise in London house prices which has taken place in recent years was particularly dramatic in Islington which, unlike Tower Hamlets, attracted a continuing flow of house buyers. Speculators were attracted too, and there were many complaints about those who 'winkled out' sitting tenants in order to sell houses with vacant possession to newcomers. Unless they had special advantages of some kind, manual workers and people in the lower half of the income distribution depended increasingly on the Borough for any improvement in their housing standards. To help them, the Borough

---

[1] For an analysis of these proposals and the difficulties of implementing them, see Michael Harloe, Ruth Issacharoff and Richard Minns, *The Organization of Housing*. Heinemann, 1974.

set about acquiring large numbers of older rented houses—some 1,700 properties in the year before this postscript was written

There is now very little slum clearance of the sort which took place on the Pleydell Estate left to be done in Islington. The quality of the worst housing and the extent of overcrowding are not as bad as they used to be. Sites for new projects are usually chosen for one of three reasons: they contain a nucleus of bad housing, due for clearance, to which neighbouring property can be added; or some obsolete property, like a disused factory or market, presents a special opportunity for house building; or the area suffers from overcrowding and other forms of housing stress to which attention has been drawn by recurring public complaints. The Council examines the possibility of rehabilitation by private owners, before resorting to redevelopment. The pros and cons of rehabilitation (as opposed to redevelopment) and the social composition of different neighbourhoods and Council estates still provoke occasional controversies within the Labour group on the Council.

The total volume of building and rehabilitation is enormously larger than it was in Finsbury: Islington is currently rehousing over 2,000 households a year, working simultaneously on about 100 different projects, and considering about forty more on which some action, possibly by private owners, must soon be taken. (The Pleydell Estate is one of these: the tenements belonging to the Guinness Trust are now being demolished and the area rebuilt at lower densities by the Trust, with some help from the Borough in the rehousing of tenants.) As the main concentration of the programme moves northwards away from the centre of London, building is restricted by the planning policies of the Greater London Council and the central government to lower densities. High buildings, of the sort that were built on the Pleydell Estate, became increasingly common during the years after our study. The Ministry of Housing and Local Government encouraged this policy (which, with hindsight, many now regard as an expensive and inhumane architectural fashion) by offering additional subsidies for high building and by requiring the Boroughs to accept, for 40 per cent of their housing programmes, industrialised methods which could only be used economically in tall blocks. The tide of fashion turned in most of the London Boroughs shortly before the disastrous collapse of a tower block at Ronan Point. The termination of special subsidies for high building powerfully reinforced the trend to lower building. Neither the adoption of high buildings nor their abandonment were based on public, reasoned analysis of their economic costs or social consequences. Islington's projects are now usually built at 136 or 100 persons per acre—Council members would often prefer still lower densities—and blocks of flats rarely go as high as seven or eight storeys.

Developing much larger numbers of smaller sites at lower densities than Finsbury could do, the Borough generally finds it easier to satisfy objectors than it was in the project we studied, and negotiating delays are less destructive of the Borough's housing programme than they were in the much smaller and more densely built Borough of Finsbury. Objections to compulsory purchase and the compensation offered are still common. The numbers of planning objections to a new development depend heavily on the outcome of recent inquiries which show whether the central government is likely to back the local authority or the objectors. There may also be further public inquiries into road closures, but those too are rarer in smaller projects.

The rehabilitation schemes which are now increasingly common pose more complex problems. The Borough takes powers for compulsory purchase if the housing is owned, or may be bought, by landlords intent on squeezing out sitting tenants to secure the higher prices which can be got for empty houses, or if the property includes vacant accommodation needed in the scheme. Later the Borough consults residents about the future of the area, and may agree to lift compulsory purchase orders if convinced that owners are improving their houses on terms which will benefit sitting tenants. In these consultations it is the owner-occupiers who generally form the first and most effective pressure groups. Tenants, happy at first to await rehabilitation or rehousing, become restive or hostile later if left uncertain about their future for too long.

In 1973 the Council came to the conclusion that this system was not well co-ordinated: it did not, for example, provide good and continuous forecasts of the needs to be met and the resources available for the purpose in public and private sectors of the market. A Housing Committee has therefore been re-created to resume general responsibility for housing—but not land-use planning as well—and a new Co-ordinator of Housing Services is being appointed. The holder of this post will be generally responsible for helping the Committee formulate the Borough's housing strategy, and for implementing it.

Conclusion

Our original study showed how independent groups in the public and private sectors of the economy interact in the course of a major housing project. There was conflict within each sector as well as between local authorities and the public. The story had a fairly constructive outcome, thanks partly to a process of bargaining which yielded benefits to all concerned, and partly to the exercise of power by local government. This postscript enables us to take the discussion a little further.

The extension of the boundaries, powers and resources of the local housing authority, brought about by the reform of London government, reduced the Borough's dependence on the Greater London Council and the Ministry, and reduced the central government's opportunity and obligation to intervene as arbitrator between contending local authorities.

Conflicts in the public sector were not eliminated—some of those which continue can be glimpsed in this brief postscript—but many of them were internalised within the Borough's enlarged sphere of action.

Other developments have made conflicts of the kind that occurred when Finsbury was working on the Pleydell Estate much less common today. As the older, inner parts of London are rebuilt, the new Borough has turned its attention to less densely packed neighbourhoods. Islington handles far more projects and has a much larger staff to do the job. Conflicts are less severe when densities are lower because it is easier to find ways of satisfying competing land users; and a Borough which is working simultaneously on many projects comes under less pressure to buy off objectors than Finsbury experienced when most of its resources were committed to one major project on which the progress of its whole housing programme depended.

Our original study showed that firms and well-organised groups of private citizens (such as the Guinness Trust tenants) wielded considerable influence on the progress and outcome of this sort of project. This postscript reminds us again that there is seldom only one public with a claim to participate in decision-making; there are usually several, and their interests (like those of the owners and tenants of housing that is to be acquired for rehabilitation or redevelopment) often conflict. Likewise there is seldom only one bureaucracy with which the public has to do business: there may be conflicts between different levels of central and local government, between different departments of the same authority and different groups within one political party.

The task of launching and completing a major project in these circumstances calls for a combination of two distinct processes: the mobilisation of commitments to act (convincing people that something must and will be done) and the specification of the action to be taken (deciding exactly what to do). Logically it might seem more rational to decide what to do before agreeing to act. But in real life the two processes advance together. Having many other things to attend to, people do not get seriously involved in a project till they are convinced that action which might affect them is imminent. Without initial commitments to act, such as the compulsory purchase of housing that is to be rehabilitated, it is difficult to start clarifying what is to be done. Until the specification grows clearer (Is it to be redevelopment or rehabilitation? Of which houses? In what order?) many who must collaborate in the venture—by improving their property, for example—will be unwilling to act. Action, once it begins, rules out some of the options hitherto available: if speculators acquire houses, their tenants may be bought out or squeezed out; if the Council acquires them instead, owner-occupiers may be precluded from moving in. Each of these participants is free to act without waiting for the others; if the Council waits too long, it may find that speculators or owner-occupiers have already moved in.

Thus public authorities cannot decide exactly what to do before acting —commitment and specification must advance together[1]—and public participation in planning and housing projects cannot be a once-for-all thing, conducted and completed at the start, before goals are formulated or commitments made. To be effective participation must be a continuing or recurring process, engaging the relevant people in discussing the right questions at the right times at intervals throughout the project, and leading to successive decisions taken by those with power to act. Since conflicting interests will normally be at work, both amongst the public and within the bureaucracy, these decisions can never satisfy all concerned.

---

[1] For a fuller discussion of this point see Peter Levin, 'Commitment and Specificity in Urban Planning', *Town Planning Review*, April 1972.

CHAPTER 8

CRISIS IN A CANADIAN SERVICE FOR CHILDREN

This study deals with a period in the history of a voluntary agency. Important developments were initiated by new members of the agency's staff, but additional resources required to sustain these innovations were not forthcoming in sufficient quantity. The financial crisis that followed compelled a reappraisal of aims and methods which revealed differing perceptions of the situation and precipitated a conflict in which a widening circle of people was embroiled. The phases of this conflict, and the character and timing of the intervention which eventually resolved it may prove instructive.

The study of a Children's Department, presented in Chapter 6, posed a number of problems which had appeared in some earlier research carried out in a similar agency in Canada. The opportunity for an international comparison and the inherent interest of the Canadian story led us to add this study to the London cases. It deals with developments in a local Children's Aid Society which took place between 1952 and 1954, and the research was done during the following months, in the course of a broader study of the social services of Brockville, Ontario.[1] These social services and the legislation on which they are based have undergone major changes since then, but no attempt has been made to bring the account up to date. The Society's Board and staff and other members of the community gave generous help in the study, and we are most grateful for their willingness to let us use what was at times a painful experience for the purposes of this research.

All those working for the Society agreed that the growing emphasis laid on 'protection services', or preventive casework, constituted the most important recent development in their agency. This is the aspect of their work that we deal with. Since the Society and its environment will be unfamiliar to many readers, this report begins with two introductory sections: an outline of the responsibilities of Ontario's Children's Aid Societies and the way in which they are administered, followed by a brief sketch of the town and surrounding district that form the setting

[1] See D. V. Donnison, *Welfare Services in a Canadian Community*, Toronto University Press, 1957.

for the events to be described in the third section. The story ends with an appraisal of the changes that occurred, followed as usual by a discussion of more general issues.

Children's Aid Societies

At the time of this study there were fifty-three Children's Aid Societies in the province of Ontario. Most of their work fell under five headings: (i) the guardianship of children committed to their care by the courts; (ii) the provision of a social work service for families that have difficulty in bringing up their children; (iii) the arrangement of adoptions, including the placing of children with prospective adopters, the supervision of these homes during a trial year, and the provision of a report for the court that made the legal adoption; (iv) the selection of foster parents and adopting parents; (v) the provision of help for unmarried mothers. The Societies did a number of other things besides. They called on parents who were seeking a divorce whenever there were children under the age of sixteen in the family, and they presented reports to the provincial Supreme Court to help it decide who should have custody of the children. They made investigations for the Department of National Health and Welfare when the Department received complaints that people drawing family allowances were not spending the allowances on their children, or were failing to send their children to school. In the few places where there was no probation service (and the area studied was at that time one of them) the Societies were informed of all children due to appear in court and they provided the courts with reports on the home surroundings of these children. They might also be asked to supervise those found guilty.

The administration of these services was a complex business, for the Children's Aid Societies retained many of the characteristics of a voluntary organisation, yet from their beginnings in the last decade of the nineteenth century they had always had certain statutory duties for which they were responsible to the Provincial Government. Their incomes which were drawn partly from voluntary sources and partly from three different levels of government, and their accounting problems, their public relations—in fact all their work—reflected this dual statutory-voluntary constitution.

The Children's Aid Society studied was typical in having a Board of not more than twenty members elected at an annual general meeting to which were entitled to come all who paid a subscription of at least one dollar a year or a life membership fee of fifty dollars. The membership of the Board was in practice decided by the Board's own nominating committee which was called upon each year to prepare a list of names for the approval of the general meeting. The Board's principal members were the President—normally serving for about three years—a Vice-President, a Secretary and a Treasurer. All of them were unpaid. There was also an Honorary President—a distinguished member of the community who occasionally presided on formal occasions.

At the time of this study the Society's paid staff consisted of an executive Director, seven case workers, an office manager, three clerical workers and a cleaner.

A Children's Aid Society only received children into its care when they had been committed to its wardship by a Juvenile and Family Court. Committal was made on grounds of neglect,[1] and might be 'temporary' (for one year at a time) or 'permanent'—which meant that the Society assumed full parental rights and duties unless wardship was brought to an end by a resolution of the Board confirmed by the Provincial government's Director of Child Welfare.[2] In practice, children were seldom brought to court for proceedings leading to temporary or permanent wardship unless the Society had already spent some time in attempting to help the parents fulfil their responsibilities. Once committed to a Society's care, children were in nearly every case placed in foster homes and supervised by the Society's workers. The costs of caring for a Society's wards were met by the municipal authorities in whose areas the children previously lived, but 25 per cent of these contributions were refunded to the municipalities by the Provincial government. The court might also order parents to contribute to the maintenance of their children. The sum to be paid to Societies for the maintenance of their wards was a fixed *'per diem* rate', determined by the local magistrate or judge. At the time of this study it was the responsibility of Boards to apply to the courts when necessary for revisions of their *per diem* rates.[3]

The work of caring for children took by far the largest share of the Societies' resources of time and money. They were responsible for this work to the Director of Child Welfare, the head of the Child Welfare

---

[1] The legal definition of 'neglect' inevitably left ample scope for interpretation According to the Provincial Child Welfare Act of 1954, which slightly extended the definitions given in the earlier Children's Protection Act, neglected children included those with no one to look after them, those whose parents or guardians were unable or unwilling to care for them properly, those whose parents or guardians permitted or encouraged them to break the law, those who associated with thieves, drunkards, prostitutes and other undesirable people, and those judged by qualified psychiatrists to be rejected or deprived of affection to a degree sufficient to endanger their emotional or mental development.

[2] At the time of the study a new Act came into force, limiting the period of temporary wardship to a total of two years and permitting Societies to terminate permanent wardship any time by bringing wards to court for the magistrate to determine whether 'the welfare of any child might best be served by the termination of . . . permanent commitment'. Child Welfare Act 1954, S. 16 (13) and S. 16 (14); Province of Ontario.

[3] Subsequent legislation required the courts to re-consider the rates annually, and provided for a standard code, drawn up by the Director of Child Welfare, for the estimation of these rates. (Child Welfare Act 1954, S. 24.)

Branch of Ontario's Department of Public Welfare. They sent monthly reports to the Branch, and the Branch issued regulations, set standards and inspected each Society at least once a year.

The Societies' 'preventive casework', directed at children living in their own homes, had always been encouraged by the Provincial authorities. As early as 1897 the Provincial Superintendent of Neglected and Dependant Children (later called the Director of Child Welfare) wrote in his annual report that 'In all child-protection and philanthropic work generally the true aim should be the conservation of family home life . . . It is true that the removal of children from the control of vicious parents is advocated, but this is only as a last resort, and when all reasonable likelihood of securing better training for the child in its own home has been given up.'[1] (An outlook that was in some ways in advance of our own Children Act of 1948.)

But in contrast to child care services, for which responsibilities and standards had long been precisely defined, preventive work had largely been left to the Societies to develop according to their own lights and resources, with some guidance and encouragement from the Child Welfare Branch's Inspectors. The Societies' Boards had to finance this work from voluntary contributions—through subscriptions, bequests, flag days and house-to-house campaigns—to which the Provincial government added two grants: a sum equal to 25 per cent of the money raised from voluntary sources, and an annual grant (which at the time of this study had been temporarily fixed according to a formula that in effect gave most to those Societies judged in the past to have been most efficient). Municipal authorities were also allowed to make grants to the Societies, and a few Societies had been able to secure generous help from this source, arguing that local authorities could save themselves the costs of child care by enabling the Societies to prevent families breaking up.

With some modifications, the Societies' adoption work followed a pattern similar to that found in adoption agencies in England, but the probationary period, when children are fostered without payment with prospective adopters, lasted a year, the Societies were not required to secure the consent of parents when arranging for the adoption of their permanent wards, and there was no 'guardian *ad litem*'. The Societies, when presenting their reports to the County Courts, acted—legally speaking—as advisers to the Director of Child Welfare whose responsibility it was to provide much of the evidence required by these courts when considering adoption applications.

The selection of foster homes and adoption homes also followed a familiar pattern, except that foster care and adoption were both pursued on a much larger scale than would be considered possible by most English Children's Departments. Thus the Society studied had some

[1] *Neglected and Dependant Children.* Ontario, Report of Superintendent, 1897, p. 6.

250 children in its care, of whom 9 per cent were in 'adoption probation homes' (thirty-one adoptions had been completed during the previous year). All but 8 per cent of these 250 wards had been boarded out, the few exceptions being children placed in mental hospitals, boarded out by other Societies or otherwise provided for. The provision of foster care as the normal—indeed, the almost universal—method of child care demanded skill and organisation on a scale that is not required in agencies whose foster care is restricted to a smaller number of foster parents who are relied on to look after a minority of children specially selected from those in the agency's care. In the larger Societies the finding of foster homes was often handled by a separate department, but this work was administratively and financially a part of their child care service.

Societies encouraged unmarried mothers to seek help early in their pregnancy, but their first contact with these clients usually arose when the Child Welfare Branch (to which the provincial Registrar-General reported all illegitimate births) passed on information about the birth to the appropriate Society whose duty it was to write to the mother offering to help her gain her legal rights and make plans for her future and the future of her child. Unmarried mothers might then call on the Society or ignore the letter. In this work, which was closely related to their child care and adoption services, the Societies again acted as the agents of the Director of Child Welfare.

This outline of the functions of Children's Aid Societies presents a simplified and somewhat unreal picture. The Societies and the problems they face vary widely. At one extreme are complex organisations, found in two or three big cities, with a large professionally trained staff, working in collaboration with family casework services, health services, public housing authorities, a probation service, child guidance clinics, children's homes of many kinds, and other agencies. At the other extreme are small Societies, thankful if one member of their staff of three or four has relevant training of some sort; these workers may be called upon to cover a sparsely populated territory of several hundred square miles—much of it impassable in the depth of winter—with the support of an equally small public health unit, a few welfare or relieving officers (typically part-timers) and no other public services except the schools, the churches and the police.

The links the Societies were called upon to sustain with other institutions should be borne in mind. They drew family allowances from the *Federal government* for all their wards and made investigations on behalf of the Department of National Health and Welfare at Ottawa. They could only be set up with the approval of the *Provincial government*, and were legally responsible to that government for much of their child care, adoption and unmarried parents' services; they sent monthly reports to the Provincial authorities in Toronto, and received regular guidance, inspection and grants of money in return. Moreover, if they failed in their duties the Provincial government had power to dissolve a Society, take over its property and direct its chief officer to carry on its statutory services. They relied on the *municipal councils* in their districts for the bulk of their incomes (in the form of payments for the maintenance of wards) and they could receive further grants from these local authorities. The councils were frequently represented on the Societies' Boards but at the time of this study there was no effective requirement that this be arranged. The Societies often appeared in *Juvenile* and *Family Courts* seeking wardship of children, and they made occasional applications to these courts for changes in their *per diem* rates; unless there was mutual trust between the Societies and the magistrates (who were professional lawyers, appointed to full-time, permanent posts by the Provincial government) neither of these procedures would work smoothly. The Societies also had frequent contact with the *County Court* (whose judges were appointed by the Federal government and therefore tended at the time of this study to differ from the magistrates in their political allegiances). In these courts they presented evidence in adoption and affiliation proceedings.

The Societies also had to maintain sound relations with the *public*— or rather with many 'publics': with adopters who tended to come from the professional and business sections of the community, with foster parents who were more likely to be lower-middle and solid working class people, with contributors drawn from all sections of the community, with Board members and others who held leading positions in voluntary and statutory welfare services, with clients who were predominantly unskilled and poorer people, and with clients' relatives and neighbours and the various professional workers (doctors, teachers, ministers, etc.) who often provided the channels through which a Society first heard of those whom it helped.

The Setting

The Society that forms the subject of this study served Brockville, with a population of about 14,000, two smaller towns each with about 4,000 people, and the two counties surrounding them—the whole area containing some 60,000 people spread over a rectangle about 50 miles long and 30 miles wide, divided between five municipal authorities. All three towns lay on the main highway that runs along Lake Ontario and the St Lawrence between Toronto and Montreal; smaller villages had grown up around road and rail intersections in the rocky or gently rolling farming country to the north. The Society's headquarters was in Brockville; other services which covered much of this area also operated from the town—the labour exchange, the Public Health Unit the Red Cross and the Canadian Legion, for instance.

Brockville is the main shopping and marketing centre of the region, an old town that grew from settlements established by United Empire Loyalists who sought refuge here after the American revolution. By the middle of the last century it had become a railway junction, a market town and a small but busy centre of industry. Later the place became famous for the great wealth of a few of its citizens—most of it earned in big cities across the American border—and for its beauty, its respectability and its tendency to stagnation. In 1906 a local journalist described the town thus:

"... while the Creator of the Universe did much in preparing a superb location for Brockville, the people whom he has honoured by sending them here to live have done and are still doing their share. It is true there is no mad, boom rush in the old town and never has been, but, like the handsome structures which grace its streets, Brockville's mercantile and business interests are mostly on a solid foundation, and unmoved by those fluctuations in trade that invariably drive to the wall the financial weaklings. Brockville's business men are neither splurgers nor plungers, nor yet are they plodders . . ."

After the second world war a new highway, the St Lawrence seaway, and the gathering pace of Canada's industrial growth brought new factories, new people and new enterprise to the district. The local 'aristocracy' was still accorded the respect due to public service and inherited wealth, but a new class of managers, business and professional men and their wives had taken over leadership of most of Brockville's institutions. Of those in proprietary, managerial, professional, commercial or clerical jobs, little more than a half had lived in the town for ten years; those holding the chief positions in the town's welfare services included an even larger proportion of newcomers. Of those doing manual work, about three-quarters had lived in the town for more than ten years.[1]

Life was comfortable by British standards, but no better than Canada's average. A quarter of the town's households lived in flats and apartments, and most of the rest lived in owner-occupied, detached houses. Practically every house had its own garden. At the time of the 1951 census, nine out of ten households had their own bath or shower, and the great majority had a washing machine, refrigerator, telephone and vacuum cleaner. There was one car for every four people. Living standards in the surrounding countryside were somewhat lower and even in the towns there were a few families living in houses scarcely better than shacks.

The district contained a few Roman Catholics and small groups of Dutch immigrants, but the population was mainly protestant and of British origin. The Loyal Orange Lodge, the Freemasons and other 'fraternal orders' still flourished.

People came and went frequently, there was no local accent and most

[1] See *Welfare Services in a Canadian Community*.

CRISIS IN A CANADIAN SERVICE FOR CHILDREN   175

of the adults were not born in the districts where they had come to live. Nevertheless there were strong local loyalties and a thriving local social life: people read the local newspaper (founded in 1820) and listened to local radio stations, and they turned out to performances of their operatic, film and concert societies in numbers that would put any British community of similar size to shame. They complained they were overrun with strangers and no longer knew their neighbours, yet even in Brockville people noted new faces and kept track of their neighbours' affairs. Thus at the time of this study the new Director of the Children's Aid Society was favourably commented upon—not because he was a good social worker or a sound administrator, but because 'he takes his (own) children to the right shows'. In the smaller towns and villages everyone seemed to know everyone. Local services were provided by a rudimentary but reasonably effective profusion of nominated and elected *ad hoc* authorities (for health, housing, protestant schools, Roman Catholic schools, recreation, etc.) and by voluntary organisations. The hierarchy of social classes was less obtrusive than England's and these distinctions were overlaid by others not of a hierarchical kind—distinctions between newcomers and local boys, between the smart set and those with more modest, frugal and sober habits, between Liberals and Conservatives, between the young and the middle-aged, and between thriving religious denominations of a dozen different kinds.

The Development of 'Preventive Casework' in the Children's Aid Society

The local Children's Aid Society was founded in 1894 when a public meeting resolved 'to bring the matter before the official member of each church in town . . . requesting them to name two gentlemen and two ladies to act as directors on the board of the proposed corporation'. Three years later the Society extended its work to the two neighbouring Counties. In 1901 the Provincial authorities urged its Board to provide a shelter for homeless and neglected children, but it was not until 1912 that the shelter was founded—through the generosity of one of the town's leading families. In 1914 the Society appointed a paid agent for the first time—a part-timer who was also the local YMCA 'boys' work secretary'. Children were cared for in the shelter, but little was done to find foster homes for them or to help the families from which they came. In 1916 the agent left to join the army.

The Society was put on its feet in 1934 when it appointed as its first full-time executive Director (or Superintendent as he was then called) a man who had for many years played a leading part on its Board. He had been the local director of an immigration society which brought children over from Britain and placed them on farms throughout the district, and his long experience of foster care revolutionised the

Children's Aid Society. The shelter was transformed into a reception and training centre (in the face of considerable opposition from local benefactors who had founded and supported it) and more children were boarded out—many of them in 'free' or 'wage' homes where they received board and lodging in return for personal service or a part of their wages. Attention was then given to the prevention of neglect and more staff had to be found. In 1935 the Society's first trained social worker was appointed—a graduate of the University of Toronto's School of Social Work. She worked with the Society until 1953 and became widely known and respected in the district. She and the Director were helped from time to time by untrained, temporary workers who were called 'case-aides'. From about 1936 onwards an appeal was made for voluntary contributions nearly every year.

The war brought new demands. The armed forces and new departments of government asked for investigation and supervision of soldiers' families and asked the Society to help with the administration of allowances paid to them. A special worker was appointed to give her full time to these duties. In a report prepared by the Director in 1944 the Society was described as 'a private organisation which could logically develop its services to a much further degree and form the backbone, particularly in rural areas, of an adequate family welfare service . . .' By 1947 the superintendent had a staff of two trained social workers, two case-aides and three clerical workers. Next year the shelter was closed. Soon after, the Society's 'Women's Auxiliary', which had devoted itself to caring for the shelter and the children who lived in it, was also brought to an end.

In September 1952 two more trained workers were appointed—two men who had just graduated from the Toronto School. They came with a firm conviction that children lost more when removed from affectionate parents than they could ever gain from the orderly and healthy conditions of a foster home, and they looked upon child care as one aspect of a wider service designed to enable families to cope with their problems and take charge of their own affairs. In their casework they were less willing than some of their colleagues to seek or use the advice of relieving officers, ministers and other 'lay' people, they refused to divulge information about their clients to people with whom these things had previously been shared, whenever possible they attempted to make appointments before calling on their clients, and they tended to use a technical language—a jargon, some people called it—largely derived from psychoanalytic sources. Both were married men in their early thirties, both had had fairly wide experience before entering social work and both had some private income. In the small and rather conservative communities of the district, their new methods and attitudes were a potentially explosive intrusion.

By this time the Director had four full-time trained caseworkers, another trained man working part-time, and two workers without professional training. The trained workers were given very wide discretion to develop their own methods.

The Director was an active but reserved man, with a strong sense of duty. He had lived in the town for about forty years and had invested some money in rented houses bought during the depression. His friends were few but loyal. He was due to retire in three years' time.

A year or two earlier the Society had acquired a new President. She was the wife of a factory manager who had come to the town about five years before. She had been a Board member for several years and had already taken the lead in establishing and running a number of voluntary organisations in the district. She was an intelligent, loquacious and compelling woman with tremendous drive and a tendency to inspire admiration or enmity among those with whom she came in contact. She was in her late forties and had a Ph.D in Sociology.

In March 1949 the Society had 305 children in its care and was working with fifty-one unmarried mothers and eighty-four 'protection' cases involving children living in their own homes. Its income, which had exceeded its expenditure by only 803 dollars during the previous year, was drawn from the following sources:

Income of the Society in 1948–9

	$	$
Provincial and municipal payments for maintenance of wards*	50,486	
Municipal grants	3,493	
Provincial grants	1,500	
Payments for services to Federal government departments	732	
Family allowances for wards*	10,957	
Total from public sources		67,168
Donations, subscriptions and bequests	4,319	
Revenue from investments	189	
Contributions from parents for maintenance of wards*	7,630	
Miscellaneous	126	
Total from private sources		12,264
TOTAL INCOME		$79,432
Surplus of income over expenditure		$803

*Items directly related to number of wards in the Society's care.

During the next few years the numbers of children in care rose slightly, but increases in income (due to larger payments from Provincial and municipal authorities) failed to keep pace with rising expenditure, and by 1952 the Society was drawing on its reserves to the extent of some $4,000 a year.

The arrival of the new men precipitated a crisis. Fewer children were committed to the Society's care, and larger numbers were returned to their own homes. This struck at all the main sources of the Society's income—maintenance payments from Provincial and municipal governments, family allowances, and parental contributions. No compensating economies were made; indeed more workers were being employed, the costs of preventive casework had increased, and foster parents were being given a freer hand in clothing and equipping foster children. A comparison with figures for 1953, presented below, shows that the proportion of income directly related to the numbers of wards in the Society's care remained unchanged (at 87 per cent of the total) during a period when the Society's resources were being increasingly turned to other work.

By 1953 the Society was going bankrupt. During the last nine months of the year[1] the Society was overspending by more than $1,000 a month. All available investments had already been sold and the bank was becoming restive about the Society's mounting overdraft. Its manager was a member of the Board. Appeals for grants were made to the municipal councils in the Society's area, but without success. The annual financial campaign for voluntary contributions was a failure, either through bad organisation or through lack of public confidence in the Society.

Meanwhile relations amongst the staff deteriorated and their disagreements were reflected among Board members. The President and some of her colleagues were convinced they should press on with the development of preventive casework, even if the resources for it were not immediately available. Her determination to back the new element in the Society and to be available to any of the staff who wished to express their views to the Board led its members to intervene in the daily work of the agency to an unusual extent; on at least one occasion the President asked a caseworker to visit a family that was already being helped by another worker. The Provincial authorities were aware of these difficulties and Supervisors from the Child Welfare Branch came down twice to discuss the situation, but little was achieved.

Possibly as a last resort, the Director suggested to one or two members of the staff that the number of wards (and hence the Society's income) might be increased if they visited certain families whose children had been in their care in the past. Increasingly disturbed by this and other developments, the two new men then called on the President to tell her it was becoming more and more difficult for them to play a constructive part in the Society: in effect they offered their resignations.

---

[1] The Society's accounting year was at this point altered to coincide with the calendar year; hence the shorter period covered by these figures.

Income of the Society, April–December 1953

	$	$
Provincial and municipal payments for maintenance of wards*	49,113	
Municipal grants	1,987	
Provincial grants	2,582	
Payments for services to Federal government departments	814	
Family allowances for wards*	7,844	
Total from public sources		62,340
Donations, subscriptions and bequests	4,198	
Revenue from investments	—	
Contributions from parents for maintenance of wards*	4,476	
Total from private sources		8,674
TOTAL INCOME		$71,014
Deficit		$10,238

*Items directly related to number of wards in the Society's care.

But they were persuaded to stay on. The President was already convinced that a new Director must be found, but she knew her Board was sharply divided on this issue. Shortly afterwards the Director himself offered to resign, saying he no longer felt he had the confidence of the Board. This offer was also refused.

Meanwhile it became clear that influential people in the municipal councils and elsewhere were not willing to rescue the Society unless changes were made in its leadership, and the Director became the focus of a good deal of unpleasant gossip. Eventually, at the end of July 1953, he again offered his resignation and this time it was accepted unanimously. The part-time trained worker (who had become a temporary full-timer and managed to remain on reasonably good terms with all concerned) was asked if he would assume the Directorship, but he refused. The Society's troubles were known in the profession, and no one would apply for the post. Eventually one of the new men was made Director, at first in an acting capacity. The Society's first trained worker (appointed eighteen years earlier) and another social worker resigned.

Meanwhile the costs of maintaining the Society's wards were rising and an application was made to the Magistrates' Court for an increase in the *per diem* rate from $1·15 to $1·41. The application was commenced on 13 October 1953, and opposed by counsel representing some of the municipal authorities which would have to pay the increased charges. After a long hearing, ending on 3 November, the Magistrate issued a detailed and carefully reasoned judgement, finding 'with some hesitation' that $1·23 per day was 'a reasonable sum to be paid by a municipality for the maintenance of a child by the Society'. His hesitations arose largely from the fact that the Society had not made (and many thought could not make) a clear distinction between the portion of its expenses incurred for 'protection' work with children in their own homes, and the portion incurred for the maintenance of its wards. He noted the 'apparent animosity between the Society and the municipal councils', and drew attention to the fact that the Society was sole judge of the way in which its work was distributed and its expenses allocated, while the councils had no control whatever over its affairs. True, the councils nominated six of the Society's Board members but 'their qualifications are questionable unless they individually subscribe and so become members'. (He probably knew that the municipal representatives did not play an active part in the Board's work.) Since the municipal liability for maintenance of wards could not be escaped, the Court held it to be the Society's responsibility to draw up accounts distinguishing clearly between the two main parts of its work and to 'limit itself in the protective and preventive aspect of its work to that which can be done with available voluntary contributions no matter how desirable an extension of that phase of its work may seem to the Society'. Meanwhile, the Magistrate pointed out, it was open to the municipal authorities to employ people to investigate wardship applications and to oppose these applications in court, to show when parents of wards were able to contribute to their maintenance, and to ensure that their contributions were fully paid. They might also reduce the numbers of children coming into the Society's care by carrying on their own preventive work or by contributing to such work done by the Society. (Taken together, these suggestions would have virtually amounted to a statutory take-over of the service.)

The Society was sinking fast, for this application had been the last shot in its locker. Questions were being asked about the uses to which family allowances had been put, for this item of income was paid into a separate trust fund which helped to reduce the interest payments on the mounting overdraft. The Honorary President (a Senator and a wealthy and respected member of the community who had given generous support in the past) complained that a large donation made for specified purposes had already been spent in other ways. He resigned, writing that he could no longer be associated with the Society. Finally the Board itself resigned in a body.

At this point the Provincial government's Director of Child Welfare had to intervene. After a preliminary and fruitless meeting with those who had been on the Board, he invited them, the staff, municipal councillors, members and supporters of the Society, to a meeting. At this meeting he urged all present to sink their differences for the good of the cause; he reminded them that he was responsible for the 250 children in their care, and suggested that he could only carry out his responsibilities at the expense of the municipal councils, with the help of a staff of social workers—probably the very people whom the Society had employed, with salaries quite as generous as those the Society had paid. Thus he made it clear that his Branch was responsible for ensuring that most of the Society's work continued and had power to fulfil these responsibilities at the expense of the local municipalities. (In fact, so drastic a step would only have been taken as a last resort. It would have been politically unpopular, and the preventive social work—which lay at the root of the crisis—would have had to be abandoned since the Provincial government had no legal powers to carry it out.)

The deadlock then broke. The Board resumed office. A new application was made for revision of the *per diem* rate, supported this time with all the statistics that could be devised and—more important—not opposed by the municipal councils. This application was successful. Some of the councils gave additional grants to the Society. The agency's premises were sold (a large house with rooms originally used for the temporary accommodation of children) and the staff moved to cramped, but businesslike, offices rented in the commercial centre of the town. Subsequent flag days and appeals were more successful, and before long the Society's finances and the morale of its Board and staff were greatly improved. Two years later the new Director joined the supervisory staff of the Provincial Child Welfare Branch and the other 'new man' succeeded him.

Reappraisal

What changes had taken place? What had this crisis been about? The growing emphasis on preventive social work was the development stressed by those leading the Society in 1954. But in fact there had not been a striking change during this period in the distribution of the Society's activities. The 305 children in the Society's care in 1949 had fallen to 248 by 1954. The 51 unmarried parent cases being dealt with had risen to 73—numbers no larger than those found on the Society's books ten years earlier. The 84 'protection' cases had risen to 103, yet the most striking increase in this element of the case-load had taken place not during this period but between 1944 and 1949, when the number of protection cases had more than doubled.

These changes were visible in the Society's accounts—but barely visible. The proportion of total expenditure devoted to 'child care' fell from 83 per cent to 76 per cent between 1949 and 1954, 'investigation and preventive field work' rose from 4 to 7 per cent, and 'administrative and other' expenses rose from 13 to 17 per cent. By 1954 the Society calculated that 30 per cent of its field workers' time, equivalent to 34 per cent of field workers' salaries, was devoted to work with children living in their own homes, and the rest to children in the Society's care. It is even less plausible to suggest that preventive casework was at this time first accepted as one of the Society's major functions: statements have been quoted which show that this was always thought to be an important function of this and every other Children's Aid Society.

There were cynics who said that nothing more than a palace revolution had occurred. The staff, and particularly the leading people among them, had changed. Yet this was no trivial change. New methods and a new approach appeared in the Society's work: something that can be illustrated more easily than measured.

The Society began as an offshoot of church and school, teaching parents and children to accept the standards for which these institutions stood. This approach, characteristic of a benevolent police force, was still reflected in the Annual Report for 1925, written by the first Director when he had been a member of the Board.

'During childhood character is in the making; good and bad tendencies are struggling for mastery; the soul is in a state of flux. Parents are entrusted with the most delicate, the most susceptible, the most precious of all raw materials. If they do not mould it, the World, the Flesh and the Devil will . . . This problem must be borne by the home, the church and the school. The Children's Aid Society exists to see that these *three agencies* have a chance to function upon every child . . . we are endeavouring by persuasion, encouragement and threats to have delinquent parents remedy the existing evils.'

By 1953 a changed emphasis was apparent. A leaflet circulated during the first campaign for voluntary contributions after the appointment of the new Director read as follows:

'Some broken homes can be rebuilt—through making the parents aware of their parental responsibilities—through assisting the parents to strengthen the emotional bonds of family living—through helping the parents to find ways and means of securing the minimum physical standards consistent with their children's health and welfare—through planning with the parents all the details, emotional and physical, necessary for the re-establishment of the home and the return of their children.'

The practical implications of this change sometimes appeared in the Society's case records. In 1944 a social worker visited some foster parents who were having trouble with one of the Society's wards. She reported that 'the foster parents have endeavoured in every conceivable way [to correct his behaviour] by not giving him spending money, sending him to bed, even giving corporal punishment—which was not approved—but with little results. [He] still comes home with pencils, erasers, etc. which belong to other children.' Ten years later the same boy was again giving trouble in another foster home. Another social worker visited him and reported: 'I tried to get [his foster father] to express what [the boy] did or did not do that "griped" him . . . he needs a man to whom he can relate and identify . . . and resents [his foster father's] rejecting attitude towards him.' The Society's aim in both cases was the same—to help the boy live happily in his foster home— but its approach to the problem was different. In 1954 the Society no longer looked merely at the foster parents' methods of discipline; it studied the unspoken feelings of the boy and his foster parents in an attempt to help them live happily with each other. The report made in 1944 might have come from an experienced layman; the report made in 1954 is that of a professional doing a job for which specific training is required, and for which—rightly or wrongly—a new language had been developed.

A similar contrast may be seen in two letters sent at different periods in the Society's history to unmarried mothers. This was the form used early in 1953:

'The registration of the birth of the above-named child to you has been reported to us as is required by law. The purpose, of course, is that there may be assurance of the welfare of the child and that our report thereon, may be placed with the Department of Public Welfare, Toronto.

'It would appear to be best in the interest of all concerned, that you would first come to see us and give us certain required information and assurance.

'It is, of course, a part of our responsibility to give you assurance of such assistance as is available under the Children of Unmarried Parents Act which we can explain when we see you.

'Please co-operate as suggested and help us to avoid the necessity of other less desirable or convenient approaches.'

This was the form adopted in the following year:

'The registration of the birth of your child has been reported to us as is required by law.

'The law provides help for you, whether or not you are keeping your baby, both in planning for your child's future and in getting financial assistance from the father of the child.

'We are required to send a report to the Provincial Director of Child Welfare. We would like, therefore, to discuss your plans for your child with you as soon as is convenient. Please be assured that all information is confidential.'

The first letter emphasises the Society's need for 'information' and 'assurance' about the welfare of the child, and threatens 'less desirable or convenient approaches' if co-operation is not forthcoming. The second offers the mother help in making plans for herself and her baby, and promises confidential treatment of the case.

The change in the Society's role in the community is best illustrated by the help its workers sought from other people. In earlier days they frequently consulted others about the families with which they were concerned. In dealing with complaints about a family living on relief a social worker noted in her report that she had asked for the help of the Relieving Officer and 'He called on Mrs Y and warned her very strongly against this drinking party in her home'. The Society sought guidance from ministers, doctors, business people and others, particularly when selecting adopting or foster parents. Later the Society still asked for the help of these people, but it was help of other kinds. It asked them to attend meetings and discuss its work, to sit on its Board, to organise its fund-raising campaigns and contribute to its funds, to adopt its children and serve as foster parents. It seldom asked for their guidance in its dealings with individual cases.

These conclusions would not be accepted by all who took part in the events described. To some, the central feature of these two years was a struggle for power that ended in victory for the President, retirement for the Director and promotion for two young men. Others saw little in the story but a financial crisis, brought upon themselves by a well-intentioned but unbusinesslike group of people. According to another version, the crisis took the Society one more step away from its origins as a local voluntary organisation, controlled and supported by a small group of local citizens, and one more step towards becoming a district office of a Provincial government service. All were agreed that a famous victory had been won, but contenders and observers gave differing accounts of who had won and what they had been fighting about. In our opinion all were at least partly right.

We made no attempt to discover whether the Society's clients were aware that any change had taken place.

DISCUSSION

When those who provide a social service become convinced that their service is bad, perhaps even inhuman, should they press on with reform and turn a blind eye to signals of approaching disruption and bankruptcy, determined that their agency should if necessary die in a good cause? When a man has done more than anyone else to raise a service to its present level and then seems to stand in the way of further progress in the last years before his retirement, should one maintain the standards of tolerance and kindness that ought to apply in relations between neighbours and fellow citizens, or should further improvement of the service come first? These are important questions, familiar to every experienced administrator. Research can only pose and clarify such problems; it cannot resolve them.

We endeavour here to identify the principal phases of the development described, and the factors that played a part in each. Developments examined in previous studies were initiated partly by changes in the resources available for the provision of a service (as in Bethnal Green's switch to slum clearance) partly by changes in the scale and character of demand for a service (as in the development of the Home Help service) and partly by changes in the number and character of the people providing the service (as in the cases of the Children's Department and, again, in the Home Help service)—though in none of these cases was the total development due to these factors alone. In the service discussed here—as in others whose character depends primarily on the people providing the service, rather than on financial resources and the terms on which they are made available—it was the growth and character of the staff that played the 'leading' part in the development of policies. But while changes in the staff initiated new developments, many other factors became important once these developments began.

Opportunity for change came with the great increase in staff and resources during the decade after the war. The training and character of the staff recruited did a lot to determine the nature of the developments that followed, but the Society did not recruit its first trained workers at this time—nor even the first from the Toronto School of Social Work. (A trained person with inadequate resources and a vast caseload is often forced to work in ways that differ little from those of the untrained.) More money, more staff, new blood and a light rein on all concerned permitted new elements to develop within the service. But these innovations were expensive, and a growing volume of resources was needed to sustain them. This phase could not continue once the Society was confronted with a growing deficit in its accounts. Differing approaches became conflicting approaches as threatened bankruptcy forced the Society to reappraise its work and its priorities.

Increased resources provide opportunities for experiment and development, but it is the scarcities that often follow from more ambitious work which compel people to choose between abandoning an experiment or accepting it as a recognised part of the service. The limitations which confront those developing new features of an agency's work may appear in the form of a lack of legal powers (as in the Children's Department case, to some extent) in the form of a shortage of staff (as in the Children's Department and Home Help cases) or in the form of other shortages—of office space or equipment, for example. In a voluntary agency, the development of whose work depends on financial resources rather than legal powers, the scope for innovation will often be determined largely by the money available—as in this case. The discretion given to the Society's social workers could not continue unrestricted and the underlying vagueness about the Society's principal functions had to be clarified when further development brought the threat of bankruptcy. Those responsible for the agency were then drawn into increasingly direct and detailed interventions in its daily work. This occurred more or less accidentally, but a tightening of central controls is a common feature in services experiencing a growth of staff and a development of functions until new conventions are established and greater discretion can again be given to field workers. (The same process occurred in the National Assistance Board case.) Clarification of the Society's aims and methods eventually emerged in the course of a struggle for power in which the Board and its staff, the municipal councils, the Provincial Child Welfare Branch, the magistrate's court and private citizens were all involved.

Economic and social changes taking place in the surrounding district exercised a considerable influence on the outcome. The 'professionalisation' of the Society's staff and its growing dependence on the Provincial government were only one small example of a similar professionalisation and centralisation of industry, commerce and government to be seen throughout the district. The 'new young men' among the Society's staff found allies among the new class of migrant middle class people who played an increasingly active and dominant part, both in the affairs of local voluntary bodies and in commercial, industrial and government institutions which were to a growing extent controlled from major centres outside the district and managed by people brought in from outside. As the wife of a migrant factory manager, the President of the Board herself illustrated and represented these economic and social changes.

But no real progress could be made towards the resolution of the Society's problems until every available gun had been brought to bear in the battle and the balance of contending forces became clear. The Provincial Director of Child Welfare provided the final impetus to a solution by threatening to take over the statutory parts of the Society's work and charge their cost to the municipalities, but it is doubtful whether this step would have proved so decisive had it been attempted before every other available solution had been tried and every other source of influence had been brought to bear. The 'timing' of his intervention was well judged. Had he acted earlier his intervention would have been regarded by many as an unjustifiable Provincial government interference in local affairs, but at the point when he called a meeting with all concerned his action merely confronted them with the ultimate consequences of continued intransigeance.

In the case of the London Children's Department it was shown that people approaching a problem with different frames of reference describe the issues at stake in different ways, but are nevertheless capable—without abandoning their different approaches—of collaborating in solutions which accord with the aspirations of each participant. Indeed, each may claim authorship of the solutions devised. In this case, too, the people involved approached a problem with different frames of reference, interpreting the issues in very different ways. But for a while no mutually satisfactory solutions could be found. Their objectives were not merely different; they were irreconcilable.

The deadlock was hardened by other features of the situation. Agencies controlling resources that were vital to the development of the Society—the municipalities in particular—had no effective channel of communication (or failed to use the channels available) for expressing their views or for learning at first hand about the Society's needs. Such a situation inevitably tended to provoke a refusal to participate—'strike action'—when the Society pressed on with developments which were not properly understood or accepted by those who had to play a part in them. In a north American community large sums of money are raised for charity, largely through the organising capacity and social pressures exerted by local leaders—frequently managers in commercial and industrial firms, who organise fund raising 'campaigns'. But these leaders show a marked reluctance to commit themselves to campaigns that are unlikely to succeed. The social and professional rewards of the heavy work involved depend on the success of the campaign. Thus a change, real or assumed, in public attitudes to a voluntary agency can very quickly have an impact on the agency's financial resources. Meanwhile several members of the staff who were most heavily involved had readily marketable professional qualifications, and three of them had private sources of income. They were thus able to accept the consequences of determined pursuit of their objectives, should resignation become necessary. A solution could only be found when some people withdrew altogether from the Society and the municipal authorities were compelled to accept that the bulk of their financial obligations were inescapable—though they might perhaps be reduced by the growth of the preventive work which the Society was endeavouring to develop.

It is tempting to suggest that the problems revealed in this case were a product of some of the distinctive and forceful personalities in the story. Personalities clearly played a major part in determining the character and intensity of the crisis, but difficulties of the kind that arose in this Society are inherent in its constitution, and the Provincial authorities have had to intervene in similar crises in a number of other Children's Aid Societies. The Society combined functions which were in England performed at this time by the Children's Departments, the National Society for the Prevention of Cruelty to Children, adoption and moral welfare agencies, and the Probation Service. Many would applaud this attempt to integrate services designed to meet closely related needs, and to cope explicitly with problems that the subdivided English system conceded. Though the stresses on those administering the services may be severe, the children probably benefit. The Society's work, however, was divided up in an odd and arbitrary fashion: a child in trouble at home constituted a 'protection' case, but when he entered the Society's wardship he turned into a 'child care' case, reverting to 'protection' when he went home again; if his sister became inadvertently pregnant she was an 'unmarried mother', and her baby might figure in the 'adoption' caseload. Each of these elements in the Society's caseload tended to become the concern of a different body. The municipal councils were responsible only for the maintenance of wards. The Provincial government's slender resources (considerably enlarged since this study was made) had to be devoted first to its limited statutory responsibilities in the fields of child care, illegitimacy and adoption. Meanwhile the Board tended to make the development of preventive work its special concern. Policies tended to be developed by the Society with guidance from Provincial authorities, while the municipalities which provided most of the Society's income had no control over either. This divorce between policy-making and financing bodies is no new thing—British universities have made a principle of it. But there are dangers in any situation where people hold power in the affairs of an organisation (in this case the power of the purse) yet have no effective communication with those holding formal authority. During a period of stability this system can work very well but when the objectives of a Society are being extended and its priorities are changing it takes exceptional leadership to maintain effective communications and to reconcile the diverse interests of all concerned.

These problems cannot be completely solved while Ontario demands social services on a scale which the taxpayer alone can finance, and maintains the structure of voluntary organisation and small-scale local government which grew up to meet the needs of another age. In less acute form, the same problems afflicted the schools, health services and public housing ventures, but these were all services which were of immediate interest to large numbers of people—for most of the population has children, and all are anxious to be healthy and well-housed. The Children's Aid movement lacked these firm roots, and had no supporting pressure groups—no equivalent to the parent-teacher associations or the numerous voluntary health associations—to provide the secure political and administrative backing it required.

The surprising thing is not that the Children's Aid Society ran into trouble, but that any organisation whose services are unrealistically subdivided, inspected and controlled by one body, financed by half a dozen, subject to arbitration from several, directed by a self-selected Board and forced to rely for the money to support an important part of its work on fluctuating voluntary contributions, should normally have functioned so smoothly and effectively.

POSTSCRIPT

Twenty years have passed since the events described in this study, but the Children's Aid Society of Brockville and the United Counties of

Leeds and Grenville thrives, the boundaries of its territory are unchanged, and with help from its Director and others we can outline the main developments which have occurred during this time. We begin by noting changes in Provincial law and practice, and then turn to the Brockville local Society.

Ontario's Child Welfare Act of 1965 took the system a step further in the directions in which we saw it moving. Indeed, some sections of the Act might have been designed to cope with situations of the sort we described. Municipal authorities in the area served by a Children's Aid Society must be properly represented on its Board. Each year the Society must send these authorities and the Provincial Director of Child Welfare an estimate of its operating costs for the following year, apportioned in a clearly prescribed way between the Province and the various local authorities in its area. If the authorities cannot accept the total budget proposed, or its apportionment amongst them, or if the Society cannot accept the Minister's decision (which may not accord with its original proposal) the whole question must be referred for arbitration to a Child Welfare Review Committee specially constituted to represent the main interests involved. The Committee must report its findings to all the parties within thirty days, and within thirty more the Minister must give a decision from which there is no appeal.[1] If at the end of any year, the Society's expenditure exceeds or falls short of its original estimate, an appropriate adjustment is made to the budget for the following year.

In tightening up the administrative and financial arrangements for child welfare, the Act of 1965 made it clear that the local Societies had to work in close collaboration with the municipal authorities in their areas, but that the Provincial Government was ultimately responsible for ensuring that a reasonably adequate service was provided, and could not allow local disagreements to obstruct it.

But the Act made no change in the functions of the local Societies: indeed, it reaffirmed them.[2] They are *Children's Aid* Societies their job is to work with families, not with anyone who might need their help (as in the English Social Services Departments described in the postscript to Chapter 6). Within the family it is the welfare of the child which is their chief responsibility. The Act confirms this principle at many points. If the court decides that a child must be removed from home because he is 'in need of protection', the Society must help his family, or some other suitable person, to resume care of him soon: temporary wardship can only be granted for twelve months, and may not be extended for longer than a total of twenty-four months consecutively. If that cannot be, he must become a 'ward of the Crown', in which case the Society and the Provincial Director of Child Welfare assume 'all the

[1] The Child Welfare Act of 1965; Part I, Province of Ontario.
[2] Part II.

rights and responsibilities of a legal guardian' until he leaves their care on marriage or at the age of eighteen. (The Society can extend its care till he is twenty-one if he has special needs which justify this.) That means, as before, that the authorities can consent to his adoption without seeking the agreement of his natural parents.[1] Conflicts over children between parents and foster parents, which have been a recurring problem in Britain, are less likely to occur in Canada because if the child is not returned fairly soon to his parents—as he normally is—they will usually lose all rights over him. He is then likely to be adopted. Judges are reminded of the primacy of the child's needs by sections of the Act which repeatedly oblige or empower them to consult children before reaching decisions.[2]

A recent report by a Task Force appointed by the Ontario Minister of Community and Social Services makes it clear, however, that most of the administrative and political problems discussed in our original study are still very much alive. For the time being, however, they recommend that 'the Ministry . . . devote its energies to seeing how far the existing system can be improved before adopting a more radical approach to reform'.[3]

At the conclusion of our original study one of the 'new men' became Director of the Brockville Society and was later followed by the other. Neither succeeded completely in gaining the confidence of the municipal authorities. The Society held costs down by a determined policy of getting children home or getting them adopted, and the numbers in care fell by 1958 to 126. But the municipalities represented on the Board were still reluctant to contribute to preventive work.

Eventually the Director resigned and his successor, who is still in the post, was specifically asked to resolve these problems by the Board who decided that he 'be appointed as Executive Director effective 1 January 1959 and that a policy be established to improve relationships with municipal, town and county councils'. The new Director set about building 'good personal relations with the key people in the communities, principally the clerk and treasurer of the City of Brockville and of the United Counties of Leeds and Grenville and we soon adopted an unwritten policy of arranging for those local critics of the Society on the councils to be appointed to the Board of the Society. It did not take long to convince them that we were making a sincere effort to do our best for children in the most economical fashion possible . . . The result was that our protection contribution from the municipalities went up from just under $6,000 in 1958 to an average of about $14,000 in the next five or six years. In 1960 we received over $18,000 and found

---

[1] Section 73(3).
[2] E.g. Sections 31(5), 37(7), 73(4) and 75a.
[3] Task Force on Community and Social Services, *Report on Selected Issues and Relationships*, January 1974, p. 61.

ourselves in the unheard position of having a considerable surplus in protection. We promptly returned the surplus to the municipalities who had contributed it and I think it was the wisest move we ever made.'[1]

The demands on the Society and the resources for meeting them still fluctuated. The population of the area rose steadily. But families receiving 'protection services' fell to well below 200 in the mid-1950s, rose to over 500 by 1969, and then declined again. Children in care rose to about 150 in 1967; then fell (owing to vigorous family casework and an ambitious adoption programme, enthusiastically supported by the public) to about 100 in 1972. Work with unmarried parents declined; but more of the children in care were teen-age boys, difficult to foster or adopt, and more expensive to care for. A new group home had to be opened for them. Since the costs of looking after illegitimate children were wholly borne by the Provincial Government but 40 per cent of other child care costs had to be met by the municipalities, this change might have strained the Society's relations with the local authorities. But the goodwill built up in that quarter enabled the Society to surmount these difficulties: between 1970 and 1972 contributions from the municipalities increased by 75 per cent to $105,000, while Provincial contributions increased by 42 per cent to $227,000.

The Director had refused to write off the debt to the Society's capital fund accumulated during the crisis years, insisting instead on charging 5 per cent interest on the loan each year against the Society's current expenditure. When the 1965 Act laid upon the various levels of government a more direct financial responsibility for the Society's work, this debt was repaid with their help. With bequests which had been carefully invested, this enabled the Society to build excellent new premises and still retain some reserves for future expansion. A family clinic has been set up with the help of local psychiatrists and others, and the Society changed its name to 'Family and Children's Services' in 1974.

The Society's staff remained for some years at the numbers reached during our original study—a Director and about seven field workers and four office workers. Expansion followed, giving the Director by 1967 a supervisor, ten field workers and four office workers. Since then, numbers have remained fairly stable, but they may increase again if negotiations now beginning for a merger with the smaller Society to the north reach a successful conclusion.

This relatively placid ending to the controversies in which the Society was embroiled was due to several causes—particularly to the efforts made to reconcile the responsibilities of the Society to the various levels of government and to clarify the obligations of each to the others, the trouble taken by the Director to build good relations with municipal officials, and his prudent financial management. Important, too, was the unchanging character—the conservatism, possibly—of the work and

---

[1] Director's letter to the author.

functions of the Children's Aid Society. Earlier troubles had been due partly to a new approach to the job introduced by new people who were compelled to seek new resources for their work in a rather conservative community which did not fully understand or trust them. The old Director probably knew he was taking a risk in recruiting them. Such risks have not been taken, and may not have been necessary, since then. The Society's resources and practice improved during the next twenty years, but its aims and methods have not changed very much. The training of its social workers accords with the conventions generally accepted by the leading staff and board members of the Society, and has generally been gained after serving an apprenticeship as untrained workers. There have been no more 'new men'.

CHAPTER 9

CONSULTATION AMONG SOCIAL WORKERS IN THE FAMILY WELFARE ASSOCIATION

This study deals with another voluntary agency. It traces the evolution of procedures for the improvement of professional skills and working methods in one of the agency's local offices. These procedures were initiated by the agency's staff, in response both to the changing demands being made on their service and to broader developments within the social work profession. The resources required for this innovation were secured from outside bodies which exercised considerable influence on the agency's work, and also through a reduction in case-loads which enabled staff to devote more time to each case. The divergent expectations of those involved and the scarcity of the resources available to them provoked conflicts somewhat similar to those seen in the previous study. The agency's administrative structure was ill-adapted for resolving these conflicts, and the loss of senior staff and committee members posed further difficulties.

The starting point for this study was one of the seven Area Offices of the Family Welfare Association: Area 4, which included the City of London and much of the north-eastern part of London County—the Boroughs of Holborn, Finsbury, Stepney, Poplar, Shoreditch, Bethnal Green, Hackney and St Pancras. The Area Secretary in charge of this Office mentioned several recent developments in her field, but it was difficult to isolate a topic for study amongst them. However, she referred frequently to the growth of 'supervision' and of procedures for the systematic discussion of cases her staff were dealing with, and she stressed the important part these developments played in the other trends mentioned. With the agreement of the Secretary and her staff this development was selected as the theme of our study which was carried out in 1958.

We shall use the general term 'consultation' to refer to these processes, meaning by this any procedure designed to enable social workers to discuss their current cases with others at regular intervals. It includes a number of different but comparable activities, all of which were intended to help social workers to improve the standards of their work: 'conferences' at which groups of caseworkers met to discuss individual cases and current problems, with or without the help of an 'expert' of some kind; 'supervision' provided by a senior person (inside or outside the normal administrative structure of the Association) who discussed cases with individual workers and took considerable responsibility for selecting the topics to be explored and posing problems for the worker to consider; and 'consultations' in which workers themselves selected cases and problems on which to seek the guidance of an expert who was normally brought in for this purpose from outside the agency. These different forms of consultation cannot be clearly distinguished since they tended to merge and alternate with each other in practice. Some of them may be termed 'supervision' but the principal purpose of all of them is not to inspect the work done or to control those who do it, but to advance knowledge and skills and to evolve common policies and codes of practice.

The policies of the Family Welfare Association had been debated for several years prior to this study, and the debate still continues. We therefore begin with a brief account of the work and structure of the Association and the changes both were undergoing at this time. We then turn to Area 4 and the development of various forms of 'case consultation' in that Office between 1954 and 1958, explaining the part played by the Association's Central Office in these developments, and concluding with an appraisal of the progress made.

This report is based on interviews with most of the staff and committee members of the Association who took part in the developments described, and on reports, memoranda and records of various kinds. One of the authors served for a period on the Association's Administrative Council and this experience also contributed to the findings presented here. The story was by no means ended when our study took place. A major review of the FWA's policies and organisation was beginning as our study closed and important changes, which we do not trace,[1] followed from it.

The Family Welfare Association

The Charity Organisation Society was founded in 1869 and renamed 'The Family Welfare Association' in 1946.[2] As late as 1944 its stated aims were still 'to organise charitable effort and to improve the condition of the poor', but wartime pressures and post-war social legislation prompted the Society to provide a full-scale social casework service later described as being designed 'to alleviate the distress which people feel when for any reason they come into conflict with their social environment . . . the phases of this method are (1) to make as thorough a study of their client as is relevant to his social situation, (2) to determine from

---

[1] They are briefly noted in the postscript to this chapter.

[2] For a history of the Society see Charles Loch Mowat, *The Charity Organisation Society, 1869–1913*. London, Methuen, 1961.

the knowledge ... available how best he and his family may be helped, and (3) finally to involve the client and his family in working towards a solution of their difficulties'. In this work the various forms of material help the Society might provide 'are a means to an end, rather than the end itself, which end is the best adjustment which can be effected between the client and his social environment'.[1]

These aims were a reinterpretation of the original objectives of the COS, but they had to be combined with many other tasks which the agency had taken on during its long history. The FWA had an Old People's Homes Committee, established to find appropriate forms of residential care for old people; it was responsible for fourteen Citizens' Advice Bureaux in various parts of London and formed the administrative channel for the distribution of funds provided for them by Metropolitan Boroughs; it undertook a similar service for two Legal Aid Centres assisted by the London County Council; it administered some almshouses, various trusts and eleven pension funds, and acted as agent for other charities; it provided an Information Service originally designed to expose fraudulent appeals but now mainly used by solicitors and others wishing to trace small charities; and it published a journal—'Social Work'—the 'Annual Charities Register and Digest' and the 'Guide to the Social Services'. More directly related to its family casework service were the Association's long-standing contribution to the training of university students and others interested in social work, and various temporary experimental projects such as those dealing with the treatment of marital disharmony, the welfare of coloured people, and the development of methods of work among 'problem families'.

The development and co-ordination of these activities were the responsibility of the FWA's Administrative Council. Under a constitution drawn up in 1950 (revised again since this study took place) this Council consisted of thirty members. Two were elected to represent each of the seven Area Committees, two practising social workers were elected by the Area Secretaries, one represented the Citizen's Advice Bureaux, and there were three ex officio members (the Chairman, Honorary Treasurer and Assistant Honorary Treasurer). The remaining ten members were co-opted—some of them from statutory social services and London University. Members of the Council were appointed, and normally re-appointed, every three years. The Council met once a month. It debated and approved policy, and followed up directions from the Annual General Meeting (to which all members of the Association who subscribed at least ten shillings a year might come) and from the special 'Domestic Meetings' of Council and staff which were supposed to be held twice yearly. It was ultimately responsible for the appointment and dismissal of the Central Office staff and all 'casework' staff.

[1] Unpublished *Review of the Family Welfare Association*, Muriel A. Cunliffe. FWA, 1960.

The Council appointed committees and delegated powers to them. The principal committees at this time were the General Purposes Committee (which dealt with most staffing and establishment matters, acted as a supervisory and informative link between the Council and the Area Committees, and dealt with urgent business arising between Council meetings), the Selection and Training Committee (dealing with training, and negotiating with universities and other bodies), the Aims and Policy Committee, and the Finance Committee. Other committees dealt with appeals, press and publicity, grants, and special services and projects such as the Information Service, the Citizens' Advice Bureaux, and placements in old people's homes. All these Committees were entitled to co-opt members in addition to the Council members serving on them. The Association's Central Office at Denison House was directed by the General Secretary, and its senior staff included the Organising Secretary (responsible for casework staff and training matters, and deputy to the General Secretary) the National Casework Secretary (responsible for dealing with enquiries about individual cases from all over the country) and the Accountant.

It can be seen that the central body in this structure—the Administrative Council—met frequently enough to play an active part in the Association's management but had a large membership representing diverse interests and including paid staff, volunteers and outside experts of various kinds. It was responsible to two different general assemblies—the Annual General Meeting and the Domestic Meeting —and carried out its work through a very large number of committees, each of which could co-opt further members.

Since 1954 the Association's casework service had been provided from seven Area Offices. Each had its own Area Committee of at least twelve members elected annually. Committee members included representatives of voluntary and statutory services and various other local interests. Under the 1950 Constitution they were required to meet between four and twelve times a year for the purpose of raising and administering funds, teaching and training workers in the principles, methods and administration of family casework (using whatever methods they thought fit), and establishing centres offering advice and guidance on matters of family welfare. They managed FWA affairs in their Areas, elected members to the central committees, and appointed representatives to the committees of other agencies. The organisation of fund-raising appeals and the supervision of Area finances was normally delegated to sub-committees. The Area Committee might also elect a 'Cases Sub-committee', not more than one-third of whose members might be co-opted from outside the Association. This sub-committee would 'consider and make decisions on all cases submitted to them but delegating authority to the Area Secretary in dealing with cases coming within the defined policy of the Association'. It, or the Area

Committee, had to authorise expenditure exceeding £35 on any one case. It had also to make recommendations to the Area Committee on all questions of policy affecting individual cases, and report any cases in which a change of policy was required or implied.

Each Area office was run by an Area Secretary who was a senior social worker responsible for directing the other caseworkers in the office, the small clerical staff, and a number of voluntary workers. She was responsible to her committee for the social work service, the training of students and general administration. Her casework staff would normally consist of one or two Assistant Secretaries, and possibly another in training. In earlier years the Association's local Areas (then called 'Districts') were smaller and more numerous—there had been twenty-one of them in 1948, and a maximum of thirty-nine during the nineteenth century. In the past their Secretaries frequently had no fully trained staff, but they could call on the assistance of a larger number of unpaid voluntary workers.

Thus at the Area level, too, the Association had made a partial but incomplete adaptation to change. The Area Committees' control of casework, training methods and the distribution of material help—originally complete—was loosened and left for each to clarify for itself. The Committees included a growing proportion of 'expert' members, employed in neighbouring social services, alongside the 'lay' volunteers who represented the traditional source of the Association's membership. The COS had always been a fairly loose federation of local units. At the time of this study the Central Office's growing control over the Areas hinged largely on its power to appoint and pay casework staff, but the Areas' capacity to raise funds of their own—and hence their real autonomy—varied considerably, though none were financially self-supporting.

At this stage in its history the FWA was responding to a number of external developments which may be briefly summarised. Full employment, rising incomes, and the establishment of the National Assistance Board and other statutory services—several of which have been described in earlier studies in this series—had deprived the Association of many of its earlier relief-giving functions. The scarcity of leisured local gentry, and the Association's growing reliance on trained social work staff shifted the balance of expenditure and power within the agency, conferring greater influence on trained social workers and the Central Office which paid their salaries. Meanwhile the gathering national drive for more trained social workers (to be most forcefully represented by the report of the Younghusband Committee[1] which was being written at the time of this study) posed serious problems for the FWA; although it had always played an active part in this campaign, the Association did not have the financial resources to compete with the salaries offered by the big statutory services, and to recruit good staff it had to offer other

[1] *Report of the Working Party on Social Workers*, Ministry of Health, HMSO 1959.

inducements such as the opportunity of doing interesting work in a professionally stimulating environment. In the past, COS workers had concentrated on helping the most 'helpable'—those whom an earlier generation described as 'the deserving poor'—but the FWA had come increasingly, though never unanimously, to concentrate on the most intractable cases for which the statutory services often proved least effective. The distribution of material help, though never an end in itself, had been the COS's best known and most extensive task; but the 'harder' cases the Association was now dealing with, coupled with the new outlook and training of many of its staff, made the skilled use of human relationships the principal instrument of its work. The COS had been suspicious of the growth of government and unwilling to render itself or its clients dependent on public money; but the FWA was gradually compelled to seek financial help from the Home Office, the Boroughs and the London County Council.

The Association's 'ordinary income' rose from £18,751 in 1946–7 to £54,504 in 1957–8, but the largest part of this increase came from central and local government grants for specific projects, while income from subscriptions and donations available to meet general expenditure only increased from £10,391 to £18,829 during this period. As a result the annual deficit fluctuated between £750 and £27,562, and had been increasing for four consecutive years at the time of this study. It was covered, thanks to a large but unpredictable flow of legacies, and net assets actually rose slightly. But to maintain this position the Treasurer was compelled to demand repeated economies.

During the decade after the war the FWA carried out successive reviews of its functions and administrative structure, and reduced the number of its Area offices—and hence its caseload—from twenty-one to seven. In 1947–8 it received 17,433 new applications for help; by 1955–6 this number had fallen to 4,059 and then continued at approximately this level.

Although the attempt to organise procedures for 'case consultation' among the staff of Area 4 was only a minor aspect of the general course of development outlined here, it nevertheless constituted a central thread in the story. The COS had provided for consultation through 'case committees' in each Area which controlled the distribution of material help and supervised the work of the staff. Since committee members were often attracted to devote their time to this task by the opportunity it provided for first-hand contact with practical social work, and since Area Committees were supposed to be ultimately responsible for their Areas' debts, the Case Committees had compelling reasons for supervising closely the work of their staff. But the assumptions and outlook underlying this system had become unacceptable to many in the FWA—particularly among the new generation of trained social workers. Thus the search for new methods of consultation was prompted

CONSULTATION AMONG SOCIAL WORKERS IN FWA 199

by a determination to work out new policies and conventions, to improve social work practice, to provide the stimulating and progressive professional environment which would encourage the new training courses to send their students to the FWA, and to attract graduates from such courses to join the staff. But the structure and traditions of the FWA could not easily accommodate consultants or supervisors, and the financial resources to employ such people were hard to come by. This case therefore throws a good deal of light on the general progress of the Association at this time and cannot be understood unless that broader context is kept in mind.

'Case Consultation' in Area 4

The FWA Area that forms the basis of this study was the product of a series of amalgamations. In 1949, after the first of these, its territory had a population of 65,000 and its staff of one senior caseworker and two juniors dealt with 1,017 new applications for help during the following year. At the end of 1950 its territory was extended again to cover two more Boroughs, providing a total population of 238,000, and the same number of staff dealt with a little over 800 new applications during the following year. In 1954 parts of two neighbouring Areas were incorporated to give Area 4 a population of 650,000 from which 689 new applications were dealt with in the following year by six trained workers, one of whom left halfway through the year. These figures, showing the increasing territory to be covered and the falling caseload (falling for the office and, even more strikingly, for its workers) indicate the changing character of the Area's work which was becoming more selective and intensive.

The amalgamation of 1954 was more than just another in the series; it was part of a bigger reorganisation which followed a comprehensive reappraisal of the FWA's aims and methods. The new Area, with an office in Myddleton Square, was one of two centres set up at this time to experiment with new ideas about social work and the organisation of a family casework service. Its paid staff of six trained caseworkers was larger than the FWA had ever envisaged before, though the size of the Area's population was equally unprecedented. These staff had been chosen to form a 'progressive' team of experienced workers, sympathetic to the aims of the new centre. All had volunteered to take part in the experiment.

In a paper presented to her committee some years later, the Area Secretary described features of the old COS from which she and her colleagues wished to break away. 'The responsibility for ensuring that clients were deserving seemed to override the normal regard for the rights of the client as an individual.' '... there was a general assumption that the Committee knew what was best for a client ... (and there were) definite standards in the minds of Committee and workers as to right and wrong.'[1] Clients were usually interviewed in rooms occupied by other workers and clients; they were asked to name two referees who would substantiate their statements, and some checking up was done without seeking the clients' consent—with the Public Assistance Committee and the Mutual Register of Assistance, for example. (Consent seems generally to have been sought, however, for inquiries among employers, landlords and others outside the social services.) Emphasis was placed upon material circumstances and honest, upright behaviour, rather than upon feelings, and relationships. Cases were often dealt with by more than one worker in order to maintain 'impartiality'. She felt that plans had been made *for* people, not *with* people.

At that time some workers formed the opinion that more attention should be paid to the feelings and motives of clients and social workers alike. They wanted to learn more about human behaviour, and make more deliberate and effective use of the relationships that developed between clients and workers. This change in outlook was linked with the spread of knowledge about psychology and psychiatric methods. In a second paper presented to the committee,[2] another member of staff outlined three principal ideas used in the new approach to family casework: the influence of unconscious forces upon human behaviour, the importance of childhood experience in determining adult personality, and the sexual origins of much human feeling. These ideas, together with an appreciation of psychological mechanisms such as 'projection', 'reaction-formation' and 'identification', were used to seek a deeper understanding of the client's needs and to attempt a solution of his problems through a controlled, professional relationship with the social worker.

The development and application of these ideas called for careful thought and expert guidance—guidance of a different kind from that provided by the weekly meetings of Case Committees still operating in several Areas. This had been recognised in 1953 in the report of a Reorganisation Sub-Committee which led to the establishment of the new experimental offices. The sub-committee quoted Dr Younghusband ('Modern casework involves practising casework under supervision and good supervision necessarily implies good casework is being done in the agency') and described consultation and supervision as 'the two essentials for good casework practice'; 'neither of these is adequately provided for in the present structure of the Association'.

These recommendations, which dealt with many other matters besides, were accepted after a good deal of argument and modification. In February 1954, just after the new Area 4 was established, a Supervisor/Consultant was appointed to work from the Central Office. (Some

[1] Mary Keenleyside: 'Development in Casework Method', *Social Work*. (October 1958, Vol. 15, No. 4, p. 516.)

[2] S. I. Briskin: 'Casework and Present Day Trends', *Social Work*. (October 1958, Vol. 15, No. 4, p. 521.)

Area Secretaries were still uneasy about the implications of the term 'supervisor'.) This step was facilitated by two other developments. The Association hoped for support from the Home Office which eventually agreed to contribute to the Supervisor's salary on the grounds that her work would provide tuition in marriage counselling. Meanwhile plans were being made for the establishment of a new training course for social workers at the London School of Economics and Political Science; the Association and the School were hoping to establish training centres in Area Offices for students on this course, and a Supervisor could help to achieve these aspirations.

The Supervisor/Consultant, a psychiatric social worker who continued at the Central Office until February 1957, was asked to devote most of her attention to the five 'ordinary' Area Offices and the two larger experimental offices saw little of her. Her appointment meant that some decision had to be taken on the future role of the Case Committees, with whom responsibility for case decisions had hitherto rested. Areas were left free to work out their own plans: to retain, modify or abolish their Cases Committees, or to supplement their work with case conferences held with the Supervisor/Consultant or other experts. At a Domestic Meeting called in April 1954 (at the request of Area 4) to discuss the Committees, the Chairman reaffirmed the Administrative Council's opinion that adaptations to new conditions were essential, but that Areas wishing to maintain their Case Committees should be free to do so. During the next two years the Aims and Policy Committee watched the variations in practice which developed in the Areas, but although experiments with case conferences were judged to have been very successful, no pressure was brought to bear on those Areas which still preferred to submit their cases to the decision of a lay committee.

The staff and committee for the new Area Office at Myddleton Square were drawn from three different Areas. One of these had followed the traditional aims and methods of the Association, in another there had been greater willingness to consider new departures, and the third provided many of the staff and committee members who had been most active in working out new ideas. The two post-war Secretaries in this third office had been unusually able and energetic, and had done much to win the co-operation of their committee. Nevertheless the committee had retained its decisive power and exercised it when necessary. In 1951, for instance, it refused to allow the staff to attempt intensive casework and provide help with household management among 'problem families' since their numbers and training were not considered adequate for this work. Their Chairman (who later chaired the new Area Committee) had had considerable war-time experience in another voluntary agency—the Personal Service League—and she had been drawn to the FWA by her interest in casework. She had herself worked in the Area for a time as a trainee, and she was an active member of the Administrative Council and several of its committees, including the Reorganisation Sub-Committee of 1953.

Staff from all three Areas had attended discussion groups on casework arranged at various times since 1948 with a psychiatrist, a psychiatric social worker on the staff of the London School of Economics, and staff of the Tavistock Clinic. The Area Secretary had been encouraged by this introduction to the application of psychiatric principals in social work to take a year's course in advanced social casework at the Tavistock Clinic, returning in time to take over the new Area.

Three months before the new Area Office opened, its staff began regular consultative meetings with a specially appointed worker. In August 1953 the General Secretary of the FWA had attended a United Nations seminar in Italy, and had there met a member of its staff—a Hungarian-born American caseworker and university teacher then working in Europe on a Fulbright scholarship. He was impressed by her teaching ability, and on his return proposed that the Council should appoint her as a temporary consultant to the staffs of the two experimental areas. She began work in October 1953, three months before the amalgamation took place, and continued until the following May. She held weekly group sessions, lasting about two-and-a-half hours, for the staff who were to be transferred to Myddleton Square. Her final report shows that she found it necessary to give consultation that was both broader in scope and more precise than she considered usual by American standards, since the staff needed to be taught something of the psychology of normal human behaviour, pathological behaviour and psychosomatic illness, in addition to casework techniques. She also found much uncertainty among the staff about future goals and prospects.

The group based their discussion on cases prepared by the workers and circulated in advance of the meetings. The consultant also read the case papers. Afterwards the workers responsible for the cases discussed made a summary of the discussion which was checked by the consultant and attached to the case papers. The topics considered included material relief-giving, the nature and use of relationships, and the psychological mechanisms underlying human behaviour. There were in all twenty-seven meetings, two on intake procedure, two-and-a-half on statistical techniques, one on material assistance, one on unmarried mothers and one-and-a-half on a self-evaluation of the group; the remaining nineteen dealt with case material and points arising from it.

The consultant felt she ought to have continuous contact with the workers in order to create the mutual trust without which it was virtually impossible to teach or to learn; she also tried to gain a thorough knowledge of the organisation and the workers in it. She concluded that the experiment had proved stimulating—workers had acquired a good deal of knowledge and had consolidated their considerable previous experience. In this sense they were more confident of themselves and of the aims and values of their profession. But the process of acquiring knowledge and developing new techniques in place of rejected ones, involving critical self-examination, produced considerable anxiety and for this reason the consultant considered it necessary for the staff to have continuous and close supervision and more teaching. While she considered group sessions better for some things, a more satisfactory integration of theory and practice would be achieved by individual supervision. She was firm in asserting that supervision 'properly conceived and executed does not undermine self development and self reliance, but enhances it by giving it guidance and encouragement . . .'

When the new Office was set up the staff persuaded a majority of the Committee to do without a Case Committee. Instead members were invited to serve on a 'Cases Advisory Panel' whose advice the staff could seek when necessary. In fact the Panel was infrequently used during the first year and thereafter fell into abeyance. In general, decisions about cases were left to the staff, after discussions with their consultant or in their own weekly staff meetings. This decision was referred to the Central Office and the General Secretary advised the Area that under the Constitution cases on which £35 or more was to be spent must be referred to the Area Committee, but that its approval could if necessary be regarded as automatic. Some Committee members still felt strongly that the change was unwise, both from the casework point of view and because it would lose local support. At least one member refused to serve on any committee whose role was advisory rather than executive. The Area staff were worried by this division of opinion, and hence asked for the Domestic Meeting mentioned previously. The Area's decision to keep decisions on cases in the hands of the staff was not seriously challenged after that, but the difficulty of maintaining the interest and full co-operation of a lay committee which had no direct contact with casework remained a source of concern.

When the temporary consultant left, the staff of Area 4 felt strongly the need for further support and teaching and asked for more group sessions with additional individual supervision—though they were aware of greater confidence in themselves and in their ability to help clients. They still felt embarrassed by the giving of material help, realising that such help was sometimes necessary and that it could be given constructively within a casework plan, but still feeling hampered by attitudes towards the provision of material help which stemmed from the days when 'relief-giving' had been a symbol of traditional COS policies. They also felt a need for help in developing satisfactory methods for their initial 'intake interviews' and for recording the work done on each case. The freedom gained by abolishing the Case Committee brought new and heavy responsibilities, for social workers alone now had to decide whom to help and whom to turn away, what help to give and what to withhold. Many of the anxieties and uncertainties they expressed at this time centred on these questions.

These views were reported to the Administrative Council and its Training and Selection Committee, together with an outline of two experiments the Area proposed to make—an analysis of intake interviews over the next three months, and the introduction of an appointments system fixing the time and duration of all but emergency interviews. Lack of funds and suitable people made it impossible to replace the Consultant when her contract ended in May 1954. The Supervisor/Consultant at Central could provide no help and for a while Area 4 was left to fend for itself. The staff derived a certain amount of support from their own weekly meetings where all matters concerning the Area were discussed: office administration, statistical and recording techniques, casework skills, cases, and policy involving relations within the Association and with outside agencies. The focus of these discussions varied with changing needs: when consultation was not available, discussion of cases predominated, although a good deal of thought was devoted to the analysis of new cases and recording processes. A recurrent topic for staff discussion throughout the period was the function of the Area Committee.

In September 1954, the Administrative Council was informed of negotiations between the FWA and the Institute of Almoners (one of whose representatives had been a member both of the Council and the Aims and Policy Committee) to obtain a grant from the Sir Halley Stewart Trust to finance a joint experiment in supervision, for which the name of an American casework consultant was put forward. She accepted the appointment for only eight months but at that time there were hopes of another American—a Fulbright scholar—being found to take her place. This project, although designed to meet the needs of the experimental Areas, was equally a reflection of the FWA's determination to maintain and develop its role as a major training body for caseworkers, both for its own staff and for students sent by the universities. The necessity for the FWA to offer two centres capable of providing training and supervision of the calibre required by the new course begun at the London School of Economics in October 1954 had been a strong argument in favour of the creation of the two experimental offices. But the Secretaries were not clear whether the new supervisor was to supervise them or train them to supervise others. Like other measures promoted by the Central Office, it was intended to do both, for the Association wanted to build up a group of supervisors among its casework staff.

Area 4 had hoped to receive both individual supervision and group sessions. After preliminary talks with the staff the new Consultant decided on the latter for the ten FWA caseworkers and the four almoners involved. She did this because the FWA staff already had experience of working in groups, and quicker results would thus be achieved in integrating theory and practice (speed was important because of the LSE students who were about to arrive), and because tuition in supervision was particularly important for the almoners.

This programme, she reported, provided 'consultation'—rather than 'supervision' in the American sense of the word. In America, 'the supervisor is a fellow member of the staff who has considerable administrative responsibility for supervisees and their work as well as that of teaching students and beginning workers and/or helping more experienced workers in their continuing professional development'. That is to say she is an administrator and policy-maker as well as a teacher. The second consultant was at least as skilled in administration as in casework, and she was able to help the staff clarify a number of administrative problems. The topics covered included the classification of cases and an experiment carried out in analysing new applications for help. The consultant pointed out that caseworkers were tending to overestimate the psychological factors in family tensions and to play down social factors. The caseworkers were ready to acknowledge this, but found it difficult to share the supervisor's horror at the poor standards of living considered acceptable by the FWA. American standards of material well-being prompted her to be more generous with material help than seemed realistic to them. They agreed, however, that research was needed to help them in assessing family budgets. The supervisor also argued that many of the Association's difficulties arose from the fact that it had incomplete control over the funds available for its work and an inappropriate administrative structure.

She approved the new aims of the FWA and, 'since organisation and administration are so closely related to creating the proper "climate" in which casework can grow and develop', suggested a thorough reorganisation aimed at 'strengthening and clarifying lines of responsibility'. 'In the present structure it may be inevitable that there will be feelings of separateness and rivalry which are not conducive to growth and progress.'

In June 1955 the consultant returned to the USA and Area 4 was once again left without supervision, although still feeling greatly in need of it. Cases came to the fore again in the discussions at staff meetings and the Area Secretary began to devote one hour a week to each of her social workers in order to discuss their work. This was an approach to supervision in the American sense, but it increased the heavy responsibilities she already carried in her own casework, in supervising students and administering the Area Office. The burden borne by Area Secretaries had been an increasing problem for a number of years; as early as July

1948 the suggestion had been made in the Council that each Area should have an administrative as well as a casework Secretary. By taking on a bigger Area Office and supervising students for the LSE the Secretary was compelled to abandon half her own casework. One social worker had left the new office six months after its creation and had never been replaced, so the Area did not have the full complement of staff planned for it. Various attempts were made to relieve the Area Secretary, by appointing an administrative worker (who left after a month, partly owing to the small salary she was paid), and by distributing some of her more routine duties among the senior staff. The latter arrangement was only partly successful, for senior workers also had little time to spare, and additional difficulties arose from the strain of experimental work on a small group in unsettled circumstances which made it hard to develop a smoothly operating team.

In July 1955 the Central Office suggested that Area 4 might receive supervision from the caseworker who had run the Association's Problem Family Project and was now on the regular staff of another Area. Area 4 considered that their supervisor should ideally be a part of their own casework team, but since this worker was known to be highly skilled and in any case there seemed to be no alternative, they welcomed the suggestion although she would not be available until the following January. Later in the year, however, it was found that her commitments were too heavy to permit this extra work, and the Area was again left without any prospect of help.

Early in June 1956 the Area Secretary talked to the General Secretary about the possibility of getting supervisory help from the Family Discussion Bureau, a marriage counselling agency originally established by the FWA in 1948 in collaboration with the Tavistock Clinic to whom it was about to be transferred owing to lack of the financial resources required for it. With the Bureau would go the Home Office grant for marriage counselling services which helped to maintain this work, and the FWA was anxious to qualify independently for such a grant by virtue of the Area's work on marital cases. The Secretaries' Meeting sympathised with this aim, and was generally eager to increase skill in marriage counselling. In July they discussed the matter with a worker from the Bureau who suggested something on the lines of the group they ran for a number of psychiatric social workers in Middlesex.

The Home Office was prepared to regard such supervision as a qualification for a grant, and the Family Discussion Bureau was willing to undertake the work, and was interested to compare this type of training with the practical course given in their own office. The Area staff were not entirely happy with the proposal—it seemed to them an expensive and inadequate substitute for what was really needed. Preliminary talks with FDB workers did not altogether remove their doubts, but the Area Secretary persuaded her colleagues to make a three months' trial from November 1956. Two members of the Bureau staff were to take a group weekly for one-and-a-half hour discussion of problems arising from difficult marital cases. One of these workers had spent ten years with the FWA as an Assistant Secretary and had transferred to the FDB when it was first started.

The staff of Area 4 then reorganised their own weekly meetings, and decided on a 'work plan' which they hoped would lead to better formulation of goals and more disciplined thinking. In this move they had been influenced by a Canadian casework tutor who had been running short courses at the London School of Economics that year. When the FDB group had been running for three months an attempt was made to assess its value. The caseworkers were still unsure—they felt there was too strict a limitation to marital cases and too few general implications were studied, and they were still worried about problems of relief-giving. They tentatively suggested a further trial period of three months. The FDB workers, on the other hand, felt the group was going well, and was useful from their own standpoint in throwing light on the treatment of marital problems in a general casework setting. Indeed, they were now inclined to think that the best preparation for marriage guidance work lay in specialised training of experienced caseworkers drawn from a general social work agency. The Area Office staff, strongly encouraged by their Secretary, 'rather lamely' agreed to continue group discussions of all kinds of personal relationship problems until the end of the University year. During the following months the group became much more effective, and by the end of the session the staff decided unanimously and with enthusiasm that it should be continued indefinitely after the summer break. (The FDB worked to university terms.)

During the year the Council's Selection and Training Committee had examined the whole question of supervision and concluded that group supervision best served the needs of the FWA. The Central Supervisor/Consultant's contract expired in February 1957, and at her own request it was not renewed. It was agreed that the duties and responsibilities attaching to the post at that time were too great to be borne by one person. The post had been advertised with revised duties and a suitable applicant found—a worker from the FDB—but by then a thorough-going review of the work of the Association had been authorised by the Council, and the appointment was therefore left in abeyance until the review should be completed. However, the applicant from FDB agreed to take over for a while a weekly case conference group in one of the Areas: and Area 7 (the second experimental Area) after a period of 'consolidation' without supervision, had arranged individual supervision at the Tavistock Clinic for its four senior caseworkers, but now wanted to set up a group similar to that in Area 4.

The Selection and Training Committee discussed plans for setting up four groups—three covering all Areas, and one for workers supervising junior staff. The latter had to be dropped for financial reasons, but the other three came into operation in the autumn of 1958 when Area 4 was joined by Area 3's staff for its group meetings with FDB workers, who also started another group with Areas 6 and 7. The other three Areas combined in a group led by a psychiatric social worker from the Tavistock Clinic.

Meanwhile Area 4 had been discussing the problem of its Area Secretary's overwork. She raised the matter with her Committee in October and November 1957, dividing her duties into the delegable and non-delegable, and proposing that the former be taken over by an Administrative Secretary. The Committee sympathised strongly with her, but were worried about the status such an officer would have, and the general feeling was that administration should remain under the control of a caseworker. A working party from the staff was set up to consider the problem, and their findings referred back to the Committee, who then submitted a plan to the Council for the appointment of an administrative officer who should not only take over routine office matters from the Area Secretary and be the office manager, but should be able to speak with authority on casework, and act as a public relations officer. A long argument about the financing of this plan ensued—the Area claiming that it could find the money from a legacy recently made to it, and the Administrative Council and its Finance Committee pointing out that all the Association's resources would be needed to weather yet another financial storm that was blowing up at this time. Eventually an outside source of funds was found to back the experiment, and the Administrative Officer—a social worker trained in the new course at the London School of Economics—was appointed in the autumn of 1958, at the time this study was being completed. At the same time a review of the Association's aims and organisation—the third major review since the war—was beginning.

Conclusion

This account of the development of case consultation is a confusing and inconclusive story. Had any other aspect of the FWA's work been examined the result would probably have been the same, for the Association itself was in a transitional stage.

Several things had been happening at once. The Association's caseload had shrunk and the needs to be met were changing, owing to rising living standards and the development of other social services. The staff found that more of their work had to be devoted to dealing with intractable personal problems calling for more skilled treatment based on a deeper understanding of human behaviour. Wider developments in the social work profession encouraged some of the staff to seek opportunities for improving their knowledge and practice, particularly with the aid of psychoanalytic insights. It may be, too, that their clients expected more considerate and sensitive treatment than they did in the past; such a development would be in line with a trend to be seen in many other spheres—in the growing interest in 'labour relations', 'public relations', 'communications' and the elaboration of 'service industries' of all kinds, as well as in the development of the social services. Advances in knowledge about human behaviour and motivation, mostly made before the war, have spread to a wider audience and gained wider application since the war, in social work as in other fields. As the Association's staff assumed more of the responsibilities originally borne by voluntary committee members, many of them became increasingly concerned about the inadequacy of their knowledge. Their search for expert guidance and training followed from all these developments. And when such help was provided it reinforced the trend, extending both their knowledge and their awareness of ignorance, and whetting their appetite for further study and more critical evaluation of their own work.

Throughout this period the FWA was engaged in a continuous struggle to redefine its functions and reorganise its structure—a struggle conducted under the shadow of bankruptcy and amidst repeated attempts to economise. Each of the groups set up to reappraise the FWA's aims and methods reached broadly similar conclusions: family casework ought to be the FWA's main function; there should be fewer Area offices, and each should have a larger and more highly trained staff who should bear full responsibility for decisions about casework; and skilled supervision should play an important part in these developments. But although a number of steps had been taken in these directions, the most striking thing about the FWA's attempts to reorganise itself was the cycle—repeated every two or three years—of crisis, reappraisal, discussion, minor modification and crisis. Why was progress so slow and uncertain—in the development of supervision as in other spheres?

There seem to be several reasons for this. It was repeatedly pointed out that the development of new and more effective forms of casework among people whose needs were not adequately met by the large statutory services was a natural evolution of COS traditions. This was true. But several aspects of this development were peculiarly difficult to reconcile with these traditions. It concentrated the agency's resources on helping the kind of people whom the COS would often have rejected as 'unhelpable' or 'undeserving'; it called for increasing reliance on paid staff and a restriction of the power of the voluntary, 'lay' committees which had formed the backbone of the COS; it conferred increasing power on the Central Office; it cost money, and compelled the Association to collaborate increasingly closely with government, and with bodies such as the London County Council and the London School of Economics—institutions which had in the distant past been the spiritual homes of some of the COS's most formidable opponents.

In considering the FWA's response to these dilemmas it must be remembered that the Association was a federation of Area Offices, financially dependent upon a Central Office, but never completely subject to central direction. The jurisdiction of Area and Central organisations had never been precisely defined; each Area had financial resources of its own and was encouraged to raise money for itself, but in the last resort the resources of all Areas could be called on to pay the Association's debts. Thus disputes about the Areas' freedom to spend their 'own' money and disputes about the Central Office's powers to appoint and move caseworkers continued throughout the period covered by this study—and indeed throughout the lifetime of the COS. Generally speaking, the Central Office tended to exercise most power at times of financial stringency and the Areas gained greater freedom once each crisis was past. The Areas with the largest resources and those individuals noted for their capacity to raise money held a stronger hand than others.

Differences in outlook and training meant that different people—among staff and committee members alike—reacted in different and sometimes conflicting ways to proposals for reform. 'Lay' committee members had little opportunity to test the new methods or convince themselves of their effectiveness; and the traditions of the Society with which they were familiar—the network of small local offices, the discriminate giving of material relief, the judgement of 'character' (with honesty, respectability and independence their recurring theme)—were all called in question by these new methods. The Chairman of Area 4, who was noted for her support of the 'progressives' within the Association, said that she herself would probably not have joined the FWA had it not been for the opportunity of serving on a Case Committee. Others who lacked her faith in the new methods were much less willing to abandon the old. The FWA was passing through a phase to be seen at one time or another in many services. It was about the beginning of the last century that the distinctive roles of 'professional' and 'lay' workers were recognised and established in civil engineering services building roads and bridges; the schools and public health departments followed suit later, and many branches of social work—beginning with the psychiatric and medical social workers—are now passing through a similar phase. It is significant that many of the committee members who took leading parts in working out new policies within the FWA were themselves professional workers (predominantly psychiatric social workers and almoners). Their role was criticised by some of the 'lay' committee members who at Administrative Council meetings in 1958 argued (unsuccessfully) that members who held staff positions in other social services should not be permitted to serve on certain committees. This criticism was not accepted at the time, but it was undoubtedly true that the FWA's attempt to incorporate new trends of thought in its management by appointing members of its own professional staff and staff from neighbouring statutory services to its Central and Area Committees sometimes led to a confusion of roles and an unhelpful identification of certain viewpoints with particular personalities or interests.

As in other federations of diverse local units (the Labour Party for example) the fact that a decision had been reached at one level of the administrative structure did not deter exponents of the defeated point of view from raising the issue again at other levels and in other committees: the primary loyalties of the members of the Association's numerous committees were often attached to the particular Area or the particular branch of the FWA's services they had been chosen to 'represent'. Such a system calls for exceptionally consistent and compelling leadership; those responsible for managing the Association could not rely on formal authority or a unitary hierarchy to impose decisions. Thus the fact that the FWA lost several of its key senior officers in the mid-1950s may help to explain why progress was somewhat uncertain at this time. The Chairman of the Administrative Council, the President, the General Secretary and the Organising Secretary all changed within two years.

Meanwhile no way of assuring financial stability could be found, and this made it difficult to pursue consistent policies. Voluntary sources of funds were inadequate to keep pace with rising costs. Modest grants were made by the Home Office, and some Area offices had occasionally received contributions of up to £250 from Metropolitan Boroughs, but it was not till the closing weeks of this study that the Association first made a more general appeal to the London County Council. The LCC had already given generous grants to other voluntary family casework services—notably the Family Service Units—but the FWA seems to have felt that a whole-hearted appeal to the local authorities should only be made as a last resort.

All these uncertainties affected the development of consultation. It was never accepted that regular and uniform procedures for consultation should be adopted throughout the Areas, and this form of help was regarded by many as an 'extra' to be provided when resources could be spared for it. Even the enlarged Area 4 may have been too small to justify an appointment for this purpose, but when a Supervisor was added to the Central staff she was unable to provide the help this Area needed. It was therefore impossible to work out and apply the 'best' methods of consultation; help had to be got from whoever happened to be available at the time, paid for with whatever funds could be found, and linked with other (and possibly irrelevant) developments in order to qualify for grants. Moreover, though caseworkers in Area 4 were agreed that the old Case Committee could not help them, they were uncertain what should take its place. When the Area Secretary herself began to provide supervision for her staff and students the resulting pressure of work became intolerable for her. Some new distribution of duties had to be worked out, and the appointment of an Administrative Officer was but the latest in a series of attempts to reorganise the structure of an Area Office in accordance with the needs of a modern social work service.

Consultation therefore developed in a groping and hesitant fashion, depending upon the help of consultants from other agencies, other countries, other professions or other branches of social work, Experiments in consultation received a mixed welcome from those they were designed to help, and when they came to an end altogether new procedures had to be set up which might owe little to the lessons of previous experience. Yet, by one means or another, the Staff of Area 4 repeatedly returned to the task of learning more about their work and seeking guidance and support in their dealings with their clients, whether through staff discussions, supervision or other methods.

DISCUSSION

The principal features of this development and many of the problems it posed have already been considered. Here we discuss some of its more general administrative implications and draw comparisons with other studies in this series. Although the evolution of consultation in this Area Office was only a minor aspect of the FWA's history, it was so closely related to the development of the whole agency at this time that it must be considered in this context.

Post-war modifications in the work of the FWA were first brought about by external economic and social changes, but their implications were rapidly taken up and developed by some of the agency's staff and committee members. As in the Children's Aid Society and the London Children's Department, changes in aims and working methods depended on the application of increased time, manpower and skill to each case. In previous cases this was achieved by an increase in staff, but the resources of the FWA permitted no general increase in manpower. The same effect was achieved in Area 4 by an amalgamation of Areas and a considerable reduction in each worker's caseload. In other Areas, where earlier patterns of social work continued unchanged, caseloads were not reduced in this way. The broad and unspecific character of a social service's aims, noted in previous studies, again appears in this case: even the new definition of the agency's principal functions, quoted at the start of this report, was open to many different interpretations. As in other developments we have traced, the interpretations were hammered out in the course of day-to-day adaptations and improvisations, punctuated by occasional more general reappraisal and debate. The three main groups of factors playing a part in this process are again familiar: the influence of outside authorities controlling resources required by the agency—the Home Office, the Family Discussion Bureau and the University, for example—the aspirations and outlook of staff and committee members actually providing the agency's services, and changes in the demands made on these services. (We have paid least attention to the demands made on the service because they played a smaller part in the particular development chosen for this study; they were a product of many factors, including social conditions in the surrounding area, the reputation of local FWA offices, the links between the FWA and the large number of agencies referring cases to it—nearly 150 different agencies referred the 2,000 cases that were 'active' at the time of this study[1]—and the priorities applied by workers responsible for selecting the cases to be served.)

Features of its situation which rendered it particularly difficult for the FWA to combine these influences and make them a basis for a consistent and continuing evolution of its policies have already been identified. The objectives to be achieved were ill-defined and controversial. The Children's Department and the Children's Aid Society, considered in previous cases, were able to develop family casework as an *adjunct* to their principal, highly practical and widely recognised job of caring for children, with less anxiety about the need for consultation and supervision—though similar demands were expressed by staff working in those agencies, too. But the FWA's staff, lacking the security provided by a central, practical task of this kind, felt greater need for discussion, guidance and education. In the Area Offices that still confined themselves mainly to the discriminating distribution of material help—also a practical and clearly understood task—there was less demand for consultation. Meanwhile the objectives of the various interests playing a part in the evolution of the FWA's work, inside and outside the agency, could not readily be reconciled. As in other cases we have considered, there were discrepancies between the formal or 'manifest' explanations of the agency's work and objectives, the practical or 'assumed'[2] interpretation of these objectives, and the future aspirations of those concerned. But these discrepancies did not lead in a cumulative, reconcilable and smoothly evolving direction; they were often contradictory.

It is at this point in the analysis that we have learnt to look for the groups and individuals whose roles compel them to contend with such conflicting pressures and produce a fruitful synthesis or compromise. But the FWA's patterns of communication and decision-making proved particularly weak at this point. Some confrontation had to be achieved between the diverse approaches to family casework, and the many other interests within the Association—the Citizen's Advice Bureaux, the Old People's Homes Committee, the Information Service, experimental

[1] *Review of the Family Welfare Association.*
[2] The terms quoted are Wilfred Brown's *Exploration in Management,* Heinemann, 1960, p. 289.

projects of various kinds and other services, all competing for a share of the same funds. Only at the level of the Administrative Council was this confrontation possible. The status and authority of such 'representative' bodies always tends to be uncertain in a voluntary association: a similar problem of sovereignty appeared in the Children's Aid Society. In the FWA a large Council was recruited in a manner designed to encourage people to represent rather than reconcile their interests, and further appeals from its decisions could then be made to the Domestic Meeting and, potentially, to the Annual General Meeting. The agency's 'federal' structure helps to explain why decisions were less authoritative, more cautious—and less disruptive—than those traced in the previous case.

Meanwhile the social workers in Area 4, like their colleagues in other studies, were passing through a phase of professional development in which they needed to identify the crucial and distinctive features of their work and concentrate upon strictly professional concerns. The structure of the Association might have been designed to encourage the less desirable features of this phase by shifting the consideration of more general questions, such as the priorities to be accorded to the agency's different activities and Areas, to a distant and indecisive forum. The consultations, staff meetings and supervisory sessions in Area 4 were not only a means of professional development but also an attempt to sort out these priorities at the local level, dealing frequently with intake procedures and the selection of cases, the role of the Area Committee, the principles to be adopted in providing material help, and so on. But if appropriate procedures for determining priorities in an agency's work are not available, decisions have nevertheless to be made—often in inappropriate places. The outcome of this continuing attempt to fashion new aims and methods, going on at the same time in many branches of the Association, emerged in the form of irreconcilable demands on the financial resources available—as it did in the case of the Children's Aid Society. This process inevitably transferred many of the ultimate decisions about the allocation of resources to those responsible for the Association's finances. The professional staff sometimes complained that decisions about the development of social work services were taken on the basis of irrelevant financial criteria, but the Honorary Treasurer retorted— justifiably enough—that he had at least to ensure that deficits on current account were restricted to a level which would in the last resort leave him two years' grace in which to wind up the Association and meet all its debts and obligations. If others could not restrict the Association's expenditure to this level, he had no alternative but to pose the problem himself, for decision by any authority capable of acting. Consultative and educational procedures for the staff in Area 4 were amongst the occasional casualties of this process.

Thus the development examined in this study was a central feature of the attempts made by the staff in one Area office to cope with changed demands on their service in the light of new ideas then developing throughout their profession. By gaining greater discretion in determining the selection and numbers of cases to be served, the methods to be employed and the aims to be adopted, these workers were able to make considerable changes in the character of their service. But the increased responsibilities they assumed in this way and the fundamental questions these developments posed about the ill-defined objectives of the service led them to seek new forms of guidance and new procedures for learning about their work. These new forms of supervision called for additional expenditure which could not be assured on a planned and continuing basis because the assumptions on which they were based were not generally understood and accepted throughout the agency. Effective procedures were not available at this time for reconciling the conflicting objectives of different branches and interests within the agency and for determining the priorities to be accorded to each. Procedures for consultation and supervision were nevertheless improvised in an intermittent fashion, largely as an adjunct to other activities and requirements of the agency. These and many other problems of the FWA were examined in the course of a major review conducted just after this study was made, and a major reorganisation has since been carried through in an attempt to resolve them.

POSTSCRIPT

The FWA is one of those organisations which has a collective 'personality', some features of which survive wholesale changes in constitution, staff and premises. Public and painful reappraisals of its own organisation and functions have been one of those recurring features. Picking up the story again in 1973, fifteen years after the point at which our original study ended, we found the FWA had published a major review of these questions—the fifth since the war.[1] This quoted from the Cunliffe Report, produced in 1960 at the conclusion of the third major review which was beginning as our study ended:

'... no individual, government or organisation is going to make any appreciable grant to the Association unless it can be demonstrated that the Association has a programme and fills a need in the community not coped with in any other way. The Association would find this hard to do at present for it has no clearly laid out policies and therefore the boundaries of its activities are frequently hazy. There has been insufficient research in order to establish needs with which the Association might deal. There has been a marked tendency for the Association to live unto itself and when making plans to have little contact with other organisations except to ask for money.'[2]

[1] Report of the Study Group. FWA, 1972.
[2] Cunliffe Report, 1960, p. 24.

This statement, said the latest Report, was 'unfortunately equally relevant to the state of FWA twelve years later'; but the Association has made considerable progress during the two years since that was written.

The consultative processes which we studied were recognised to be crucial to the Association. 'Because working with clients at depth is personally very demanding', said the Report of 1972, 'it is important that the workers should be supported. Professional support is built into the system in the casework department, each worker having regular supervision with the principal social worker and the principals deriving group and individual support from the Casework Consultant.' ('Principal' was the new title for Area Secretary.) The Study Group drove home the need for this sort of support, or care, by quoting from an experienced social worker who had previously been on the Association's staff: 'The caring in the organisation is absolutely vital, if one is to care anywhere near adequately for one's clients.'[1]

By 1973 the FWA was working in a new environment. It had grown increasingly dependent on the local authorities. As we have explained in the postscripts to Chapters 5 and 6, the Children and Young Persons Act of 1963 gave the Children's Departments greater powers to do preventive work and provide material help for families in difficulties of many kinds. The London County Council was abolished in 1965 and its responsibilities for personal social services were transferred to the 32 Greater London Boroughs. In 1971 these responsibilities had been brought together from the Boroughs' Health, Welfare and Children's Departments to form the new Social Services Departments. With an enlarged and better trained staff of social workers, these Departments had powers to help virtually anyone. More and more people who might previously have sought help from charities turned to the Supplementary Benefits Commission, set up in 1966 as a successor to the National Assistance Board. In addition to its regular benefits, the Commission could make grants and weekly allowances for exceptional needs of many kinds. Thus the FWA had stronger competition to contend with. Meanwhile many social work services were turning away from the kind of intensive casework on which the FWA had built its reputation.

Internally, the Association had been transformed. Its worst financial problems were solved, for some years at least, by the sale of its old central office—a lugubrious mausoleum close to Victoria Station in the middle of Westminster. The Association's new headquarters was in a businesslike, two-storey office behind a shop-front on a main road in Dalston, one of the less fashionable parts of inner London. After acquiring and converting the new building and paying off its overdraft, the sale left the FWA with a quarter of a million pounds for the development of its work. These large reserves, held by the Central Council, may

[1] Report of the Study Group, p. 4.

have helped to unify the Association and check tendencies to separatism in the Areas.

A succession of internal conflicts and resignations led in 1972 to a recasting of the Association in the form of a limited company with charitable status, no share capital, and a simplified constitution. The Association's main purposes remained, as before, 'to provide a casework service for people with difficulties especially in personal relationships; to teach and train persons in the principles, methods and administration of social work . . . ; to promote, encourage or undertake organised research or experimental work . . . ; to act as trustee of, and to administer charitable and other trust funds; and to establish, support or assist Citizens' Advice Bureaux and other centres for giving advice and guidance'.[1] Henceforth its affairs were managed by a Council which was elected from three sources: an annual general meeting of members (the majority), Area Committees, and other relevant organisations. Some of the Area Committees remained an active force within the Association, but all were more clearly subordinated to the Central Office than they had been fifteen years earlier. Their social work staff were neither obliged to consult them about individual cases nor to seek their approval before making grants to clients.

The seven Area Offices were retained—Area 4 covering the same territory as before. Most of them had more staff and (with a total FWA caseload of under 1,000) fewer cases to handle than they had at the time of our original study. Area Offices took a more standardised pattern— not unlike the one originally pioneered by Area 4. Each was led by a Principal Family Social Worker who was assisted by about four other social workers. All were professionally trained caseworkers and between a third and a half had undergone an analysis. Their work was based on psychoanalytic assumptions about human motives and behaviour. It was intensive, and tightly organised: a typical social worker with two years' experience would do fifteen one-hour interviews in the course of a thirty-five-hour week. Clients—about thirty per worker—would be seen at least once a fortnight. Most of these interviews took place in the office, but unsupported mothers and others who had difficulty in getting out were still visited at home.

About two-fifths of the people helped by the FWA came on their own initiative, about one-third—a growing proportion—were referred by local authority services, and the rest came on the advice of doctors, medical social workers, employers and others. A few were middle class, but the majority were poorer working-class people. The 'presenting problems' were marital in at least two-fifths of cases, financial in one-fifth, and the rest included a wide range of family, personal, housing and other difficulties.

The consultative processes which we studied were financed from

[1] Memorandum and Articles of Association.

regular, current expenditure, no longer from special grants. The senior person responsible for what was now described as 'supervision' was the Casework Consultant—a senior member of the Central Office staff. He had previously been the Principal of the Southwark Area Office. He was responsible for recruiting all the Association's social caseworkers. He ran courses of ten to twelve sessions with groups of new staff, but caseworkers relied mainly on their own Principals for supervision—usually in weekly sessions. The Consultant met Principals fortnightly in small groups, partly for administrative and partly for 'therapeutic' supervision. Students from social work training courses—about forty coming each year, usually for nine to ten months—were supervised by the more experienced caseworkers in Area Offices to whom they were individually attached.

The difficulties which staff experienced with those whom they tried to help and the feelings involved in their relationships with clients and colleagues provided the main themes of supervisory sessions. The purpose of these discussions was to make social workers' relationships with their clients therapeutically more productive.

Some uncertainties remained about the functions of supervision, and particularly about the job of the Casework Consultant himself. In the course of the latest review he had recommended that his role as spokesman for the social casework 'interest' within the FWA should be recognised by renaming his post 'Head of Social Work' and making Principals and their social caseworkers responsible to the Director of the FWA through him. But the majority of the Study Group, on which he had served, recommended that the Director's position should be strengthened, and that the Consultant should shed management tasks, such as the appointment and deployment of staff, and become 'Chief Professional Adviser' to the Director and the Association.[1] Influential academic members of the Study Group continued to serve on the Council's Organisation Committee (successor to the Reorganisation Committee in our original study) which was looking into these problems when this postscript was being written. At that time the Committee proposed to the Central Council that the Consultant become 'Assistant Director (Social Work)'. His responsibilities under that title would be broadened because he would 'be accountable for social work in the areas *and* for helping the Director establish consistent social work policies throughout the whole of the Association'.

Conclusion

What conclusions can be drawn from this brief glimpse of the FWA's recent development? The main trends traced in our original study have gone a lot further. Although the Association still has multiple functions, social casework is more clearly than ever its main task. Those who do

[1] Report of the Study Group, p. 12.

this work—previously a somewhat motley group, with various kinds of training or none—are all now trained in a distinctive, psychoanalytic professional tradition. The Area Committees, originally one of the main sources of power in the FWA, are now generally confined to tasks such as raising funds for general use and informing central office about local needs. The new Director is herself a social caseworker (the first to hold this post) who was trained within FWA. And although there may be some controversy about the Casework Consultant's role it is generally accepted that he is the main spokesman for social casework within the Association. The consultative processes we studied have become a central and permanent feature of the Association's organisation and working methods.

It is recognised, too—as it was not at the time of our original study—that the FWA's future will depend increasingly on the support of the local authorities and their Social Services Departments. The authorities' grants now meet two-thirds of the FWA's current expenditure, and the Association is already asking for 75 per cent. To retain that support it must show that it complements the local authorities' services in valuable and irreplaceable ways. Owing to small caseloads, good training and careful supervision, FWA staff can generally give people more intensive help over longer periods than would be feasible in the public services. They can reach some clients who might not be willing to approach the authorities. They can help others who could not be given the time they need by hard pressed public services: one of the FWA's offices runs a fee-charging casework service for the middle class. The Association also helps universities and colleges to train students who later enter many different kinds of social work.

While the Social Service Departments and the training courses are overwhelmed by the new demands laid upon them, there is an assured demand for the FWA—escaped at last from its debts and its dusty Victorian offices. But many recognise that the Association will have to reconsider its policies as time goes by. It has adopted what might be described (by management consultants) as a '*process*-oriented' strategy, focusing increasingly specialised, psychoanalytic attention upon fewer clients. The achievements of this process are difficult to measure. Some would argue that a briefer intervention, focused on more concrete and clearly defined tasks, agreed with the client, would be more effective—and cheaper.[1]

The present lengthy and labour-intensive service is likely to become increasingly expensive in relation to other goods and services as incomes rise. A '*market*-oriented' strategy—alert to changing needs and demands and quick to devise new ways of satisfying them—might lead to a wider

---

[1] For a survey of some research which underlies such thinking, see W. J. Reid and Ann W. Shyne, *Brief and Extended Casework*. Columbia University Press, 1969.

variety of interventions, including group work and community development, advocacy of welfare rights and 'task-oriented' social work.

The Director noted these possibilities when she addressed the Association's annual general meeting in January 1974. 'We are going to look at effectiveness and I hope do some research. We have the confidence to explore Family Therapy and Group Work methods—and if there are any other methods coming along in future I think we should have them too.' What they can have will depend increasingly on what the taxpayer's representatives in local government are prepared to pay for.

CHAPTER 10

FORMULATING A POLICY FOR SECONDARY EDUCATION IN CROYDON

This study deals with an attempt to adapt a social service to changes in the demands being made upon it. But the major development proposed by the director of the service in response to initial expressions of public concern could not begin without the participation of the principal people providing the service and the consent of others capable of influencing its growth. Thus conflicts which emerged at a later phase in other cases we have studied had here to be resolved at the outset. This study traces the course of these negotiations and the parts played in them by the various groups involved. A growing circle of outside interests was brought into the debate and a determined drive for decisions made it difficult for the governing body of the service to maintain an independent standpoint or to formulate a fruitful synthesis from the diverse views presented to it.

This study deals with two attempts to recast the system of secondary education in a County Borough. The first took place between 1954 and 1956; the second began in 1961 and was still under discussion in 1964 when the study ends. The study was carried out by a Borough Councillor[1] and has the advantage—and possibly some of the disadvantages—of being based largely on a diary and on current records assembled by an active participant in some of the events to be described. Unlike most of the previous studies, this case deals with the preparation of plans for a new development, not with their implementation. These plans called for a wholesale reorganisation of complex and firmly rooted institutions, a reorganisation which could not be worked out gradually and pragmatically; major decisions had to be taken about the future structure of the system before any reform could begin. The case deals with negotiations, still in progress, which may eventually lead to new developments. The social services considered in most of the previous cases had something like a monopoly of the particular type of service examined; in this case the Education Department was collaborating closely (and some of its schools were competing directly) with a parallel system of private schools, and these relationships with

[1] Kenneth Urwin.

outside bodies played a considerable part in the story. Yet, despite these distinctive features, many elements of the story will already be familiar from the analysis of previous cases: the initial recognition of stresses calling for reappraisal of the system, the formulation of different—and sometimes conflicting—interpretations of this situation among groups with divergent frames of reference, the involvement of a widening circle of interests capable of exercising influence on the decisions to be made, and the concentration of pressures focused upon the body responsible for those decisions—all these phases of the policy-making process will be familiar. The way in which they were handled by the Education Authority provides distinctive variations on this theme, and may account for the Authority's failure—thus far—to bring about any major reform.

Croydon and its Secondary Education

Croydon has a population, according to the 1961 census, of 252,500: by the middle of 1963 this figure was estimated to have risen to 254,100 —an addition due to a birth rate that is well above the average for England and Wales. Croydon is an integral part of the London conurbation. Its centre lies ten miles south of Charing Cross. But, like West Ham and East Ham in the same conurbation, it constituted a separate County Borough for local government purposes at the time of this study. Thus its immediate neighbours—Beckenham and Bromley in Kent, Mitcham and Sutton in Surrey—had limited powers and were subject to the Kent and Surrey County Councils for many purposes. But Croydon's Council was responsible for all local government functions within its territory. Under the reorganisation of Greater London government, due in 1965, the boundaries of the local authority are to be substantially enlarged.

The town is not merely a dormitory suburb of London. Despite its large commuting population, it has a strong commercial position in its own right. Its manufacturing industries include electrical components, computers and electronic gear, small cars, and so on—a variety of fairly specialised engineering enterprises. But commercial undertakings now hold pride of place. With the steep rise in rents in central London, more and more companies have sought out the office space which Croydon's own schemes of development have recently offered. In 1956 (when its existing office accommodation was almost negligible) the town promoted in Parliament a private Bill which triggered off major re-development in the central area. Early projects—the fruit of collaboration between the Council and private developers—coincided with the Government's growing determination to discourage further office development in Central London; and Croydon's stake has since grown to such an extent that the Location of Offices Bureau expects the town to rank as the fifth largest commercial office centre in the country by 1970—its office population, then numbering between 25,000 and 30,000, would be exceeded only by those of London, Birmingham, Manchester and Liverpool. As the developers include considerable shopping areas in their office blocks, Croydon also has a growing reputation as a shopping and service centre.

The town returns three members to Parliament and has since 1950 been represented by Conservatives, with majorities ranging in the 1959 Election from 6,000 to 10,000. The balance on the Borough Council swung to give the Labour group a slight edge in 1963, with twenty-five elected representatives to the Conservative-Independents' twenty-three. But the allocation of aldermanic seats prevented the Labour group from taking control.

The Council of Croydon is the accredited Local Education Authority —one of 146 in England and Wales. For most practical purposes the responsibilities of the Council are vested in its Education Committee, made up of eighteen Councillors and Aldermen. The terms of membership of the Education Committee differ from those for other Committees of the Council, in that its members serve for three years at a time, six being elected each year. The Committee normally meets every four weeks, and it has a number of sub-committees whose meetings also follow a regular cycle. These deal with Schools, Further Education, the Youth Service, Youth Employment, Reconstruction, and Finance and General Purposes. The agenda on each occasion is drawn up by the senior officers of the Education Department, normally after consulting the elected Chairman—though any member may request in advance that a specific item come up for discussion. The meetings of the Education Committee—but not of its sub-committees—are open to the public and the press. Exceptionally, as in the matter under review here, a special ad hoc sub-committee may be created, reporting direct to the full Committee. All policy recommendations must receive the final ratification of a majority vote in Council.

The Education Committee's professional advisers consist of administrators with substantial teaching experience, and a number of expert technical officers. There is also a local Inspectorate. The Chief Education Officer's principal colleagues are the Deputy Education Officer and the Chief Inspector. The Principal School Medical Officer, who is also the Borough's Medical Officer of Health, is responsible for medical matters. The Chief Inspector has a staff of five Inspectors, and other senior officials include the Principal School Architect, two Assistant Education Officers responsible respectively for Schools and Further Education, the Supplies Officer, the Youth Officer, and the Youth Employment Officer.

Education is compulsory from the age of five years. This means that the Education Authority is responsible, under the 1944 Education Act, for providing schools of different kinds for children from five to the statutory school leaving age of fifteen. A considerable number of children will choose to stay at school beyond this age, and the Authority must provide schooling for those who want it until the end of their eighteenth year. Croydon's experience in this respect is important, for the proportion of the town's children staying into their fifth, sixth and seventh year of secondary schooling is well above the national average. Comparable figures for London, and for Boroughs about the same size as Croydon are shown in the accompanying table.

PERCENTAGE OF CHILDREN REMAINING AT SCHOOL BEYOND MINIMUM SCHOOL LEAVING AGE, 1963

Numbers in age-groups shown, as percentages of same groups at the age of thirteen

	15-year-olds		16-year-olds		17-year-olds	
	Boys	Girls	Boys	Girls	Boys	Girls
Croydon	64	54	35	26	27	10
London County	51	49	27	25	13	11
Leicester	38	28	20	14	12	6
Stoke-on-Trent	22	19	16	11	10	7
Newcastle-on-Tyne	34	31	17	14	9	6
Counties	44	42	24	22	12	10
County Boroughs	38	33	20	17	11	8
England	42	39	23	20	12	10

Source: Ministry of Education, *Secondary Education in Each Local Education Authority Area*. List 69. HMSO, 1964.

In this table the figures refer to pupils for whom the Authorities had direct financial responsibility. The majority of these pupils were in the Authorities' own schools—the 'maintained schools'. A few of them had places, by the deliberate choice of the Authority concerned, in independent and direct grant schools[1] of the neighbourhood and their fees were paid by the Authority. In Croydon the population of children so placed in any year is over 5 per cent of the total number for whom the

[1] An 'independent school' is one financed solely from endowments and fees for pupils. Normally no Authority would buy places at an independent school unless the school is a good one—at least being 'recognised as efficient' by the Ministry. The independent schools in which Croydon takes free places are two prominent boys' public schools (one within, the other just outside, the Borough boundaries) and four denominational schools, one Anglican (girls) and three Roman Catholic (two for boys, one for girls). Normally 'direct grant schools' are one-time independent schools now receiving a grant from the Ministry of Education in return for an arrangement to receive free-place pupils from Local Authorities. Croydon takes a substantial number of places at two such schools, one for boys and one for girls.

Authority is financially responsible: this relatively high figure indicates a marked wealth of opportunity in Croydon's own situation, for in and around the Borough are 9 independent and direct-grant schools, 5 for boys and 4 for girls, all of them with a long educational tradition, where the Authority contracts to take free places for some of its pupils. These places are allotted to children gaining a high position in competitive transfer tests set by the Authority in the last year or so of the primary school: every parent of a primary child can express preferences for particular schools in the secondary range, but the child's ranking in the transfer tests is the principal means of selection.

A number of parents choose to pay fees for education at secondary schools not provided by the Authority, either for religious reasons, or because they feel that private schooling has special advantages. These children may at any time transfer to a maintained school, but their placing will be at the discretion of the authority.

In this study we are concerned with the pattern of secondary education which developed in Croydon after the 1944 Act, and with Croydon's own evaluation of the selective processes which largely determined the placing of children within that system. Broadly speaking, this system is divided into three parts: Grammar, Technical, and Modern. Two 'maintained' grammar schools, one for boys and one for girls, were already in existence in 1944, and these were continued. As the school population grew, and as it became obvious that many more children could cope with work at least up to 'Ordinary' level, so other secondary schools were converted into grammar schools, further 'selective' schools (including technical schools) were created, and finally 'academic' courses with 'O' level objectives were begun in a limited number of 'non-selective' secondary modern schools. This enlargement of selective education continued throughout the post-war period, and by 1963 there had been added to the two 'maintained' and one 'aided' grammar schools existing in 1944: five new grammar schools (ex-'central' schools), a selective school without a sixth form (ex-secondary modern), two technical schools with sixth forms, and academic courses leading to 'O' level examinations in ten secondary modern schools. By 1963 the thirteen-year-olds for whose education Croydon was responsible were distributed in the manner shown in the table overleaf. In comparison with other authorities, Croydon had an exceptionally large number of children in independent and direct grant schools, and an average proportion in grammar schools; but the smaller numbers in intervening types of school left a proportion in the secondary modern schools that was also larger than average.

Each school has a considerable measure of independence, and the Authority is at pains to interfere as little as possible in their internal administration. Their development therefore reflects a delicate balance between head teacher and staff, parents and pupils, and the Borough

PERCENTAGE DISTRIBUTION OF THIRTEEN-YEAR-OLDS BY TYPE OF SCHOOL, 1963

	Primary (all-age)		Secondary Modern		Technical		Comprehensive		Other Secondary		Grammar		Direct Grant		Independent	
	Boys	Girls	Boys	Girls	Boys	Girls	Boys	Girls	Boys	Girls	Boys	Girls	Boys	Girls	Boys	Girls
Croydon	0	0	67	69	8	*	1	1	3	4	16	20	2	6	4	1
London County	1	*	15	15	2	*	48	46	19	21	15	17	1	1	1	*
Leicester	0	0	73	71	6	0	0	0	6	7	15	22	0	0	*	*
Stoke-on-Trent	2	1	49	54	7	3	0	0	29	30	11	10	2	2	0	0
Newcastle-on-Tyne	4	6	55	51	17	18	7	7	0	0	13	14	4	3	0	2
Counties	2	2	65	64	2	2	6	6	5	5	19	20	1	1	1	1
County Boroughs	3	3	63	64	6	4	5	4	4	6	16	17	2	2	*	1
England	2	2	65	64	3	2	6	5	5	5	18	19	2	2	1	1

*Less than 0·5 per cent.

Source: Ministry of Education, *Secondary Education in each Local Education Authority Area*. List 69. HMSO, 1964.

Inspectorate. A Governing Body, normally composed of eight members headed by an Alderman or Councillor, is established for each school, and its members appointed every three years by the Council. Membership of these bodies tends to follow the lines of political grouping in the town, though non-political organisations may offer nominees to the Council. In the case of schools with a denominational background which are now aided or controlled by the Authority, members are appointed to represent the denominational interest. The duties of Governors are restricted mainly to the school, and they have no part in shaping the overall policy of the Authority, though they may legitimately comment on the application of that policy to their own school.

Behind these local groups intimately connected with each school—Council and Education Committee, Governing Body, administrators, teaching staff and parents—stands the Ministry of Education (since renamed the Department of Education and Science). The Minister has considerable powers to maintain standards in individual schools. The 1944 Act required him to 'secure the effective execution by local authorities, under his control and direction, of the national policy for providing a varied and comprehensive educational service in every area'. Thus every Authority had to produce a Development Plan, indicating in detail the siting, area and general character of its schools, actual and potential. But despite the intentions of the Act, a Development Plan has no force in law. Section 12 of the Act, which empowered the Minister to make 'local education orders', has not been applied. Under Section 13 an Authority must consult the Ministry about any proposal to establish a new school or to close an existing school, and the Minister is empowered to veto or modify proposals of either type; and under Section 67 (4) he has on occasion prevented expansions of existing schools which appeared to him to amount to the establishment of a new school. Croydon was never certain whether its plan for reorganising secondary education required the Minister's approval or not.

HM Inspectors of Schools—who are appointed by Order in Council and technically independent of the Ministry—provide advice and a means of informal consultation linking the Ministry and the Education Authorities. The Ministry used also to distribute the funds provided for the Authorities by the Treasury, but since the Local Government Act of 1958 this function has been exercised by the Ministry of Housing and Local Government whose general grants cover about 60 per cent of the Authorities' current expenditure on education.

A school has real, if limited, independence. But it operates within a framework determined by the Council and its committees, who depend on the advice of the administrative officers and inspectors in the town hall; it is influenced by the Ministry and the central government's inspectors, the professional associations to which its staff belong, the parents of its children, and sometimes an association of old pupils. All these bodies play some part in the study that follows.

The main features of Croydon's situation may be summarised before proceeding to the developments to be traced in this study. The Borough had a rapidly increasing and reasonably prosperous population, depending mainly on work in central London or in local commercial, service and engineering industries. A large proportion of these people were determined to secure the best available education for their children. (The demand for selective secondary education was much greater here than in the other two County Boroughs in the London area.) The selective procedures which determined educational opportunities—mainly in the children's eleventh year—had thus assumed major economic and social significance, and were followed with the keenest interest. The existence of an exceptionally large number of independent and direct grant schools in and around Croydon and the opportunity for securing free places in them, sharpened the comparisons made—by parents and teachers alike—between the relative merits of different secondary schools. The independent and direct grant schools provided a small but enormously important part of Croydon's secondary system, yet they were in no way under the Borough's control, and could only be aligned with any general reform by their own agreement. The Council might decide to reduce the numbers of children it sent to these schools, but their places could readily be filled from other sources. A considerable number of influential people in the town had themselves attended the better known schools in the district and could not regard debates about their future as an abstract or remote question of educational policy. The Borough Council and its officers worked in close proximity to the Ministry, and also to the London County Council—which at this time was pressing on with the creation of an entirely different pattern of secondary education relying mainly on comprehensive schools. Croydon's Council was jealous of its independence, but aware of national and regional developments which constituted a potential challenge to its own policies. These policies assumed the basic soundness of the structure bequeathed from the pre-war period, and were designed to provide an increasingly generous variety of secondary education within the framework of a conventional tripartite division between grammar, technical and modern schools—helped out at the 'top' end with places in the independent schools. This system was described by the Borough's new Chief Education Officer as 'the first thoughts of most Authorities on their obligations under the 1944 Act to make secondary education for all a reality'. What were to be Croydon's second thoughts?

First Attempt at a Reform

In July 1954 the Council accepted a motion put forward by two members of the minority (Labour) group. It read: 'As the number of grammar school places in Croydon is already below the national average both for boys and girls, the Education Committee is requested to inform the Council what steps it proposes to take—within, say, the next three years—to provide the extra grammar school places which Croydon obviously needs if it is to take its proper share in making provision for the education and well-being of the nation.' This proposition raised questions both about the quality of non-selective secondary schools and about the scarcity of selective places.

To this motion the Education Committee reacted in September with a preliminary report, prepared by its officers, indicating some limited steps which could help make good the deficiency in selective places; and in October it set up a special sub-committee to review the grammar school situation on a broad front. Late in November a memorandum signed by the Chief Education Officer (who had held his appointment only a few months) and by the Chief Inspector was made public. The timing of its appearance was probably an accident, due to a leak of information to the local press, but the fact of its publication at a premature point—before even the sub-committee had considered it—produced immediate difficulties. The document in fact put forward an imaginative scheme for amalgamating the sixth forms of grammar schools in Croydon to form a two-year 'Junior College'; this college would provide places for pupils from all the sixteen maintained schools in which 'O' level examinations offered access to more advanced work. The creation of such a college, it was argued, would result in the kind of economies of staffing and equipment which the situation in Croydon called for, and would afford students of sixteen to eighteen years a wider variety of courses than could be provided by any one secondary school.

The memorandum had not been discussed with any representative group of teachers. They were unaware that these ideas were being considered and it thus became a focus of contention in educational circles. The Chief Education Officer recognised that 'a revolutionary change from the present pattern of the English Grammar School' was being proposed. *The Times Educational Supplement* described the plan as 'a proposal to interfere with the best of our English schools to meet a particular difficulty'. The grammar school heads in Croydon wrote defensively: 'The sixth form is the backbone of every grammar school. Its standard reflects the standard of the school as a whole.'

Representative deputations of teachers—not all of them unsympathetic to the proposal—then met the sub-committee. The following spring the Director of the Oxford University Institute of Education was invited (at the personal invitation of the Chief Education Officer) to advise the sub-committee as a consultant. By November the sub-committee, having met seven times, had reached a considered (though not unanimous) opposition to the project, and this view ultimately prevailed in the Council debate. The Education Committee's report to the Council stressed that their consultant had advised solely from the educational and not from the economic angle. It quoted him as favouring the idea of a pooling of teaching resources at sixth-form level, but as opposed to the plan as it stood. In a letter to *The Times Educational Supplement* the Consultant outlined his objections thus:

(a) A sixth form depends on continuity with what has gone before.

(b) Sixth form teaching is best given by those who are concurrently teaching at different levels.

(c) A sixth form should include opportunities for those who would never qualify for the intellectual hotbed of a junior college.

(d) A feeling of responsibility and the exercise of authority is important in the intellectual development of a young person.

The Chief Education Officer had, of course, touched on some of these points in making his case. Thus he had argued that pupils between sixteen and nineteen (with 'A' or 'S' level objectives) would be able to work most satisfactorily in a new kind of teaching institution. 'He or she (the sixteen-year-old) has emerged from the age of adolescence and can be said to have reached a stage of early manhood or womanhood. It is usually in these years, when the young person is conscious of becoming an integrated adult personality, that the foundations are laid for real intellectual or cultural achievement in later life. For those who might aspire to first-class intellectual attainment it is quite essential that their education during these early adult years should be in competent hands, under the guidance of men and women of high intellectual qualifications'. The Chief Education Officer was prepared for sixth form pupils to get away from the often unacceptable idea of 'staying on at school'. 'They would', he wrote, 'be going on to a college which might in a very short time be able to establish for itself a considerable cultural and intellectual reputation . . . The young adult of seventeen wishes to be treated as an adult and to have a different relation with his leaders from that of the adolescent . . . Five years in one school is long enough, and the growing personality is stimulated by changes of environment, so long as they are not too frequent.'

His memorandum had criticised the prevailing organisation of sixth form work as wasteful of staff, space and equipment. Because of these defects, he thought, pupils were being refused their first choice of 'A' level subjects because facilities in their school were not available; and he suspected that some who left at sixteen might have given up because of the known difficulty of providing certain courses. While minority subjects demanded special attention, no school, he wrote, could afford to divert staff to take charge of them to the extent of arranging whole periods of individual tuition.

He entered an interesting caveat against any assumption by the grammar schools that they could emulate public schools in their sixth form work. (His own teaching experience had been gained in a well-known public school.) The fact was that the public school would always carry a sixth form proportionately larger. 'For reasons which are in large part historical, the grammar school, in competition with the large public school in gaining University places, is at a permanent disadvantage . . . One might use the touchstone of Oxford and Cambridge awards . . . In competition for these the pupil from an independent school has a better chance . . . This is not due to any prejudice on the part of the Universities in favour of certain schools . . . Nor, surely, could it be contested that the native ability of the boys at independent schools is higher than the others.' The advantage of large numbers, he suggested, accounted for the better quality of sixth form work within the public schools.

This proved to be a far from convincing argument, and the comparison with public schools served further to alienate grammar school opinion within the town. In fact, at local level the grammar schools might with some justice regard themselves as impoverished to the exact proportion that neighbouring independent and direct grant schools were enriched. For these latter received the considerable asset of able free-place pupils—almost certainly potential sixth form material of good calibre. The grammar schools, competing for good pupils and striving to offer opportunities for all-round development to all of them, could not avoid emulating the public schools in their approach to advanced work. The threat of 'decapitation'—as the loss of sixth forms came to be called—appeared devastating. As the grammar school heads wrote in a second brief: 'The sixth form develops in gifted boys and girls an astonishing maturity. A break at sixteen would cut across the intentions of the GCE course—which envisage "O" and "A" level work as part of the same continuous undertaking; would hamper the transition from an imposed discipline to self-discipline; and would mean a loss of roots without time in six terms to put down new ones.'

One corollary of the junior college project in Croydon was that the heads of the non-selective schools might reasonably expect the Authority —if it accepted the proposal—to carry through a reappraisal of their part in the secondary pattern. On the one hand they might pillory—as some did—the anxieties which the grammar school heads expressed about the social effects of co-education (in the junior college): one-third of the non-selective schools were co-educational. A majority of the non-selective heads welcomed the Chief Education Officer's plan. They argued that the more capable children in the non-selective range would merit still larger opportunities of achieving 'O' level standards and so of finding a place in the junior college. They recognised that with this end in view the Authority would seek to strengthen their staffing and improve their equipment. However, their expectations could not be too sanguine. It had to be accepted that even with a radical change of policy in Croydon it would take a generation to bring all the older schools up to a reasonable standard in buildings and equipment. Moreover teachers do not live for ever. In default of tangible evidence that the Authority was able to plan extensive re-building schemes—and no such opportunity was open to any authority—the grammar schools would maintain many of their preponderating advantages. There were those too who remarked that the consultant had shown no enthusiasm for the demise of the grammar school: they regretfully summed up his intervention as that of a distinguished but remote Oxonian who, like the Devil invoking Einstein against Newton on another occasion, had shouted 'Ho'—and restored the status quo.

Thus the Council, at the end of this first series of discussions, acquiesced in very restricted change. The imminent closure of two Polytechnics provided room for a physical expansion of grammar school work, and Croydon's selective intake grew in 1956 and subsequent years to about 30 per cent of the age-group concerned. At the same time 'academic' courses were planned in certain of the non-selective schools.

Progress thus far may be briefly summarised. A new Chief Education Officer and his immediate colleagues took the opportunity provided by the Council's first serious expression of dissatisfaction with the secondary system to propose far-reaching reforms which would have created a new type of sixth form college at the cost of 'decapitating' the Borough's grammar schools. These proposals were supported by a considerable wealth of statistical—and emotive—argument. They provoked immediate opposition in the schools most obviously due to suffer from such a change, and after considerable discussion and a generally unfavourable report from an outside consultant they were abandoned. The arguments advanced so far were mainly derived from two fundamentally different points of view. Those concerned with the development of education throughout the Borough dwelt on the wider educational opportunities, the more efficient deployment of teaching resources, and the more acceptable educational environment which the reform would offer in the long run. Those concerned with the development of existing grammar schools dwelt on the serious damage such a reform would bring about in those schools in the immediate future. Many more arguments were to be advanced in subsequent years, but these basic differences in outlook still constituted the principal obstacle to agreement. Though the Council and its committees had been given a great deal of evidence to consider, no serious attempt had yet been made to achieve a reasoned reconciliation of views and interests among the schools themselves. Prolonged and detailed discussion of these questions would be required before any progress could be made.

FORMULATING A POLICY FOR SECONDARY EDUCATION 233

A Second Attempt

Croydon's second investigation of its secondary education began at Committee level in 1961. This time the initial problems provoking discussion were different: they were the unreliable selection procedure, and the apparent waste of grammar school places. By now the principle and practice of competitive selection at eleven plus had been called in question in many parts of the country. Croydon's contribution to the national debate was to correlate transfer test results with the subsequent scores of pupils at 'O' level. This investigation showed how uncertain a predictor the eleven plus procedure was: there were disturbingly poor 'O' level achievements among grammar school pupils, and signs of good 'O' level potentialities among a limited number of children in non-selective schools. At the same time the Chief Education Officer's passionate interest in the junior college scheme reasserted itself, and he tried to build a new and stronger case for the junior college upon opposition to the eleven plus.

The papers prepared by the administration from 1956 onwards all showed concern at the quality of response to grammar school opportunity as evinced by those with a poor record in examinations for the General Certificate of Education. These inquiries deserve special mention. What the administration did was to establish its own yardstick of reasonable achievement within the grammar school. This was to be two or more passes at 'O' level in English Language, Mathematics, a Science, or a Foreign Language—so-called 'basic' subjects. Such a criterion can be challenged, but no other systematic method of evaluating the performance of grammar school children was seriously proposed. Those who felt that the yardstick of GCE success was a poor one would assert that to restrict the analysis to 'basic' subjects was even less revealing.

These points emerged from the analyses made by the Education Department:[1]

(a) In 1956 and 1957, only 10 per cent of maintained school entrants passed in the four 'basic' subjects.

(b) In 1958, the figure was higher at 14 per cent, but there were 41 per cent who passed in one subject only or in none.

(c) The children taking free places in independent and direct grant schools did considerably better, on average, than those in maintained schools.

(d) When the assessment of IQs quoted at the time of the transfer tests was correlated with GCE 'O' level results five years later, the following pattern emerged for the maintained schools.

There is no reliable basis for a comparison between the results obtained in selective and non-selective schools. Until recently, for

[1] 'Secondary Education in Croydon. A Consolidated Report.' July 1962.

IQS AND 'O' LEVEL RESULTS

IQ level at transfer	Average passes in 'basic' subjects		Average passes in all academic subjects	
	Boys	Girls	Boys	Girls
127+	2·3	3·2	4·7	5·2
123–6	2·35	2·6	4·0	4·4
119–22	2·3	2·1	4·5	3·7
115–18	2·0	1·7	3·2	3·0
111–14	1·6	1·5	2·7	2·5
107–10	1·65	1·4	2·6	2·6
103–6	1·7	0·9	2·4	1·0
99–102	1·4	1·1	2·2	2·2

example, there had been no provision for foreign language work to 'O' level in non-selective schools. However, in one year, 1958, ninety-four pupils in non-selective schools took 'O' level subjects. The results achieved by these children are shown below. The ranking of the 'catchment' pupils in the original transfer tests had not justified any expectations of a useful result in 'O' level work five years later, yet they, and fifty-six other pupils, had achieved encouraging results.

	No. of children	Average passes in academic subjects	Average IQ
'Selected' for academic course	19	3·4	108
Recommended by Junior School Heads	37	3·2	107
'Catchment' pupils	38	3·2	100

Now a grammar school place at eleven plus was a prized social asset, and 84 per cent of Croydon parents opted for grammar school at the time of their child's transfer. But in the light of these findings the Chief Education Officer wrote in 1961: 'A considerable proportion of pupils in grammar and selective schools have failed to some degree in a curriculum which they might have been expected to tackle . . . It might be held that unless after five years in the secondary school a pupil can obtain a pass in two or more of these basic subjects, he has not in the event justified his place in the grammar school or selective school course . . . What emerges therefore is the need to retain flexibility within the secondary school course, since to make too rigid a division at eleven plus means subsequent wastage in both directions (i.e. children selected and failing to justify their selection, other children making a presentable showing in GCE work despite having been unselected).'

These reports, and the administration's recommendations based on them, went to a new sub-committee of the Education Committee which began seriously to consider the problem in June 1961. In April the Education Committee had asked for a general report on 'the state of the schools'. The sub-committee was made up of four members of the majority group and two of the minority. Their objective was to consider the whole character of secondary schools in Croydon and to propose some change in pattern. The trend of the administration's proposals was towards common secondary schools, capped as before by a junior college; but there were sidelong glances at other possibilities of reform which came to assume greater importance as the discussions went on.

The Chief Education Officer submitted his reports to the Director of the National Foundation for Educational Research, and to the Director of the London University Institute of Education. In his comments, the former stressed the advantages of the large school—with eight-form entry as a desirable size—and urged flexibility of curriculum, especially during the first three years of secondary education. The Director of the Institute made written observations and visited Croydon, at the suggestion of the Chairman, to speak to the Education Committee. He was concerned that the present structure of secondary education fixed things too soon and too finally; he appreciated the merits of 'academic' streams in non-selective schools, but recognised the difficulties of making proper provision at the top end of secondary schools without a very large entry at their base. So (while disclaiming any intimate knowledge of Croydon's secondary pattern) he felt that: (a) four-form entry common schools might be educationally satisfactory until choice of subjects had to be made at about fourteen plus; (b) some selection would have to follow 'O' level, and this fact might lead a pioneering authority towards a junior college. To this extent, at least, he presented views at variance with those of the consultant who had advised the Council seven years before.

The Chief Education Officer was at this time trying to drive matters rapidly to a conclusion, urging the sub-committee to make a recommendation about the general lines on which change in Croydon could be based, and leaving to future consultation with head teachers the detailed work of implementation. This was considerably further than the sub-committee was prepared to go. The staffs of schools had at no point been officially advised of the administration's reports and had therefore been offered no opportunity to comment upon them. It was unthinkable that far-reaching decisions by the Education Committee could be envisaged while teachers remained entirely outside the discussions.

However, the draft of the report of the sub-committee in July 1962—incorporating most of the administration's findings and the views of the two consultants—was positive in its tone and detailed in its manner of presentation. It prompted conjecture that decisions had already been taken since it stated: 'They (the sub-committee) consider that it should be the Council's policy to move progressively towards the pattern of a common school at the secondary school stage between eleven and sixteen, so that competitive selection at eleven plus may be suspended ... They consider establishing a new pattern of work for GCE 'A' level and for University admission, and have returned to the proposal discussed seven years ago ... for the pooling of this work for all maintained secondary schools in the borough.' The report included a sketch timetable by which the early stages of the plan could be made effective. Its publication gave rise to the widespread impression—shared by such papers as *The Times Educational Supplement* and the *Observer*—that the 'Croydon Plan' was being put into effect.

But the scheme outlined was prefaced by the words—'The sub-committee have in mind ...'—and when the report was presented to Council the Chairman of the Education Committee emphasised that no final decision was being sought. The Committee recommended discussion of the proposals with the Ministry of Education, and meetings with head teachers to consider both the principles involved in the proposals and the methods by which they might be implemented. The Chief Education Officer proceeded to make personal contact with heads of schools to acquaint them with the background to the whole enquiry.

At the beginning of the new term in September deputations representing staff in the schools moved in upon the sub-committee. Initial reactions followed the same kind of alignments as in 1954–5. But public, as distinct from professional, comment was more favourable to change than it had been during the earlier debate. Thus the *Croydon Advertiser* declared: 'When seven years ago, we opposed the idea of a sixth form college in Croydon, absorbing and replacing the sixth forms of the existing grammar schools, we were wrong. It was a judgement based too much upon a sentimental attachment to the established order, too little upon an appreciation of desirable developments to meet new needs ... The arguments now put forward to support it are convincing, even, virtually, unanswerable.'

In all, four deputations met the sub-committee. They came from the Head Teachers' Association, from the National Union of Teachers, from the Joint Four Association—staffs of maintained grammar, independent and direct grant schools—and from the National Association of Schoolmasters. The Head Teachers' group, divided as it was along expected lines, could give no impression of unity: their representatives put forward divergent views, with the primary heads eager for the ending of competitive selection, the secondary non-selective heads supporting the tentative plan, and the grammar heads arguing the merits of a seven-year course and preferring—if change there had to be—fully multilateral or comprehensive secondary schools. The deputations from the Joint Four Association and from the NUT could claim near unanimity among their members—the former opposing the plan, and the second supporting it. But while the Joint Four ignored their dissentients, the NUT actually included in their deputation a grammar school spokesman to represent their minority viewpoint. The NAS speakers put individual rather than corporate points.

Written memoranda were also sent to the sub-committee. Some of these reflected the concern of the governing bodies of selective schools that their voice be heard. Others had a political orientation, and local ratepayer, Labour, Liberal, and Communist groups ventilated their judgements. A newly formed Croydon branch of the Association for the Advancement of State Education set up a working party which prepared an analysis of the Report, but considered it inappropriate to express an opinion on the merits of the scheme.

The most incisive statement opposing the plan for reorganisation was prepared by the headmasters of two long established and widely respected boys' schools of Croydon, sharing the same well-endowed Foundation. The first Whitgift School was founded in 1600 by John Whitgift, Archbishop of Canterbury. In 1837, when national ferment about educational provision was beginning to grow, the Charity Commissioners began an enquiry into the school's work, and as a result a decision was made in 1853 to divide the school into a 'Middle' school and a 'Poor' school. The significance of these titles has long since faded. One (Whitgift School) is now independent, the other (Trinity School of John Whitgift) has direct grant status: both depend substantially upon fee-payers, the first to the extent of 90 per cent and the second to the extent of 45 per cent of its boys.

The Whitgift Foundation, by the very strength of its tradition, has come to claim a dominant place in the educational life of Croydon. Its Governors tend, in the main, to be closely identified with the civic life of the town, and the Chairman of the Foundation was for many years —in a different capacity—leader of the majority group on Croydon Council. The Council for its part nominates three Governors to the Foundation. Nevertheless, the two schools stand quite outside the sector of maintained schools and are in no way subject to the Council's control. It was to be expected that their headmasters would play a forceful part in the controversy.

One of the basic administrative problems facing a local education authority, they wrote, is to decide on the age at which to 'select' its pupils. They noted the diversity of practice in developed countries: if Western European countries still hold to selection about eleven, the USA and USSR select very much later—the USA, in effect, as late as the second year at University. The heads accepted the need for early selection if it met the ever-growing need for highly educated men and women, and they went on to argue that an alliance of independent, direct-grant and grammar schools was essential to this end.

They stressed that the Report contained two major propositions which did not cohere. The first dealt with the problem of 'overlap'—the discrepancy between eleven plus performances and 'O' level results among children selected and not selected. The authors of the Report clearly saw this overlap as cause for grave concern; but the heads replied that four-fifths of selective school entrants appeared to justify their places. The second proposition in the Report was its call for a major reorganisation, and this, said the heads, could not be founded merely upon the problem of the overlap. Hence they argued that the Report was lame in its more important leg: for reorganisation—especially in the drastic form proposed—could not be justified if Croydon's own analysis of its situation was all that could be found to justify it.

The Whitgift heads saw the 'common school' as a direct threat to the proper education of Croydon's more able children. 'The Report,' they wrote, 'shows a lamentable lack of concern about the likely effect on the able children whose needs are so well met by the grammar school pattern. Social justice for them demands that they shall be put in as favourable a position academically as their counterparts in the independent and direct grant schools. There *is*, pace the Report, a type of child who can fairly be described as academic in the sense that his abilities and inclinations are, on the whole, mainly intellectual. How is their lot going to be improved by attendance at an unselective school? It is absurdly unrealistic to suppose that such a school, shorn of its sixth form, will attract the service of able graduates. The admirable general-degree man . . . is not the answer for the abler child, who must if possible be taught by teachers whose academic horizons are as distant as his own will eventually become. The independent and direct grant schools work on this assumption, and, equally, nothing less than the best available is good enough for the grammar school child. In short, they need as lively a milieu as can be found for them . . . Academic quality, which is more hardly won in the maintained grammar school than in the independent school, takes years to build up. To disperse it is folly.' They concluded that the age of eleven was by no means too early a point to find and encourage the abler child, and called for an extension of the practice of arranging later transfers at thirteen for those missing the first opportunity. (But Croydon's experience with late transfers, whether at thirteen or at 'O' level, has shown how difficult to operate this procedure can be. The brighter children in secondary modern schools are handicapped because they have not followed a full grammar school curriculum. Meanwhile the attempt to develop more academic teaching in these schools may be frustrated by the loss of their best pupils.)

This line of reasoning pursued by the Whitgift heads served to reiterate in Croydon's situation a recent judgement of Sir Edward Boyle, Minister of Education, whose actual words they quoted with approval. 'The grammar schools are still the strongest and most valued elements in our system of state education . . . We should not destroy them, but they in their turn must show themselves responsive to the times and must learn to deal with the less bright boys and girls, who can, none the less, gain by working in an intellectual atmosphere.'

The publication of this paper was an important stage in the discussion of proposals for a change. Yet it was significant as much for the areas of the Report on which it did not comment as for those on which it did. The Chief Education Officer, in a memorandum replying to the two heads' observations which he prepared for the sub-committee, noted that a concern for 4,300 children in Croydon's grammar schools could apparently be advanced as a reason for ignoring the 31,000 other children for whom the Education Committee was responsible. He came more and more to base his own case upon the inequities of eleven plus selection. 'The concept behind the proposals is the absolute necessity in the state educational system of retaining flexibility in secondary education between the age of eleven and the normal school leaving age (about sixteen in Croydon) . . . The present pattern results in an alarming waste of latent ability and an inefficient use of teaching power.' He chided the Whitgift heads for their attachment to educational patterns designed to meet bygone social and economic needs. 'We are going through a period when the accepted social and economic pattern is disintegrating . . . The countries whose methods are disparaged in the Whitgift report, the USA and USSR, are the very ones who in their different ways seems to have grasped the significance of the present changes better than the older countries of Europe, and are forging ahead. For ourselves it is clear that overall educational standards have got to be raised higher than we have ever before imagined: and we cannot afford a system which does not leave the doors of educational opportunity open as long as possible.'

This written debate between the Whitgift heads and the Chief Education Officer went to the heart of the whole controversy. An analysis of the other memoranda received by the sub-committee reveals nothing quite as provocative. Save for a representative group of primary school heads, no one troubled to comment on the quality of the junior school in Croydon or tried to relate the secondary school to its junior school foundations. This may not be surprising as the whole exercise bore upon the future of the secondary schools, but the absence of any reference to the ethos of junior schools suggests that the task of preparing the child for transfer to secondary school—as distinct from helping him to follow a curriculum to an agreed level—was not seen to present any special difficulty. Several papers deprecated the effect upon individual children of competitive transfer testing. Thus, the Advancement of State Education group wrote: 'The use of a test for transfer at eleven plus imposes psychological strains on some children, mostly as a result of parental anxiety.' The non-selective school heads wrote of the tests as 'bringing a sense of failure and denial of opportunity to those who do not pass'.

The prospect of common schools in the Borough worried the grammar heads, particularly in view of the proximity of their competitors, the independent and direct grant schools. 'We shall have independent and direct grant schools providing one kind of education and one kind of staff, and common schools providing a quite different kind of education, with a different quality of staff.' Moreover, the loss of sixth forms would be irreparable: the connection between the sixth form and the rest of the school was held to benefit the sixth former, the pupil on his way to the sixth, and the pupil who was never going to reach the sixth. The non-selective heads, by contrast, had no fears of the common school concept. The schools, they argued, would be integrated social groups; there would be more effective deployment of staff; girls (in mixed schools) would have real opportunities of technical education for the first time; the ladder of attainment would be there for all who could to climb.

In October 1962 three members of the sub-committee and the Chief Education Officer discussed their tentative plan with representatives of the Ministry of Education, among them the Under-Secretary of the Schools Branch and the Chief Inspector for secondary schools. The Ministry spokesmen indicated that Croydon's experience of difficulties in the grammar schools was by no means unique and did not in itself make a compelling case for the total abrogation of seven-year courses. They said there was not, in Croydon's presentation of its arguments, any integral relationship between its concern about the inequities of competitive transfer at eleven plus and its interest in the 'device' (the Ministry's word) of a junior college. Further, as Croydon representatives already knew, the approach of reorganisation in Greater London meant that a new London Borough of Croydon—including Coulsdon and Purley, then still part of Surrey—would be responsible for implementing any plans which might be agreed. Thus the final formulation of a scheme would have to wait upon the creation of the new Borough, whose members would be elected in 1964, and representatives of the existing Coulsdon and Purley area would at that point have a voice in determining both the principle and the detail of organisation in the new Croydon's schools.

This point had not been lost on Croydon. It tended now to slow down the tempo of discussion. And a further development imposed new delay. The Chief Education Officer's health broke down, and he was intermittently absent over a period of several months. Eventually, in the summer of 1963, he had to retire from office on grounds of ill health. A new judgement—that of the Deputy Education Officer—was brought to bear on the situation: without prior commitment to any plan, but with increasing command of the issues to be resolved. He was appointed

FORMULATING A POLICY FOR SECONDARY EDUCATION

Chief Education Officer in November. He and a new Chief Inspector wrote an additional report in which four separate schemes of reorganisation were set out.

These were: (a) the original proposal, i.e. common schools from 11 to 16 with a Junior College after 16; (b) a plan to model Croydon's pattern of schools on the Leicestershire experiment, with a break at 14; (c) a mixed scheme founded both on 11–14 year schools and on 11–16 year schools, to be followed jointly by grammar schools and a junior college; and (d) a proposition that existing schools could be grouped to form large multilateral units, with 9–12 form entry and sixth forms. By the end of the year the sub-committee had asked the Chief Education Officer to concentrate his study on the second and third of these proposals, and to consider the additional possibility of one multilateral school with a seven-year course.

Under the Leicestershire scheme, existing non-selective schools in Croydon would become junior secondary schools for pupils from 11 to 14, and existing selective schools would become senior secondary (or grammar) schools for those from 14 to 18 plus. Though the character of schools and the age of their pupils would change, each school could remain in its existing building, with few exceptions and a minimum of modifications. It was calculated that sixth forms in the senior schools would be of the order of 120 pupils, which was less than the administration would ideally recommend.

The other 'composite' plan envisaged the establishment of relatively large secondary schools for pupils of 11 to 16 through amalgamations of schools whose buildings were close enough to each other. Smaller and more widely separated schools would become, as in the Leicestershire project, junior secondary schools for pupils from 11 to 14, with a natural sequence to similar sized schools catering for those between 14 and 18. A junior college would be founded to provide post 'O' level facilities for pupils from the first group of schools. In effect, therefore, the Borough would have two parallel kinds of sixth form at work, and it was argued that there could be flexibility of entry arrangements to suit pupils' objectives.

Early in 1964 the framework of these two schemes (together with the possibility of a multilateral school for children between 11 and 18) was outlined to the teachers' organisations of the Borough, and a series of consultations was held between the administration and teachers' representatives. On this occasion the Governing Bodies of the denominational schools within the Borough were approached for their views. But neither scheme found real favour with any section of teacher opinion. Since the first round of meetings with teachers' representatives in the autumn of 1962, three new points of resistance had clarified themselves. First, the teachers who opposed most actively the continuance of competitive selection were dismayed at the prospect of a surviving 5 per cent selection for independent and direct grant places: they argued that this destroyed the main virtues of the reform since pressures within the junior school would be even further intensified by competition for the few remaining selective places. Second, the Borough's non-selective schools were becoming increasingly concerned about the loss of their 'academic' work—to 'O' level standard. Although some non-selective schools still provided no 'O' level opportunities, the great majority hoped they might, and thus even within a year had found new reasons for cherishing some aspects of the status quo. Third, the notion of a distinction between common schools (implicit in the composite scheme which provided for some schools dealing with the ages from 11 to 14 and others dealing with the ages from 11 to 16) was repugnant, for it suggested yet another hierarchy within the authority's pattern of schools—a hierarchy for which there was no sort of justification.

The teachers were not in a position to obstruct all change in the Borough. Firm positions had not been taken up, and the arts of persuasion may still bring about some modification of these views. But in face of the collective opposition of the teachers' associations—with whom unanimity is a rare phenomenon—the sub-committee and administration had again to go back over their tracks. The sub-committee continued to search for a formula which it could commend to the new Croydon without in any way committing its successors. In the end, however, it had to be content with a statement of principle. This was accepted by the Education Committee, whose report to the last meeting of Croydon Council before the elections for the new Borough stated: 'Because the Committee recognise that it will be for the Council of the London Borough of Croydon to decide on the form of Secondary organisation, they are not recommending a particular scheme, as they are of the opinion that the Council of the new Borough should have the opportunity of examining possible schemes. They do, however, consider that they should express themselves on certain matters of principle and conclude:

1   That selection at eleven plus for maintained schools should be abolished;

2   That the Authority must continue to take place at Direct Grant and Independent Schools:

3   That any scheme of reorganisation adopted must be shown to be superior to the present tripartite system in that:

    (a) it allows to every pupil that opportunity in terms of his age, ability and aptitude which the 1944 Act laid down as a principle;

    (b) it recognises that this opportunity must be made real for pupils of all degrees of ability; and

FORMULATING A POLICY FOR SECONDARY EDUCATION 243

(c) it must be flexible enough to permit a pupil that rate of progress through a secondary course which his ability demands.

4 That as planning for additional secondary schools must begin within the next year, it is essential to establish principles according to which new secondary school places must be built.'

The Council, by fifty-five votes to one, accepted this Report, with its implications for an eventual reorganisation of secondary education to produce secondary schools providing for a full range of ability. Its four conclusions were commended to the new Borough of Croydon.

This second attempt at reform originated from a more general concern with the inadequacies of the educational system, and developed against the background of nationwide discussion of the same issues. By 1961 it was becoming clear that further expansion of existing forms of selective education—the only positive outcome of the first attempt at reform—would not resolve the problems. Indeed the record of 'O' level performances in the enlarged grammar schools suggested this form of development might even make matters worse. A system of common primary schools, succeeded at the age of eleven by a tripartite pattern which owed more to the accidents of past history than to the Borough's current needs and potentialities, called for more radical reforms. The negotiations that followed during the next three years produced no such reform. But they were not altogether fruitless. Before its amalgamation with neighbouring local authorities, the County Borough had resolved that means must be devised to abolish competitive selection tests at the age of eleven. This procedure would be maintained for places in direct grant and independent schools only. This decision, limited and negative though it might be, was a long step forward in the process of formulating a policy for secondary education. It remains to be seen how it will be received by the representatives of the new London Borough of Croydon.

DISCUSSION

Although the negotiations traced in this study failed to produce any conclusive result during the period covered, they nevertheless provide a revealing glimpse of the policy-making process and an opportunity for applying some of the concepts derived from previous studies in this series. The form and character of an educational system changes slowly and is always liable to be rendered obsolete by continuing economic and social development. Croydon lies in one of the more prosperous segments of the London suburbs and is thus affected by all the social changes occurring in this most rapidly developing region of the country. There are several long established schools of high reputation in the district, and the Borough's system of secondary education owes a great deal to the traditions they have helped to create. The task of adapting this system to the social changes proceeding around it is thus likely to be peculiarly difficult.

The inadequacy of the system and the need for reappraisal and reform was forced upon public and professional attention in a number of ways. The scarcity of opportunities for academic education, the increasing competition for places in selective schools, and the waste of talent among potentially able pupils excluded from these schools; the difficulty of providing more advanced and specialised teaching in schools too small to support an adequate sixth form, and the wasteful use of the sixth form teaching resources available; the inefficiency and unpopularity of selection procedures at the age of eleven, the distortions of primary education they produced, and the difficulty of arranging any effective opportunity for selection at later stages of schooling; the need to provide for the education of growing numbers of 'young adults', many of whom preferred to escape from the restrictions imposed by traditional forms of schooling and seek the freedom offered by the labour market: these were among the problems to be contended with.

When his Council expressed concern about some of these issues, the new Chief Education Officer seized the opportunity to propose a radical reform of the whole system. Such a reform called for a wholesale reorganisation of many well established institutions and could not be brought about without the support of at least a large proportion of the people directing these institutions. Some of the most influential schools playing a part in the system were not maintained by the Borough, and the constitution of the others could not be radically altered without the consent of the Ministry. It was clear that the interests of those who would have to participate in this reform were liable to conflict; these interests, moreover, were represented in a number of well entrenched professional associations. An attempt would therefore have to be made to find some common ground between them, and to work out a reconciliation of divergent aspirations through the formulation of plans that would offer advantages of some kind to most of those concerned. This might have been the point at which representatives of those providing the service—administrative and technical officers, inspectors and head teachers—could have been brought together in working parties to formulate viable solutions. But that step was not taken, and the anxieties of many of these people were sharpened by premature publication of proposals to be considered by elected members. Thus key people among the providers of the service were compelled to present their views in the form of an attack on these proposals, and to commit themselves to an increasingly public opposition both to each other and to the administration. An outside consultant was then brought in to advise the Council in a situation which forced him to assume the role of an arbitrator. He was not prepared to support the reform proposed, and

FORMULATING A POLICY FOR SECONDARY EDUCATION 245

the Education Committee was unwilling to press on with it. In any case this proposal for reorganisation, whatever its long-term value, did not promise any immediate solution to the particular problems the Council had originally posed for discussion.

The second attempt at a reappraisal of Croydon's secondary education followed a remarkably similar course until the point at which the Chief Education Officer resigned owing to ill-health. Once again an expression of concern about specific problems arising from the general structure of Croydon's system of secondary education was taken as an opportunity for proposing the same reforms. Once again the Education Committee and its sub-committee were called upon to discuss these proposals before the staff actually providing the service had a chance to consider them; and again a plan for reform was published in a manner that provoked opposition to the administration and dissension between those who would have to collaborate in implementing it. Two new consultants were called in to give their verdict—a rather more favourable one this time. The arguments presented on all sides were elaborated at greater length, and public attitudes to the problem had changed since the earlier date. A new group of citizens, concerned with the advancement of state education, appraised the administration's scheme in a balanced fashion; but the Council—which had so far reached no decision of policy—made no attempt to enlist such public support. The Whitgift Schools, though entirely independent of the Borough's education service, threw their formidable weight against the plan. Meanwhile the fundamental differences between the outlook of the principal groups involved remained much the same as in the previous negotiations. Head teachers were concerned with the development of their own type of school and the opportunities of the children they were immediately responsible for. Their differing responsibilities led them to favour or oppose different features of the administration's proposals; but none of them were able to consider the evolution of the *whole* system and the educational opportunities of *all* Croydon children—those in school and those at work—in quite the comprehensive manner in which these questions presented themselves to the Committee and its senior officers. All these points of view were reasonably clear by the time the Authority consulted the Ministry, and the Ministry's officials refused to support the proposed reform, commenting that the Borough had not demonstrated that this was the only solution for the recognised difficulties it faced.

With a change in its leadership the Education Department reconsidered its plans for the future, and a more flexible and varied choice of solutions was formulated. But by now the interests involved were publicly committed to a number of conflicting aspirations and it proved as difficult as ever to secure agreement. This was the point at which the forthcoming reform of local government interposed a pause in the drive for decisions which may yet provide opportunities for a reconsideration of these issues and the modification of intransigent standpoints.

The course of these events suggests that despite the wealth of telling statistics prepared by the Education Department, those providing the service—both in the schools and in the town hall—were never enabled to formulate a common approach to the problems confronting them. Complete agreement might have proved impossible, but the course adopted compelled them to approach the problem, not as teachers sharing a common concern for education throughout the Borough, but as exponents of different types of schooling. The Council had shown itself to be concerned about particular problems, but had not expressed any general preference for solutions. Its role might therefore have been to define broad objectives and to consider alternative means proposed for attaining them; but it became involved in the detailed formulation of one solution and allowed itself to be aligned with certain interests within the service before rival interests had been heard. It is proper for the officials who are responsible for the development of a social service to 'educate' their governing body and urge particular courses of action upon it, but they should do their utmost to secure agreement among their colleagues before involving their masters in controversy. Consultation with the Ministry, which bore the final responsibility for arbitrating in cases of dispute, was postponed until late in the proceedings—perhaps too late to be of much value. A variety of alternative solutions were then examined and time will tell whether these may offer an escape from the deadlock. Nevertheless, despite their inconclusive outcome, these negotiations had at least brought about a widespread recognition—publicly endorsed by the Council—that the existing pattern of secondary education was no longer adequate. This consensus may yet form the basis for a major new departure.

Previous studies have shown that the staff providing a social service, those controlling the resources required for it, and those determining the demands made upon it must all play a part in any major development of the service. The general objectives of the social services are often ill defined and capable of being interpreted in diverse ways. This diversity need provoke no conflict provided the aspirations of participants are satisfied to a sufficient extent. But when important groups among those providing the service suffer, or expect to suffer, a serious loss of resources, powers or status, conflicts arise among them which will spread, if pressed sufficiently far, to a widening circle of outside interests capable of influencing the development of the service. The timing of decisions about this development then calls for sensitive judgement. For premature attempts to resolve such conflicts may commit those responsible for these decisions to standpoints which provoke unnecessarily intransigent opposition among those who must eventually play a part in the evolution of the service. Major participants in this evolution may then be compelled to resign, or evolution itself may be brought to a halt.

POSTSCRIPT

The new London Borough of Croydon took over in April 1965, incorporating Coulsdon and Purley. These were politically Conservative districts to the south of the town on the fringe of Greater London, which had been classed among the 'exclusive residential suburbs' by Moser and Scott in a book categorising British towns.[1] The reform of London government increased the Borough's population by 32 per cent and deprived it of some of the old County Borough's powers—its more strategic town planning responsibilities for example. But the administration of education, and the Chief Education Officer himself, continued unchanged. Six months earlier a Labour Government, committed to comprehensive reorganisation of secondary education, had been returned to power at Westminster.[2]

A third attempt to reorganise Croydon's schools began. It is still too early to say how it will end, but the log-jam has been broken and major changes are now taking place. This postscript records the main events in a complicated story.

In October 1964 the new Borough accepted without debate the policy statement bequeathed to it by its predecessor, including the crucial first clause recommending 'that selection at eleven plus for maintained schools should be abolished' (see page 242 above). Although the Conservatives had a majority on the Council, these proposals were not then regarded primarily as a Party matter. The Education Committee asked the Chief Education Officer to set up a working party of teachers to prepare 'a practical scheme of reorganisation' which would satisfy the criteria in this statement. The main teachers' associations were represented on the working party; the Joint Four, the National Union of Teachers, the National Association of Schoolmasters, the Croydon Head Teachers' Association, and the Association of Teachers in Technical Institutions. One teacher was added to represent the Borough's two secondary technical schools. After thirteen meetings the teachers' representatives produced a scheme designed to offer something for everyone: there would be selection at eleven plus for direct grant and independent schools only, further selection by 'guided choice' at thirteen and at sixteen for some selective schools, and opportunities for every secondary school to have its own sixth form. These proposals were clearly unworkable: they were quietly dropped by the Education Committee and the teachers.

[1] C. A. Moser and W. Scott, *British Towns*. Oliver & Boyd, 1961.

[2] For an account of the development of education in London during these years see David Regan and Sam Hastings, 'Education', in Gerald Rhodes (ed.), *The New Government of London:The First Five Years*. Weidenfeld & Nicolson, 1972.

The Committee and its officers then prepared a scheme of their own which was taken by the Chairman and the Chief Education Officer to the Department of Education and Science where officials, now given a clear brief to bring about comprehensive reorganisation, encouraged them to go ahead. This scheme was presented to a meeting of all heads of schools and then to area meetings of teachers. It was published in the Press and sixteen public meetings were held to discuss it in the closing weeks of 1965 and early 1966. The Chief Education Officer or his representative outlined the scheme at each meeting—the Chief speaking to the teachers' meetings and to ten of the public meetings. After this introduction, members of the Special Sub-Committee on Reorganisation answered questions at each meeting on points of policy, often against noisy competition. Circular 10/65, sent out the previous July, calling for an end to eleven plus selection and asking education authorities to adopt one of six types of reorganisation, had made comprehensive education a frankly political issue. Shaken by the outcry against it, the Education Committee rejected the scheme in January 1966, and the Council confirmed their decision in March. Nothing more could be done for the time being. The Leader of the Council encouraged the Chief Officer to accept a Commonwealth University Fellowship in Canada for three months.

From mid-1966 until the summer of 1967 the Education Committee thought in terms of 'pilot' schemes. Then, in the autumn of 1967, Croydon was prodded into action again by Miss Alice Bacon, one of the Education Ministers, who had herself been a teacher. She pointed out to the Leader of the Council that something had better be done if the Borough was to get her Department's approval for badly needed secondary school building programmes. She was not prepared to let local authorities use resources for separate secondary modern and grammar schools when it was Government policy to press for comprehensive schools. They had 'a friendly talk', and the Leader of the Council agreed to see what could be done.

A mixed scheme of reorganisation, incorporating different kinds of schools, was then prepared, accepted in principle by the full Council, and presented for public discussion and representations. This time a different sort of debate followed. People were invited to write to the authority, and about a dozen deputations were received at the town hall. Public opinion was better informed and more favourable: discussion concentrated mainly on the 'nuts and bolts' of the scheme, not the principles. Councillors were prepared to advocate the principles while their officials expounded the details. Hitherto, officials who tried to explain the principles—coolly, as officials should—had been exposed to passionate opposition without adequate political support. This time they were supported—by Conservatives.

The scheme was finally recommended to the Council, which in March

1968 debated a proposal that two schools be excluded from it. Their exclusion would, in effect, have wrecked the plan. But on a vote the scheme was accepted. That spring Labour lost all representation on the Council except for one councillor and two aldermen.

The new scheme provided for transfer either to schools covering the age range eleven to fourteen which were linked to a top tier of fourteen to eighteen schools, or to schools covering the age range eleven to sixteen which gave opportunities of moving into the upper half of a fourteen to eighteen school or—for those properly qualified—to the Technical College or the College of Art. All three types of secondary school were described as 'high schools'. They were to be fairly large, with between five and twelve forms (150–360 pupils) entering each year. Selection at the age of eleven was to continue for direct grant and independent schools and, more temporarily, for voluntary aided grammar schools belonging to the Churches. The Whitgift Foundation's Trinity School discarded direct grants and assumed a wholly independent status at about this time. The sixth form or junior college, central to Croydon's previous plans for reorganisation, had disappeared—although they were by now reappearing in the reorganisation schemes of many other authorities. Earlier debates had left their mark, however, in the husbanding of sixth form teaching resources, and the channelling of pupils from a large number of secondary schools into a smaller number in which sixth form work was to be concentrated.

This scheme was approved by the Department of Education and Science in September 1968. It was to come into force in 1970, but restraints on school building imposed during these years of recurring economic crises compelled the authority to postpone that for a year. Meanwhile a team of seven of Her Majesty's Inspectors of Education from the central government came to Croydon to help the authority and the heads of its schools plan curricula and organisation for the new schools.

Then in June 1970 the Conservatives returned to power at Westminster and Mrs Thatcher became Secretary of State for Education and Science. Circular 10/70 was despatched from the Department a few days later. 'Circular 10/65' it said, 'is withdrawn. Consequential restrictions on the character of secondary building projects will no longer apply... Authorities which have had reorganisation plans approved by the Department may either proceed to operate them unchanged or notify the Department of their wish to modify them.' Croydon's scheme was re-examined yet again by the full Council in October, but the Chairman of the Education Committee urged his colleagues to stand by it and no concessions were made.

It will be a long time before Croydon has a completely comprehensive system of education. The Roman Catholic grammar schools are working out ways of participating in such a system, and negotiating the complex property transactions involved, but the Anglicans sit tight, refusing to implement the reorganisation they originally agreed to. Mrs Thatcher was still Secretary of State when we returned to the Borough at the end of 1973, and no one put any pressure on them to conform because it was well known that she would support an Anglican grammar school in any conflict with the authority. The numbers in Croydon secondary schools are rising owing to the raising of the minimum school leaving age, the growing proportions who stay on beyond that age, and the continuing increase in the Borough's population: only two of the education authorities in Greater London have had a faster growth in their school populations.[1] But a smaller proportion of children go to selective independent and direct grant schools from the authority's primary schools, because the numbers of places available in these schools have not increased. As Catholic schools come into the reorganised system these numbers will fall. In 1966, 7·1 per cent of primary school leavers took free places in independent or direct grant schools; by 1973 the proportion had fallen to 5·1 per cent. Each time a proposal to pay increased fees at direct grant and independent schools comes before the Committee, there are likely to be fresh debates about the need for these places. As the local authority's schools gain strength and public recognition it may become increasingly difficult to demonstrate that the independent and direct grant schools offer a service which is not available elsewhere. The problems facing this sector were discussed by the Public Schools Commission which reported on the direct grant and independent day schools in 1970. 'We have repeatedly found', they said, 'that where reorganisation of secondary education has been pressed furthest without the participation of non-maintained schools, the formulation of a policy for these schools tends to be hardest to devise and apply. A policy of "wait-and-see" designed to "keep the options open" . . . would be disastrous.'[2]

Conclusion

Much more research has been done on the reorganisation of secondary education since our study was made.[3] We refer to some of it in the last chapter of this book. Here we will only consider what this postscript adds to our original conclusions. The picture conveyed, perhaps more vividly than before, is of a body of officials in the education department and their senior colleagues throughout the schools endeavouring to

[1] They were Brent and Sutton. See Regan and Hastings, op. cit., pp. 157–61.
[2] *Second Report of the Public Schools Commission.* HMSO, 1970, para. 183.
[3] For example, David Peschek and J. Brand, *Policies and Politics in Secondary Education* (Greater London Papers No. 11, London School of Economics and Political Science, 1966); Richard Batley, Oswald O'Brien and Henry Parris, *Going Comprehensive. Educational Policy-making in Two County Boroughs* (Routledge & Kegan Paul, 1970); and Rene Saran, *Policy-Making in Secondary Education. A Case Study* (Oxford University Press, 1973).

formulate and implement new policies within a changing world. They made increasingly determined attempts to consult representatives of all the different kinds of teachers who would eventually have to play a part in the scheme: the anxieties and conflicts provoked by Croydon's first attempt to reorganise secondary schools without proper consultation were never forgotten.

As the debate grew more heated it might have seemed attractive to take the issue 'out of politics' and ask the professionals to settle it. But the teachers could not formulate workable proposals for solving these essentially political problems. When invited to try in 1965, they attempted to satisfy every branch of the profession and ended up by producing a scheme which would have been disastrous for their pupils. (That has always been the danger of syndicalism.) It was the Council itself—working mainly through its Education Committee—which had to approve and register, though rarely formulate, policy decisions. And it is the Council which must ultimately defend them in public. Only when councillors were prepared to do this—as at last they were in 1968—could administrators make their own most effective contributions to innovation.

This service faced a public which was probably better informed about its work and certainly more demanding than the public opinion related to other services we studied. That is a fairly recent development.[1] Parents and the public at large can question, protest, and advocate particular points of view most effectively on matters which arise at smaller scales demanding smaller resources than those in this case study—in the management of primary schools, for example. They cannot set new developments in motion although they may contribute to the pressures which will in the longer run do so. Usually they respond to proposals and initiatives of the bureaucracy and are often most effective when exerting pressure through councillors who have, as elected representatives, a right to be heard and a legitimate authority which individuals and pressure groups lack. The public, along with everyone else concerned in this story, was capable of learning more about the problems being debated. That process of education, which produced in 1968 a perceptible shift in the general climate of opinion, operates on a national as well as a local scale. Similar changes in the assumptions and tone of debate about secondary education were to be seen in many other places at this time.[2]

Any formulation of the process of public participation in the administration of schools as a conflict between *the* public and *the* bureaucracy

---

[1] This development and its impact on educational administration is discussed by Maurice Kogan *et al.* in *County Hall. The Role of the Chief Education Officer.* Penguin, 1973; e.g. pp. 58–60.

[2] See *Second Report of the Public Schools Commission*, Chapter 7, for a summary of the debates at this time.

is misleading, for there are many publics with divergent interests, confronting many branches of the service with potentially conflicting aims serving different groups of clients. The Council and its Education Committee were responsible for reconciling these conflicts and arbitrating between them. They may have been reluctant to offend local interests to which they were sympathetic, such as churches or independent schools, but once committed to a policy they did their best to follow it in ways that improved the performance and reputation of their own schools, even if that meant neglecting their friends in the private sector.

In this case, the Council and its staff operated within constraints which left them little room for manoeuvre in the short run. The initiative and responsibility for innovation lay with them, but they depended on the Department of Education and Science for authority to reorganise schools, and for money for their school building programme; and that, at crucial points, meant dependence on alternating parties and changing Ministers with a sharp eye on local political interests. The central government's officials could help the authority in many ways but, on issues as politically sensitive as those in this case, only when given a clear brief to do so by the party in power. Ministers could prod the authority to act, as Miss Bacon did in 1967, or restrain it, as Mrs Thatcher did later. Either way, they may be best viewed as important but changing parts of the environment in which the education authority had to operate.

CHAPTER 11

TAKING DECISIONS IN A UNIVERSITY

This study, published for the first time, deals with events in a university. Although that setting is quite different from tnose of previous studies, many of the problems and processes explored will already be familiar. New work—an experimental training course—was initiated by University staff, and shaped partly by those controlling the complex resources needed for the job and partly by demand for the service offered—demands from students and their future employers. Many people and institutions outside the University had a stake in the outcome of the experiment. When a decision had to be made about its future it became clear that those responsible for the course were competing for resources and opportunities with colleagues doing other work. Different teachers gradually formulated divergent accounts of the issues at stake, each assembling supporters in the process. When the head of their department tried to resolve the conflict, a widening circle of interests, extending well beyond the university, exerted pressures on him and then on the Director of the college. A final decision could not be reached until every available gun had been brought to bear.

This study was made at the same time as the others presented in this book. With the exception of much of the last chapter, our previous studies dealt mainly with past events, viewed from the 'outside' and pieced together later by interviewing participants and reading the records available. We wanted to make a study of the University because it would enable us to trace a current development with 'inside' knowledge as it unfolded from day to day. The choice of a development was easy, for in the Department of Social Administration at the London School of Economics and Political Science, where these studies were made, there was no doubt which development was then demanding most attention, and one of the authors was participating actively in it. This report is based on his diary of the proceedings, other documents, and discussions with participants. All the main participants commented seven years later on a draft of this chapter, and many commented again on a subsequent draft ten years after that.

The story deals with the introduction of a new course of training for social workers, and the Department's attempt to reach a decision about the future of this and other courses for social workers which it was then providing. Historians of social work will be most interested in the origins of the new course and the later dissemination of its influence through the profession. This study has the much more modest aim of recording the LSE's attempt to make a particular decision during the academic year 1956–7. It ventures into earlier and later history only so far as that is necessary to make sense of its more limited topic.

This chapter throws some light on others in the book. Two of the training courses described were preparing students for the kind of work done by the LCC Children's Department and some of their students were trained in the Area 5 Office, described in Chapter 6. The reorganisation of the FWA's Area Offices, described in Chapter 9, was brought about with the encouragement of those responsible for the new LSE course, partly for the purpose of providing supervised field work for their students. The new course drew heavily on North American ideas about social work. Those who have read Chapter 8 will be familiar with some of these ideas and the disturbing impact they can make. In view of all these reasons for making and publishing the study along with the others in this book, it will be asked why it was originally omitted. Not because of any University veto: the heads of the Department and the School both gave their permission for publication, provided it was made clear—as it should be—that this was a most unusual example of university administration. But no one could produce a generally acceptable account of these events and some of the author's colleagues felt his would be hurtful to themselves and others, and would make it harder for them to do their jobs. He decided they might be right. Moreover, he had by then become a Professor, responsible for making their work easier, not harder. Now that all the participants have left the School that obligation is lifted. But the reader should bear in mind their concern: this chapter was written by a participant in the events to be recounted who may have failed to understand important aspects of the story and who cannot wholly shed his own biases. Other participants would have each written different stories.

The Problem Posed

In 1956, when this study began, the Department of Social Science and Administration of the London School of Economics and Political Science (to give them their full titles) provided three professional training courses for social workers. One of these—the Course in Applied Social Studies—had been set up on an experimental basis in 1954 with the aid of a grant from the Carnegie United Kingdom Trust sufficient to run it for four years. At the end of that time the School would have to decide whether to continue this Course, with or without some modification, and how to pay for it. It was understood by all concerned that the LSE would continue the experiment in some way if it succeeded; but in what way, and how 'success' was to be measured, had yet to be determined. Before describing how these decisions were made we must explain the organisation of the Department and its social work courses, and their place within the School.

The LSE is one of the Colleges of the University of London. It is divided into a number of Departments, although in 1956 no formal recognition was given to this fact. At that time the Social Administration Department, as it was usually called, had 22 academic staff: a Professor, a newly appointed Reader, a Lecturer with the title of 'Senior Tutor',[1] 11 other Lecturers, 6 Assistant Lecturers (2 of whom devoted half their time to other Departments in the School) and 2 Research Officers. They were helped by an Administrative Assistant and a number of secretarial staff.

The Department was teaching about 300 students at this time: about sixty were taking the Social Administration options in the second and third years of a course leading to an Honours Degree in Sociology, ninety were taking a two-year course leading to the Certificate in Social Science (later renamed the Diploma in Social Administration) and twenty-five graduate students were taking the same course in one year. The Department also provided four one-year professional training courses, designed in the main for graduates in the social sciences: the Personnel Management Course for about twenty-five students, the Mental Health Course for about thirty-five students training for psychiatric social work, the Child Care Course for about twenty students training to work in the local authorities' Children's Departments and in voluntary child care organisations, and the Applied Social Studies Course for about twenty-five students entering various branches of social work. A number of graduate students were reading for higher degrees, and various others were temporarily attached to the Department.

The general pattern of degree courses was determined by University Boards of Studies consisting of the more senior teachers in relevant subjects from all Colleges participating in the degree concerned, but certificate courses of the kind we shall be mainly concerned with were administered independently by the University's Colleges and Schools. The School had a Director, and its management was conducted with the aid of administrative staff through a considerable number of committees, the most important of which consisted at that time of Professors presided over by the Director. The principal decisions on most issues affecting the development of the School—other than decisions about appointments and promotions—had to be ratified by the Academic Board, a general assembly of nearly all the academic staff convened once a month during term-time.

[1] She had been the senior teacher of Social Administration before the appointment of a Professor and Reader. Her title was inherited from pre-war times when much of this teaching had been done by 'tutors' who were paid less than lecturers.

At the head of the Department was the Professor of Social Administration who had been appointed in 1950—the only one in the country at that time. He had no experience of University administration, not having worked in a University before, but he had been assured by the Professors who persuaded him to come to the School that the Department virtually ran itself and he would be able to devote most of his energies to research. He was a scholar whose perceptive and humane analysis of controversial questions of social policy had gained him an international reputation. He was widely regarded as the outstanding thinker and teacher in his field. Until 1950 his Department had been a fairly small group, who managed their affairs fairly informally with the help of fortnightly meetings under the supervision of one of the Professors of Sociology who had also done distinguished work in the field of social policy. The group had an honourable history, tracing its origins to the School of Sociology which was founded at the initiative of the Charity Organisation Society (later renamed the Family Welfare Association) in 1903, and brought to the LSE in 1912. Clement Attlee had been one of its teachers (Hugh Dalton was runner up for the post). But little research was being done when the Professor took up his Chair, and the Department's academic status was not high within the School. The Department grew considerably in the years that followed, attracting younger men to do research on problems of social policy, and an increasing number of visiting scholars from overseas. The growing size and complexity of the Department called for more systematic procedures of communication; staff meetings were minuted and decisions were more often committed to paper. But formality was still kept to a minimum. University teachers are in principle equal; once confirmed as lecturers, they can continue in their posts until retirement. The authority of a head of a Department depends largely on his personal influence, his reputation as a scholar and teacher, and his power to make recommendations to professorial committees and other bodies determining the allocation of resources and the appointment or promotion of staff.

The informal and non-hierarchical character of this group must be constantly borne in mind. In this chapter individuals will be distinguished by titles indicating their responsibilities—as they have been in our other studies. But such titles give a misleading impression of the Department's ethos: its staff in fact referred to each other not as 'Lecturers in Charge' of particular courses, but by their names—usually their first names. In normal circumstances no group of teachers could have been kinder to newcomers and to each other. Their sunny, informal character made it all the more difficult for them to cope with conflict when it came, or to make fiercely contested decisions about the allocation of power; they lacked procedures and a tone of voice for such occasions.

Teaching for the Sociology Degree and the Social Science Certificate had to be organised in collaboration with other Departments in the School and elsewhere in the University, but the four professional courses were left almost entirely to the staff concerned with them: it was they who provided most of the teaching and arranged for the contributions made by other lecturers who were drawn mainly from outside the School. Several of these staff had joined the School some years before the Professor. Each was accustomed to running her own Course on behalf of the School and to having direct access to its Director if she needed it. More recent recruits, attracted by the reputation of the Professor to join a School which had grown a good deal larger, had stronger loyalties to the Department and to him personally.

The Personnel Management Course, which is not directly involved in this study, worked on fairly conventional academic lines; its students were required to work in industry for part of their vacations, and to carry out brief research projects the findings of which were examined at the end of the year. The three Professional Courses in social work—to be referred to in this study as 'the Professional Courses'—made greater use of field work in the social services, supervised by carefully chosen staff in these services whose reports played a major part in the final assessment of students. In the Mental Health and Applied Social Studies Courses students spent three days a week in the field during term time, and in all three Courses most of the vacations were devoted to field work.

The Professional Courses' involvement with the outside world posed special problems for the University. They depended on the continuing support of the local authorities and central government departments which provided the grants to enable students to attend them, the social services which provided supervised field training, the supervisors themselves, central government departments which occasionally contributed to the salaries of these supervisors, and professional associations (such as the Association of Psychiatric Social Workers and the Institute of Almoners) which recognised University qualifications as entitling people to membership and hence to certain posts and salary scales. A determined refusal to co-operate in any of these quarters could bring a course to an end. The LSE's Department of Social Administration had long experience of working with these bodies, many of whose senior members were its own graduates. Nevertheless, the development of professional education in this field called for a delicate balance between the different interests involved—for social workers, their employers and their various professional associations might disagree with each other as well as with the School—and a reconciliation of academic freedoms with professional and administrative rights and duties. Advisory Committees attached to the Courses were designed to help maintain this balance, and the uncertainty of their functions was perhaps a necessary feature of the balancing act.

Thus far we have not tried to distinguish these Courses, but each differed from the others in important ways. The Mental Health Course —the first of its kind in the country—had been set up in 1929 with the help of American funds and guidance, and provided a widely recognised training for social workers with at least two years' experience and (usually) a University qualification in the Social Sciences. Its students, therefore, tended to be older and more experienced than those on the other two Courses. Some of them worked subsequently in other services and other countries besides the British child guidance clinics and mental hospitals for which their training was primarily designed. Although there were three smaller courses of this kind in other Universities, most of the social workers qualifying and practising in this field came from the LSE, and all five of the staff teaching social casework in the School had at some time taken the Course. University teachers of social work throughout the country had generally trained as psychiatric social workers, and PSWs wrote most of the more important articles in the social work journals. There was an advisory committee attached to the LSE Course—the Mental Health Course Committee—consisting of some of the Department's staff, two well-known psychiatrists and several senior psychiatric social workers, under the Chairmanship of the Professor. This Committee had not met since 1954 but the Professor and the Lecturer in charge of the Course knew its members and maintained informal contact with them. The Lecturer in Charge—who will be referred to in this study as 'the Lecturer in Charge (MH)'—was well known as a teacher and organiser, and for her general contribution to the profession, which included the establishment and editing of the only monthly journal then published for readers in all branches of social work. Yet despite her very practical contributions to the whole field of social work the dominant position of her Course gave its graduates an élite status which engendered in some quarters the kind of hostility that any Brigade of Guards provokes.

The Child Care Course was set up, along with similar courses in other Universities, at the time of the Children Act of 1948 to help meet the new Children's Departments' urgent need for staff. Besides taking students from University courses in the social sciences, the Course accepted a few others, such as health visitors and teachers, experienced in working with children. Those responsible for it had always been more willing than their colleagues in the other two Courses to adapt the resources of the University to meet the immediate needs of their service, and in this new field there had been less opportunity to build up a network of trained supervisors for their students. The Lecturer in Charge felt that one of the groups of potential supervisors she had worked to create had been taken over by the new Applied Social Studies Course. At the time of this study there were only two other Child Care Courses of this kind in the country and all three were conducted with the support of the Home Office's Central Training Council in Child Care, consisting of representatives from the Home Office, the Universities and the local authorities, who met about twice a year. Strictly speaking, the School did not award a qualification to students completing this Course but recommended successful candidates for the award of the Central Training Council's Certificate in Child Care. The current agreement with the Home Office was due to come to an end in 1958 and the School would then have to decide, in consultation with the Home Office, whether to continue this training or bring the course to a close. The 'Lecturer in Charge' (CC)', as we shall call her, was an experienced social worker with a flair for teaching who was well known throughout the Children's Departments. The success of the Course rested largely on her personal contribution as a teacher. Few though they were, her published articles conveyed some of the most perceptive insights about social work contributed by anyone in Britain. But she did not enjoy administration, and she hated conflict.

The Applied Social Studies Course was also the first of its kind in Britain. It drew, like the Mental Health Course a generation before, on American experience, and like that Course it was designed to link theory and practice more effectively. It was designed to equip students for all branches of social casework, other than psychiatric social work. The staff manning it were working very hard to build up a team of supervisors in a variety of services who collaborated closely with them, met once a fortnight at the School, and attended some of the lectures with their students. The Course took students who had studied Social Administration direct from the Universities' degree and certificate courses, together with a number of more experienced students with similar University qualifications. Students and their teachers were keenly aware that the Course was on trial—financed by a grant which was due to come to an end in 1958. (If the Mental Health Course was the Brigade of Guards, these were the Commandos.) The staff prepared annual reports for the School to send to the Carnegie Trustees, and kept in touch with a Consultative Committee consisting of representatives of the Department and of bodies employing and training social workers—the Probation and Children's Departments of the Home Office, the Ministry of Health, the Institute of Almoners (later Medical Social Workers) and the Family Welfare Association—who met about once a quarter under the chairmanship of the Professor. The 'Lecturer in Charge (ASS)' had been a member of the Department for some twenty-five years. She was a well-known juvenile court magistrate, and had an international reputation for the contribution she had made to the development of training for social work through her published works and the leadership she had given to public and international bodies of many kinds. Of all those teaching regularly on these three Courses, she was the only one who was not herself a trained social worker. But she had been on the School's staff for longer than any of the others, and she was the only one personally familiar with the United States. She was unquestionably an 'authority'—with a Florence Nightingale touch which inspired devotion in many quarters, and provoked opposition elsewhere. Her style and social origins gave her access to the power structure through networks which were personal rather than professional. Other teachers in the Department lacked these assets and felt it was somewhat unprofessional to operate in this way.

The grant which made the Coursepossible was secured by the Professor and the Director of the LSE who represented the School at what they regarded as the crucial meetings with Trustees, after discussions with staff throughout the Department. All three Lecturers in Charge had helped to plan the new Course, but it is clear from their papers that the Trustees regarded it as the personal creation of the Lecturer in Charge (ASS); although she had been in the USA when the final decision was taken to go ahead and start it in 1954, she had been at earlier meetings with the Trustees, and was mainly responsible for negotiations with the Government departments and professional associations whose willingness to recognise the Course was essential for its success. The curriculum and organisation of the Course were based on ideas which had first been publicly discussed in two reports she had prepared for the Trust in 1947 and 1951. The Course, as she saw it, was based on the assumption that social work in all branches of the social services should be a distinctive professional activity, with aims, methods and theories of its own which would be independent of the service in which it was performed. Although considerable progress had already been made in professional training, social work had been most fully developed for settings such as hospitals and psychiatric clinics where social workers operated as an adjunct to other professions providing other services. Thus, it was argued, teachers had been compelled to think too much about the settings for which their students should be trained, and too little of the human and social problems about which they should become educated. Those responsible for the other Courses would not accept that they had failed their students in these respects.

The teachers running these three Courses were a small group. The Mental Health Course had three staff and the Child Care Course had two. All but one of these played some part in teaching students in the Department's 'basic' Certificate or Degree courses. The Applied Social Studies Course had two staff who did not teach on other courses. Other lecturers teaching on all three courses came from outside the Department. But these numbers do not convey the importance of the Courses. Each year the Department produced twice as many students from all its Courses as the next largest Departments of this kind in the country, and its professional training courses held an even more dominant position, producing well over half the total of trained social workers coming from British Universities at this time. There are now far more University courses for social workers, and the LSE no longer dominates the field. Then, as now, many other students were trained outside the Universities. In the 1950s the largest courses outside the Universities were provided by the Institute of Almoners, and for probation officers by the Home Office. Although the LSE's contribution was a small one, it was well known that any experiment conducted at the School would later affect social work throughout the country. Yet social work led a precarious existence within the School.

To many, within the LSE, these Courses appeared to involve much irrational duplication of effort. This attempt to organise intensive and closely integrated teaching to prepare students for different branches of social work within a year of completing their 'basic' Courses had produced minor differences between the professional Courses which were held to justify separate teaching by different lecturers of similar subjects such as social work, law and psychology. Likewise the students' supervised field work, though designed to achieve the same general objectives, had developed on different lines, and was related to different patterns of teaching within the School. Staff on each professional Course sought similarly qualified supervisors for their own students; they conducted independently the complicated negotiations required with the agencies in which students would do similar field work, and they arranged similar seminars with supervisors to equip them for their work and keep them informed about teaching going on in the School.

There were doubts about the academic quality of the work. Intensive teaching, coupled with field work in term time and vacations, did not leave the students as much time for reading, or as many opportunities for critical questioning of their teachers as graduates working at the LSE would normally expect. Teachers themselves had little time for research, and few of them produced the kind of publications which would secure promotion within the School. So much the worse for the School, some would say, but there was no doubt that many features of these Courses would excite suspicion within the University—particularly their procedures for assessing students which relied partly on the judgement of supervisors who were not on the staff of the University (and in some cases not graduates of any University). Whatever their views about the justice of these criticisms—and there was plenty of disagreement about that—no one in the Department wanted to expose these sensitive problems to the more powerful and conservative academic authorities in the LSE.

The Department depended on the benevolent support of powerful groups in the School. Although with 20 teachers and some 300 students it was larger than the average LSE Department, it had very few senior staff—1 Professor, 1 Reader and no Senior Lecturers. The Reader was new to the School, having joined the Department that year at the age of thirty after two years' work in Canada. All this put an exceptional burden on the Professor. By contrast, the Law Department at that time had 4 Professors, 3 Readers and 8 other teachers, the Anthropology Department had 2 Professors, 1 Reader and 3 other teachers: and each of these Departments was responsible for a much less diverse and complicated array of courses. This study deals only with the three Professional Courses in social work, but it must be remembered that they constituted only a small part of the responsibilities carried by the Professor, inside and outside the School. He had the difficult task of developing the Department's research and teaching, and securing the resources for this in competition with other Departments. The School Committees which allocated these resources consisted of Professors who were appointed in their personal capacity, for the existence of 'Departments' was not formally recognised at that time. This system called for much time-consuming negotiation because a Department with one Professor could do nothing without the support of other Departments. His success in achieving a relatively rapid expansion of his Department was due partly to the support of a sympathetic Director.

The main priorities for the allocation of financial resources within the School were reappraised every five years when the quinquennial grants distributed through the University Grants Committee and the University were determined. The next round of negotiations over the School's quinquennial plans was due to take place this year—1956. In these negotiations the Professor had to bear in mind that his Department's claims would be weakened if it appeared to be running three similar courses side by side, with the aid of similar and rather expensive teaching provided by occasional lecturers from outside the School, or if the development of the Department's work appeared to be dictated by outside interests. These anxieties were sharpened by the fact that the Director was due to retire at the end of 1956. His successor's views were unknown. They were unlikely to be as influential as those of the retiring Director who had been a power in the School for many years.

We have tried to set the scene. In the centre of it stands a Department consisting of three loosely related enterprises which were, in ascending scale: a Course in Personnel Management, a school of social work (though no one would have called it that) providing three separate Courses and a group of teachers studying various problems of social policy and providing, in collaboration with other Departments in the School, a general introduction to the social sciences in courses for graduates and undergraduates.

Although no one clearly foresaw this, the Applied Social Studies Course introduced in 1954 was a time bomb which was bound to produce major repercussions. The Course was based on the assumption that social workers in a wide variety of fields could be trained together, with a minimum of specialisation (though appropriate options were included to suit students entering different branches of the profession). The Course took students entering the child care field and could potentially take psychiatric social workers too, as such courses already did in the United States. If it was a success the future of the other two Courses would inevitably be in question. The LSE's dominant position in the training of social workers made it impossible for the Department to experiment independently and privately; anything it did would eventually affect social work and social workers throughout the country. All concerned were well aware of this competitive situation and its national implications. Among the observers of this experiment were people in the central and local authorities and the social work professions, without whose continuing support none of the three courses could survive. Each Government department and each branch of the profession was in competition with the others, knowing its future prospects depended on the number and quality of the students training to enter its part of the field. In social work journals at the time, the term 'profession' was still usually applied to specific branches of social work, such as almoning or probation—not to social work as a whole. Within the LSE, teachers who were not directly involved in the Professional Courses were beginning to note that degree and certificate students in the 'basic' courses were showing a growing preference for the Applied Social Studies Course. Leaving aside any assessment of the relative merits of the Course, there were obvious attractions in a qualification which could be taken without prior practical experience and would eventually give its bearers access to several different branches of social work.

Everyone knew that a decision of some kind would soon have to be made. The new University quinquennium, the forthcoming renegotiation of the Home Office grant for the Child Care Course, and the termination of the Carnegie Trust's grant for the Applied Social Studies Course together made that decision urgent.

A First Attempt at a Decision
When the new Course was set up in 1954 the Professor asked the Lecturers in Charge of all three to collaborate in working out plans for their future development. He foresaw the need for some sort of amalgamation, but he was not a social worker himself and he intended that they should sort out what ought to be done. Communication between staff of the new Applied Social Studies Course and those responsible for the other two was difficult from the start. A well-known American Professor in the field of social work education spent some time at the School that year and it was hoped that she would help all concerned, but the meetings she held only made matters worse. Her advice about teaching was widely respected, but her inflexible commitment to American ways of organising a course reinforced fears that an American doctrine was to be imposed on the British.

Next year, in October 1955, the Professor asked the three Lecturers in Charge to prepare memoranda outlining the form the Courses might eventually take. Their proposals held out hopes of agreement on the main issues: all accepted the necessity for some degree of unification. The Lecturer in Charge (ASS) proposed a gradual integration that would eventually produce one Course with a curriculum similar to that being developed in her own. The Lecturer in Charge (CC) was critical of the assumption that social workers in different fields could be given similar training but was prepared to consider a partial amalgamation of the Child Care and Applied Social Studies Courses, provided she was not called upon to take part in it. She argued that the Mental Health Course should continue independently, providing an advanced training for more experienced social workers. The Lecturer in Charge (MH), though critical of certain features of the new Course, welcomed a common basic training for social workers—pointing out that the Mental Health Course, whose ex-students worked in many fields, had already gone some way to achieving that. She proposed that the Applied Social Studies Course take over the training of child care officers and later include some of the less experienced students entering psychiatric social work, leaving the Mental Health Course to concentrate increasingly on more advanced students and research in all branches of social work. Any proposals of this kind would have to be discussed with administrative and professional authorities outside the School who would be concerned about the quality and relevance of training, and the number of places to be offered to each branch of social work.

When a new Readership was created in January 1956 the first holder of this post was asked to devote special attention to these problems by the Professor who frankly confessed he was at his wits' end. The Reader did a little teaching on these Courses, attended classes and lectures, and talked with the staff. After consulting him, the Professor later proposed to announce a gradual amalgamation of all three Courses and a reallocation of duties, giving each of the Lecturers in Charge responsibility for a part of the curriculum rather than for a separate Course. After talking with the Reader and the Senior Tutor he decided this might prove too radical a change and no announcement was made, but he took a step in this direction by setting up three 'working parties', each including staff from all three Courses, to discuss different parts of the curriculum under the Chairmanship of one of the Lecturers in Charge. The Lecturer in Charge (MH) was to be responsilbe for 'social work theory and practice', the Lecturer in Charge (CC) for 'human growth and behaviour' and the Lecturer in Charge (ASS) for 'social administration'. The Reader was to convene occasional meetings of all the staff concerned. By this time the Lecturer in Charge (CC) had fallen seriously ill; she recovered, but later suffered a bereavement which threw heavy domestic burdens on her. She decided to take a year's leave of absence in the autumn. General meetings of the professional courses' staff began in May 1956, and the working parties started their discussions in July, dealing with teaching practice in each Course and the steps that would be required to achieve common patterns of lectures, class work and field work. The Reader did his best to learn the points of view of all concerned and prepared a paper on different approaches to unification which was later discussed at a general meeting of the whole Department in November 1956. On 19 December an encouraging report was submitted by the professional courses' staff to the Professor showing that agreement had been reached on the following points.

1 Changes must be made in field teaching for students in the Child Care Course to bring it up to the standards expected in the other Courses. Little could be achieved until that was done. Although she was on leave, the Lecturer in Charge of this Course had herself outlined plans for such a development which had been discussed with her colleagues. There were few supervisors in Child Care capable of doing the job: thus a temporary course would be arranged for staff in the Home Counties' Children's Departments who would later supervise the field work of Child Care students. This proposal had already been tentatively discussed with representatives of the Home Office who approved its general principles.

2 The Courses should not concentrate too heavily on social casework with individuals. Further work was needed to improve teaching on social work with groups and the study of human behaviour in groups.

3 Some joint teaching could be arranged at once for students in all three Courses, and there was no objection in principle to closer integration of all the Courses, though much more study of the problem would be needed.

4 Closer links should be established between staff in the Department and supervisors of their students in the field.

5 There should be a reorganisation of clerical and administrative staff to provide a joint service for all three Courses.

So far, so good: but there were also disagreements. Staff of the Applied Social Studies Course placed greater emphasis on the standards and character of the training to be provided, and less on the practical and immediate problems of undermanned services in the field. Thus they insisted on qualifications for teachers of social casework which others thought unrealistic or too rigidly exclusive; the requirements proposed would in fact have excluded three of the Department's staff who were already teaching the subject. Staff of the new Course also expected to provide a full-time one-year Course for future child care supervisors, while others assumed that a part-time Course would be sufficient for these fairly experienced social workers.

At this point all concerned agreed that no more could be done until the Professor decided the future pattern of these Courses. Staff in the Applied Social Studies and Child Care Courses were anxious to know whether their work was to continue after the summer of 1958, eighteen months hence; negotiations with the Home Office over the proposed Course for supervisors were held up until the future was clear; the Lecturer in Charge (CC) was uncertain whether to return to the School at the end of her year's leave of absence; one of the staff on the Mental Health Course was considering an attractive job offered to him by another University; and those responsible for the Applied Social Studies Course had plans for the recruitment of an additional teacher for their course. These and lesser problems were all waiting on the decision.

The decision was delayed until mid-January when the Senior Tutor returned from four months' sabbatical leave in the United States. This gave the Professor and the Reader time to reconsider the situation. Although a number of important practical proposals were now agreed, nothing could be done, they believed, till decisions were made about the future responsibilities of the people concerned. The main issue was no longer what should be done but who should do it. Meanwhile relationships were deteriorating. The Professor said he had been exposed to repeated complaints and several offers of resignation over the past three years. (That is denied by the people concerned, but it certainly describes how he *felt*.) It was damaging to the Department that different members of its staff should negotiate—unknown to each other—with the same people about the supervision of students' field work and other matters. One person, the Professor, Senior Tutor and Reader agreed, must have general responsibility for these Courses and the delicate task of integrating them. No money was available to bring in an 'overlord' or 'co-ordinator' from outside, who would in any case take a considerable time to familiarise himself with a situation in which prompt action was needed. The Reader was not a trained social worker, and did not want the job. He intended to do research on broader questions of social policy which would be very difficult to pursue if he had to devote his attention wholly to these Courses. One of the Lecturers in Charge was ill, and had said she did not want the job. Thus it had to be one of the other two. The selection of either would probably entail one or two resignations.

The breakdown of communication between the principal participants which led to this impasse was repeatedly referred to by all of them, with bewilderment and a deep sense of injury. Since they were unusually intelligent and civilised people with long and successful experience of public affairs and wide circles of friends—good communicators, in fact—this was an important and puzzling feature of the situation. We will discuss it later.

In January 1957 the Professor, with the agreement of the Reader and Senior Tutor, informed the three Lecturers in Charge individually that all three Courses would be unified by stages. The main steps to be taken were: the setting-up of a temporary course for child care supervisors, to be run by the Lecturer in Charge (CC), and the development of shared teaching on certain subjects for students in all three Courses in 1957-8; the amalgamation of the Child Care and Applied Social Studies Courses in 1958-9; and the development of research and teaching in the field of administration which would be the special responsibility of the Lecturer in Charge (ASS). Starting in 1958-9 the same document would be awarded to successful candidates for the certificates of all three Courses. The Mental Health Course would be combined with the other two as soon as possible. In May 1957 the Lecturer in Charge (MH) would become 'Lecturer in Charge of Professional Education for Social Work'. This was the crucial decision.

Many concerned with social work inside (and later outside) the School were upset because these decisions had been taken 'without consultation'. The Professor and his closest colleagues felt he had been consulting all concerned within the School for years and had reached an impasse which could not be broken till this decision was made. They did not believe it would have been proper to consult outsiders before taking such decisions.

After some ten days of rather confused discussions the two Lecturers responsible for the Applied Social Studies Course informed the Professor that they would both resign at the end of the academic year. The Lecturer in Charge welcomed the decision to integrate teaching but felt the choice of her colleague from the Mental Health Course as 'Lecturer in Charge of Education for Social Work' showed a lack of confidence in her own contribution. The Lecturer in Charge (MH) was herself dismayed at what seemed to her a sudden decision, which gave her responsibility for Courses whose future shape she had not been consulted about. That was important because the plans proposed could not be put into practice without the agreement of outside bodies with whom she would have to negotiate. When the resignations were announced her first thought was to offer her own resignation too, but after thinking it over and seeking the advice of the new Director she resolved with his encouragement and that of most of the Professional Course teachers to attempt the tasks assigned to her, partly because she was unwilling to abandon her own long established Course—particularly at a time when the Report of a Royal Commission expected next year held out hopes of the biggest reform in mental health services to be attempted for a generation. (The reform came later in the Mental Health Act of 1959).

Finally, in response to protests and rumours, a revised version of the original announcement was given to the staff of the three Courses, and then sent simultaneously to all members of the Department and a large number of people outside the University directly concerned with the three Courses. This statement, dated 20 February, was significantly less specific than the first draft, speaking of 'unification of the three Courses by stages'. 'The first step will be some planned co-ordination of teaching in the three Courses. The next stage will involve the amalgamation of the Applied Social Studies and Child Care Courses. The relation of the Mental Health Course to this Course will be a matter for further discussion as plans develop.' The Lecturer in Charge (MH) was to 'become lecturer in charge of professional education for social work' on 1 October, and there would be no 'other major changes in the distribution of teaching responsibilities'. The statement concluded with the announcement of the two resignations, to take effect on 30 September. It paid tribute to the contribution those resigning had made to social work education in the School, and expressed the hope that some way might still be found to enable them 'to continue to be associated with the work of the Department'. This letter prompted as many questions as it answered. Most of those who received it knew perfectly well that the Applied Social Studies Course could not go on if deprived of both the teachers responsible for it.

One thing, however, was clear. The Professor, Reader and Senior Tutor were henceforth firmly committed to supporting the Lecturer in Charge (MH). They had asked her to do a difficult job which was bound to put her in a painful position. Another thing would soon be clear, too. Up till then they had been mainly concerned with the development of their Department and its place within the School. Henceforth they would have to devote increasing attention to social workers and the social services—bodies outside the University, without whose support the professional Courses could not survive. Meanwhile interviews and correspondence for the selection of students to come in the following October continued.

The Issues at Stake

To understand how this conflict developed and what happened next calls for sympathetic appreciation of the points of view of the people concerned; otherwise their disagreements appear to be no more than a struggle for power—and they were more than that. Conflicting views were never very clearly formulated and communication between the main participants broke down (we were repeatedly told) long before the author came on the scene. Thus we can only try to outline some of the things which were regarded as most important by the main groups involved in a summary which grossly over-simplifies the differences within each group. These groups were the Professor and those closest to him; the three groups responsible for each of the Professional Courses, the rest of the teachers in the Department; and various groups outside the University who were associated with the Courses. Each perceived the issues at stake in different ways.

The Professor and his younger lecturers saw these events as being initiated and conducted by their Department within the University, with the help of outsiders. They had an academic frame of reference. Teachers responsible for the Professional Courses saw the LSE as a stage on which to provide training initiated and sustained by many interests in the social work field to meet the needs of that field. They had a social work frame of reference. For those running the old Courses —particularly the Mental Health Course—who had existing commitments to defend, it was a conservative frame of reference (not in the party political sense: in that respect they were further to the Left than their competitors). Those running the new Course had a radical frame of reference, for they sought to change the whole system of training (and their leader later went on to play an increasingly important part in doing that). The frames of reference for groups outside the Department, ranging from Professors in other Departments to social workers, civil servants and trustees of charitable foundations, depended on their commitments to those on the centre of the stage and on their own interpretations of events.

Since it was their main job to help the Department develop its teaching and research, the Professor, Reader and Senior Tutor perceived the conflict in the context of the School and its committees which together formed the arena in which they had to secure resources for the Department. They were probably more keenly aware than their colleagues of the situation later noted by the School's new Director in a letter to the author. 'When the Carnegie grant expired the Course could be continued only at the cost of School general funds, on which it would be an additional burden. It ... was going to be in competition with developments which other academic departments might desire to make. During the earlier part of the Session 1956–7 we were with increasing anxiety awaiting news of our grant for the new quinquennium [to begin on 1st August] and when we finally received that news on 22nd June 1957 it became clear that the increase over the previous grant was going to be small; it would not leave room for much new development, and the competition to which the Course was going to be subject was that much increased. I think that there may have been indications in the earlier part of 1957 that this was likely.'[1]

The Professor and his closest colleagues were convinced that a gradual integration of the different forms of training for social work was needed, and that the School would rightly refuse to take on a new Course unless the Department moved convincingly in that direction. Not being trained social workers themselves, they lacked the knowledge or the authority to decide exactly how that should be done. That, they felt, was the job of the staff running the Courses. But although the need for integration was generally accepted, these social work teachers had

[1] Letter dated 4 June 1964.

repeatedly failed to agree about the steps to be taken. They had asked the Professor to make decisions about the allocation of responsibilities among them—that was not particularly surprising: sub-departments within an organisation scarcely ever amalgamate voluntarily—hence he had to choose one of them to lead the group towards unification. He chose the one who seemed to him to have the strongest roots in British social work and its professional organisations. The decision gave him—prematurely, as it turned out—a cathartic sense of escape from years of destructive controversy.

Those responsible for the new Applied Social Studies Course, including the students' supervisors in the field, would not have devoted themselves to the enormous task of 'creating a tradition in two years' (as one of them put it) if they had not been dissatisfied with older traditions. Like those responsible for the other Courses, they perceived the conflict in a professional context: it was important because of its ultimate bearing on social work, and its outcome would ultimately be decided in the field. Several of these people had originally trained as psychiatric social workers, and between them they had experience of many branches of social work. They were risking their professional reputation and future by trying to create a new training which, if it succeeded, would make all others obsolete. When they first decided, with close colleagues in the field, to commit themselves to setting up the Course they knew it would make them unpopular in many quarters and described their decision as 'the suicide pact'. What was needed, they felt, was a new kind of professional education which would equip students to work in a variety of fields, rather than specialist training to work (often as junior partners) in one field. That education should be based on a closer integration of theory and practice; it should deal with human relationships and the workings of the family; it should help social workers to take action, not just to make—or help others make—'diagnoses'. While they found American social work education and its psychoanalytic insights often gave them fruitful guidance, their experience in many other parts of the world convinced them that their principles were not culture-bound to any particular country. They feared the long-established psychiatric social workers who dominated the profession and whose training, they felt, remained too closely tied to the needs of powerful medical groups and institutions. They believed it to be desperately important to assure the continuation of their own Course, which would enable other branches of social work to escape from second class status; and they feared that a unification of responsibilities for teaching would leave them at the mercy of powerful and fundamentally hostile groups within the profession. The Lecturer in Charge of the Mental Health Course might not herself be hostile, but she could scarcely avoid acting from time to time as spokesman of those who were.

Those responsible for the Mental Health Course felt they were trustees of a tradition well rooted in the field and in the academic world. The little research and writing which had been done by social workers had mainly come from psychiatric social workers. Students coming to the LSE Course were better qualified and more widely experienced than those entering any other social work course in the country. Many went on to leading positions in other branches of social work. A new Mental Health Act, when it came, would make urgent demands for training in this field which were bound to fall heavily upon the LSE. This was no time to rock the boat. Staff running the Course had been accustomed, until recently, to communicate informally with the Director, unobstructed by the Departmental hierarchy which was now beginning to emerge. But their main base was in the field, not the School, and they believed that lasting changes there had to be brought about by working patiently through representative professional and political organisations, not by personal influence or *ad hoc* decisions. They were suspicious of the newcomers' passionate enthusiasms and their reliance on American doctrines which were often ill-suited, they felt, to British traditions. They recognised, however, that major steps would soon have to be taken to rationalise the different forms of social work training. The new Course was already depriving the other two of good candidates. The Child Care Course could not long survive in competition with the Applied Social Studies Course which offered a more widely usable version of the same qualification. The Mental Health Course would probably have to cater increasingly for the more experienced students, if ways could be found to train younger PSWs in an enlarged version of the Applied Social Studies Course. (That was not an idea that appealed to the 'radicals' because it would preserve the first-class status of social workers trained in the Mental Health Course.)

Those responsible for the Child Care Course shared many of these views. Their leading figures were PSWs themselves, and personal relations between them and those responsible for the Mental Health Course were friendly. But the Lecturer in Charge and her immediate colleagues had more fundamental criticisms to make of the 'generic' approach to social work represented by the new Applied Social Studies Course. Overemphasis on the generic element in social work, they argued, encouraged people to regard the social services as a base from which they could deploy their skills. These services had specific, practical help to offer the people whose representatives created them, and it was the social worker's first duty to provide the help and protection which Parliament had intended. There was so much more to be learnt about the practical work and statutory duties of a child care officer, and the acquisition of 'human relationship skills' should not be the main purpose of training. It was widely (and probably rightly) assumed that the Lecturer in Charge had no ambition to run a larger empire. That may explain why she felt, with some justification, that she was not consulted as plans for the future of the Course took shape. Instead, she had sometimes learnt by accident of major decisions affecting her Course and herself, and was then compelled to react more aggressively than she would have wished. Supporters of her Course in the child care services were worried lest an amalgamation of Courses would compel them to accept the same number of places for students that almoners, probation officers and others had, instead of the much larger share they now had.

The remaining Lecturers in the Department—about a dozen of them —fell approximately into two groups: the older generation (mostly women) who were particularly (though not only) concerned with the personal social services and the preparation of students for work in this field; and the younger generation (mostly men) who were particularly (though again not only) concerned with a broader range of social problems and academic teaching without any specific vocational commitments. The professional loyalties of the latter were directed more strongly to the Department and the academic world in general to which they looked for promotion in future. Most of the former were disturbed by a conflict which divided old friends, but their allegiances probably depended more upon their personal relations with the people concerned than upon their views about social work. The younger generation became involved in the argument more reluctantly, if at all. When compelled to take sides, they tended to support the Professor, partly because they felt he had particularly heavy burdens to bear—including recurring ill health—and should not be distracted from academic work which they regarded as more important (in 1956 he had published a seminal paper, still quoted, on the social division of welfare, and important books were to follow) and partly because many of them were suspicious of what they regarded as American-style social casework. Some of them, too, did not want to be identified with social workers and the 'outsiders' they brought into the University.

Thus the new Applied Social Studies Course and the idea underlying it were not strongly rooted in the Department or the School. Apart from the staff directly responsible for it, the Course's most determined backers were outside the School, among field supervisors, officials of central and local government, and members of the professional associations who had together helped to found it. Senior social workers in the Home Office and the Ministry of Health believed the Applied Social Studies Course could make an important contribution to training for their services and to the general development of social work. Senior people in the Institute of Almoners had already resolved to bring their own fairly large training courses to an end and hoped this Course and its successors elsewhere would provide adequate alternatives within the Universities. The social caseworkers of the Family Welfare Association

TAKING DECISIONS IN A UNIVERSITY 273

were also looking to the new Course to provide a continuing flow of well-trained recruits to their kind of work.

This outline of the ways in which different people perceived the issues at stake may help to explain *how* the conflict developed, but it owes a good deal to hindsight. Right or wrong, it is a clearer formulation of the issues than anyone could have given in the heat of battle. *Why* the conflict occurred is a different question to which we return at the conclusion of this chapter.

Further Negotiations

The decisions announced by the Professor provoked varied reactions. All were dismayed at the loss of valued colleagues and the friction this would cause in a generally happy Department. In the course of many private discussions and one long staff meeting (held on 4 March 1957 without the Professional Course teachers) groups began to form within the Department seeking to supplant or support these decisions. It was the dissatisfied who had to make the running at first.

The Lecturer in Charge (MH) sought to meet the supervisors responsible for field training in the Applied Social Studies Course but instead they wrote to the Director (in February) expressing dismay at the turn of events and asking to see him. He agreed to meet them as soon as they had discussed the situation with the Head of the Department. After a meeting with the Professor and Reader and much further discussion, they decided not to see him. They feared their Course would be jeopardised if it was combined with others in a way that deprived them of the support they had previously been given by its teachers—particularly the Lecturer who was 'second in command' of the Course and their main link with the School. They made it clear that they could not continue to work on the Course unless at least one of the two Lecturers responsible for it returned to collaborate with them. They refused, for the time being, to discuss the situation with the Lecturer in Charge (MH) who was to have general charge of professional education for social work.

Senior officials of the agencies in which the supervisors were employed wrote to the Director of the School and the Professor. They expressed somewhat similar fears and were particularly concerned at what seemed to them an abrupt decision, taken without consultation with outside bodies.

The Secretary to the Trustees financing the Course wrote, on 21 February, expressing concern and implying that his Trustees were likely to withdraw the grant from which the Course was financed. After further correspondence with the Professor and the Lecturer in Charge (ASS) they agreed, on 11 March, to continue the grant provisionally. But their Secretary set inquiries in train which encouraged many concerned with the new Course to write to him. He did not consult their opponents.

On 4 March the Professor sent a further statement to all who had received his letter of 20 February. This briefly explained the background to his original decisions and outlined the distribution of responsibilities he envisaged for the future. The Lecturer in Charge (MH) would not 'take over' the running of the Applied Social Studies or Child Care Courses: her responsibilities would be for 'setting these developments [i.e. integration of the Courses] on foot and co-ordinating the many negotiations involved'—negotiations which in practice would often 'have to be left to others'. This, he assumed, would in any case be the normal academic practice. Integration would be worked out with 'the general agreement of those responsible for all three Courses' by 'an *ad hoc* committee of all the staff concerned', to be presided over by the Reader if the Committee wished. If agreement could not be reached in this Committee, decisions would have to be taken by the Head of the Department. There would have to be close consultation with the existing Consultative Committees to the Professional Courses which might be 'combined and reconstituted'. No decision had been taken about the person to be responsible for running the single combined Course which would eventually emerge. The statement ended with an appeal to those who had resigned to reconsider their decision.

A week later the Lecturer in Charge (ASS) sent a reply to this statement to all those outside the School to whom the letter of 4 March had gone. She concentrated on two problems: consultation, and the future role of the Lecturer in Charge (MH). Questions of 'timing and consultation, which were . . . one of the main reasons for our final resignations', would depend on 'the exact nature of the *ad hoc* committee which we would see as performing important functions'. She felt that the future responsibilities of the Lecturer in Charge (MH) had been modified by the letter of 4 March, but not sufficiently to enable her to withdraw her resignation: 'If I were to be asked to continue in charge of the Course next session to work under [her] in all the planning and negotiations which must be done if the Course is to become permanent, this would be generally regarded as an expression of lack of confidence in my previous conduct of these negotiations, as well as of my general planning of the curriculum . . .' She suggested that the Lecturer in Charge (MH) should 'under a reworded title, continue to retain her present responsibility for the Mental Health Course and also act as secretary to the committee proposed'.

Where others regarded the 'unification' or 'planned co-ordination' of all three Courses as the principal issue at stake (as in the Professor's statement of 20 February, for example) this letter and other statements by those sympathising with its standpoint described the same process as the Applied Social Studies Course 'becoming permanent' and regarded the continuation or termination of this Course as the focal point of dispute. To defend what they had created, the advocates of a unified generic training were, for the time being, calling for a new and separate specialism.

The Consultative Committee to the Applied Social Studies Course met on 20 March. The non-University members of the Committee were worried and somewhat hostile, but uncertain how best they could contribute to the solution of these problems. Some resented the cancellation of an earlier meeting at which the Professor's decisions might have been discussed before they were announced. Those responsible for training were anxious to know whether a Course would be run next year and who would staff it. One of the Home Office representatives gave warning that her Ministry might withdraw its support from the Course. An attempt was made to explain some of the background to the decisions but the Committee was persuaded not to make a detailed inquiry into the reasons for the resignations. The only positive action taken was to arrange an extra meeting of the Committee to be held on 8 May.

On the same day, supervisors to the Applied Social Studies Course wrote to the Director (without warning or consulting the Head of the Department) asking that a 'professional courses development council' be set up. They took this direct action because they were still unwilling to meet the Lecturer in Charge (MH) and felt the Professor had left them no alternative. Its immediate result was a stiffer attitude on the part of the Professor to whom this appeared a stupid intrusion into the affairs of the School, likely to discredit those who were doing their best to gain a sound footing for social work education there. He wrote final letters two days later to those resigning, offering to withdraw the words 'in charge' from the title of the new post but reasserting his determination to support its holder 'to the full', saying she must have 'conditions of responsibility and initiative in which to work'. He said that new methods of consultation with supervisors and others outside the School would have to be worked out, and concluded with another appeal for the withdrawal of the resignations. He then left on 28 March to spend two months in the United States where he had agreed, many months before, to give a number of lectures.

The Reader took over responsibility for these negotiations. Until then his task of acting as adviser and go-between had compelled him to maintain a certain detachment in order to communicate effectively with all concerned. Henceforth he was compelled to take decisions and commit himself. Since his responsibility was for the Department as a whole, rather than for one Course within it, and since he felt unable (even had he wished) to modify the distribution of duties outlined in the Professor's statement of 4 March, those concerned mainly for the future of the Applied Social Studies Course gained the growing impression thereafter that their communications with him were 'breaking down'. His objectives were reasonably clear: to reassert on every appropriate occasion the decisions announced on 4 March, to develop closer collaboration with outside bodies whose support was required by the Professional Courses, to arrange terms for the withdrawal of both resignations if possible, and to ensure that the Applied Social Studies Course continued—which meant that the 'second in command' on this Course must return to the School for at least one more year, if necessary without the Lecturer in Charge. The former had already made it clear that since her first loyalty had to be to the Course itself she would be prepared to consider returning to the School without the latter—though only with the utmost reluctance. The Lecturer in Charge (ASS) wrote to the Reader on 1 April, welcoming the plan for a consultative committee and explaining that decisions about her own future could only be made 'as part of a total plan worked out and agreed by all those directly concerned'.

In a succession of meetings, running through April, May and June, starting with senior Professional Course staff and including a successively wider range of staff, supervisors and senior officials from the social services, plans were worked out for the establishment of an Advisory Committee to assist the School in the development and integration of all three Courses. The existing Advisory Committees would be abolished, the new Committee would be entitled to advise on any aspect of professional education for social work, and all those teaching on the Professional Courses would hold regular staff meetings of their own. At first many of the Department's staff—and particularly those supporting the decisions so far made—were suspicious of this Advisory Committee and feared it might infringe academic prerogatives. They had some reason for their concern: at one stage a constitution was proposed under which teaching plans would be worked out with the guidance of a sub-committee of the Advisory Committee which would consist largely of people drawn from outside the University—not an arrangement which the School would accept. But agreement became easier when this proposal was dropped, when it was appreciated that the large number of outside interests involved would compel the appointment of a large Advisory Committee that would have to rely heavily on the academic staff, and when officials and social workers participating in the discussions showed themselves to be experienced administrators, with genuine respect for the rights of the University, who were mainly concerned to ensure that professional training developed successfully in the School.

The day after the Head of the Department left for the United States the Secretary of the Carnegie United Kingdom Trust wrote to the Director saying how deeply concerned his Trustees were about staff changes on the Course and the lack of consultation with 'the professional bodies whom the Trustees regard as partners in this important experiment'. As a result of various discussions they had had with people concerned with the Course the Chairman of the Trust and the Convener of the Trust's Education Committee had decided to recommend that 'the Trust's grant for the session 1957–58 be suspended until the Trust is satisfied that the Course will proceed into its fourth year without drastic changes in the teaching staff and with the goodwill and confidence of the professional agencies'.

A number of discussions followed between the Director and members of staff, and the Director and representatives of the Trustees. Their outcome was summarised by the Director when talking with the Reader and Senior Tutor on 24 April. He said he had come to doubt whether a University was the proper place for the Applied Social Studies Course. But if the University continued to run a Course of this kind then funds must be found for it, whether or not the Trust was prepared to provide them. In any case he was not prepared to discuss the staffing of the School with the Trustees. Later there were more discussions with the Trustees who finally agreed to make the remainder of their grant available.

Through these weeks the Reader was trying to bring affairs to a head. It was high time to inform students who had been accepted for next year's Applied Social Studies Course whether there was to be a Course for them to attend. People concerned with training at the Home Office, the Family Welfare Association, the Institute of Almoners, and the Universities were growing increasingly worried about these students and asking increasingly insistently for a decision. Meanwhile if replacements were to be found for staff intending to resign in October, the vacant posts would have to be advertised without delay.

No final decisions could be made about the Course until the position of the Lecturer in Charge (ASS) was clarified and this now depended on the functions to be allotted to the principal members of staff concerned. Many discussions took place on these matters and it was eventually agreed with the Director that: (a) the other Lecturer on the Applied Social Studies Course would run it for a trial year; (b) a new Lecturer would be recruited (and all the Lecturers in charge of the three Courses were agreed on the person to be invited to take this post); (c) the future distribution of places on the Professional Courses to students specialising in different branches of social work would be settled in consultation with the proposed Advisory Committee (a question of vital importance to the social services and professional associations concerned); (d) all new field training units would be agreed jointly by the Professional Courses staff, again in consultation with the Advisory Committee; (e) the School would give sympathetic consideration to the appointment of a new Administrative Assistant to act for all three Courses, and to a reallocation of rooms which would place staff on the three Courses closer to each other. These agreements cleared much of the ground and, in a final attempt to resolve the situation so that decisions might be taken on the Professor's return, the Reader helped the Director to prepare a statement, dated 15 May, which they and the Senior Tutor believed would be acceptable to all concerned and provide a basis on which the Lecturer in Charge (ASS) could return—as a part-time Lecturer, acting as 'adviser on general policy in relation to the Applied Social Studies Course'. She raised two queries about this statement which presented no problem, and one which revealed the unbridgeable gulf still remaining. In place of a statement explaining that the Lecturer in Charge (MH) 'will assume the leadership and co-ordination of these developments as explained in [the Professor's] letter of 4 March' she proposed the words 'will act as secretary to this committee' (i.e. the new advisory committee to be established for all three Courses).

Final Decisions

That at least made it finally clear that no agreement could be reached between the people involved in these negotiations. They defined and interpreted 'the developments' referred to in the latest statement—indeed, the whole problem under discussion—in different ways. For one group the question to be decided was the continuation or termination of the new Course. Later, they probably assumed, it would become the basic model for the future of professional training in social work. For others the decision to develop and integrate the three Courses—which might or might not eventually become completely united—was the main issue. Warning of this continuing disagreement had been given, though not fully grasped, by a misunderstanding arising at this time. In making plans for the appointment of a new lecturer it was proposed by the Reader and others that the newcomer would teach on 'the Professional Courses'—since he would be appointed to the Department which was concerned with all three Courses. This proposal, ineptly made without consulting them, greatly dismayed the two Lecturers responsible for the Applied Social Studies Course who had assumed the new appointment was designed to develop their own form of training. (The man in view for the appointment was one of their own supervisors.)

By the time the Professor returned on 27 May, other aspects of the situation were clear too. The Director was prepared to go no further in finding avenues of escape from the impasse: talking about the Applied Social Studies Course to the Reader he said: 'I don't want to kill the thing, but I am no longer disposed officiously to keep it alive.' This resolve was hardened in various quarters by the realisation that the School's financial position during the next quinquennium would be unexpectedly tight: there were no resources to spare and Professors in other Departments were looking around for economies which would save them from having to accept cuts in their own development plans. Sensing this change in climate perhaps, a growing body of people outside the School—including many of the officials and social workers who had opposed the original decisions—were prepared to sink their differences and make any contribution they could to ensure the Course survived.

The Professor discussed the position with the Director and his principal colleagues as soon as he returned to London. The Director made it clear on 5 June that no firm assurances could be given about the appointment of an additional Lecturer (the man originally in view for this post had turned it down because the School could not offer him as much as he was already earning in the probation service) and added that anyone appointed would be attached to the Department and not to any particular Course within it. The two Lecturers responsible for the Applied Social Studies Course offered, for the second time, to surrender half their own salaries to make such an appointment possible, but this offer was refused. After further discussions the following announcement was made by the Professor, with their agreement, to a Departmental Staff meeting on 12 June. He had already made it clear privately that the only alternative available to him was to close the Applied Social Studies Course.

It has been decided that the Course in Applied Social Studies should be run next session. I want, therefore, to summarise briefly the present position as regards staff and other matters.

'After my return from the United States [the Lecturer in Charge (ASS)] who had already decided that she did not wish to return to the School in more than a part-time capacity, indicated her willingness to accept an offer of an appointment for next session as adviser and part-time lecturer to the Course in Applied Social Studies. Subsequently, she suggested to the School that her salary should be made available to secure a sufficient margin for the appointment of a full-time teacher. [Her] offer has been accepted. Both the Director and I very much appreciate the spirit in which [she] has made this suggestion and agree that it could form a helpful contribution towards the solution of our present difficulties. Although her teaching connection with the Course will cease at the end of the present session, we shall hope to continue to have the benefit of her help and advice on the new Advisory Committee on questions of social work and education which she herself has worked so hard to advance. I respect her for the offer she has made, and thank her, in particular, for all she has done for the development of the Course in Applied Social Studies.

'[The other Lecturer on the Applied Social Studies Course] has accepted an appointment for next session as Lecturer in Charge of the Course in Applied Social Studies. To assist her, an additional full-time lecturer will be appointed and the School hopes to make a further announcement on this in the near future.

'Pending the return of [the Lecturer in Charge (CC), the other Lecturer on this Course] will be in charge of the Child Care Course.

'It is intended, early next session, to consider the future of the

Course in Applied Social Studies and its relationship with the courses in Mental Health and Child Care. Accordingly it is necessary, as indicated in my letter of 4th March, to make internal arrangements for the co-ordination of discussions that will be involved in considering the problems of integrating these courses. To this end, it has also been decided to establish a new Advisory Committee to help in discussions of policy.

'In pursuance of these arrangements [the Lecturer in Charge (MH)] will, in addition to continuing to be in charge of the Mental Health Course, be responsible for the co-ordination of the necessary discussions of future policy and will, from the date of the inauguration of the new Advisory Committee, serve as its executive secretary.[1]

'The Committee will it is hoped, be the principal forum for discussion of plans and policies in relation to the three Courses. This Committee will include people drawn from training and employing bodies, professional associations, field work agencies, the supervisors and the staff of the Department. I believe it could play an important and effective part in the development of our teaching. We intend to set it up as soon as possible.'

POSTSCRIPT

We should note a few of the main developments which have occurred since 1958 before discussing the conclusions to be drawn from this study. 'Generic' courses, like the Applied Social Studies Course, grew up during the next decade in other Universities and later in the Technical Colleges. Many adopted the same name. But most of them offered qualifications only for a limited range of specialisms, such as child care, probation and medical social work for instance. They were 'generic' in philosophy and methods rather than unspecific in professional terms. Some of the new postgraduate courses combined, in eighteen or twenty-one months, a basic introduction to social administration and the social sciences with a professional training in social work. Meanwhile more specialised social work courses did not disappear; indeed, they grew in numbers—particularly for probation officers. These arrangements depended on the support which different Government departments could offer for training in various branches of social work, and the Universities' response to these offers.

The introduction of the new Social Services Departments in 1971, recorded in postscripts to previous chapters, helped to lower the barriers between different specialisms. Without the generic courses, that unification is unlikely to have been achieved. (The Seebohm Committee, whose report[2] led to this development, included among its

[1] This was crucial for the Lecturer in Charge (MH) who "fully intended to be the *executive* secretary, and was". (Letter to the author.)
[2] Report of the Committee on Local Authority and Allied Personal Social Services Cmnd 3703, 1968.

members graduates of the LSE's Mental Health and Applied Social Studies Courses.) An equally important contribution to this unifying trend was the creation in 1970 of the British Association of Social Workers to represent branches of the profession previously represented by the associations speaking for medical social workers, psychiatric social workers, child care officers, mental welfare officers, moral welfare workers and family caseworkers, and the Association of Social Workers. Of the major groups of social workers, only the National Association of Probation Officers stayed out.

The most important development in training for social work during these years was the creation, under the Health Visiting and Social Work (Training) Act 1962, of a large number of two-year training courses outside the Universities leading to the Certificate in Social Work (now replaced by the Certificate of Qualification in Social Work[1]). Shorter, part-time and in-service training also began to develop for welfare assistants and others in the social services. These developments followed from the report of a Committee of Inquiry working under the Chairmanship of the Lecturer in Charge (ASS) which was published in 1959. Another initiative proposed in this Report was the establishment of a National Institute for Social Work Training which was set up with support from charitable trusts and the central government. She and her colleague, who took over the Applied Social Studies Course from her, both joined the staff of this Institute. Meanwhile a number of Universities, with the LSE among them, developed Master's and Doctoral Degrees which were intended to provide opportunities for more advanced work in this field. Gradually a pattern of training was growing up in which 'vertical' divisions between specialisms were giving way to 'horizontal' divisions between less advanced and more advanced qualifications, with opportunities for their holders to progress from one to another. But the pattern remains fairly confused, for these courses serve a continually evolving field. Every time training for social work seems to be settling into a stable pattern, new courses and specialisms appear—in residential work, community work, administrative studies and so on.

While some of these more recent innovations have left their mark on the LSE, none of them began there. At the School, things have moved more slowly since the events described in this chapter. The new Lecturer in Charge—previously 'second in command'—took the Applied Social Studies Course forward for one year and then left. The Reader took over for the year 1958–9, when the Child Care Course was amalgamated with the Applied Social Studies Course. Thereafter the Lecturer in Charge (MH), now Lecturer in Charge of Social Work Education, assumed general responsibility for both the remaining Courses. She was

---

[1] *Social Work. Setting the Course for Social Work Education*, First Report of the Central Council for Education and Training in Social Work, 1973.

made a Senior Lecturer, and later Reader in Social Work. Arrangements for shared teaching developed slowly. For a while staff of the Mental Health Course devoted part of their efforts to training experienced mental welfare workers who were assuming heavier responsibilities under the new Mental Health Act. Then a small-scale course, offering no formal qualification, was set up for experienced, professionally qualified staff. (The Area Officer of the LCC Children's Department, who figured in Chapter 6, joined this group as a student when she left her subsequent post as Children's Officer for Tower Hamlets.)

Progress towards unification of the Diplomas (as they were renamed in 1962–3) in Mental Health and Applied Social Studies can be traced in the convergence of their examination requirements. These can be abstracted in tabular form from the Calendars of the School. Progress was slow until the late 1960s. The titles of their examinations were then as follows:

	Mental Health	*Applied Social Studies*
1967	1 Mental disorder 2 Mental health in childhood and adolescence 3 Casework and administration 4 Current psychological and social problems	1 Human behaviour and casework 2 Social administration and casework
1968 to 1970	1 Human growth and behaviour 2 Casework and administration 3 Mental disorder	1 Human growth and behaviour 2 Casework and administration 3 Social work and social problems

Then in the year 1970–1 a combined Diploma in Social Work Studies superseded both Courses, with examinations in:

    1 Human growth and behaviour
    2 Social work and social administration
    3 Social pathology

Numbers on these Courses have grown slowly. In 1957–8 there were seventy-three students taking the three Courses. By 1973–4 there were 90 on the combined course, including 25 taking a Master's Degree in this field. The School's Advisory Committee on Social Work Education, after a year of frequent and active discussions, met rarely and was then quietly disbanded.

DISCUSSION

It is when things 'go wrong' and unforeseen conflicts disrupt a hitherto orderly scene that processes which normally flow unnoticed through the usual channels of an organisation break surface and become visible to the research worker. Extraordinary though its events seemed to the participants, this case illustrates processes which can be more dimly discerned in other situations we studied. We note a few of these processes here and examine them in greater detail in our final chapter.

In research of this kind it is particularly important, and difficult, to define the centre and boundaries of the action to be studied. To explain how the Professor's decisions of June 1957 were reached (which is the question we started from) we chose his Department as the focal group for research (instead of the smaller number of people staffing the Professional Courses, the larger numbers constituting the whole School, or other groups extending beyond the School which might have been chosen). That choice does not define the cast for the play: the people who actually played a part in bringing about the decision to be studied included many outside the Department and excluded some of those inside it. But it fixes the author's standpoint and determines who are to be described as 'insiders' and 'outsiders', 'senior' and 'junior', 'those responsible for providing' a course and 'those controlling the resources they need'—terms which are all morally loaded in subtle ways. Such standpoints have to be chosen pragmatically. We cannot prove that ours was 'correct': we can only argue that it was the most revealing available—and note the biases it may introduce. (Some would argue that the story has been told from a point of view more sympathetic to the Head of the Department than to other participants. Defining his Department as the focal group for the study may encourage a bias of that kind.)

An innovation (the new Applied Social Studies Course) was begun by staff within the Department. To achieve that they had first to secure more resources: the only alternative strategy would have been to cut down on other work which many people were doing. The resources needed in this case were very complex. They included staff and their salaries, grants for students, supervisors in the social services, recognition of qualifications by employers and professional associations, authorisations from LSE authorities to appoint staff and accept students, and so on. These resources were secured, thanks to an expanding and relatively benign environment in and around the LSE, and thanks to the talents of the Professor and his colleagues, and the support of the Director. But, as in other cases we studied, a price had to be paid for these resources in assurances and claims of various kinds which satisfied those from whom they were sought. The Course had to be recognised by the relevant Government departments and professional associations (a point on which the Carnegie Trust was insistent and initially sceptical); it had to provide sufficient instruction about the nature of health and disease (to satisfy the Institute of Almoners); it had to produce a sufficient number of child care officers (to satisfy the Home Office); and so on. Senior staff operating on the boundaries of the organisation played, as usual, the main parts in these transactions—people such as the Director, the Professor and particularly the Lecturer in Charge of the new Course.

Further constraints were imposed by the potential customers of the service—in this case candidates for the Course and others, like their University tutors and future employers, who helped to shape their demands. Students were impressed by the hope—advertised each year in the School's Calendar—that the Applied Social Studies Course would enable them to work in various branches of the social services, not only in one setting. Their tutors believed the Course was intellectually superior to alternative options for probation officers and others, and were interested in other features, such as the possibility that a common training would in future make co-operation between different social services easier.

To accommodate all these expectations and retain some freedom of action, the innovators kept their aims sufficiently vague (the new Course was to be 'experimental') to leave them a good deal of discretion. The growth which followed did not proceed evenly, 'to scale': that is to say, it enlarged the opportunities, status and powers of some people more than others—or (which is more important) it provoked anxieties that it might do so. Conflict (over students, the agencies and supervisors for students' field work, the descriptions of courses and posts) began early, not at the top but at a working level within the organisation. It was some time before those directing the Department and the School were aware of these stresses, and they probably never understood them fully. Other conflicts we have studied followed similar patterns, and led to similar appeals for arbitration and decisions directed to people in senior positions—initially to the Head of the Department in this case. He tried to persuade his colleagues to reach decisions among themselves, but the competitive and non-hierarchical situation in which they were placed made that impossible. So he took decisions of his own. His premature attempt to resolve the problem led to appeals, counter-appeals and threats of resignation—whether explicit or implicit does not greatly matter. There followed interventions, first by insiders and then by outsiders: supervisors, professional associations, central and local government officials and charitable trustees—anyone capable of bringing pressure to bear on successively higher levels of the decision-making hierarchy.

Throughout these discussions the issues at stake were uncertain and confused and people constantly complained that 'communications had broken down'. *Defining* the issue became, in a sense, *the* issue. One definition of the question (Is the new Course to continue?) would pose different problems, polarise participants in different ways, and produce different reactions from other definitions (such as: Are the three Courses to be combined? Who is to be in charge of professional education? Are outsiders to dictate to the University—or the University to outsiders?). This is a recurring feature of such conflicts. People cannot decide where they stand or discover who stands with them till they define the issues at stake and the frame of reference from which those issues are to be interpreted. As they try to clarify the issues, communication between them breaks down because they are, literally, talking about different things. And when decisions are reached at the end of the day, participants give different accounts of what those decisions were really about.

The conflict was in this case particularly difficult to resolve because participants were playing a 'zero sum game': any gains made by one had to be at the expense of others—or that, at least, was how they felt. Mutual understanding and goodwill, and all the consultation in the world, would not have resolved the conflict—though they might have changed its form, location and tone. Conflict of some kind was inevitable because the main participants were committed to conflicting objectives with the support of various groups outside the University whose divergent interests would have to break surface somewhere, sooner or later. As often happens in zero sum games, the main participants appeared 'bloody minded' because their rational course of action was to decline compromises until the alternatives were clear: there were no mutually advantageous bargains available. Clarification could not be achieved until every available influence had been brought to bear. As soon as that point was reached, a solution quickly followed. That again is a common pattern: after so long a battle, further dispute may prove disastrous for all concerned.

But solutions reached in this way are never the end of the story. History unfolds and its eventual outcome depends on the people who stay in post, the changing pressures on them, changing attitudes and the lessons that everyone learns from their experience.

CHAPTER 12

CONCLUSIONS

Before drawing conclusions about innovations in social policy from the few we have studied, we must note the character of our evidence, the methods by which it was assembled, its limitations and likely biases. That is what we try to do in the first section of this chapter.

In the second section we consider the 'stage' on which the events to be studied were enacted. Defining the people and activities—the 'action space'—on which our research was focused is more than a methodological problem, for the way we do that goes far to shape our understanding of the process by determining what is to be studied, what excluded and where the centre of the action lies. These dramatic metaphors are appropriate, for it is a central theme of our conclusions that we are studying, not continuous, marginal adjustments to impersonal forces, but the endeavours of people, or actors, who bring about changes in the course of a process, or drama, which leads through successive phases, or acts, in which participants play recognisable roles. Others have shown how organisations survive or decay, and how markets operate to allocate resources through marginal, equilibrium-seeking adjustments; but—useful though their research has been—these are not the essential questions to ask if you want to know how innovations in social policy come about.

Having described the stage, we turn to the 'cast', trying to identify the people involved in the events to be studied, and to generalise as simply as possible about their interests, the way in which they may be grouped, and the relations which develop between them.

Next we describe the 'action', generalising about the way in which the various groups involved in the process interact with each other to bring about changes in the social services, and the successive phases, or acts, through which the process leads.

In the fifth section of this chapter we discuss cases in which the muted controversies to be found in all these stories broke into open conflict. These cases were particularly interesting because they show features of social innovation, often unperceived, which should be better understood; they were unusual examples of essentially normal processes.

If we succeed in enabling our readers to gain a clearer understanding of the processes we have studied they will know best how to use that

CONCLUSIONS

knowledge. We cannot formulate conclusive prescriptions for action from a few case studies. But we should ask ourselves what practical lessons can be learnt from this research. In the next section, entitled 'Some Local Implications', we try to answer that question.

Finally we return to the questions posed in the first chapter of this book. In what rational sense, if any, is it possible to make the world a better place? And whose rationality gains a hearing? Our case studies cannot answer such big questions, but we should consider whether our research has taught us anything about them, and contribute what we can to the larger debate before drawing this book to a close.

The Changes We Studied

We must pause to recall what kinds of changes we have studied before summarising the evidence about them and considering its implications. We took as our point of departure nine local units of the social services —interpreting those terms broadly to include a teaching department within a university, a borough housing department, and an area office of a central government service. All but one of them operated in London, mainly in the inner parts of the town, east of the centre; the exceptions were the Croydon Education Department in south London and the Children's Aid Society in Canada.

All but one of these organisations provided specific services for identifiable individuals and families: education, housing, domestic help, child care and social work—but not parks or law enforcement, or regulatory functions, such as rent control or the inspection of slaughterhouses. The partial exception was the National Assistance Board which helped to administer the Legal Aid Service provided by the Law Society, but was not itself giving this service to litigants. These distinctions may not be profoundly important, for several of the organisations had responsibilities of the kinds we excluded: the redevelopment which follows major slum clearance schemes is intended to improve the environment for all who live or work in the city, not only for the families rehoused; and local health authorities inspect and regulate foster homes, shops, houses, and many other things. All these organisations do other work which we did not study—the University does research, the National Assistance Board provided a cash assistance, and the Family Welfare Association administers citizens' advice bureaux, for example.

The cases we studied were picked by asking the heads of the local services which formed our point of departure what were 'the most important developments or changes' which had occurred in their organisations during the last few years. In a few cases they could think of nothing worth studying—or nothing, perhaps, which they could safely expose to research—and in several the development or developments actually chosen for study were defined in the course of discussions in which we, as research workers, must have exercised some influence.

We made no attempt to evaluate the changes we studied: we did not ask, for example, whether the elderly ladies who became the home help service's main customers were satisfied with the service they got or whether they, or society at large, would gain more from this distribution of the service than from other distributions which might be envisaged. In only two of these studies (the Croydon and University cases) was the researcher himself a participant in the events to be described and in those he only saw a small part of the action. In all of them we depended heavily for our evidence upon the papers and recollections of people who had played a part, as professional staff, administrators, committee members and so on, in bringing about the changes we were studying.

Together these observations suggest that our findings may best fit organisations which deliver services directly to customers—their pupils, clients, tenants, claimants or patients. They may also best fit developments which are regarded as important and successful by the directors of such services, although several of those we traced were not in fact regarded as success stories by their principal characters. (Croydon's attempts to reorganise its secondary schools were a complete failure during the period covered by our original study, and our case study of a University was felt by some of the principal participants to be too painful to publish.) Our studies were conducted from the bureaucrats' side of the counter; thus they may underemphasise aspects of social policy and administration which would seem more important to people on the customers' side of the counter. They tell us little about inaction: changes which unroll imperceptibly without anyone taking deliberate steps to bring them about (of which the Home Help Service was our main example) were also under-represented, although they can be as important as the more striking developments we concentrated upon.

These studies may nevertheless be revealing, provided their biases are cautiously noted. Services of these kinds are increasingly important in Britain. Housing, education and health services, personal social services and the National Assistance Board were the points of departure for our research. Together they account for the great bulk of the country's expenditure on social services. Although London differs in many ways from the rest of Britain, the conclusions we draw from these studies do not appear to apply only in the capital (indeed, most of them apply equally well to a Children's Aid Society in a small Canadian town). Several of our cases were miniature in scale but although some recount the doings of only a handful of people, developments of this kind—chosen because they seemed important to senior staff in the social services of the metropolis—often prove to be the leading edge of much larger changes. Revisiting the scene a dozen years later, we show in our

CONCLUSIONS 289

postscripts how often the innovations traced in our original studies have since become nationwide orthodoxy. (Bethnal Green was one of the first housing authorities to resume what became a nationwide programme of slum clearance; Finsbury was one of the first to build tower blocks of flats—as its successors in the new Borough of Islington have since been among those leading the way back to low-rise high density housing. Current patterns of social work training throughout the country owe a lot to the experiment made by a handful of people whose conflicts and dilemmas we recorded seventeen years ago at the LSE; the Area Office of the FWA which we studied was reorganised at that time to provide field training for students on lines now widely adopted elsewhere. The growth of an increasingly coherent and confident social work 'interest' concerned with the welfare of the whole family, which we observed in the London County Council's Children's Department, helped to lay the foundations for reforms later proposed by the Seebohm Committee, whose members included graduates from the training courses we studied at the LSE. Even local failures may exert a nationwide influence: proposals for sixth form colleges, long debated but never adopted in Croydon, helped to formulate a model now well established in many other places throughout the country.) If we approached a new sample of such services today and asked them to identify the 'most important developments or changes' in their work we would again find similar pointers to the future.

In recent studies[1] of larger innovations in social policy introduced through Parliament on a national scale, Professor Roy Parker and his colleagues concluded that governments choose issues for action on three main grounds: *'legitimacy'*—'is this an issue with which government considers it should be concerned?'; *'feasibility'*—'the possibility (or the assumed possibility) of taking steps to deal with a problem'; and public *'support'* for action on the issue and, more diffusely, for government in general. The local developments which we have studied are an earlier, not a more trivial, phase of the processes of trial and error which ultimately help to give proposals for social reform the legitimacy, feasibility and support they must have if they are to be applied on a nationwide scale. The more dramatic events cannot be understood without studying these, their less dramatic, forerunners.

The Stage
Everyone who studies innovation in the output and policies of human organisations has trouble in defining these organisations. Burns and Stalker in their pioneering work on *The Management of Innovation* deal sometimes with 'concerns' which 'were only small parts of their parent organizations', and sometimes with groups of 'several separately

[1] Phoebe Hall, Hilary Land, Roy Parker and Adrian Webb, *Change, Choice and Conflict in Social Policy*. Heinemann, forthcoming.

incorporated companies'.[1] They were quite right not to tie themselves to any definition, for such definitions determine the stage on which the central part of the action is to take place, and, by implication, who should be regarded as 'up-stage', 'down-stage' or 'off-stage'. They determine frames of reference and the reference groups which go with them. The action itself—in our case the innovations to be studied—must first be defined; only then can a stage suitable to accommodate it be identified. The stage will never be exactly coterminous with administrative organisations such as a Social Service Department or one of its area offices; and even when an 'action space' has been chosen it may remain controversial because the choice implies a particular interpretation of the nature of the innovation, the issues at stake, and the roles of the actors concerned. (In our study of the FWA, some of the Association's members treated it for most purposes as a fairly loose federation of Area Offices, each subject only to its own Committee: for them, the Area Office generally constituted the stage. But in times of financial crisis all had increasingly to defer to headquarters and treat the FWA as 'the organisation' to which they belonged. In the University case some people were convinced their Department within the London School of Economics was the central stage for the action and its Professor the leading actor, with the implication that others, off-stage, should not too rashly intrude into affairs which were essentially 'academic'. Others had a different stage in mind on which lecturers in charge of courses were the leading actors; it included a section of the Department but extended outside the School to include administrative, professional and other bodies which played major parts in the training of social workers.)

Almost by definition, innovations in policy call for some modifications of frames of reference which may previously have been accepted without much question. Thus for the research worker exploring such innovations there can be no objective or authoritative definition of the organisation he is to study. He has to use his judgement, try to grasp the issues at stake, and focus on whatever stage or action area seems best suited to them, noting ways in which this frame of reference may bias his account, and telling the story from several different points of view (as we tried to do in the previous chapter) when that is the only way to convey an understanding of the action.

Our concern about the importance and the difficulties of defining the 'stage' or central focus of the action to be studied will seem overanxious academicism to some, but the problem has far-reaching implications. It explains, for example, why so much of the sociological literature on bureaucracy and the economic literature on the theory of the firm is of so little help to anyone trying to learn how the policies, aims and functions of the social services evolve. Most of this literature starts

[1] Tom Burns and G. M. Stalker, *The Management of Innovation*. Tavistock Publications, 2nd edn, 1966, p. 77.

from a predetermined concept of the organisation to be studied—useful for its own purposes, but ill-suited to ours. Its authors are asking, not what do people do, but how does their organisation survive?

The Cast

Each of the developments we studied called, by definition, for changes in the volume, character or distribution of services to be delivered to the public, which could not come about without changes in the behaviour of the people who did the work of providing the service. They had to make the changes happen. Sometimes they responded to opportunities and pressures, without recognising at the time that they were making a change. (Staff of the home help service laboured consciously enough to increase its size, but came to concentrate increasingly upon the elderly without deliberately planning that outcome; they were simply responding day by day to needs, demands, and pressures of various kinds.) More often, however, the principal people providing the service had to work long and hard to bring about an innovation, and to change their colleagues' behaviour in the course of it. (Developments such as those we traced in the LCC Children's Department, the Canadian Children's Aid Society, and the University placed enormous strains on the key actors and would never have happened if these people had not been deeply committed to making them come about.) The 'providers' of the service, and their leading figures in particular—those who played leading parts in the development, whatever their position in the bureaucratic hierarchy—are the central actors in the cast.

In the previous edition of this book we concluded that it is usually these providers of the service who initiate changes.[1] Dr Rene Saran,[2] who compared our findings with work which she and others have done in the highly politicised field of secondary education, rightly pointed out that the providers often respond to external pressures from politicians and others. We could not disagree with the final conclusion she reached in her own field: 'decisions about changes in policy and in administrative practice are closely related to changes in informed opinion. Indeed, these two factors reinforce each other'.[3] It can be difficult to tell whether the providers lead or follow informed opinion: often they do both.

In the majority of our studies (most clearly in the LCC Children's Department, the Canadian CAS, the FWA, and the University) the major initiatives for change were taken by paid staff of the service. That, we pointed out in our previous book, is most likely to happen when the providers are 'trained and skilled, when they are given considerable

---

[1] Page 239 et seq.
[2] *Policy-Making in Secondary Education. A Case Study.* Oxford University Press, 1973.
[3] Ibid., page 274.

discretion in the practice of their own work, and when the services they provide depend largely on their own direct contacts with those served', rather than on 'costly capital investment or the provision of cash payments'.[1] Where massive resources are required for a development (as in the reorganisation of a Borough's housing programme or its secondary schools) the central government and the elected members of local government must be involved at a fairly early stage.

Some students of British government would argue that its paid officials have long played a major part in developing its policies and functions. Professor Oliver MacDonagh, in his study of the Passenger Acts of the nineteenth century which eventually protected emigrants travelling by sea, pointed out that 'dramatic or political themes, and especially those linked with great persons or ideas, are naturally the first to attract attention from scholars'. But it is not to be assumed that subjects like his own, which 'rarely engaged the attention of public men or parliament, and never entered party politics', are 'a-typical and unrepresentative'—or unimportant. His study deals with a classic conflict between the principles of free trade and the progress of collectivism. In this field, he concludes, 'generally speaking, the agents of the change were the professional administrators, and the lesser and least distinguished administrators at that ... The men who made the revolution were the humdrum executive officers, and career civil servants who never rose above the height of assistant under-secretary.'[2]

But argument about the sources of innovation in social policy will usually be a chicken-and-egg affair because new deveopments cannot begin without a response from many others besides the providers of the service. (It would not be profitable to argue whether Bethnal Green's switch to slum clearance was due to an outside stimulus—the shortage of building sites within the Borough—or to the advice given by officials contending with that problem, or to their Council's determination to go on building which compelled them to approve these proposals: clearly all were essential parts of the story.)

To carry out the innovations we studied, the providers of services always needed resources of some kind—often of many kinds: authorisations, money, staff, office space, and so on. There was insufficient slack in the system—too few unused resources under their own control—to get far without seeking extra resources, outside the providing group. For that they had to seek the support of a second group of people who controlled these resources. Others capable of influencing the resource controllers often played a part in the story too. We illustrate these processes from our own cases below.

To bring about a change in the volume, character or distribution of their services, the providers had also to elicit a response of some kind

---

[1] Page 238.
[2] *A Pattern of Government Growth. 1800–60.* MacGibbon & Kee, 1961, p. 327.

from their customers: innovation called for more or fewer or different customers, or customers accepting a different kind of service. These customers were a third group, again external to the providers, who played an essential part in the story. Others who mediated in various ways between customers and providers usually played a part too.

Thus the three essential participants in the innovations we studied were (a) the providers of the service, (b) those who controlled the resources they needed for the job, and (c) their customers. Normally found, but not logically essential, were various mediators between these parties.

In their relations with the other two groups the providers of the service were always competing, explicitly or implicitly, with rivals who could put the resources they needed to other uses, or win customers away from them. Anthony Downs[1] called these competitors 'allocational rivals' and 'functional rivals' respectively. The same people or institutions may play both parts.

Downs also identified other actors, such as a 'sovereign'—the director, council, or committee to whom a 'bureau' is responsible—and 'beneficiaries' and 'sufferers' from the bureau's work who extend beyond the direct customers of its services. His analysis is revealing, but for our purposes there is no point in multiplying entities unnecessarily. Indeed, to assume there must be *a* 'bureau' subject to *a* 'sovereign' is already to fall into the trap of identifying the stage before the cast. If we want to understand innovations in policy, rather than the growth and behaviour of organisations, we must start with the action to be studied and then discover who plays a part in it, before considering where it is to be located in organisational space. If there is *a* 'bureau', rather than several —which often happens—we may find that important members of the providing group work from outside it, their rivals may work from within it, and there may be several sovereigns with competing jurisdictions.

The Action

Thus far our account has been simple and fairly unassailable—much of it true almost by definition. But to generalise revealingly about the process of innovation in local units of the social services we must now take greater risks. Firm conclusions about anything so complex cannot be derived from nine rather obsolete case studies. However, we may be able to identify recurring features and phases of this process, and show the roles which people tend to adopt and the interaction which typically unfolds between them in successive phases. While we cannot prove that such patterns always occur, we must at least show that convincing illustrations of all our generalisations can be found in our studies. The reader who starts at this end of the book will have to refer back to the studies if he finds the argument unconvincing.

[1] *Inside Bureaucracy*. Boston, Mass., Little, Brown, 1967, p. 45.

Before innovation begins the providers of a service tend to be fully engaged in coping with their existing responsibilities: their work has expanded, or been compressed, to fit the time and other resources available to them. In the course of this work they have accumulated commitments to institutions, interests and individuals outside the providing group—their customers, their suppliers and supporters, and those who play mediating roles of various kinds in their work. Thus the providers have few resources to spare and they usually have difficulty in redeploying existing resources without upsetting someone. (The FWA was a partial exception to this rule because much of their short-term and somewhat inarticulate clientele for charitable grants had gradually been taken over by statutory services—the NAB and other functional competitors—which offered these people more acceptable forms of help. Thus the Association could reduce its caseload, close Area Offices, and concentrate staff on new kinds of work. But even in this case, such changes provoked complaints from members of Area Committees and others who valued the old ways. The University case was more typical of the usual pattern. Until a grant of money and many other resources could be found, the teachers were fully employed in providing courses for social workers which entailed many commitments to outsiders—to future students and the tutors who advised them, central and local government departments which wanted trained staff, field supervisors and the agencies employing them who expected a continuing flow of students to come to them in future, and so on.)

But the aims and responsibilities of a service are usually defined in very general terms, as a glance at the opening clauses of many Acts of Parliament will show, and that gives leaders of the providing group ample scope for new interpretations of their functions when opportunities for reinterpretation arise. (We quoted a good example of such a statement of aims from the Rushcliffe Committee which defined the purposes of Legal Aid as being 'to enable persons of small or moderate incomes to obtain, as of right, all those services of a solicitor and barrister which a prudent man who had sufficient means to do so would obtain at his own expense'—marvellously compendious lawyer's language from which can be unpacked inexhaustible opportunities for innovation and development.)

How are specific proposals for innovation produced? They may be generated by new recruits with a new outlook or training (as in the Canadian and the Children's Department cases), they may emerge in response to externally generated changes in resources, demands or opportunities (as in the FWA, Bethnal Green and Finsbury cases to varying extents) or they may be the product of new thinking by existing staff, which probably calls initially for a good deal of 'overtime' effort (as in the University case, the Children's Department and the FWA). Typically, several of these sources of innovation will be found, for

CONCLUSIONS 295

innovation is easier when all parts of the system are in some sense ready for it.

Although the aims of a social service are usually imprecise, that does not leave its providers free to do whatever they like. Apart from constraining commitments accumulated from past work, they usually have an ideology of some sort—a closely related set of aims, assumptions and professional loyalties—which excludes many courses of action which might otherwise be considered. These ideologies may be derived partly from the surrounding community and its accredited spokesmen (as in Bethnal Green when there was never any doubt that a Labour Council would go on building houses while any slums remained in the Borough to be cleared, and in Croydon where many people held strong, and conflicting, views about the aims of their schools) or they may be derived from the professional training and traditions of the providers (as in the social work cases—and in Croydon too).

But ideologies do not evolve simultaneously and uniformly like a smoothly flowing river. The glacier cracks and groans. Proposals for innovation usually imply there is some conflict between new and old ideologies within the providing group (as in the LCC, Canadian, University and Croydon cases), or between the ideologies of providers and those of political leaders through whom they secure power and other resources which they need. (Something of this sort happened in Tower Hamlets when staff accustomed to the ways of the LCC Children's Department came up against an older, working-class ideology about children and families which differed from that of the newer, middle-class socialism of the LCC.)

Any important conflict within the providing group (even a potential rather than an explicit one) is related to similar conflicts outside the group. These links may be clear and direct (as in the University, Canadian and Children's Department cases: the LSE formed the stage on which much larger external conflicts were enacted; the Board of the Children's Aid Society and others in the community were deeply involved in controversies among their staff; and in the Tower Hamlets Children's Committee, which took over the LCC service, divergent views of Catholic and Jewish councillors about family obligations were related to divisions among their staff). But sometimes the links between internal and external conflicts are implicit and scarcely perceived by the people concerned. (It was not widely foreseen that the closure of housing waiting-lists in Bethnal Green would switch opportunities from young and increasingly crowded families waiting their turn for a house to slum dwellers, many of whom were older people who had long had a home of their own, inadequate though it might be. Later, other departments of local government became involved: pressures arising from decisions in the Housing Committee obliged Welfare and Children's Departments to care for homeless families which might in other Boroughs have been sheltered by the Housing Department.) Conflict is endemic whenever changes are being made. We consider the typical course of such conflicts shortly. But first we must resume our attempt to trace the normal course of innovation.

Before they can get far, the providers must secure additional resources —or, to be more exact, there must be a positive shift in the balance between the current supply of resources for the service and the demands made upon them. To take on new tasks, the providers must shed old ones or secure the extra resources required to do more work: the only other alternative—an increase in productivity—is in the social services, difficult to achieve in the short run, although it can happen over the longer run (it did in the NAB, which improved and hastened its assessment procedures).

The providers must secure the assent of those who control the resources they need for new work and for any work they intend to shed. The process is typically diffuse and lengthy. Key people among the providers—typically their most senior people—must gain agreements from others who exercise some control over the resources they need. These resource controllers are outside the providing group, not directly responsible for its services, and generally have many other concerns on their minds. Such controls operate in many ways. They may be derived from formal authority (of the kind held by a central government department, or by the Treasurer and Establishments Officer of a municipal council) or from well established procedures of varying degrees of formality (such as regular meetings of chief officers, designed to ensure that each proceeds with the agreement of his senior colleagues) or from personal, political or professional influence (based on the personal status and connections of local councillors, professional leaders and others) or from the choices made by able people who must be persuaded to join the providing group before the desired development can be brought about (for authority to appoint additional staff will be of little value unless good recruits can be found). To gain the support of all these people the providers must commit themselves to achieving certain objectives regarded as valuable, or at least acceptable, by those controlling the resources they need. To this extent they must sacrifice some of the freedom to run the service in their own way which they would retain if they chose the quieter life available to a group that seeks no major changes or developments in its work.

The providers may be compelled at this stage to commit themselves to general objectives (such as 'reducing the numbers of children coming into public care', or 'abolishing the eleven plus examination') or to more specific objectives (such as providing particular facilities sought by a leaseholder who is capable of delaying or blocking a development, as in the Finsbury example). Commitments and claims, offered as an inducement to secure the resources required at this stage, tend either to be specific but unimportant, or important but ill-defined. This is because the providers seek to retain as much control of their service as possible, and because the interests whose support they require are often so diverse that objectives which are important and precisely specified would be likely to alienate some of them. (The proposals made by the Chief Education Officer in Croydon were in fact so radical and specific that they provoked insuperable opposition. Likewise, in the High Flats case, the attempt to satisfy both a leaseholder and a tenants' association led to serious trouble, and further delays arose before the conflicting interests of the Ministry of Housing and Local Government and the County Planning Department could be reconciled). But more general commitments—to 'preserve the family', for example, or to 'advance knowledge about marital problems' (seen in the Children's Department, Children's Aid Society and FWA cases) are less likely to prove disruptive or too precisely binding. Mediators of various kinds may play important parts at this stage. (In our study of a University, the LSE's negotiations with a charitable trust and various central and local government departments and professional associations illustrate the process of securing the assent of resource controllers with the aid of influential mediating figures, and the complex claims and commitments made in return for their help. The Finsbury architect's negotiations with LCC and central government departments, land-owners and others offer similar examples.)

As they secure extra resources, or shed demands, the providing group has to convert resources into services, usually by modifying, expanding or redeploying existing services. The eventual outcome—the change in policy actually realised—often takes years to emerge and is difficult to predict with any precision. That is because the conversion of marginal increments of money, labour, materials and equipment into a service is a complex and gradual process. It depends on the people who do the work and the relationships they establish with each other and with those who use the service and the mediators who help to shape and regulate demands for it. Exchanges on the margins between the providers and their customers continually mould the character of the service, extending it in some directions and eroding it elsewhere—rather as wind and tide shape a coastline over the years.

The providers' relationships with their customers are in the long run as important as their relationships with resource controllers in determining the character and distribution of the service, but their influence tends to be more diffuse and harder to trace. Price mechanisms often play a part in the story. (The changing distribution of the home help service was shaped partly by the insistent demands for help from elderly people and the lack of demand from families with children. That in turn was due partly to the higher cost of the service to families, who often needed many hours of help each day if the service was to be any use to them, and who paid full fees because they normally had full-time earners in their households.) But price rarely performs a market clearing function in the social services. Their providers thus have more potential candidates for the service than they can satisfy. Thus the outlook and methods of the providers may go far to shape the demands that reach them and the priorities accorded to each. (In the case of the home helps it was clear that the staff and the councillors to whom they were ultimately accountable felt more comfortable with their elderly customers than with families in which house-keeping standards might be low and mothers might be away in hospital.) Those who mediate the demands of customers by providing information, referring them to the service or advocating their claims may play an important part in the process. (In the Home Help case again, the hospital consultants who had to get old people home in order to empty the beds needed for new patients, and the general practitioners and medical social workers who sought help for them when they got home, both exerted an influence on the distribution of the service which may have been all the more powerful because the service was in its earlier days located in the Health Department.) Many other mechanisms played a part in generating, restricting and shaping demands for the services we studied. (Our study of the high flats built in Finsbury showed that such structures must usually be designed many years before the buildings are completed and then help to determine the kinds of household which can be accommodated on the site for sixty years or more to come.) But research which was conducted on the bureaucrats' rather than the customers' side of the counter cannot throw much more light on these processes.[1]

Both in their continuing bids for resources and in their relations with customers, the providers of a service are always in competition with allocational and functional rivals. Although this competition usually operates only over small margins of the service, it nevertheless imposes constraints on what the service—and its rivals—can do. (Thus the Law Society and the Lord Chancellor's Advisory Committee at first opposed the provision of Home Office grants for voluntary law centres which they saw as competing with their own services. Those engaged in reorganising Croydon's maintained secondary schools had carefully to consider the effects of competition from independent and direct grant schools: although only 7 per cent of primary school leavers entered these schools in 1966 they included a much higher proportion of those willing to become the sixth formers so badly needed by the Borough's new high schools. If that proportion had risen appreciably by 1973—instead of falling to 5 per cent—the Borough might have had to reconsider some of its policies to prevent further losses to independent schools. In the LCC the Health and Children's Departments were providing very similar intensive family casework services and each was aware of their competitive

[1] For a revealing discussion of the whole problem, see Professor R. A. Parker's article 'Social Administration and Scarcity', in *Social Work*, April 1967.

CONCLUSIONS 299

relationship which was only brought to an end, when, in the new Borough of Tower Hamlets, both were combined in the Social Service Department in which the child care staff tended to dominate the providing group. The FWA has been well aware in recent years that its claims on public funds depend on finding tasks which the Social Service Departments want it to do, but cannot themselves so readily perform. At the LSE, one of the developments which precipitated a crisis was competition for students between older training courses and the new Applied Social Studies Course which began to bid students away from its rivals.) In many of these cases the service's functional competitors were also allocational competitors bidding, implicitly at least, for resources which it might need. Beyond these clearly identifiable allocational competitors there was the unlimited range of competing uses to which public and charitable resources can be put—including leaving them in the hands of the taxpayers and donors. Thus the providers of every service were constrained by the knowledge that they were operating in two kinds of competitive market—the market for resources and the market for customers. (Consolidation of hitherto separate services within the new Social Service Departments will internalise some rivalries within these larger groupings and shift the boundaries across which others are played out, but it will not eliminate the competition.)

These are the essentials of the process we have been studying Whether they initiate new developments or not—and they often do—the people who do the work of providing a social service have to carry these developments out, consciously and deliberately as a rule, but occasionally in response to external pressure which lead them in directions they do not perceive till later. The lines of action they take usually depend heavily on what Dr Saran called 'informed opinion' in their field, and the commitments already made to outsiders which are often the institutional source and expression of these opinions. There will usually be more than one set of opinions or ideologies to draw on within the providing group where lie the seeds of conflicts which have their external counterparts to which they can readily be linked. To bring about a new equation between the resources used by the service and the customers it serves—usually increasing both—the providers have to operate in two competitive markets: the markets for resources and for customers. In each they have to make commitments and provide services sufficient to secure the participation of resource controllers, customers and those who mediate their relations with each. We have described innovation as a process in which the main initiatives usually spread outwards from a central providing group; but the causal directions can be reversed, so that the providers respond to initiatives taken by resource controllers, customers or others mediating between them. In every case we studied external forces had an important influence on the outcome.

In real life innovation is a less orderly process than this formulation suggests. Several innovations of varying strength and duration may be working their way through a service at the same time. They seldom have a clear start or finish. Once a new development has begun it often produces further off-shoots and calls for yet more resources. Indeed there are signs that continuous modification and development of a social service are most likely to occur when those providing it secure a continuous increase in resources—because the process of growth ensures there is always a margin of unused human resources available for planning, promoting and developing new things, in the confidence that risks can be taken today because there will be new opportunities tomorrow. If the increase in resources comes to an end, or if new recruits are so inexperienced and untrained that they demand a great deal of supervision from more experienced staff (which amounts to the same thing) then there is no longer any margin of time and energy available for innovating activities. Thus the process of *growth* (meaning an increase in resources) and the process of *development* (meaning changes in the character of the service) tend to be linked—growth promoting development—especially in the types of service in which innovatory powers cannot be centralised and innovation calls for active contributions from a considerable number of professionally trained staff.

Conflict

We explained, early in the previous section of this chapter, that innovations in social policy always bring the threat of conflicts, inside and outside the group providing the social service in question. Here we try to explain how such conflicts develop. The examples on which we base this account were unusual—fortunately innovations do not all provoke bitter public controversy—but they were special cases of a normal process. Conflict reveals patterns and problems which are also present, if harder to perceive, in more peaceful conditions. This makes these cases particularly interesting, and we are particularly grateful to the battle-scarred participants who tried to help us understand them.

Growth and change do not proceed at a uniform pace or scale throughout the providing group and their associates. They produce uneven development of the service and of the group providing it. The actual aims and organisation of the service diverge increasingly from the official accounts of these things, and some people gain aspirations for the future which diverge even further.[1] Sooner or later a reappraisal must be made, and new procedures and doctrines agreed: without it, further development is likely to produce a tendency to overspend the

---

[1] For a revealing discussion of the differences between these ways of looking at an organisation see Wilfred Brown's *Exploration in Management* (Heinemann, 1962) which contrasts 'extant' (actual), 'manifest' (officially prescribed), and 'requisite' (desirable) accounts of an organisation.

budget, a scarcity of staff at points in the structure which were not expanded sufficiently to cope with the extra work being generated at other points, or a tendency to outstrip the legal or constitutional powers of the agency. (The Children's Aid Society clearly ran into a situation of this kind.) Often it is only when confronted with the limitations on their resources that the providers explicitly accept—or reject—a change in policy. (The University crisis arose when it became clear that it would no longer be possible to maintain three Courses unchanged.) This phase may prove disruptive, or it may pass off smoothly. How soon and how sharp its impact comes will depend partly on the providers themselves—particularly on their more senior members—and partly on the rate at which they can acquire additional resources to sustain continued development of all activities without having to discriminate explicitly against any of them.

It is those amongst the providing group who are most directly affected by the changes proceeding or threatened—people usually working at modest levels of the bureaucratic hierarchy—who first perceive a need for a 'decision' on policies, priorities, responsibilities or the distribution of resources, as caseloads or overtime increase, rumours circulate, personal relations deteriorate or other signs of stress appear. They begin to form groups and cliques which define the problem and the 'issues at stake', and canvass solutions. Different interpretations of the situation, different aspirations and different personalities do *not* necessarily produce conflict, provided all concerned can satisfy their aspirations within the same general pattern of development (as we found in the LCC Children's Department). If their objectives can be reconciled in this way, people with divergent views have a remarkable capacity for supporting—and indeed for claiming to have originated—developments whose purpose and significance they describe in very different terms. Conflict only begins seriously when different interests and aspirations cannot be reconciled in this way; when someone *has* to suffer, or be excluded from the group providing the service concerned. Contending groups then seek the support of those responsible for taking the 'decisions' they ask for. This may be the first that senior staff of the service hear of the conflict. A polarisation of opinions follows. The contenders search for satisfactory definitions of the issues at stake among like-minded associates, rather than among their opponents; and having established a circle with a common outlook on these issues they appraise and evaluate any solutions proposed by the response accorded to it in this circle. The Children's Aid and University cases showed that deciding what the 'issue' *is* tends at this stage to become *the* issue. For that goes far to determine the frames of reference and reference groups of the contenders, and the external interests which are likely to support or oppose them. They are formulating, and fighting about, ideologies and alliances.

If no decision is made, or if the decision proves unsatisfactory to some, those most dissatisfied tend to seek the support of outside groups capable of exerting influence on the decision. Typically these outsiders will be found amongst those controlling resources required by the providers, but the pleas of customers may be brought to bear too. 'Outward' appeals of this kind encourage others amongst the providers to make counter-appeals to outsiders likely to support alternative points of view. A widening circle of interests may then be brought into play, and their influence is concentrated on those responsible for a decision, and subsequently on those at more senior levels of the hierarchy who are capable of reversing that decision. (Pressures switched at this stage from the Head of the Social Administration Department to the Director of the LSE, from the Director of the Children's Aid Society to his Chairman and the Provincial Government's Director of Child Welfare, and from Croydon's Chief Education Officer to his Council and the Ministry of Education.) If the conflict is pursued to extremes, those with authority to take the necessary decisions have to wait until all available guns have been brought to bear in the battle. To take a decision sooner only invites attempts to modify or reverse it which may disrupt the agency and discredit authority (as happened in all three of the cases just mentioned). Some reconciliation of conflicting interests and aspirations may be achieved at any stage; it may, for example, prove possible to find additional resources which satisfy the aspirations of all concerned. If no reconciliation is possible on these lines a solution will have to be achieved through the exercise of authority or through a bargaining process which establishes the balance of power between contending forces. These bargaining strengths depend on the distribution of formal authority, the value of individual participants' contributions to the service, the ease with which substitutes for their contributions can be found, the strength and character of loyalties to the agency, and other factors. A lot will depend on the participants and the conventional patterns of authority previously established among them.

A decision must eventually be reached if the service is to continue. Though the formal approval of such decisions by an appropriate authority may simply set a seal on a much lengthier process of development, negotiation and conflict, the announcement of it is often the first that the public at large will hear of the decision in question. The eventual outcome, however, may not accord closely with this decision: it will depend heavily on the people who are left in positions which give them effective responsibility for implementing it. Many a point sacrificed by compromises made in the course of a conflict has been recovered, when the opposition resigns.

Provided they are kept within bounds, uncertainty about the future and the anxieties it provokes, encourage innovation and enable people to adapt to change. But when heightened in the course of conflict they may have the opposite effects. People who have for long treated each

CONCLUSIONS 303

other as colleagues, and even as friends, may find that the situation compels them to adopt the altogether different relationships of formal authority or competitive bargaining. Such relationships, which may be acceptable in the army or the marketplace, can prove peculiarly harrowing and destructive in the settings we studied. When people are compelled by bitter public controversy to formulate their views at length and defend them with determination it becomes increasingly difficult for all concerned to change their minds—at least while they remain among familiar colleagues. Memories of the pain inflicted by conflict may discourage them from risking another conflagration or the changes that might provoke one. This may explain why the two services we studied which were most sharply afflicted by conflict (the University social work courses and the Canadian Children's Aid Society, in each of which important changes were followed by two resignations) moved into a conservative 'post revolutionary' phase which continued for many years after. They grew in scale, but the more important innovations in their field henceforth began elsewhere.

The paucity of our evidence means that this can be no more than a speculation—a speculation which suggests that those who can manage conflicts without destructive and humiliating confrontations are best equipped to keep innovation going. Advocates of more aggressive styles of action should bear in mind that conflict, even if it achieves short-term changes, sometimes leads to longer-term paralysis.

Some conflicts can be settled by negotiations from which all parties can derive satisfying outcomes. They are 'positive sum games', thanks to the growth of resources and opportunities, the complementary nature of people's aspirations, the good temper of the participants, and so on. (This was achieved in the LCC Children's Department and in the building of Finsbury's flats.) Other conflicts are 'zero sum games' in which the gains of winners can only be achieved at the cost of losers. It then becomes rational for all who fear they may lose—which soon means everyone—to exert every possible influence to defeat their opponents. Inaction is preferable to the wrong action. Such conflicts can only be resolved when it is clear that every available influence has been brought to bear. They can then be very quickly resolved. (That is what happened in the Canadian and the University cases, and the failure to reach that stage during the period of our original study in Croydon explains why no solution of that conflict could be reached at that time.)

The main conclusions we want to draw from this analysis of conflict are that competition for resources and customers, the reformulation of ideologies, and the struggle for power are not distinct activities. They evolve together as different aspects of a continuing process. (When the heads of primary schools, supported by the National Union of Teachers, made their voices heard in the debate about the reorganisation of Croydon's secondary schools—a debate hitherto dominated by secondary school heads and their unions—they were not only seeking their share of power. They helped to reformulate the issues being debated as questions about the future of all children in the Borough, not only questions about the future of its grammar schools. When radical lawyers, impatient with what they regarded as the slow dissemination of free legal advice through conventional solicitors' practices, advocated the creation of legal centres in poor neighbourhoods, to be staffed by full-time salaried lawyers, they were not only bidding for resources which might have been used in other ways, but were helping to reformulate the issues being debated as a matter of assuring the civil rights of the poor, in addition to enabling the poor to use legal services which have grown up to meet the needs of the rich.)

Some Local Implications

We turn now to discuss some of the implications of this account, starting with points which may interest those concerned with local services of the kind that we have studied. In the next and last section of this chapter we consider some broader implications. In this section we note points which bear on different participants in the process, starting with the customers of the social services.

It is clear that the selection of the social services' customers merits far more detailed study than we have been able to attempt. All the services we have examined faced a bigger demand than they could meet and we know little in detail of the processes that determine which customers are selected and which services these people actually get. Moreover a social service frequently benefits several people simultaneously, even if only one of them would be recognised as its client in a particular 'case'; thus the distribution of help amongst those involved in one case also calls for careful study. (The social worker in a Children's Department may be called upon to help children, their parents and foster parents. The Children's Aid Society's services for unmarried mothers involved responsibilities to the mother, her baby and the Provincial Child Welfare authorities. The National Assistance Board officer dealing with Legal Aid Assessments is serving the Law Society for whom these assessments are made, but in practice we found he could not simply disregard the needs of the people whose resources he was assessing. The Home Help Organiser knows that her service may be of vital importance, not only to old people and their families, but also to hospitals, general practitioners, old people's homes and other social services.) Thus the character and development of a social service depends on the willingness of customers to use such agencies and the selection they make of the services available, the procedures bringing customers to the attention of those providing the service—procedures often reflecting the needs of other services—the selection of applicants made by those providing the service and the manner in which the providers interpret their responsibilities to the various people who may be concerned in one 'case'.

What has been said about the customers indicates the complexity of the jobs to be done by those directly providing services for them—particularly when these services give wide discretion to the staff concerned. The aims of such services cannot be considered in isolation from the attitudes and methods of those who provide them. (Quotations from the files of the Children's Aid Society showed how much the character of a service may alter when there are changes in the outlook, methods and skills of its staff.) The capacity of field staff to handle and develop their relationships with staff in other agencies may play as large a part in this process as their capacity to deal directly with clients. Formally approved 'changes in policy' announced by the governing body may simply recognise and codify a process worked out over several years by people at humbler levels of the providing group.

The next group of participants to be considered appear at the middle and more senior levels of the social services' management. They are not empowered to make major decisions but they have considerable discretion to allocate the resources required for the service and to control and supervise the uses to which they are put. Their responsibilities frequently place them at 'junctions' in the communication system linking specialists and sub-groups who have divergent interests and aspirations. They act as selective 'filters', choosing and interpreting information which passes up and down the hierarchy and between one agency and another. They must be capable of speaking and understanding the different professional and administrative 'languages' of those with whom they communicate and reconciling divergencies among them. They often prepare the plans and the memoranda relied on by politicians or more senior staff—who may subsequently be given the credit (or the blame) for them. They are sufficiently close to the field staff and to those at the top of the hierarchy to be familiar with the weaknesses of both, yet they must be prepared to shore up such weaknesses in unobtrusive ways if the service is to develop effectively. They must learn a sensitive appreciation of the aspirations and trends of development likely to prove acceptable to various participants. They may have begun their careers as general administrators or as professionally qualified specialists, but to be fully effective they must have developed loyalties to the fields in which they work—loyalties which transcend the horizons of a particular agency or profession. (The Deputy Town Clerk in Bethnal Green, the Senior Child Care Officer in the Children's Department, the Secretary to the Lord Chancellor's Advisory Committee on Legal Aid, and the Architect in Finsbury all bore such responsibilities in different ways, and the progress of the developments in which they were engaged owed a great deal to them. It may not be a coincidence that no one appeared to fill this role effectively in the cases in which more serious conflicts and difficulties arose.) Studies of administration tend to deal with the top or bottom levels of the structure: democratically elected bodies and their chief officers at one end; clients and those who serve them at the other. We neglect the levels between at our peril.

It should now be clear that the role of the directors of social services, though important, is a restricted one. The influence exerted on the development of a social service by those already considered, and the fact that staff in these services cannot normally be removed from their posts except in cases of the gravest error or scandal, gives chief officers limited room for manoeuvre. They generally bear the principal responsibilities for dealing with outside interests controlling the resources required for the service. They are called upon to convey, inside and outside the providing group, a sense of purpose and direction, and of the value and importance of what is being done, and to shape the general level of aspiration amongst those providing a service. If they fail to secure the support of those controlling the resources required for expansion—including potential recruits to the agency—the services they provide are unlikely to develop, though the existing pattern may become or remain efficient. They are called upon to look further ahead than any of the other participants we have considered, fostering fruitful lines of innovation (which will often be initiated by more junior staff). The commitments they enter into with senior colleagues, the procedures they sanction for the evaluation of their services, the recruits selected to join their staff, the resources acquired for their agency—all these must be chosen in a manner that opens rather than closes the doors for future development (development for which their successors will often gain the credit). The timing of crucial decisions made at this level of the hierarchy often calls for exceptional skill, and our studies suggest that the temptation to make prompt and explicit decisions may be as seductive and dangerous as the temptation to procrastinate. Chief officers are responsible for the agencies they direct, and are naturally proud of their reputations. But our studies show that some of the social services' most important tasks are performed by groups of people scattered in different agencies, and the more important innovations always call for collaboration with many people outside the agency. The term 'service' is commonly used to refer both to an agency and to the work it does, and it can be peculiarly difficult for chief officers to appreciate the distinctions between these concepts. Fruitful development of the work calls for a capacity to subordinate the interests of the agency to those of the people to be served.

Because they must play a leading part in continually developing and interpreting the aims of their service for their colleagues, their governors and the public at large, chief officers need to sense just how far they can go in defining and publishing these aims. Unnecessary vagueness encourages slipshod work and the neglect of the more easily forgotten customers; it also makes any evaluation of the service's working methods and general progress impossible. But there are 'good'—that is, rationally defensible—reasons for caution about excessive public precision about aims. Three of these reasons should be noted: (a) Social services have to operate in conditions of uncertainty: at any moment demographic, economic, political and other changes may produce unexpected needs, opportunities or dangers in the markets for resources and for customers to which the services must be alert. They must therefore retain sufficient room for manoeuvre to respond to these changes. (b) Professionally trained staff play increasingly important parts in most of the social services. To secure the best and to enable them to give of their best, they must have increasing discretion to develop their work in their own way: with professionalisation goes devolution of powers to area offices, working groups and individual staff. This is where innovations will increasingly begin. Aims must be clarified in ways which focus effort without destroying initiative. (c) The social services are often riddled with potential conflicts of interest and ideology within and between different agencies. Their directors should be continually formulating longer-range aims for these services: that is why they are paid more than their junior colleagues who can often do other parts of their job better than they can. But these longer-range aims may call for new legislation, a take-over bid for services provided by a neighbouring agency, an increase in the rates, a retirement or two within their own departments and a new chairman of their committee. If all that were made explicit, the aims are most unlikely to be achieved. Thus chief officers must be capable of consistently conveying and adapting the aims of their service in terms which different audiences can understand and support, while allowing for uncertainty, preserving proper discretion, and knowing when to resist temptations to be too explicit too soon.

The role of an agency's governing body varies widely according to its constitution and traditions, and it is difficult to generalise fruitfully about it. Only in the Croydon and Finsbury cases could an elected Council or Committee be said to have initiated the developments we have studied. But in several of the other cases such bodies played an important part at a later stage. The Board of the Children's Aid Society exercised considerably influence on the character and outcome of the development studied; and the Housing Committee in Bethnal Green established a general climate of opinion which gave a firm foundation for the work of their officials.

Because the members of these bodies are elected by the public—or by the fairly small minority which chooses to vote in local elections—they are sometimes expected to conduct a direct 'democratic' management of their services in accordance with the wishes of voters and taxpayers. Commentators then make depressing references to the 'encroachment of bureaucracy' or the 'decay of local democracy' when the reality turns out to be different. A century and more ago the members of vestries, boards of guardians, charitable committees and similar bodies themselves carried out much of the daily work they were responsible for, and faint traces of this tradition are still to be seen in our study of the Family Welfare Association. But the assumptions encouraged by such folk memories are liable to be misleading and needlessly derogatory to those who now perform the difficult and time-consuming duties of committee membership.

In fact, the governing body of a social service is only one of the channels of communication between the public and those providing the service, and 'the public' is itself an abstract or latent entity consisting of many potentially conflicting groups, each of which may at some stage become active as customers, supporters, rivals, critics, taxpayers, voters, or in other ways. (The Architect in the Finsbury case had to deal with the County Council and the Ministry, representing respectively a regional and a national 'public'; the Borough's Housing Manager had to deal with the tenants originally living on the site and those subsequently selected for the new flats; and other participants had to deal with neighbouring land owners and leaseholders—all 'publics' of different kinds. The Children's Aid Society had to deal with private donors and subscribers, several municipal Councils, departments of the Provincial and Federal Governments, foster parents, adopters, and the families it served. *Some* of the Society's communications with *some* of these 'publics' were channelled through its Board.) Examples could be multiplied indefinitely, but these may show that the distinctive features of the governing body's role do not arise from any monopoly of relationships with the external community that uses and pays for a social service.

The governing body may be accountable to voters and taxpayers in the sense that its tenure of office depends, formally speaking, on re-election, and it is formally responsible for approving the taxes to be levied each year. But the committees of the two voluntary bodies we have studied selected themselves, in effect; and among the local authorities dealt with in our original studies, only the Croydon Council had suffered a turnover of members since the war which was sufficient to threaten the position of its majority party. Meanwhile a large part (and often the majority) of the tax revenues required for their services was levied by other bodies—typically by the central government. No one would deny that elections do sometimes bring about important changes in the policies of local social services (our postscript on Islington, successor to the old Borough of Finsbury, provides an example—though scarcely a dramatic one.) We only wish to establish that such changes often—perhaps usually—originate from other sources, that the role of governing bodies does not consist mainly of initiating or directing

CONCLUSIONS

changes in policy, and that others engaged in providing the service may be at least equally active in communicating with the public, and equally anxious about the quality of their relationships with the public. When political initiatives, based on an electoral mandate, do become important, these will often be taken by central rather than local government. (Our postscripts on Croydon and Islington give examples.)

Meanwhile governing bodies have many other responsibilities. They are particularly concerned with establishing and maintaining relationships with those who control the resources required for their services, and they form one (but only one) of the principal channels of communication with such groups. They often devote moré effort to keeping the public informed about the service than to keeping its providers informed about public opinion. They constitute a means of arbitrating between contending interests amongst the providers, and the existence of this 'court of appeal' may be very important, even in an agency where people always choose to settle out of court. They also perform certain formal duties which have symbolic importance—inaugurating new institutions, receiving distinguished visitors, bidding farewell to retiring members of staff, and so on.

But when dealing with the type of development we studied, the governing body's principal role was to approve, modify or reject decisions which commit the providers to significant changes in their objectives, to courses of action which involve risks or impinge on other services, and to significant expenditures or redistributions of resources. Such decisions may call for consideration of technical evidence, but they require more than an appraisal of facts and methods; they require a judgement about priorities, objectives and risks. The staff providing a service are not compelled to consider the other services which may have to be foregone if their own is to expand, nor to determine how much it is worth paying to minimise certain risks inherent in their proposals, nor to weigh the effect on neighbouring services of precedents (in their methods of dealing with clients, the salary scales of staff, or payments to foster parents, for example) which they propose in their own service. They may indeed consider all these things, but they are not compelled to do so; they are often ill equipped to weigh and appreciate the factors involved, and it might be inappropriate for them to devote too much energy to such tasks. It is the responsibility of social workers, engineers, doctors, teachers and others who work in the social services to concentrate on providing and perfecting the service they are capable of; no one else can do that for them. But someone does have to consider what sacrifices should be made to secure these standards. The governing body, provided it is adequately informed and advised, should be equipped for this purpose. Their staff need a sensitive appreciation of this role if they are to distinguish the things the governing body should consider from the things it need not be aware of.

It is often difficult to secure and maintain a clear appreciation of these distinctions. The governing body's members may understandably wish to 'keep in touch' with the operations of the services for which they are responsible. For this and other reasons they may be tempted to spend a lot of time on executive or near-executive work which confuses their role and wastes their energies. (The Family Welfare Association's local Case Committees, the Finsbury Housing Committee's personal participation in the selection of tenants, the time spent by Children's Committee members on the Managing Committees of residential homes and schools, and the Croydon Education Committee's detailed analysis of proposals for reforms that had not yet been considered by senior staff in their own service—all these appear to be examples of such confusion.) The governing body's job is not to provide the service, but to find staff who can do this—and, if necessary, to remove those who cannot. Its work is as difficult, in its own way, as the tasks of managing the service, and it should offer a sufficiently satisfying challenge.

Equally damaging confusions arise if the staff providing a service 'counter attack' by assuming some of the responsibilities of the governing body. (The attempt by Croydon's Education Officer to reorganise secondary schools without first gaining the whole-hearted backing of his Council illustrates some of them.) Sometimes they evade or delay action the governing body has resolved upon. More often they submerge the governing body in a mass of confusing detail because they do not know how to pose clearly the questions which a committee really needs to consider, or simply because they feel that sufficient material must somehow be found to fill every meeting.

These comments on the roles of participants in the administrative process have tended at points to become prescriptive—even hortatory. Our evaluation of administrative structure is based on the assumption that innovation and development are its most important tasks, and that effective means must be found for completing each phase of the processes outlined earlier. Whether particular innovations and developments are good or bad is a different question which our study was not designed to answer.

Larger Implications

In conclusion we look back to some of the questions posed in the opening chapter of this book. In what rational sense, if any, is it possible through social policies to make the world a better place? Whose 'rationality' gains a hearing, and who gets neglected? Or are social plans and policies no more than the temporary outcome of a continuing struggle for power? Our studies were not designed to answer these large questions; they had a more modest, descriptive purpose. But they may throw some light on them. We will confine ourselves to a few comments prompted by this evidence.

CONCLUSIONS

Local innovations in social policy of the kinds we traced develop in an environment where competition is endemic, in the public as much as in the private sector. The aims of social services and the agencies responsible for them are ill-defined and will always remain so. There is no dominant, comprehensive social ideology commanding universal assent —or, if there is, it operates on too abstract a plane to provide any lasting consensus about developments of the sort that we studied. Conflicts about social policy, implicit if not explicit, are normal inside and outside the social services. In short, this is in many ways a pluralist world which evolves in a disjointedly incremental fashion, and decision-makers must do their best to muddle through.

That does not mean there is no scope for more 'rational' decision-making. At other scales of organisation and debate, which we have not studied, there is scope for a more rigorous 'systems approach'. That kind of analytical rigour is best suited to occasions when the problems to be solved call for the formulation of better methods to attain agreed ends with resources within the control of the organisation to be studied. With caution, a systems approach can also help to explore and clarify larger options open to policy-makers in situations of risk and uncertainty, but its absence from our studies was not only due to the (very natural) lack of such techniques in the social services of ten years and more ago. Every innovation we studied called for action by people in various organisations, subject to no single direction: never were the key actors all employed within one organisation. Every innovation called for the acquisition of resources and customers in competitive markets; and since these markets had no market-clearing price mechanism to conceal the fact, any allocation of resources they produced posed controversial problems of equity or social justice for which there was no intellectually or technically authoritative solution. In such conditions, systems analyses can perform a useful service by furnishing parts of the information to be considered before the essentially political decisions about policy are taken. Responsible advocates of the systems approach would claim no more.

Nevertheless the process we studied was no mere power struggle between contending interests exerting pressures on the 'responding system' of government, as some pluralist accounts have suggested. To start with, people providing the social services, right down to fairly humble levels of the administrative hierarchy, played important parts in formulating, initiating, interpreting and developing their own policies and functions. If government consists largely of the management of contending interests, then in this field the institutions of government—the managers themselves—are often the most important interests involved.

It would be equally mistaken to assume either that the competition for resources and opportunities which runs through these cases is non-ideological—a mere power struggle—or that ideologies can be formulated and reformulated without a good deal of competition and conflict. In the previous sections of this chapter we gave examples to show how the development of cliques and alliances, competition for resources, and the formulation of ideologies all evolve together as different aspects of a single, larger process.

There are real debates about questions of principle to be discerned in this competitive world—debates which matter profoundly to the participants. But whose voices are heard, and whose neglected? The providers of the services play a central part. New initiatives frequently originate with them, often in the course of conflicts between different interests within the providing group. Even if change originates elsewhere, it is the providers who actually have to carry out new developments, often reinterpreting them along the way. Formal and binding decisions about new policies seldom precede action: they generally follow long periods of groping experiments by the providers. But the providers operate within constraints imposed by central and local politicians, by scarcities of resources, and by competition for customers. They are also guided and constrained by ideologies—their own, and those to be found amongst 'informed opinion' in their field. These ideologies are generally humanitarian, and often egalitarian too.

It is difficult to distinguish which of these influences is most important: they may only be different ways of describing the same fundamental realities. (Political constraints are severe, because the service costs so much, because the customers cannot be expected to pay for it, because...) But in the short run the most important constraints on the aspirations the providers have for the development of their service usually appear in the guise of scarcity of resources. Hence the interests and attitudes of the people who control these resources are vital. Their influence, operating from the 'top' of the organisation charts, was generally more important than the influence of customers at the 'bottom'. The needs of customers were not forgotten, but they could in the short run be neglected with greater impunity.

In studying the ways in which ideas, practices and priorities evolve within the social services, we have gained a glimpse of the processes which can ultimately make 'the ideas of the ruling class . . . the ruling ideas'. For the interlocking network of political, professional, financial and administrative constraints within which a particular service operates is part of a larger network which constitutes the governing processes of the nation. That network is fortunately a fairly 'open' one, in the sense that it harbours competing and changing interests—repeatedly generating, or penetrated by, new ideologies. And, good or bad, it is a network which grows out of the realities of organisation and management within the public services of urban, industrial societies. These realities doubtless work in different ways under different regimes, but we cannot assume—without far more evidence—that political revolution

CONCLUSIONS

would necessarily have a liberalising or humanising influence upon these processes. (Nor should we assume they are incapable of improvement, with or without revolution.)

We have said that the controllers of resources often dominate the scene in the short run. But do the customers exert more influence in the long run, through the continuing pressures of their demands, or through political action which captures fresh resources or steers existing resources in new directions? We have shown that the demands of customers did exert important influences on the development of some of these services. But they were controlled and sometimes distorted by mediating systems of information, advice and referral (particularly for social work and health services), by means tests (for Legal Aid), waiting-lists (for housing) and academic selection tests (for education). Once the rationing and allocative effects of a price mechanism have been cast off, other kinds of rationing must take their place. But together these procedures may manage demands in ways which neglect the needs of some people or of whole classes of people. To generalise about that would call for fresh research: here we can only say that the processes of demand management vary from one service to another, and their effects are varied and very important.

Popular influences exerted through the democratic procedures of local government clearly play a major part in the longer run. The Boroughs of Bethnal Green and Finsbury and their larger successors, Tower Hamlets and Islington, have gradually acquired and rebuilt a large part of their stock of housing; indeed Tower Hamlets will in time rebuild most of its territory. To manage the housing for populations of some 150,000 people without regard to profit, and to allocate it in an honest if crude attempt to meet needs, are remarkable achievements which would not have occurred without the determination of local Labour Parties and the wider pressures of the Labour movement.

Parliamentary majorities and their programmes are important too: successive changes in the attitude of the central government's officials to Croydon's proposals for the reorganisation of its secondary schools which followed the alternation of Labour and Conservative Governments at Westminster were the most obvious examples of that in our studies. But the transformation wrought by the creation of the Social Services Departments and the massive expansion of Legal Aid and Advice remind us that some of the biggest changes brought about by Parliament are not a matter of controversy between the political parties.

Croydon's experience shows that party politics work in complex ways. Each case must be studied before we can decide who is likely to gain or lose from such interventions. The old and the new Croydon both had Conservative Councils: their attempts to reform secondary schools were seriously disrupted when the Labour Party took up on a national scale proposals of the sort which the Borough was already considering. The Labour Party's intervention may have been needed to achieve reorganisation on the national scale, but it did little for this cause in Croydon.

Before concluding that party politics will in the long run exert a dominant influence, we should recall that the most successful of the services we studied—if success is measured by its rates of growth in resources or in numbers of its customers—was the Legal Aid and Advice scheme which was carried forward by civil servants, lawyers and other professional people who did their best to keep the issue out of party political controversy in order to secure the support of lawyers and Lord Chancellors in successive governments. In this they succeeded, but at the cost, to the poor, of a set of priorities which appear to be more closely attuned to the needs of lawyers—the principle resource controllers—than to those of their poorer clients. No one could say with confidence whether the poor would have gained more from this fairly rapid expansion of the scheme into areas with which lawyers serving the affluent were already familiar, or from a probably slower expansion into areas which were of greater interest to the poor.

To tackle a single issue, capable of solution within a short period, it can be useful to secure the support of a political party—provided the party gains power and takes prompt action. But the support of one party generally provokes the opposition of others. Thus for a programme of action calling for continuous development over many years, more consistent support based on a broader consensus is needed. That consensus may then become too closely tied to the existing power structure and its professions to give the greatest benefits to poverty-stricken people. This is one of the recurring dilemmas of reformers.

Reformers have also learnt that if they are mainly concerned about the poorest people they should not rely uncritically on movements accountable to mass electorates. The Trade Unions have been noticeably unenthusiastic about the extension of free Legal Advice which appears to compete with their own advisory services. Tower Hamlets, wholly dominated by the Labour Party, was notoriously reluctant to help families, regarded as 'feckless', who became homeless because they failed to pay their rents. The hardships of the poorest people are often partly due to their exclusion from programmes introduced, often by socialist movements, to serve the mass of the population.

If neither mass movements nor party politics can be trusted to protect the poor, will more direct attempts to open the debate about social priorities to the customers of the social services prove more effective? As our studies show, the promotion of public participation in government is a difficult task, greatly complicated by the fact that it is never simply a matter of communication between *the* customers and *the* bureaucracy. In every service there are conflicts, latent or overt, amongst its providers, and between them and their colleagues in neighbouring

CONCLUSIONS

services. These conflicts are related to others outside the providing group between the different interests to be served among the public—conflicts between customers of different kinds, between customers and non-customers, between beneficiaries and taxpayers, and so on. The intervention of the local Association for the Advancement of State Education in public debate about secondary education in Croydon, previously dominated by professional organisations, was a step toward public participation in this development. But that kind of thing may do little more than create a more open political market place in which those who do best in economic market places still tend to come out on top. The Croydon AASE had progressive views about the reorganisation of secondary schools, but it was not a working-class organisation. A more sophisticated strategy was emerging in the attempts of Islington Borough, briefly glimpsed in our postscript to the Finsbury case, to secure greater public participation in redevelopment schemes within a framework which clearly retained general responsibility for the whole scheme in the hands of the authority.

The main choice to be made is not between *more* public participation or *less*, but between *newer* styles of participation by customers and others directly affected by a service, and *older* styles of participation designed to make the service accountable to all the voters and taxpayers —usually of a larger area. New and old will both continue: the question is how to combine them most fairly and effectively. Participation should make the services more responsive to the needs of those they were intended to serve; sometimes, too, it should enable the customers to provide services for themselves. But it should not relieve public authorities of the obligation to decide priorities, or deprive them of the power to put their policies into practice. The Croydon case showed that the widest consultations with teachers, educational administrators and the public failed to produce cogent and feasible policies until the Education Committee took a convincing lead in outlining and defending the principles it intended to follow; and it was the Committee, not the staff providing the service, which had to assume that responsibility.

In our studies, experiments in engaging customers in debate about the policies of the social services, few and frail though they were, had thus far been confined mainly to the fields of education and housing—major services which affect very large numbers of people. The customers of smaller services dealing with more vulnerable or deviant groups (services such as the Children's Department, the FWA, the Children's Aid Society, or even the larger Legal Aid scheme) had seldom gained any explicit hearing in discussion of needs and priorities.

These conclusions leave us searching for a precarious combination of interests and influences. Social services for the mass of the population, demanding massive resources, can only be carried forward effectively with the support of the working-class movements: their development will be frustrated and distorted unless they retain the support of these movements and the general body of customers and taxpayers who make up the electorate. Yet if the social services are shaped only by popular demands, unmediated by the innovating capacity and the humanitarian ideologies of 'informed opinion' among the social service professions, they will be liable to stagnate and vulnerable minorities may be neglected. But if the development of the social services is shaped entirely by the staff who provide them and those who control the resources they need, social policies will be confined too closely to the ideologies of the ruling classes. Humane though they will often be, that is a prescription more likely to relieve immediate, short-term distress than to eliminate its fundamental causes. The voice of the customers—and particularly the more vulnerable of them—is therefore the third influence which must be brought to bear. Difficult though that is, the attempt to gain them a hearing should be a continuing theme in the development of social policies.

INDEX

Abel-Smith, Brian 35n, 79n
Adoption of Children (Regulation) Act, 1939 104
Almoners 272, 280–81
Almoners, Institute of 204, 257, 259, 261, 272, 277, 283
Altshuler, Alan A. 41n
Architects 51–2, 57, Chap. 7, 139, 305, 308
Area Health Authority 63
Ashworth, William 39n
Assistance Board 64. See also National Assistance Board, Unemployment Assistance Board
Association for the Advancement of State Education (Croydon) 237, 239, 315
Association of Municipal Corporations 80
Association of Psychiatric Social Workers 257
Association of Social Workers 281
Association of Teachers in Technical Institutions 247
Attlee, Clement 256
Auditor See District Auditor
Australian National University, Research School of Social Sciences Pref. 1974
Aves, Geraldine Pref. 1964

Bacon, Alice 248, 252
Bagehot, Walter 17
Banfield, Edward C. 33n, 41
Bar Council 80
Barrington, Mrs. Russell 17n
Barry, Brian 33n
Batley, Richard 250n
Beckenham 222
Bell, David 34n
Bentham, Jeremy 24, 30–1
Bethnal Green, Metropolitan Borough of Chap. 3, 50, 60, 86–7, 89, 126–132, 161, 163, 185, 193, 289, 292, 294–95, 305, 307, 313
Bevan, Aneurin 48
Beveridge Committee, Report 20
Board of Guardians 106
Boucher Committee, Report 95

Bowlby, John 121
Boyle, Edward 238
Brand, J. 250n
Braybrooke, David 29n, 30–1
Brent, London Borough of 250n
Briskin, S. I. 200n
British Association of Social Workers 281
Brockville Chap. 8
Bromley, London Borough of 222
Brown, Wilfred 213n, 300n
Building Research Station 134
Burnham, James 39n
Burns, Tom 290n

Camden, London Borough of Pref. 1964n
Canadian Legion 173
Carnegie United Kingdom Trust 254, 259–60, 263, 269, 273, 276–77, 283.
Central Advisory Council for Education (England) See Plowden
Central Council for Education and Training in Social Work 281n
Central Training Council in Child Care 259
Centre for Environmental Studies Pref. 1974
Centre for Organisation Analysis Pref. 1964n
Chadwick, George F. 26, 40
Chaloner, W. H. 18n
Chapman, Valerie Pref. 1964
Charity Commissioners 237
Charity Organisation Society Chap. 9, 256. See Family Welfare Association
Child Care See Children's Services
Child Poverty Action Group 38
Child Welfare Act, 1954 (Ontario) 170n
Child Welfare Act, 1965 (Ontario) 189
Child Welfare Review Committee (Ontario) 189
Children Act, 1948 104–05, 113, 121–22
Children and Young Persons Act, 1933 104
Children and Young Persons (Amendment) Act, 1953 122
Children and Young Persons Act, 1963 126, 132

318 INDEX

Children and Young Persons Act, 1969 126
Children's Aid Societies, C.A.S. of Brockville and United Counties of Leeds and Grenville Chap. 8., 212–14, 287–88, 291, 294–95, 297, 301–05, 307–08, 315
Children's Protection Act (Ontario) 170
Children's Services, Departments, Committees, Officers 22, 60, 65, 86, 88, 91, 94, 98, 100, 102, Chap. 6, 168, 171, 185–87, 212–13, 216, 254–55, 258–59, 272, 280–82, 289, 291, 294–95, 297–99, 301, 303–05, 310, 315
Church Commissioners 146–47
Citizens' Advice Bureaux 195–96, 213, 217
City of London 87–89, 134–35, 138, 193
Clerk's Department See Town Clerk
Communists, Communist Party 60, 127, 154, 237
Conservative Political Centre 80n
Conservatives, Party, Government, etc. 79, 130, 162–63, 223, 247–49, 313
Cook, Frances Pref. 1974
Coulsden 240, 247
Council of Social Service 63
County Councils' Association 80
Courts and Magistrates 19, Chap. 4, 68, 79, 82. See also Law Centres, Legal Aid
Courts, Canadian 169–71, 173, 179–80, 186, 189–90
Crewe 17
Criminal Appeal Act, 1907 65n
Criminal Justice Act, 1967 76, 77n
Croydon, County and London Boroughs of 80, Chap. 10, 240, 242–43, 247–52, 287, 289, 294–95, 297–98, 302–04, 307–10, 313–15
Croydon Advertiser 236
Cunliffe, Muriel A. 195n
Cunliffe Report 215
Curtis Committee, Report 22n

Dahl, Robert 31
Dahrendorf, Ralf 38–39
Dalton, Hugh 256
Defense Department, U.S.A. 27
District Auditor 155
District Valuer 137
Divorce Reform Act, 1969 77
Dixon, Julia 19n
Donnison, D. V. 48n, 60n, 168n

Donnison, Jean Pref. 1974
Downs, Anthony 31, 292
Duncan, Graeme 34n

East Ham, County Borough of Chap. 4, 222
Easton, David 28, 30, 32
Education, Services, Departments, Committees, Officers, etc. 18–19, 22–23, 86, 105–07, 113, 115, 118, 120, 122, Chap. 10, 287–88, 297, 302, 310, 313, 315
Education Act, 1944 223, 225, 228, 242
Education and Science, Department of Chap. 10, 302
Eltham 96
Emberton, Franck and Tardrew Chap. 7
Engels, Frederick 35, 42
Engineer, Borough, District 136, 139, 151, 155
Establishments Officers, Committees, etc. 113–14, 122, 296
Eversley, David 60n

Fabian Society 80n
Family Allowances (Canadian) 172, 177
Family Discussion Bureau 206–07, 212
Family Service Units 94, 113, 114n, 211
Family Welfare Association Chap. 9, 254, 256, 259, 272, 277, 287, 289, 290–91, 294, 297, 299, 308, 310
Finance Departments, Committees, etc. 63, 114, 296
Finsbury, Metropolitan Borough of 50, 60, Chap. 7, 193, 289, 294, 296, 298, 303, 305, 307, 308, 310, 313, 315
Flew, Antony Pref. 1974
Ford, Donald 106
Forrester, Jay 40–41
Franck, C 134n
Freemasons 174
Friend, J. K. 26
Friendly Societies 19

Gas Board, South-Eastern, 149, 158
Glacier Institute of Management Pref. 1964
Grand Junction Railway Company 17
Greater London Council 60–62, 161–67
Greater London Boroughs 216. See also names of Boroughs
Greve, J. 19n, 60n, 62n
Greve, S. 19n, 60n

Guinness Trust and Tenants' Association 134, 139, 147–48, 154–55, 164, 166
Gulick, L. 72n

Hackney, Metropolitan Borough of 49n, 50, 193
Hall, Penelope 16n
Hall, Phoebe 289n
Hampstead, Metropolitan Borough of 50n
Harloe, Michael 63n, 163n
Harris, Margaret 60n
Hartshorn, Alma Pref. 1974
Harvey, David 41–43
Hastings, Sam 247n
Head Teachers' Association (Croydon) 236, 247
Health, Ministry of Pref. 1964, 48, 50, 84–86, 91, 93–95, 99, 130, 259, 272. See also Health and Social Security, National Health and Welfare, Public Health Services
Health and Social Security, Department of 75, 129–30, 132
Health Services 17–18, 20–21, 288. See also Public Health
Health Visiting and Social Work (Training) Act, 1962 281
Heclo, Hugh 26
Hill, Octavia 23
Hirschman, Albert O. 32
Hobsbawm, E. J. 34n
Holborn, Metropolitan Borough of 134, 193
Home Help Services 60, 65, Chap. 5, 121, 125–26, 129, 185, 288, 291, 297–98, 304. See also Institute of Home Help Organisers
Home Office 80, 82, 118, 121–22, 198, 201, 206, 212, 259, 261, 263, 265–66, 272, 275, 277, 284, 298
Housing Services, Committees, Departments, etc. 18–19, Chap. 3, 113, 136, 287–88, 295–96, 307–08, 310, 313, 315. See also Housing and Local Government
Housing Act, 1949 48
Housing Advice and Aid Centres 62–63
Housing and Local Government, Ministry of 49–51, 54, 57, 113, 122, Chap. 7, 164, 227, 297, 308
Housing Finance Act, 1972 61, 163
Housing (Finance and Miscellaneous Provisions) Act, 1946 48

Housing (Financial Provisions) Act, 1938 48
Housing (General Purposes) Act, 1958 151
Housing of the Working Classes, Royal Commission on the, 1884–85, 23
Housing Repairs and Rents Act, 1954 48–49
Housing Subsidies Act, 1956 48–49, 55, 142
Housing (Temporary Provisions) Act, 1944 48
Huws Jones, Robin Pref. 1964

Institute of Education See University of London
Institute of Home Help Organisers 84–85, 96–97. See also International Council of Home Help Services
International Council of Home Help Services 97
Isle of Dogs 62
Islington, London Borough of 60–62, 128, 161–67, 289, 308–09, 313, 315
Issacharoff, Ruth 63n, 163n

Jessop, W. N. 26
Joint Four Association 236–37, 247
Jones, David Pref. 1974

Keenleyside, Mary 200n
Kent, County Council of 222
Kogan, Maurice Pref. 1974, 251n

Labour and National Service, Ministry of, Labour Exchanges 85, 89; (Canadian) 173
Labour, Movement, Party, Group, Government, etc. 16, 23, 52, 58, 60, 79, 126–27, 132, 141, 154, 161–63, 211, 223, 228, 237, 247, 295, 313–14
Lambeth, London Borough of 63n, 128
Lancet Sanitary Commission 20n
Land, Hilary 289n
Lands Tribunal 78, 82
Lansbury, George 130
Law Centres, Legal Centres, Legal Aid Centres 78, 81–82, 195
Law Society Chap. 4, 81, 287, 298, 304
Legal Action Group 77, 82
Legal Advice and Assistance Act, 1972 78, 82
Legal Aid Act, 1960 69
Legal Aid Act, 1964 80n

Legal Aid and Advice, Services, Scheme, etc. Chap. 4, 287, 294, 304–05, 313–15. See also Law Centres
Legal Aid and Advice Act, 1949 65
Legal Aid Centres. See Law Centres
Lewis, Philip 82n
Liberal Party 237
Liberalism, Liberals 15, 25, 35, 42
Lindblom, Charles E. 29n, 31
Local Authority Social Services Act, 1970 127
Local Education Authorities. See Education
Local Government and Planning, Ministry of 50
Local Government Act, 1958 227
Local Government Board 85, 130
Local Government Operational Research Unit 28
Location of Offices Bureau 222
London Building Act, 1930 136, 146, 155
London County Council 50–58, Chaps. 5 & 6, 195, 198, 209, 211, 216, 228, 291, 295, 297–98, 301, 303, 308
London Electricity Board 149–50
London Government Act, 1963 59, 61
London School of Economics and Political Science See University of London
Lord Chancellor, Lord Chancellor's Department, Advisory Committee, etc. Chap. 4, 65, 70, 75–76, 298, 305
Loyal Orange Lodge 174

MacDonagh, Oliver 24, 292
Mackenzie, Norman 35n
Macpherson, C. B. 37n, 38n
Marris, Peter Pref. 1974
Marshall, T. H. 25, 37
Marx, Karl 34, 37
Maternity and Child Welfare Act, 1918 85
Matthews, E. J. T. 76n, 78n, 82n
McDougall, Kay Pref. 1974
McGregor, O. R. 17n
McLeod, Iain 16n
McLoughlin, Brian 40
Meacher, Michael Pref. 1964, 133n
Meals on Wheels 131
Medical Officer of Health See Public Health, Society of Medical Officers of Health
Medical Social Work See Almoners and Institute of Almoners
Mental Health Act, 1959 267, 282

Metropolitan Standing Joint Committee for Parking 146
Metropolitan Water Board 149, 153, 158
Meyerson, Martin 33n, 41
Michels, R. 39n
Milner Holland Committee 162
Ministry of Education See Education and Science, Department of
Minns, Richard Pref. 1974, 63n, 163n
Mishra, R. C. 21n
Mitcham 222
Moser, C. A. 247n
Mowat, Charles Loch 194n

National Assistance Act, 1948 64
National Assistance Board Chap. 4, 92, 186, 197, 287–88, 294, 296, 304
National Association of Local Government Officers 97
National Association of Probation Officers 80, 281
National Association of School Masters 236–37, 247
National Council for Civil Liberties 38
National Foundation for Educational Research 235
National Health Service Act, 1946 88–89
National Health and Welfare, Department of (Canada) 169, 172
National Institute for Social Work (Previously National Institute for Social Work Training) Pref. 1964 & 1974, 281
National Institute of Houseworkers 86
National Society for the Prevention of Cruelty to Children 187
National Union of Teachers 236–37, 247, 303
Nevitt, Della Adam 60n, 161n
New Towns 17
Newman, Derek Pref. 1964
Newman, John Henry 23
Ney, Elizabeth 128n
Nightingale, Florence 20
Northern Ireland 79
Nunn, T. Hancock 21n

Oakeshott, Michael 30
O'Brien, Oswald 250n
Observer Newspaper 236
Ontario, Government of Chap. 8, 302 304
Oulton, Derek Pref. 1974 76n, 78n, 82n

INDEX

Page, D 19n, 60n
Paine, Tom 23
Parker, Roy A. Pref. 1964 126n, 128n, 289, 298n
Parker Morris Report 160
Parkin, Frank 38n
Parris, Henry 250n
Pensions and National Insurance, Ministry of 65
Personal Service League 201
Peschek, David 250n
Pleydell Estate 139, 164, 166
Plowden Council, Report 22
Pollock, A. F. Seton 78n
Poor Law, Poor Law Infirmaries 17, 20, 23, 91, 118
Poplar, Metropolitan Borough of 49n, 50, 60, 86–87, 126–132, 193
Popper, Karl 30
Powell, Enoch 16n
Probation Services, Officers, etc. 116, 126, 169, 187, 259, 261, 272, 279–80, 284
Psychiatric Social Workers 201, Chap. 11
Public Assistance Committee 200
Public Health, Local Services, Departments, Committees, etc. Chaps. 3 & 5, 105, 113–14, 118, 120–22, 126, 132, 138, 155, 173, 223, 298
Public Health Acts, 1936 85
Public Health (London) Act 1936, 104
Public Schools Commission 250, 251n
Public Works Loan Board 51
Purley 240, 247

Rawls, John 14n
Red Cross, Canadian 173
Regan, David 247n
Registrar-General (Ontario) 172
Reid, W. J. 219n
Rent Act, 1957 56
Rhodes, Gerald 60n, 126n, 161n, 247n
Ronan Point 164
Royal Navy 19
Rushcliffe Committee, Report 71, 78–79, 294

St. Marylebone, Metropolitan Borough of 50n
St. Pancras, Metropolitan Borough of 193
Saran, Rene 250n, 291, 299
School Attendance Officers 19
Schultze, Charles, L. 27n
Scott, W. 247n

Sears, Angela Pref. 1964, 133n
Seebohm Committee, Report 127, 132, 280, 289
Sharpe, L. J. 33n
Shelter 38
Shoreditch, Metropolitan Borough of 49n, 50, 193
Shyne, Ann W. 219n
Simon, Herbert A. 28
Sir Halley Stewart Trust 204
Smith, Jef Pref. 1974
Social Security, Ministry of 74
Social Security Act, 1966 74
Social Services Departments, Committees, etc. 62, 126–132, 163, 189, 216, 219, 280, 290, 299, 313
Social Welfare Department, Welfare Services 91, 98, 100, 105, 111, 126–28, 131, 295
Socialist Commentary 81
Society of Medical Officers of Health 97
Solicitor-General 77
Sosnovy, Timothy 42n
Soviet Union 42
Stalker, G. M. 290n
Stepney, Metropolitan Borough of, 49n, 50, 60–61, 86–87, 89, 96, 126–132, 193
Stevens, Robert 79n
Stewart, J. D. 27, 29
Stowe, K. R. 73n
Stretton, Hugh 39–40
Summary Jurisdiction (Appeals) Act, 1933 65n
Supplementary Benefits Commission 75–83, 216
Surrey, County Council of 222
Surveyors, Borough, District 52, 136, 139, 149, 155
Sutton 222, 250n

Task Force on Community and Social Services (Ontario) 190
Tate, Betty 126, 128n
Tavistock Clinic 202, 206–08
Thatcher, Margaret 249–50, 252
Times Educational Supplement 229–30, 236
Titmuss, Richard M. 25, 37
Tomlinson, David F. 128n
Tomlinson, George 48
Tower Hamlets, London Borough of 60–63, 102, 126–132, 163, 282, 295, 299, 313–14
Town and Country Planning Act, 1947 50

Town Clerk, Clerk's Department Chap. 3, 52, 63, 95, 104, 115, 122, 141, 143, 148, 155, 162, 305
Trade Unions 314
Treasury 65, 70, 81, 227
Treasurers' Departments See Finance
Trinity School of John Whitgift See Whitgift

Unemployment Assistance Board 64
United Empire Loyalists 174
University Grants Committee 262
University of Bristol Pref. 1964n
University of London 195, 213, Chap. 11, 294–95, 301, 303
London School of Economics and Political Science Prefs. 1964, 1974, 13, 81, 131, 201–02, 205–07, 209, Chap. 11, 290–01, 297, 299, 302
Institute of Education 235
University of Oxford Institute of Education 229
University of Toronto 176, 185
Urwick, L. 72n
Urwin, Kenneth Pref. 1964

Valuer See District Valuer

Webb, Adrian Pref. 1974, 289n
Webb, Sidney & Beatrice 20, 24
Welfare Services See Social Welfare
West Ham, County Borough of 57, 222
Westminster, City of 86
White, Richard 82n
Whitgift Foundation, Schools, Trinity School of John Whitgift 237–38, 245, 249
Wolman, Harold Pref. 1974
Wingo, Lowdon 33n
Willmott, Peter 60n
Wildavsky, Aaron 27n
Women's Royal Voluntary Service 86
Woolwich, Metropolitan Borough of 50
Works, Ministry of 48

Young, Michael 60n
Younghusband, Dame Eileen Pref. 1974, 200
Younghusband Committee, Report 197
Youth Service 223

Zander, Michael Pref. 1974, 81–82